D0535167

3 1215 00021 1661

OCRAN'S ACRONYMS

OCRAN'S ACRONYMS

A DICTIONARY OF ABBREVIATIONS AND ACRONYMS USED IN SCIENTIFIC AND TECHNICAL WRITING

Emanuel Benjamin Ocran

ROUTLEDGE & KEGAN PAUL
London, Boston and Henley

First published in 1978

by Routledge & Kegan Paul Ltd

39 Store Street,

London WClE 7DD,

9 Park Street,

Boston, Mass. 02108, USA and

Broadway House

Newtown Road,

Henley-on-Thames,

Oxon RG9 1EN

Printed in Breat Britain by

Lowe & Brydone Printers Ltd

Thetford, Norfolk

Reprinted with corrections 1980

British Library Cataloguing in Publication Data

Ocran, Emanuel Benjamin
    Ocran's acronyms.
    1. Science - Abbreviations   2. Technology -
    Abbreviations
    I. Title
    501'.48   Q123   78-40463

    ISBN 0 7100 8869 8

To Eunice

CONTENTS

INTRODUCTION

Abbreviations and acronyms, pronounceable words of conven-
ience formed from initial letters of other words, are
frequently used in scientific and technical writing to concentrate the mind wonderfully on the written subject.   The
rate of growth is so prolific that it is essentially neces-
sary to categorize their usefulness into subject groupings.
To lump them together in a general purpose dictionary is
less helpful to the subject specialist who undoubtedly
would find abbreviations and acronyms organized into
subject headings much more useful.   This dictionary has
been compiled to fulfil a subject approach - an organized
subject order for abbreviations and acronyms.

SELECTION OF ENTRIES

Journal articles in bound volumes of hundreds of journals
were examined for abbreviations and acronyms and coverage
was limited to two to five years of back issues of bound
volumes plus current issues where possible.   Hundreds of
technical reports, especially on aeronautics and computer
sciences, were also examined for entries.   Foreign abbreviations and acronyms are largely excluded and so are symbols
and nomenclature in scientific and technical reports.

With a few exceptions abbreviations and acronyms for associations, institutions and governmental bodies are also excluded. Those included are considered purely on subject merit.

There is a wide subject coverage as shown in Part one of the dictionary. Only those subjects shown with asterisks in Part one are listed alphabetically with their abbreviations and acronyms in Part two. The heading GENERAL is used in the dictionary for those items with no subject predominance but suited to many subject fields.

DETERMINATION OF SUBJECT FIELDS

To illustrate how subject fields were determined for the abbreviations and acronyms, take the following paragraphs from a technical report:

The B-52 Load Alleviation and Mode Stabilization (LAMS) program is an example of research conducted to advance a control system technology. Results from this study led to the B-52 Control Configured Vehicle (CCV) program, conducted jointly by the United States Air Force Flight Dynamic Laboratory (AFFDL) and the Wichita Division of the Boeing Company...

Under this program, in cooperation with the AFFDL, and the CCV program flutter mode control (FMC), vertical ride control (VRC) and maneuver load control (MLC) system are being tested on a NASA one-thirtieth scale

B-52 aeroelastic mode....

Wind tunnel tests of the FMC and VRC systems have been completed, and testing of the MLC and VRC system testing are discussed in the following paragraphs (AGARD-CP-175).

The title of the paper from which these paragraphs are taken is 'Wind tunnel investigation of control configured vehicle system'. The obvious subject fields for the abbreviations and acronyms obtained from this paper are aerodynamics and aeronautics. The dominant subject field by choice is aeronautics in Part two but both subjects appear in Part one. To determine the subject field, the title of the paper as well as the clientele to which the paper is written are deciding factors

DESCRIPTION OF ENTRIES

Abbreviations and acronyms listed are capitalized without stops and a few are in lower case letters. Corresponding letters to show the meaning of abbreviations and acronyms are capitalized but a few are spelled out as part of a word and are not capitalized. This is common in the Biological and Medical Sciences. Some meanings are suffixed by country to show where the listed item is commonly used e.g. (Aust.) for Australia, (Fr.) for France, (Ger.) for Germany, (Jap.) for Japan, (UK) for United Kingdom and (US) for United States. SF under listed items in Part one stands for Subject Fields and alongside in alphabetical order are listed the subject fields in which the abbreviations and acronyms are used. The subject listings are by no means exhaustive but are judged to be pertinent to the abbreviations and acronyms.

ARRANGEMENT

All entries in Part one are arranged in alphabetical order according to the abbreviation and acronyms. In Part two, entries are arranged alphabetically under their broad alphabetic subject headings.

ACKNOWLEDGMENTS

The bulk of entries in the dictionary were obtained from journals on open access at the Science Reference Library, Patent Office and the author wishes to express his gratitude to this fine library. Thanks are also due to the Civil Aviation Authority Library, London, for making it possible to examine many of their technical reports. It is inevitable that there will be a number of omissions and errors in a dictionary of this nature and to improve and extend the usefulness of this dictionary, I should be grateful to receive suggestions and additional material.

American spelling has been retained for American organizations but not necessarily for abbreviations and acronyms found in American material.

Part One

ABBREVIATIONS AND ACRONYMS

A   All Around
    SF   *Metallurgy and Metallography
        Metalworks
A   Ammeter
    SF   *Electronics and Electrical
        Engineering
a   Anode
    SF   *Electronics and Electrical
        Engineering
AA   Anti Aircraft
    SF   *Aeronautics
        *Military Sciences
AA   Armature Accelerator
    SF   *Aeronautics
AAA   Anti Aircraft Artillery
    SF   *Aeronautics
        *Military Sciences
AAAS   American Association for the
        Advancement of Science
    SF   *General
AABP   Acetylaminobiphenyl
    SF   Biochemistry
        *Biological and Medical Sciences
AAC   Air Approach Control
    SF   *Aeronautics
AAC   Automatic Approach Control
    SF   *Aeronautics
AACB   Aeronautics and Astronautics
        Coordinating Board
    SF   *Aeronautics
        *Astronautics and Astrophysics
AACC   American Association of Cereal
        Chemists
    SF   *Agricultural Sciences
        Cereals
AACD   Antenna Adjustable Current
        Distribution
    SF   *Engineering
        Radio Engineering
        *Telecommunications
AACO   Arab Air Carriers Organization
    SF   *Aeronautics
AACS   Airways and Air Communications
        Servics
    SF   *Aeronautics

AACS   Asynchronous Address Communications
        Systems
    SF   *Engineering
        Radio Engineering
        *Telecommunications
AAD   Advanced Ammunition Depot
    SF   *Military Sciences
AADA   Anti Aircraft Defended Area
    SF   *Aeronautics
        *Military Sciences
AADC   All Applications Digital Computer
    SF   *Computer Sciences
        *Electronics and Electrical
        Engineering
AADC   Anti Aircraft Defence Commander
    SF   *Aeronautics
        *Military Sciences
AAF   Acetylaminofluorene
    SF   Biochemistry
        *Biological and Medical Sciences
AAFCE   Allied Air Force Central Europe
    SF   *Aeronautics
        *Military Sciences
AAFNE   Allied Air Force Northern Europe
    SF   *Aeronautics
        *Military Sciences
AAFSE   Allied Air Force Southern Europe
    SF   *Aeronautics
        *Military Sciences
AAG   Air Adjutant General
    SF   *Aeronautics
        *Military Sciences
AAH   Advanced Attack Helicopter
    SF   *Aeronautics
        *Military Sciences
AALC   Amphibious Assault Landing Craft
    SF   *Military Sciences
AALMG   Anti Aircraft Light Machine Gun
    SF   *Aeronautics
        *Military Sciences
AAM   Air-to-Air Missile
    SF   *Military Sciences
AAMC   Association of American Medical
        Colleges
    SF   *Biological and Medical Sciences

AAOO   American Academy of Ophthalmology
    and Otolaryngology
   SF   *Aeronautics
    Noise
AAOR   Anti-Aircraft Artillery Operations
    Room
   SF   *Military Sciences
AAP   Apollo Application Program
   SF   *Astronautics and Astrophysics
AAPP   Auxiliary Airborne Power Plant
   SF   *Aeronautics
AAPU   Airborne Auxiliary Power Unit
   SF   *Aeronautics
    *Military Sciences
AAS   Atomic Absorption Spectrophotometer
   SF   *Photography
AAS   Atomic Absorption Spectroscopy
   SF   *Brewery
AASHO American Association of State
    Highway Officials
   SF   *Transportation
AASR   Airport and Airways Surveillance
    Radar
   SF   *Aeronautics
AAT   Analytic Approximation Theory
   SF   Elementary Particles
    *Nuclear Sciences
AATC   Automatic Air Traffic Control
   SF   Aeronautics
AATMS Advanced Air Traffic Management
    System
   SF   *Aeronautics
    Air Traffic Control
AATO   Army Air Transport Organization
   SF   *Aeronautics
    *Military Sciences
    *Transportation
AB   Alcian Blue
   SF   *Biological and Medical Sciences
    Cytochemistry
AB   Aminoazobenzene
   SF   Biochemistry
    *Biological and Medical Sciences
AB-AF Alcian Blue-Aldehyde Fuchsin
   SF   *Biological and Medical Sciences
    Cytochemistry
ABC   Advanced Booking Charter
   SF   *Aeronautics
    Air Transport
ABCC   Atomic Bomb Casualty Commission
    (Jap.)
   SF   *Biological and Medical Sciences
ABCCC Airborne Battlefield Command and
    Control Center
   SF   *Aeronautics
    *Military Sciences
ABCS   Advisory Board for Cooperative
    Systems
   SF   Industrial Property
    *Patents

ABL   Atlas Basic Language
   SF   *Computer Sciences
    Data Processing
ABM   Anti Ballistic Missiles
   SF   *Military Sciences
ABMA   Army Ballistic Missile Agency
   SF   *Military Sciences
ABP   Aminobiphenyl
   SF   Biochemistry
    *Biological and Medical Sciences
ABRES Advanced Ballistic Reentry System
   SF   *Military Sciences
    *Space Sciences
ABS   Acrylonitrile-Butadiene-Styrene
   SF   *Non-metallic Materials
    Polymers
ABTA   Allied Brewery Traders' Association
   SF   *Brewery
ABU   Asian Broadcasting Union
   SF   *Communication Systems
    *Copyright
    Patents
AC   Acetic Acid
   SF   *Agricultural Sciences
AC   Adaptive Control
   SF   *General
    Instruments
AC   Advisory Circular
   SF   *Aeronautics
AC   Air Conditioning
   SF   *Metallurgy and Metallography
    Metalworks
AC   Alternating Current
   SF   *Aeronautics
    *Electronics and Electrical
     Engineering
    *Mathematics
AC   Ammonium Citrate
   SF   *Nuclear Sciences
    Reactors
AC   Anti-coincidence Counters
   SF   *Nuclear Sciences
    Measurements
ACA   American Communications Association
   SF   *Computer Sciences
    Data Processing
ACA   Aminocephalosporanic Acid
   SF   Biochemistry
    *Biological and Medical Sciences
ACA   Ammoniacal Copper Arsenite
   SF   *Engineering
    *Metallurgy and Metallography
ACA   Armament Control Agency
   SF   *Military Sciences
ACAU   Automatic Calling and Answering Unit
   SF   *Computer Sciences
    Data Processing
ACB   Army Classification Battery
   SF   *Management
    *Military Sciences

ACC   Abort Guidance Computer
        SF   *Computer Sciences
             Data Processing
             Navigation
ACC   Acid Copper Chromate
        SF   *Engineering
             *Metallurgy and Metallography
ACC   Air Control Centre
        SF   *Aeronautics
ACC   Air Coordinating Committee
        SF   *Aeronautics
             Air Traffic Control
ACC   Area Control Centers
        SF   *Aeronautics
             Ground Communication Networks
ACCA   Asynchronous Communications Control
          Attachment
        SF   *Computer Sciences
             Data Processing
ACD   Acid Citrate Dextrose
        SF   *Biological and Medical Sciences
             Blood Preservation
ACDO   Air Carrier District Office (US)
        SF   *Aeronautics
             *Transportation
ACE   Airspace Coordination Element
        SF   *Aeronautics
             Air Traffic Control
             Flight Paths
ACE   Allied Command Europe
        SF   *Military Sciences
ACE   Altimeter Control Equipment
        SF   *Aeronautics
ACE   Area Control Error
        SF   Cybernetics
             *Electronics and Electrical
               Engineering
ACE   Automatic Clutter Eliminator
        SF   *Aeronautics
             Navigation
             Radar Detection
ACE   Automatic Computing Engine
        SF   *Aeronautics
             *Computer Sciences
ACF   Air Combat Fighter
        SF   *Aeronautics
             Aircraft
             *Military Sciences
ACF   Autocorrelation Function
        SF   *Engineering
             Radio Engineering
             *Telecommunications
ACF   Avion de Combat Futur
        SF   *Aeronautics
             *Military Sciences
ACGB   Aircraft Corporation of Great Britain
        SF   *Aeronautics
ACGIH   American Conference of Governmental
          Industrial Hygienists
        SF   *Biological and Medical Sciences

AcH   Acetylcholine
        SF   *Biological and Medical Sciences
             Cytochemistry
AChE   Acetylcholinesterase
        SF   *Biological and Medical Sciences
             Cytochemistry
ACI   Adjusted Calving Interval
        SF   *Dairy Sciences
ACI   Army Council Instruction
        SF   *Military Sciences
ACIC   Aeronautical Chart and Information
          Center (US)
        SF   *Aeronautics
             Navigation
ACID   Automated Classification and
          Interpretation of Data
        SF   *Computer Sciences
             Data Processing
ACIGY   Advisory Council of the International
          Geophysical Year
        SF   *Geosciences
ACIR   Aviation Crash Injury Research
        SF   *Aeronautics
ACL   Application Control Language
        SF   *Computer Sciences
             *Electronics and Electrical
               Engineering
ACLANT Allied Command Atlantic
        SF   *Military Sciences
ACLS   Automated Control Landing System
        SF   *Aeronautics
             Approach and Landing
ACM   Air Chief Marshal
        SF   *Aeronautics
             *Military Sciences
ACM   Air Combat Maneuvering
        SF   *Aeronautics
             Naval Aviation
ACM   Association for Computing
          Machinery (US)
        SF   *Computer Sciences
             Data Processing
ACM   Associative Communication
          Multiplexer
        SF   *Computer Sciences
             Data Processing
ACN   Asbestos Cloth Neck
        SF   *Metallurgy and Metallography
             Metalworks
ACOS   Assistant Chief of Staff
        SF   *Military Sciences
ACP   Allied Communication Publication
        SF   *Military Sciences
ACP   Azimuth Change Pulse
        SF   *Aeronautics
             *Electronics and Electrical
               Engineering
             Navigation

ACPA   Association for Computer Programmers
           and Analysts
       SF   *Computer Sciences
ACR   Approach Control Radar
       SF   *Aeronautics
ACRS   Advisory Committee on Reactor
           Safeguards (US)
       SF   *Nuclear Sciences
           Reactors
ACRT   Analysis Control Routine
       SF   *Computer Sciences
           Data Processing
ACS   Adrenocortics Steroids
       SF   *Aeronautics
           Aviation Medicine
           *Biological and Medical Sciences
ACS   Aerodrome Control Service
       SF   *Aeronautics
           Airports
ACS   Altitude Control System
       SF   *Aeronautics
           *Space Sciences
ACS   Automatic Control Systems
       SF   *Engineering
           Radio Engineering
           *Telecommunications
ACSM   American Congress of Surveying
           and Mapping
       SF   *Engineering
           Instruments
           Photogrametric Engineering
ACT   Activity Center Transportation (Ford)
       SF   Automotive Industry
           *Transportation
ACT   Automatic Code Translation
       SF   *Computer Sciences
           Data Processing
ACTF   Altitude Control Test Facility
       SF   *Aeronautics
ACTH   Adrenocorticotrophic Hormone
       SF   *Biological and Medical Sciences
           Cytochemistry
           Pharmacology
ACTH   Adrenocorticotrophin
       SF   Biochemistry
           *Biological and Medical Sciences
           Pharmacology
ACTICE Authority for the Co-ordination
           of Inland Transport in Central
           Europe
       SF   *Military Sciences
           *Transportation
ACTISUD Authority for the Co-ordination
           of Inland Transport in
           Southern Europe
       SF   *Military Sciences
           *Transportation
ACTP   Advanced Computer Techniques Project
       SF   *Computer Sciences
           Data Processing

ACU   Arithmetic Control Unit
       SF   *Computer Sciences
           Data Processing
ACU   Automatic Calling Unit
       SF   *Computer Sciences
           Data Processing
           *Electronics and Electrical
               Engineering
ACV   Air Cushion Vehicle
       SF   *Aeronautics
ACV   Armoured Command Vehicle
       SF   *Military Sciences
ACW   Aircraft Control Warning
       SF   *Aeronautics
           *Military Sciences
AD   Access Door
       SF   *Metallurgy and Metallography
           Metalworks
AD   Account Directory
       SF   *Computer Sciences
           Data Processing
AD   Adaptive Control
       SF   *Engineering
           Instruments
A/D   Analog-to-Digital
       SF   *Computer Sciences
ADA   Action Data Automation
       SF   *Computer Sciences
           Data Processing
ADA   Adenosine Deaminase
       SF   *Biological and Medical Sciences
ADA   American Dairy Association
       SF   *Dairy Sciences
ADA   Automatic Data Acquisition
       SF   *Computer Sciences
           Data Processing
ADA   Azodicarbonamide
       SF   *Agricultural Sciences
           Milling
ADAC   Analytical Development Associates
           Corporation (US)
       SF   *Nuclear Sciences
ADAC   Automated Direct Analog Computer
       SF   *Computer Sciences
           Data Processing
ADAR   Advanced Design Army Radar
       SF   *Aeronautics
ADAR   Advanced Data Acquisition Routine
       SF   *Computer Sciences
           Data Processing
ADBMS Available Data Base Management
           System
       SF   *Computer Sciences
           Data Processing
ADC   Aerodrome Control
       SF   *Aeronautics
ADC   Air Data Computer
       SF   *Aeronautics
           *Computer Sciences

ADC   Air Defense Command
       SF   *Aeronautics
             *Military Sciences
ADC   Analog-to-Digital Converter
       SF   *Computer Sciences
             Data Processing
ADCC   Air Defense Control Center
       SF   *Aeronautics
             *Military Sciences
ADD   Activated Dough Development
       SF   *Agricultural Sciences
             Milling
ADE   Air Defense Emergency (US)
       SF   *Aeronautics
             Military Sciences
ADEPT Automated Direct Entry Packaging
       Technique
       SF   *Computer Sciences
             Data Processing
ADEU   Automatic Data Entry Unit
       SF   Aeronautics
             Data Processing
ADF   Acid Detergent Fiber
       SF   *Agricultural Sciences
             *Dairy Sciences
ADF   Aerial Direction Finding
       SF   *Aeronautics
             Navigation
ADF   Automatic Direction Finder
       SF   *Aeronautics
             Approach and Landing
             Navigation
ADG   Average Daily Gain
       SF   *Agricultural Sciences
ADH   Antidirectional Hamiltonian
       SF   *Mathematics
ADH   Antidiuretic Hormone
       SF   Biochemistry
             *Biological and Medical Sciences
             Pharmacology
ADI   Accepted Daily Intakes
       SF   *Dairy Sciences
             *General
ADI   Alternating Direction Implicit
       SF   Civil Engineering
             *Engineering
ADI   Altitude Direction Indicator
       SF   *Aeronautics
             Instruments
ADI   Automatic Direction Indicator
       SF   *Aeronautics
ADIS   Automatic Data Interchange System
       SF   *Aeronautics
             Ground Communication Networks
ADISP Aeronautical Data Interchange
       Systems Panel
       SF   *Aeronautics
ADIZ   Air Defense Identification Zone
       SF   *Aeronautics
             *Military Sciences

ADO   Air Defense Officer
       SF   *Aeronautics
             *Military Sciences
ADOC   Air Defense Operations Centre
       SF   *Aeronautics
             *Military Sciences
ADP   Adenosine Diphosphate
       SF   *Agricultural Sciences
ADP   Automatic Data Processing
       SF   *Computer Sciences
             *Electronics and Electrical
                Engineering
ADPESO Automatic Data Processing Equipment
       Selection Office
       SF   *Computer Sciences
             Data Processing
ADS   Accessory Drive System
       SF   *Aeronautics
ADS   Advanced Dressing Station
       SF   *Aeronautics
ADS   Air Defence Ship
       SF   *Aeronautics
             *Military Sciences
ADS   Air Defence System
       SF   *Aeronautics
             *Military Sciences
ADS   Aircraft Development Service
       SF   *Aeronautics
ADS   Automatic Depressurization System
       SF   *Nuclear Sciences
             Reactors
ADS   Automatic Door Seal
       SF   *Aeronautics
ADSA   American Dairy Science Association
       SF   *Agricultural Sciences
             *Dairy Sciences
ADSM   Air Defence Suppression Missile
       SF   *Aeronautics
             *Military Sciences
ADSS   A Diesel Supply Set
       SF   *Telecommunications
ADSTAR Automatic Document Storage and
       Retrieval
       SF   *Computer Sciences
             *Information Retrieval Systems
ADT   Admission Discharge and Transfer
       SF   *Computer Sciences
             *Information Retrieval Systems
ADT   Average Daily Traffic
       SF   *General
ADU   Automatic Data Unit
       SF   *Computer Sciences
             Data Processing
ADV   Acid Degree Values
       SF   *Agricultural Sciences
             *Dairy Sciences
ADX   Automatic Data Exchange
       SF   *Computer Sciences
             Data Processing

AE	Architect Engineer		AES	American Electrochemical Society
	SF Civil Engineering			SF *Aeronautics
	*Engineering		AES	Artificial Earth Satellite
AE	Atmospheric Explorer			SF *Space Sciences
	SF *Aeronautics		AES	Atmospheric Environment Service
	*Space Sciences			SF *Geosciences
AE	Auxiliary Equation			*Telecommunications
	SF *Mathematics		AES	Auger Electron Spectroscopy
AEC	American Engineering Council			SF *Nuclear Sciences
	SF *Engineering		AES	Auger Electron Spectrum
AEC	Aminoethyl Cellulose			SF *Electronics and Electrical
	SF *Agricultural Sciences			Engineering
	*Dairy Sciences			Instruments
AEC	Aminoethyl-Cysteine		AEW	Airborne Early Warning
	SF Biochemistry			SF *Aeronautics
	*Biological and Medical Sciences		AEWC	Airborne Early Warning Control
AEC	Atomic Energy Commission (US)			SF *Aeronautics
	SF *Nuclear Sciences		AF	Air Filter
	Reactors			SF *Metallurgy and Metallography
AECL	Atomic Energy of Canada Limited			Metalworks
	SF *Nuclear Sciences		AF	Aldehyde Fuchsin
AED	Automated Engineering Design			SF *Biological and Medical Sciences
	SF *Computer Sciences			Cytochemistry
AEDC	Arnold Engineering Development Center		AF	Alternating Fields
	(US)			SF *Lunar Sciences
	SF *Aeronautics		AF	Angle Frame
	*Engineering			SF *Metallurgy and Metallography
AEEC	Airline Electronic Engineering			Metalworks
	Committee		AF	Audio Frequency
	SF *Aeronautics			SF *Communication Systems
	*Electronics and Electrical		AFA	Air Force Association
	Engineering			SF *Aeronautics
AEEMS	Automatic Electric Energy Management			*Military Sciences
	System		AFA	Army Flight Activity
	SF *Aeronautics			SF *Aeronautics
	Aircraft			*Military Sciences
AEG	Active Element Groups		AFAR	Advanced Field Array Radar
	SF *Aeronautics			SF *Aeronautics
	Avionics			Radar Detection
AEG	Allgemeine Elektrizitatts Gesellschaft		AFB	Air Force Base
	(Ger.)			SF *Aeronautics
	SF *Nuclear Sciences			*Military Sciences
	Reactors		AFB	Anti Friction Bearing
AEI	Aerial Exposure Index			SF *Aeronautics
	SF *Photography		AFBMD	Air Force Ballistic Missile Division
AEI	Associated Electrical Industries			SF *Aeronautics
	SF *Electronics and Electrical			*Military Sciences
	Engineering		AFC	Amplitude Frequency Characteristics
AEI	Automatic Error Interrogation			SF *Telecommunications
	SF *Telecommunications		AFC	Autocorrelation Functions
AEOC	Aminoethylhomocysteine			SF *Engineering
	SF Biochemistry			Radio Engineering
	*Biological and Medical Sciences			*Telecommunications
AEP	American Electric Power		AFC	Atomic Fluid Cells
	SF *Electronics and Electrical			SF *Biological and Medical Sciences
	Engineering		AFC	Automatic Frequency Control
	Power Systems			SF *Aeronautics
AEROSAT	Aeronautical Satellite			*Communication Systems
	SF *Aeronautics		AFCAC	African Civil Aviation Commission
	Air Traffic Control			SF *Aeronautics
	*Communication Systems			Air Traffic Control

AFCAL Association Franchise de Calcul
    SF *Computer Sciences
       Data Processing
AFCE Allied Forces Control Europe
    SF *Military Sciences
AFCENT Allied Forces Central
    SF *Military Sciences
       *Transportation
AFCRL Air Force Cambridge Research
      Laboratory
    SF *Aeronautics
       *Military Sciences
AFCS Air Force Communications Service
    SF *Aeronautics
       *Communication Systems
       *Military Sciences
AFCS Automatic Flight Control System
    SF *Aeronautics
       Air Traffic Control
       Navigation
AFCS Avionic Flight Control System
    SF *Aeronautics
       Avionics
AFF Above Finished Floor
    SF *Metallurgy and Metallography
       Metalworks
AFF Army Field Force
    SF *Aeronautics
       *Military Sciences
AFFDL Air Force Flight Dynamics
      Laboratory (US)
    SF *Aeronautics
       *Military Sciences
AFFF Aqueous Film Forming Foam
    SF *Aeronautics
       Aircraft Fires
       Fire Fighting
AFFTC Air Force Flight Test Center
    SF *Aeronautics
       *Military Sciences
AFG Analogue Function Generator
    SF *Computer Sciences
       Data Processing
AFGP Antifreeze Glycoproteins
    SF *Biological and Medical Sciences
AFGWC Air Force Global Weather Center (US)
    SF *Geosciences
       *Meteorology
       *Military Sciences
AFHRL Air Force Human Resources Laboratory
    SF *Aeronautics
       *Military Sciences
AFI Automatic Fault Isolation
    SF *Computer Sciences
       Data Processing
AFIPS American Federation for Information
      Processing Societies
    SF *Computer Sciences
       Data Processing
       *Information Retrieval Systems

AFIT Air Force Institute of Technology
      (US)
    SF   Civil Engineering
       *Engineering
       *Military Sciences
AFLC Air Force Logistics Command (US)
    SF *Aeronautics
       Civil Engineering
       *Engineering
       *Military Sciences
AFLCM Air Force Logistics Command Manual
    SF *Aeronautics
       *Military Sciences
AFM Air Force Manual
    SF *Aeronautics
       *Military Sciences
AFM Analysis and Forecasting Mode
    SF *Computer Sciences
       Data Processing
       *Management
AFMDC Air Force Missile Development
      Center (US)
    SF *Aeronautics
       *Military Sciences
AFMED Allied Forces Mediterranean
    SF *Military Sciences
AFML Air Force Material Laboratory
    SF *Military Sciences
AFMTC Air Force Missile Test Center
    SF *Military Sciences
AFN American Forces Network
    SF *Military Sciences
AFNORTH Allied Forces North
    SF *Military Sciences
AFP Adiabatic Fast Passage
    SF *Engineering
       Instruments
AFPAM Automatic Flight Planning and
      Monitoring
    SF *Aeronautics
AFPAV Airfield Pavement
    SF *Aeronautics
       Airports
AFPRO Air Force Plant Representative Office
    SF *Aeronautics
       *Military Sciences
AFQT Armed Forces Qualification Test
    SF *Military Sciences
       *Training
AFR Air Force Regulation
    SF *Aeronautics
       *Military Sciences
AFR Amplitude Frequency Responses
    SF *Engineering
       Radio Engineering
       *Telecommunications
AFRCE Air Force Regional Civil Engineer
    SF   Civil Engineering
       *Engineering
       *Military Sciences

AFRTC Air Force Reserve Training Center
    SF *Aeronautics
       *Military Sciences
AFS Aeronautical Fixed Service
    SF *Aeronautics
AFS Air Force Specialty
    SF *Aeronautics
       *Military Sciences
AFS Air Force Supply
    SF *Aeronautics
       *Military Sciences
AFS Army Fire Service
    SF *Military Sciences
AFSATCOM Air Force Satellite Communications
    SF *Aeronautics
       *Communication Systems
       *Military Sciences
AFSC Air Force Systems Command
    SF *Military Sciences
AFSC Armed Force Staff College
    SF *Military Sciences
AFSCM Air Force Systems Command Manual
    SF *Aeronautics
       *Military Sciences
AFSE Allied Forces Southern Europe
    SF *Military Sciences
AFSR Argonne Fast Source Reactor
    SF *Nuclear Sciences
       Reactors
AFSWC Air Force Special Weapons Center (US)
    SF *Aeronautics
       *Military Sciences
AFT Adaptive Ferroelectric Transformer
    SF *Electronics and Electrical
         Engineering
       Solid-state Circuits
AFTN Aeronautical Fixed Telecommunications
    Network
    SF *Aeronautics
       *Telecommunications
AFV Armoured Fighting Vehicle
    SF *Military Sciences
AFWL Air Force Weapon Laboratory
    SF Civil Engineering
       *Engineering
       *Military Sciences
AFWTR Air Force Western Test Range
    SF *Aeronautics
       *Military Sciences
AGARD Advisory Group for Aeronautical
    Research and Development
    SF *Aeronautics
       *Space Sciences
AGC Automatic Gain Control
    SF *Aeronautics
       *Computer Sciences
       Data Processing
       *Electronics and Electrical
         Engineering
AGCA Automatic Ground Controlled Approach

    SF *Aeronautics
AGD Axial Gear Differential
    SF *Aeronautics
       Instruments
AGDS American Gage Design Standard
    SF *Aeronautics
AGE Aerospace Ground Equipment
    SF Civil Engineering
       *Engineering
       *Space Sciences
AGL Above Ground Level
    SF *Aeronautics
       Aircraft
AGL Acute Granulocytic Leukaemia
    SF *Biological and Medical Sciences
       Cytochemistry
AGL Altitude above Ground Level
    SF *Aeronautics
AGMA American Gear Manufacturers'
    Association
    SF *Engineering
AGOS Air Ground Operations Section
    SF *Aeronautics
AGR Advanced Gas-cooled Reactor
    SF *Nuclear Sciences
       Reactors
AGRA Army Ground Royal Artillery
    SF *Military Sciences
AGRE Army Ground Royal Engineers
    SF *Military Sciences
AGS Air Gunnery School (UK)
    SF *Aeronautics
       Navigation
       *Training
AGS Aircraft General Standards
    SF *Aeronautics
AGS Automatic Gain Stabilization
    SF *Aeronautics
AGSAN Astronomical Guidance System for
    Air Navigation
    SF *Aeronautics
       Navigation
AH   Ampere Hour
    SF *Electronics and Electrical
         Engineering
AH   Analog Hybrid
    SF *Computer Sciences
       *Electronics and Electrical
         Engineering
AHCT Ascending Horizon Crossing Time
    SF *Astronautics and Astrophysics
       Navigation
AHP Aniline Hydrogen Phthalate
    SF *Agricultural Sciences
AHQ Allied Headquarters
    SF *Military Sciences
AHRS Altitude Heading Reference System
    SF *Aeronautics
       Navigation

AHS   Airborne Hardware Simulator
      SF *Aeronautics
          Navigation
AHU   Accumulated Heat Units
      SF *Agricultural Sciences
AHU   Air Handling Unit
      SF *Metallurgy and Metallography
          Metalworks
AHU   Antihalation Undercoat
      SF *Photography
AHWG Ad Hoc Working Group
      SF   Logistics
          *Military Sciences
AI   Airborne Interception
      SF *Aeronautics
          *Military Sciences
AI   Annoyance Index
      SF *Aeronautics
          Aircraft Noise
AI   Anti Icing
      SF *Aeronautics
AI   Area of Intersection
      SF *Nuclear Sciences
AI   Artificial Insemination
      SF *Agricultural Sciences
          *Dairy Sciences
AIA   Aerospace Industries Association
      SF *Aeronautics
          *Space Sciences
AIAA Aerospace Industries Association of
      America
      SF *Space Sciences
AIAA American Institute of Aeronautics and
      Astronauts
      SF *Aeronautics
          *Space Sciences
AIB   Accidents Investigation Branch (UK)
      SF *Aeronautics
          Aircraft Accidents
AIB   Agency Investigation Board
      SF *Aeronautics
AIB   Aminoisobutyric Acid
      SF *Agricultural Sciences
AIBN Azobisiobutyronitrite
      SF *Non-metallic Materials
          Polymers
AIC   Aeronautical Information Circular
      SF *Aeronautics
AIC   Ammunition Identification Code
      SF *Military Sciences
AIC   Automatic Intersection Control
      SF *Aeronautics
          Air Traffic Control
AICBM Anti Intercontinental Ballistic
      Missile
      SF *Military Sciences
          *Space Sciences
AID   Agency for International Development
      SF *Engineering
          Engineering Consultancy

AID   Automatic Interrogation Distorted
      SF *Engineering
          Radio Engineering
          *Telecommunications
AIDAS Advanced Instrumentation and Data
      Analysis System
      SF *Aeronautics
          Instruments
AIDATS Army In-flight Data Transmission
      System
      SF *Military Sciences
AIDE Automated Image Device Evaluation
      SF *Electronics and Electrical
          Engineering
AIDJEX Arctic Ice Dynamic Joint Experiment
      SF *Communication Systems
          *Geosciences
AIDS Airborne Integrated Data System
      SF *Aeronautics
          Navigation
AIEE American Institute of Electrical
      Engineering
      SF *Aeronautics
          *Electronics and Electrical
          Engineering
AIET Average Instruction Execution Time
      SF *Computer Sciences
          Data Processing
AIG   Accident Investigation
      SF *Aeronautics
          Aircraft Accidents
AIIC Army Imagery Intelligence Corps
      SF *Military Sciences
AIL   Airborne Instruments Laboratory
      SF *Aeronautics
          Instruments
AILAS Automatic Instruments Landing System
      SF *Aeronautics
          Approach and Landing
AILS Advanced Integrated Landing System
      SF *Aeronautics
          Approach and Landing
          Instruments
AIM   Aerial Independent Models
      SF *Photography
AIM   Airman's Information Manual
      SF *Aeronautics
AIM   Alarm Indication Monitor
      SF *Aeronautics
AIMIS Advanced Integrated Modular Instrument
      System
      SF *Aeronautics
          *Electronics and Electrical
          Engineering
AIMS Automatic Industrial Management System
      SF *Computer Sciences
          *Electronics and Electrical
          Engineering
AIP   Aeronautical Information Publication
      SF *Aeronautics

AIP   Allied Intelligence Publication
      SF *Aeronautics
          *Military Sciences
AIPPI International Association for the
        Protection of Industrial Property
      SF *Copyright
          Marks
          Patents
AIR   Airborne Intercept Radar
      SF *Aeronautics
AIR   American Institute of Research
      SF *Aeronautics
          *General
AIRLO Air Liaison Officer
      SF *Aeronautics
AIRPASS Airborne Interception Radar and
        Pilot's Attack Sight System
      SF *Aeronautics
          *Military Sciences
AIS   Advanced Instructional Systems
      SF *Training
AIS   Aeronautical Information Service
      SF *Aeronautics
AIS   Altitude Indication System
      SF *Aeronautics
          Avionics
AIS   Automatic Inter-city Station
      SF *Engineering
          Radio Engineering
          *Telecommunications
AIT   Advanced Individual Training
      SF *Training
AIT   Architect in Training
      SF Civil Engineering
          *Engineering
          *Training
AIT   Autoignition Temperature
      SF *Aeronautics
AITE Aircraft Integrated Test Equipment
      SF *Aeronautics
          Instruments
AITE Automatic Inter-city Telephone
        Exchange
      SF *Engineering
          Radio Engineering
          *Telecommunications
AITS Automatic Integrated Telephone System
      SF *Engineering
          Radio Engineering
          *Telecommunications
AIW   Auroral Infrasonic Wave
      SF Atmospheric Sciences
          *Geosciences
AJ   Area Junction
      SF *Engineering
          Radio Engineering
          *Telecommunications
AJ   Area Junction
      SF *Engineering
          Radio Engineering
          *Telecommunications

AL   Amplitude Limiter
      SF *Engineering
          *Telecommunications
AL   Artificial Lines
      SF *Engineering
          Radio Engineering
          *Telecommunications
ALA   Aminolaevulinate
      SF *Biological and Medical Sciences
ALAI International Literary and Artistic
        Association
      SF *Copyright
          Industrial Property
          Patents
ALARM Air Launched Advanced Ramjet Missile
      SF *Aeronautics
          *Military Sciences
ALARR Air Launched Air Recoverable Rocket
      SF *Aeronautics
          *Military Sciences
ALATD Assumed Latitude
      SF *Aeronautics
          Navigation
ALB   Albumen
      SF Biochemistry
          *Biological and Medical Sciences
ALBM Air Launched Ballistic Missile
      SF *Aeronautics
          *Military Sciences
ALC   Adaptive Logic Circuit
      SF *Computer Sciences
ALC   Automatic Level Control
      SF *Aeronautics
          Instruments
ALCC Airborne Launch Control Center
      SF *Aeronautics
          *Military Sciences
ALCH Approach Light Contact Height
      SF *Aeronautics
          Approach and Landing
ALD   Automatic Louver Damper
      SF *Metallurgy and Metallography
          Metalworks
ALFCE Allied Land Forces Central Europe
      SF *Military Sciences
ALGOL Algorithmic Language
      SF *Computer Sciences
          Data Processing
ALHT Apollo Lunar Hand Tool
      SF *Astronomy and Astrophysics
          *Lunar Sciences
ALL   Acute Lymphoblastic Leukaemia
      SF *Biological and Medical Sciences
ALM   Applied Laboratory Methods
      SF *Biological and Medical Sciences
          *Dairy Sciences
ALMS Aircraft Landing Measurement System
      SF *Aeronautics
          Approach and Landing

ALOND Assumed Longitude
    SF   *Naval Sciences
         Navigation
ALOTS Airborne Lightweight Optical Tracking
      System
    SF   *Aeronautics
         Approach and Landing
ALPA Airline Pilots' Association
    SF   *Aeronautics
ALPA Alaskan Long Period Array
    SF   *Geosciences
         Seismic Detection
ALPAC Automatic Language Processing
      Committee
    SF   *Computer Sciences
         Data Processing
ALPS Advanced Linear Programming System
    SF   *Computer Sciences
         Data Processing
ALQAS Aircraft Landing Quality Association
      Scheme
    SF   *Aeronautics
         Approach and Landing
ALRR Ames Laboratory Research Reactor
    SF   *Nuclear Sciences
ALS Antilymphocyte Serum
    SF   *Biological and Medical Sciences
         Drugs
ALS Approach Light System
    SF   *Aeronautics
         Approach and Landing
ALS Automatic Landing System
    SF   *Aeronautics
         Approach and Landing
         Instruments
ALSEP Apollo Lunar Surface Experiment
      Packages
    SF   *Astronautics and Astrophysics
         Lunar Sciences
         *Telecommunications
ALSS Airborne Location and Strike System
    SF   *Military Sciences
ALT Airborne Laser Tracker
    SF   *Military Sciences
         Missile Systems
ALTA Association of Local Transport
      Airlines
    SF   *Aeronautics
         *Transportation
ALU Arithmetic and Logic Unit
    SF   *Computer Sciences
         Data Processing
         *Electronics and Electrical
          Engineering
AM   Airlock Module
    SF   *Astronautics and Astrophysics
         Spacecraft
AM   Amplitude Modulation
    SF   *Computer Sciences
         *Electronics and Electrical

         Engineering
         *Telecommunications
AM   Analog Monolithic
    SF   *Electronics and Electrical
          Engineering
AM   Associative Memory
    SF   *Computer Sciences
         Data Processing
AMA Air Materiel Area
    SF   *Aeronautics
         *Military Sciences
AMA American Management Association
    SF   *Computer Sciences
         Data Processing
AMAD Aircraft Mounted Accessory Drive
    SF   *Aeronautics
AMBD Automatic Multiple Blade Damper
    SF   *Metallurgy and Metallography
         Metalworks
AMC Aetylmethlcarbon
    SF   *Agricultural Sciences
         *Dairy Sciences
AMC Aircraft Manufacturers Council
    SF   *Aeronautics
AMC Army Materiel Command
    SF   *Military Sciences
AMC Army Missile Command
    SF   *Aeronautics
         *Military Sciences
AMC Automatic Monitoring Circuit
    SF   *Engineering
         Radio Engineering
         *Telecommunications
AMCA Advanced Materiel Concept Agency
    SF   *Military Sciences
AMCP Abnormal Milk Control Program
    SF   *Agricultural Sciences
         *Dairy Sciences
AMCP Allied Military Communications Panel
    SF   Aeronautics
         *Military Sciences
AMCS Airborne Missile Control System
    SF   Aeronautics
         *Military Sciences
AMEDD Army Medical Department (US)
    SF   *Biological and Medical Sciences
         *Military Sciences
AMEDS Army Medical Science
    SF   *Biological and Medical Sciences
         *Military Sciences
AMF Acid Modified Flour
    SF   *Agricultural Sciences
         Cereals
AMHIC Automatic Merchandising Health-
      Industry Council
    SF   *Agricultural Sciences
         *Dairy Sciences
AMINCO American Instrument Company
    SF   Instruments
         *Nuclear Sciences

AMIS Aircraft Movement Information Service
    SF *Aeronautics
       Air Traffic Control
       *Communication Systems
AMK Anti Misting Kerosine
    SF *Aeronautics
       Fuels
AMMoL Acute Myelomonoctic Leukaemia
    SF *Biological and Medical Sciences
       Cytochemistry
AMMRC Army Materiels and Mechanics Research
    Center
    SF *Engineering
       Chemical Engineering
       *Military Sciences
AMO Air Ministry Order (UK)
    SF *Aeronautics
AMoL Acute Monocytic Leukaemia
    SF *Biological and Medical Sciences
       Cytochemistry
AMP Adenosine Monophosphate
    SF *Biological and Medical Sciences
       Cytochemistry
       *Dairy Sciences
AMPI Associated Milk Producers'
    Information (US)
    SF *Agricultural Sciences
       *Dairy Sciences
AMPR Aeronautical Manufacturers Planning
    Report
    SF *Aeronautics
AMPSS Advanced Manned Precision Strike
    System
    SF *Aeronautics
       *Military Sciences
AMR Atlantic Missile Range
    SF *Military Sciences
AMR Automatic Message Routing
    SF *Computer Sciences
AMRL Aerospace Medical Research Laboratory
    (US)
    SF *Biological and Medical Sciences
       Aviation Medicine
AMS Aeronautical Material Specification
    SF *Aeronautics
AMS Aerospace Material Specification
    SF *Non-metallic Materials
       Plastics
       Polymers
AMS Air Mail Service
    SF *Aeronautics
       *Telecommunications
AMS Army Medical Service
    SF *Biological and Medical Sciences
       *Military Sciences
AMS Army Map Service
    SF *Military Sciences
AMSL Above Mean Sea Level
    SF *Geosciences
AMSP Allied Military Security Publications

    SF *Military Sciences
AMST Advanced Medium STOL Transport
    SF *Aeronautics
       Aircraft
       *Military Sciences
AMT Audio Magneto-telluric
    SF *Oceanography
AMTCL Association for Machines Translation
    and Computational Linguistics
    SF *Computer Sciences
       Data Processing
AMTRAC Amphibian Tractor
    SF *Military Sciences
AMU Astronaut Maneuvering Unit
    SF *Space Sciences
       Space Simulation
AMVER Automated Merchant Vessel Reporting
    SF Navigation
       Shipping
       *Transportation
AN Ammonium Nitrate
    SF *Agricultural Sciences
ANBS Air Navigation and Bombing School
    SF *Aeronautics
       Navigation
       *Training
ANC Air Navigation Commission
    SF *Aeronautics
       Ground Communication Systems
       Navigation
ANC Air Navigation Conference
    SF *Aeronautics
       Navigation
ANC Army Nurse Corps
    SF *Biological and Medical Sciences
       *Military Sciences
ANCU Airborne Navigation Computer Unit
    SF *Aeronautics
       Navigation
       Testing
AND Air-Force Navy Design
    SF *Aeronautics
       *Military Sciences
ANDB Air Navigation Development Board (US)
    SF *Aeronautics
       Air Traffic Control
       Radar Beacon Systems
ANFCE Allied Naval Force Central Europe
    SF *Military Sciences
ANG Air National Guard
    SF *Aeronautics
       *Military Sciences
ANG-CE Air National Guard Civil
    Engineering
    SF *Aeronautics
       Civil Engineering
       *Engineering
       *Military Sciences
ANI Annular Isotropic Source
    SF *Nuclear Sciences

	Radiation
	Reactors
ANIM	Association of Nuclear Instrument
	Manufacturers
	SF *Nuclear Sciences
ANIP	Army Navy Integrated Presentation
	SF *Aeronautics
	*Military Sciences
ANIP	Army Navy Instrumentation Program
	SF *Aeronautics
	Instruments
	*Military Sciences
ANL	Argonne National Laboratory (US)
	SF *Biological and Medical Sciences
	*Nuclear Sciences
ANMC	American National Metric Council
	SF *Engineering
	Mechanical Engineering
ANO	Air Navigation Order
	SF *Aeronautics
	Navigation
ANOVA	Analysis Of Variants
	SF *Photography
ANOVA	Analysis Of Variation
	SF *Agricultural Sciences
	*Dairy Sciences
ANP	Allied Navigation Publication
	SF *Aeronautics
	Navigation
ANPP	Army Nuclear Power Program
	SF Civil Engineering
	*Engineering
	*Military Sciences
	*Nuclear Sciences
ANRC	American National Red Cross
	SF *Transportation
ANS	Air Navigation School
	SF *Aeronautics
	Navigation
	*Training
ANS	American Nuclear Society
	SF *Nuclear Sciences
ANS	Aniline Naphthalene Sulfonate
	SF *Dairy Sciences
ANS	Astronomical Netherlands Satellite
	SF *Astronautics and Astrophysics
	*Telecommunications
ANSI	American National Standards Institute
	SF *Aeronautics
	*Standards
ANSL	American National Standard Labels
	SF *Computer Sciences
	Data Processing
ant	Antenna (Aerial)
	SF *Communication Systems
	*Engineering
	Radio Engineering
ANTAC	Air Navigation Tactical Control System
	SF *Aeronautics
	Navigation

ANU	Airplane Nose Up
	SF *Aeronautics
	Aircraft
AOA	American Ordinance Association
	SF *Military Sciences
AOC	Air Officer Commanding
	SF *Aeronautics
	*Military Sciences
AOCI	Airport Operators Council
	International
	SF *Aeronautics
AOD	Advanced Ordnance Depot
	SF *Military Sciences
AOEW	Air Operating Empty Weight
	SF *Aeronautics
AONS	Air Observers Navigation School
	SF *Aeronautics
	Navigation
	*Training
AOP	Air Observation Post
	SF *Aeronautics
AOP	Allied Ordinance Publication
	SF *Military Sciences
AOPA	Aircraft Owners' and Pilots'
	Association
	SF *Aeronautics
AOS	Air Observer's School
	SF *Aeronautics
	Navigation
	*Training
AOT	Alignment Optical Telescope
	SF *Naval Sciences
	Navigation
AOU	Automated Offset Unit
	SF *Computer Sciences
	Data Processing
AOV	Analysis of Variance
	SF *Agricultural Sciences
AP	Air Publication
	SF *Aeronautics
AP	Alkaline Permagnate
	SF *Nuclear Sciences
	Nucleonics
	Reactors
AP	Alkaline Phosphatase
	SF *Biological and Medical Sciences
	Biochemistry
AP	Anterior Pituitary
	SF *Biological and Medical Sciences
	Cytochemistry
AP	Application Programs
	SF *Computer Sciences
	Data Processing
AP	Array Processor
	SF *Computer Sciences
	Data Processing
AP	Assumed Position
	SF *Aeronautics
	Navigation

AP   Autopilot
        SF   *Aeronautics
             *Computer Sciences
             Data Processing
APA   Amino Penicillanic Acid
        SF   *Biological and Medical Sciences
             Biochemistry
APAC   Alkaline Permagnate Ammonium Citrate
        SF   *Nuclear Sciences
             Nucleonics
             Reactors
APACS   Airplane Position and Altitude Camera
          System
        SF   *Aeronautics
APAM   Array Processor Access Method
        SF   *Computer Sciences
             Data Processing
APATS   Automatic Programmer and Test System
        SF   *Aeronautics
             *Computer Sciences
             Data Processing
APB   Antiphase Boundary Dormain
        SF   *Lunar Sciences
APC   Aerobic Plate Counts
        SF   *Agricultural Sciences
             *Dairy Sciences
APC   Amplitude Phase Conversion
        SF   *Engineering
             Radio Engineering
             *Telecommunications
APC   Area Position Control
        SF   *Aeronautics
             Air Traffic Control
APC   Armoured Personnel Carrier
        SF   *Engineering
             Mechanical Engineering
             *Military Sciences
APC   Automatic Pressure Control
        SF   *Aeronautics
             Ground Equipment
APCS   Associative Processor Computer
          System
        SF   *Computer Sciences
             Data Processing
APD   Avalanche Photodiode
        SF   *Engineering
             Instruments
APDC   Ammonium Pyrrolidine Dithiocarbamate
        SF   *Agricultural Sciences
             *Brewery
APDT   Allowed Project Time
        SF   *Computer Sciences
             Data Processing
             Operational Research
APEX   Advanced Purchase Excursion
        SF   *Aeronautics
             Air Transport
APFD   Autopilot Flight Director
        SF   *Aeronautics
             Instruments

APFD   Automatic Program Generation
        SF   *Computer Sciences
             Data Processing
APG   Azimuth Pulse Generator
        SF   *Aeronautics
             Radar
APGC   Air Proving Ground Center
        SF   *Aeronautics
API   Air Position Indicator
        SF   *Aeronautics
             Instruments
API   Armour Piercing Incendiary
        SF   *Aeronautics
             *Military Sciences
API   Automatic Priority Interrupt
        SF   Measurement Systems
             *Nuclear Sciences
APICS   American Production and Inventory
          Control
        SF   *Computer Sciences
             *Information Retrieval Systems
APIS   Army Photographic Interpretation
          Section
        SF   *Aeronautics
             *Military Sciences
APL   Applied Physics Laboratory
        SF   *Physics
APP   Approach Control Office
        SF   *Aeronautics
             Approach and Landing
APP   Auxiliary Power Plant
        SF   *Aeronautics
APPG   Adjacent Phase Pulse Generator
        SF   *Electronics and Electrical
               Engineering
APPLE   Associative Processor Programming
          Language Evaluation
        SF   *Aeronautics
             Air Traffic Control
             *Computer Sciences
approx Approximately
        SF   *General
APR   Airborne Profile Recorder
        SF   *Photography
APR   Alternate Path Retry
        SF   *Computer Sciences
             Data Processing
APRFR   Army Pulse Radiation Facility Reactor
        SF   *Nuclear Sciences
             Reactors
APRIL   Aqua Planning Risk Indicator for
          Landing
        SF   *Aeronautics
             Approach and Landing
APRL   Automated Primate Research Laboratory
        SF   *Biological and Medical Sciences
APRT   Adenine Phosphoribosyltransferase
        SF   *Biological and Medical Sciences
APSA   Automatic Particle Size Analyzer
        SF   Test Equipment
             *Testing

APSP   Array Processor Subroutine Package
        SF   *Computer Sciences
             Data Processing
APT   Advanced Passenger Train
        SF   *Transportation
APT   Advanced Passenger Transport
        SF   *Transportation
APT   Airman Proficiency Test
        SF   *Aeronautics
APT   Armour Piercing Tracer
        SF   *Military Sciences .
APT   Automatic Picture Transmission
        SF   *Computer Sciences
             Data Processing
             *Telecommunications
APT   Automatic Position Telemetering
        SF   *Aeronautics
             Navigation
APT   Automatic Programmed Tool
        SF   *Computer Sciences
             Data Processing
APTS   Automatic Picture Transmission
          System
        SF   *Photography
APU   Auxiliary Power Unit
        SF   *Aeronautics
             Aircraft
AQ   Aminoquinoline
        SF   *Biological and Medical Sciences
             Biochemistry
AQE   Airman Qualifying Examination
        SF   *Aeronautics
             *Training
AQL   Acceptable Qualify Level
        SF   *Computer Sciences
             Data Processing
AQO   Aminoquinoline Oxide
        SF   *Biological and Medical Sciences
             Biochemistry
AR   Aerial Refuelling
        SF   *Aeronautics
AR   Antireflection
        SF   *Physics
             Quantum Electronics
AR   Arithmetic Register
        SF   *Computer Sciences
             *Electronics and Electrical
              Engineering
AR   Army Regulation
        SF   *Aeronautics
             *Military Sciences
AR   Associative Register
        SF   *Computer Sciences
             *Electronics and Electrical
              Engineering
AR   Autoregressive
        SF   *Mathematics
ARA   Aircraft Research Association
        SF   *Aeronautics
ARADCOM Army Air Defense Command

        SF   *Aeronautics
             *Military Sciences
ARAP   Aeronautical Research Associates of
          Princeton
        SF   *Aeronautics
ARB   Air Registration Board
        SF   *Aeronautics
ARB   Air Research Bureau
        SF   *Aeronautics
ARC   Advanced Reentry Concept
        SF   *Astronautics and Astrophysics
             Spacecraft
ARC   Aeronautical Research Council (UK)
        SF   *Aeronautics
ARC   Aircraft Radio Corporation
        SF   *Aeronautics
             *Communication Systems
ARC   Airworthiness Requirements Committee
        SF   *Aeronautics
             Inspection
ARC   Atlantic Research Corporation
        SF   *Aeronautics
             *Astronautics and Astrophysics
ARC   Augmentation Research Center (US)
        SF   *Computer Sciences
             Data Processing
ARC   Automatic Remote Control
        SF   *Aeronautics
             *General
ARCAS   Automatic Radar Chain Acquisition
          System
        SF   *Aeronautics
ARCH   Articulated Computer Hierarchy
        SF   *Aeronautics
             *Computer Sciences
ARDA   American Railway Development
          Association
        SF   *Transportation
ARDC   Air Research and Development
          Command (US)
        SF   *Aeronautics
             *Photography
ARDS   Advanced Remote Display Station
        SF   *Engineering
             Mechanical Engineering
ARE   Asymplotic Relative Efficiency
        SF   *Communication Systems
             Navigation
ARGUS   Automatic Routine Generating and
          Updating System
        SF   *Computer Sciences
             Data Processing
ARHCO   Atlantic Richfield Hanford Company
        SF   *Nuclear Sciences
             Reactors
ARI   Airborne Radio Instrument
        SF   *Aeronautics
             *Communication Systems
             Instruments

ARIA Advanced Range Instrumented
        Aircraft
      SF *Aeronautics
ARIA Apollo Range Instrumented Aircraft
      SF *Astronautics and Astrophysics
          Spacecraft
ARINC Aeronautical Radio Incorporated
      SF *Aeronautics
          *Communication Systems
          Navigation
ARIS Advanced Range Instrumentation Ship
      SF *Astronautics and Astrophysics
          Spacecraft
ARL   Aerospace Research Laboratory (UK)
      SF *Aeronautics
          *Space Sciences
ARM   Accumulator Read-in Module
      SF   Measurement Systems
          *Nuclear Sciences
ARM   Anhysteretic Remnant Magnetization
      SF *Lunar Sciences
ARM   Anti Radar Missile
      SF *Aeronautics
          *Military Sciences
ARNG Army National Grid
      SF   Logistics
          *Military Sciences
ARNOT Area Notices
      SF *Aeronautics
          Ground Communication Systems
AROD Airborne Range and Orbit Determination
      SF *Aeronautics
          Navigation
ARODS Airborne Radar Orbital Determination
        System
      SF *Aeronautics
          Navigation
AROM Associative Read Only Memory
      SF *Computer Sciences
          Data Processing
ARP   Advanced Reentry Program
      SF *Astronautics and Astrophysics
          Spacecraft
ARP   Air Raid Protection
      SF *Aeronautics
          *Military Sciences
ARP   Azimuth Reset Pulse
      SF *Aeronautics
          *Electronics and Electrical
             Engineering
          Navigation
ARPA Advanced Research Projects Agency
      SF *Communication Systems
          *Computer Sciences
          Data Processing
ARQ   Automatic Repeat Request
      SF *Communication Systems
ARQ   Automatic Request for Repetition
      SF *Computer Sciences
          *Electronics and Electrical
             Engineering

ARQ   Automatic Response Query
      SF *Aeronautics
          *Communication Systems
ARRL American Radio Relay League
      SF *Telecommunications
ARS   Air Rescue Service
      SF *Aeronautics
ARS   Automatic Recovery System
      SF *Astronautics and Astrophysics
          Spacecraft
ARSR Air Route Surveillance Radar
      SF *Aeronautics
          Air Traffic Control
          *Communication Systems
ART   Advanced Research and Technology
      SF *Computer Science
          Data Processing
ART   Average Retrieval Time
      SF *Information Retrieval Systems
ARTC Addiction Research and Treatment
        Corporation
      SF *Biological and Medical Sciences
ARTC Air Route Traffic Control
      SF *Aeronautics
          Air Traffic Control
ARTC Aircraft Research and Testing Committee
      SF *Aeronautics
ARTCC Air Route Traffic Control Center (US)
      SF *Aeronautics
          Air Traffic Control
          *Communication Systems
ARTG Azimuth Range and Timing Group
      SF *Aeronautics
          Radar
ARTOC Army Tactical Operations Centre
      SF *Aeronautics
          Air Traffic Control
          *Military Sciences
ARTS Automatic Radar Terminal System
      SF *Aeronautics
          Air Traffic Control
          *Communication Systems
ARU   Audio Response Unit
      SF *Computer Sciences
          Data Processing
ARV   Armoured Recovery Vehicle
      SF *Astronautics and Astrophysics
          Spacecraft
AS   Ascent Stage
      SF *Space Sciences
          Spacecraft
AS   Automatically Switching
      SF *Engineering
          Radio Engineering
          *Telecommunications
ASA   Air Security Agency
      SF *Aeronautics
ASA   American Standards Association
      SF *General
          *Standards

ASA   Army Security Agency
        SF   *Military Sciences
ASAP   Applied Systems and Personnel
        SF   *Computer Sciences
             Data Processing
ASB   Air Safety Board
        SF   *Aeronautics
ASB   Asbestos
        SF   *Metallurgy and Metallography
             Metalworks
ASC   Advanced Scientific Computer
        SF   *Computer Sciences
ASC   American Standard Code
        SF   *General
             *Standards
ASC   Automatic Sensitivity Control
        SF   *Aeronautics
ASC   Automatic Switching Center
        SF   *Communication Systems
ASCA   Automatic Subject Citation Alert
        SF   *Information Retrieval Systems
ASCC   Air Standardization Coordinating
        Committee
        SF   *Aeronautics
ASCENT Assembly System for Central
        Processor
        SF   *Computer Sciences
             Data Processing
ASCET   American Society of Certified
        Engineering Technicians
        SF   Civil Engineering
             *Engineering
ASCII   American National Standard Code for
        Information Interchange
        SF   *Computer Sciences
             Data Processing
ASCVD   Arteriosclerotic Cardiovascular
        Disease
        SF   Biochemistry
             *Biological and Medical Sciences
             Pharmacology
ASD   Aeronautical Systems Division
        SF   *Aeronautics
ASDE   Airport Surface Detection Equipment
        SF   *Aeronautics
ASDIC   Anti-Submarine Detection Investigation
        Committee
        SF   *Aeronautics
             *Military Sciences
ASDIC   Armed Services Documents Intelligence
        Center
        SF   *Aeronautics
             *Military Sciences
ASEB   Aeronautics and Space Engineering
        Board
        SF   *Aeronautics
             *Engineering
             *Space Sciences
ASEE   American Society of Engineering
        Education

        SF   *Engineering
             *Training
ASET   Aeronautical Services Earth Terminal
        SF   *Aeronautics
             *Communication Systems
ASG   Aeronautical Standards Group
        SF   *Aeronautics
             *Standards
ASH   Assault Support Helicopter
        SF   *Aeronautics
ASI   Advanced Scientific Instrument
        SF   *Aeronautics
             Instruments
ASI   Air Speed Indicator
        SF   *Aeronautics
             Approach and Landing
ASIP   Aircraft Structural Integrity Program
        SF   *Aeronautics
ASIR   Air Speed Indicator Reading
        SF   *Aeronautics
             Instruments
ASLT   Advanced Solid Logic Technology
        SF   *Computer Sciences
             Data Processing
ASM   Air-to-Surface Missile
        SF   *Aeronautics
             *Military Sciences
ASM   Apollo Service Module
        SF   *Astronautics and Astrophysics
             Spacecraft
ASM   Apollo Systems Manual
        SF   *Astronautics and Astrophysics
             Spacecraft
ASMC   Automatic Systems Management and
        Control
        SF   *Aeronautics
             Aircraft
ASME   American Society of Mechanical
        Engineers
        SF   *Engineering
             Mechanical Engineering
ASMI   Airfield Surface Movement Indicator
        SF   *Aeronautics
ASMP   Air Sol Moyenne Portée
        SF   *Military Sciences
ASMS   Advanced Surface Missile System
        SF   *Aeronautical Sciences
             *Military Sciences
ASNDT   American Society for Non Destructive
        Tests
        SF   Non-destructive Evaluations
             *Nuclear Sciences
ASO   Aviation Supply Office
        SF   *Aeronautics
ASOP   Automated Structural Optimization
        Program
        SF   *Aeronautics
             Aircraft
ASP   American Society of Photogrametry
        SF   *Engineering

Instruments
Photogrametric Engineering
ASP Ammunition Supply Point
  SF *Military Sciences
ASP Antisera Seminal Plasma
  SF *Dairy Sciences
ASP Attached Support Processor
  SF *Computer Sciences
      *Electronics and Electrical
        Engineering
ASPR Army Services Procurement Regulations
  SF Contracts
      *Military Sciences
ASPR Average Specific Polymerization Rate
  SF *Non-metallic Materials
      Polymers
ASR Airport Surveillance Radar
  SF *Aeronautics
      Air Traffic Control
      Instrument Flying
      Radar Beacon Systems
ASR Automatic Send/Receive
  SF *Computer Sciences
      Data Processing
ASR Aviation Safety Regulation
  SF *Aeronautics
ASROC Anti Submarine Rocket
  SF *Aeronautics
      *Military Sciences
ASRS Automatic Storage and Retrieval
      System
  SF *Computer Sciences
      *Information Retrieval Systems
ASST Advanced Supersonic Transport
  SF *Aeronautics
ASSU Air Support Signal Unit
  SF *Aeronautics
      *Military Sciences
AST Advanced Supersonic Technology
  SF *Aeronautics
      Aircraft Engines
AST Automatic Shop Tester
  SF *Engineering
      Testing
AST Auxiliary Segment Table
  SF *Computer Sciences
      *Electronics and Electrical
        Engineering
ASTA Association of Short Circuit Testing
      Authorities
  SF *Standards
ASTC Airport Surface Traffic Control
  SF *Aeronautics
      Air Facilities
ASTF Aero-propulsion System Test Facility
  SF *Aeronautics
      Aerodynamics
      Testing
ASTM American Society for Testing Materials
  SF *Engineering

Mechanical Engineering
Testing
ASTP Apollo Soyuz Test Project
  SF *Astronautics and Astrophysics
      *Space Sciences
ASTRA Application of Space Techniques
      Relating to Aviation
  SF *Aeronautics
      Communication Systems
ASU Automatic Switching Units
  SF *Engineering
      Radio Engineering
      *Telecommunications
ASV Automatic Self Verification
  SF *Computer Sciences
      Data Processing
ASW Anti Submarine Warfare
  SF *Military Sciences
ASWG American Steel Wire Gage
  SF *Engineering
      *Metallurgy and Metallography
AT Air Temperature
  SF *Aeronautics
      *General
AT Aminotriazole
  SF *Biological and Medical Sciences
      Cytochemistry
AT Anti Torpedo
  SF *Military Sciences
AT Atomic Time
  SF *Naval Sciences
      Navigation
AT Audit Trail
  SF *Computer Sciences
      *Electronics and Electrical
        Engineering
ATA Actual Time of Arrival
  SF *Aeronautics
      Air Traffic Control
ATA Air Transport Association
  SF *Aeronautics
      *Transportation
ATA American Taxicab Association
  SF *Transportation
ATA American Transit Association
  SF *Transportation
ATAA Air Transport Association of America
  SF *Aeronautics
      *Transportation
ATAC Air Transport Advisory Council
  SF *Aeronautics
      *Transportation
ATAF Allied Tactical Air Force
  SF *Military Sciences
ATB Access Type Bits
  SF *Computer Sciences
      Data Processing
ATB Air Transport Board
  SF *Aeronautics
      *Transportation

ATC   Acoustical Tile Ceiling
      SF *Metallurgy and Metallography
          Metalworks
ATC   Air Traffic Control
      SF *Aeronautics
          Navigation
ATC   Air Traffic Controller
      SF *Aeronautics
ATC   Air Training Command
      SF *Aeronautics
          *Military Sciences
          *Training
ATC   Aircraft Technical Committee
      SF *Aeronautics
ATC   Armament Training Camp
      SF *Aeronautics
          Navigation
          *Training
ATC   Army Training Center
      SF *Aeronautics
          *Military Sciences
          *Training
ATC   Automatic Through Centers
      SF *Engineering
          Radio Engineering
          *Telecommunications
ATCA Automatic Tuned Circuit Adjustment
      SF *Engineering
          Radio Engineering
          *Telecommunications
ATCAA Automatic Tuned Circuit Adjustment
          Amplitude
      SF *Engineering
          Radio Engineering
          *Telecommunications
ATCAC Air Traffic Control Advisory Committee
      SF *Aeronautics
          Air Traffic Control
          Navigation
ATCAP Air Traffic Control Automation Panel
      SF *Aeronautics
ATCBI Air Traffic Control Beacon
          Interrogator
      SF *Aeronautics
          Radar
ATCC Air Traffic Control Center
      SF *Aeronautics
ATCCC Advanced Tactical Command and Control
          Capability
      SF *Computer Sciences
          Data Processing
ATCO Air Traffic Control Office
      SF *Aeronautics
ATCRBC Air Traffic Control Radar Beacon
      SF   Aeronautics
          *Communication Systems
ATCRBS Air Traffic Control Radar Beacon
          System
      SF *Aeronautics
          Navigation

ATCS Air Traffic Control Service
      SF *Aeronautics
ATCS Air Traffic Controller Specialist
      SF *Aeronautics
          Aviation Medicine
ATCSS Air Traffic Control Signaling System
      SF *Aeronautics
          Air Traffic Control
          *Communication Systems
ATCT Air Traffic Control Tower
      SF *Aeronautics
ATDA Augmented Target Docking Adapter
      SF *Aeronautics
          *Astronautics and Astrophysics
ATDS Air Tactical Data System
      SF *Aeronautics
          Naval Aviation
ATE   Advanced Technology Engine
      SF *Aeronautics
ATE   Automated Test Equipment
      SF *Computer Sciences
          Testing
ATEC Automated Technical Control
      SF *Computer Sciences
          Data Processing
ATEC Automatic Test Equipment Complex
      SF *Aeronautics
ATG   Air-To-Ground
      SF *Aeronautics
          *Military Sciences
ATGSB Advanced Test for Graduate Study in
          Business
      SF *Engineering
          Engineering Consultancy
ATI   Army Training Instruction
      SF *Aeronautics
          *Military Sciences
          *Training
ATIS Automatic Terminal Information
          Service
      SF *Aeronautics
          *Information Retrieval Systems
ATJ   Automatic Through Junction
      SF *Engineering
          Radio Engineering
          *Telecommunications
ATK   Along Track Distance
      SF *Aeronautics
          *Computer Sciences
          Data Processing
ATK   Available Tonne-Km
      SF *Aeronautics
ATLAS Abbreviated Test Language for Avionic
          Systems
      SF *Aeronautics
          Avionics
          *Computer Sciences
          Data Processing
ATLB Air Transport Licensing Board
      SF *Aeronautics

*Transportation

ATM   Apollo Telescope Mount
     SF   *Astronautics and Astrophysics
       *Communication Systems

ATN   Augmented Transition Network
     SF   *Computer Sciences
       Data Processing

ATO   Aircraft Transfer Order
     SF   *Aeronautics

ATO   Assisted Take-Off
     SF   *Astronautics and Astrophysics

ATO   Automatic Trunk Offices
     SF   *Engineering
       Radio Engineering
       *Telecommunications

ATOM   Apollo Telescope Orientation Mount
     SF   *Aeronautics
       *Astronautics and Astrophysics

ATP   Accepted Test Procedure
     SF   *Aeronautics

ATP   Adenosine Triphosphate
     SF   *Agricultural Sciences
       *Biological and Medical Sciences

ATP   Allied Technical Publication
     SF   *Aeronautics
       *Military Sciences

ATP   Army Training Plan
     SF   *Military Sciences

ATPI   American Textbook Publishers
      Institute
     SF   *Copyright

ATR   Advanced Terminal Reactor
     SF   *Nuclear Sciences
       Reactors

ATR   Air Traffic Regulations
     SF   *Aeronautics

ATR   Air Transport Radio
     SF   *Aeronautics
       Communication Systems

ATR   Aircraft Trouble Report
     SF   *Aeronautics

ATR   Anti Transmit Receive
     SF   *Aeronautics
       *Communication Systems

ATRAN   Automatic Terrain Recognition and
      Navigation
     SF   *Aeronautics
       Navigation

ATREM   Average Time Remaining
     SF   *Computer Sciences
       Data Processing

ATREPS   Air Traffic Control Representatives
     SF   *Aeronautics

ATS   Advanced Technology Satellites
     SF   *Meteorology
       *Space Sciences

ATS   Air Traffic Service
     SF   *Aeronautics

ATS   Anti-Thymocyte Serum
     SF   *Biological and Medical Sciences

Physiology

ATS   Applications Technology Satellite
     SF   *Aeronautics
       *Communication Systems
       *Space Sciences

ATS   Armament Training Station
     SF   *Aeronautics
       Navigation
       *Training

ATS   Army Transport Service
     SF   *Aeronautics
       *Military Sciences

ATS   Astronomical Time Switch
     SF   *Astronautics and Astrophysics

ATSD   Airborne Traffic Situation Display
     SF   *Aeronautics
       *Communication Systems

ATSU   Air Traffic Service Units
     SF   *Aeronautics
       Soaring

ATT   Advanced Technology Transport
     SF   *Aeronautics
       *Transportation

ATTITB   Air Transport and Travel Industry
      Training Board
     SF   *Aeronautics
       *Transportation

ATTP   Advanced Transport Technology Program
     SF   *Aeronautics
       Aircraft

ATU   Aerial Tuning Unit
     SF   *Communication Systems
       Radio Engineering

ATV   All-Terrain Vehicle
     SF   *Metallurgy and Metallography
       Metalworks
       Welding

AU   Amplifier Unit
     SF   *Electronics and Electrical
         Engineering

AU   Arithmetic Unit
     SF   *Computer Sciences
       Data Processing
       *Mathematics

AUM   Air-to-Underwater Missile
     SF   *Military Sciences

AURA   Association of Universities for
      Research Astronomy
     SF   *Astronautics and Astrophysics
       *Engineering
       Mechanical Engineering

AUTEC   Atlantic Undersea Test and Evaluation
      Center
     SF   *Military Sciences

Auto   Automatic
       *General

AUTODIN   Automatic Digital Network
     SF   *Computer Sciences
       Data Processing

AUTOMAP   Automatic Machining Program

```
          SF  *Computer Sciences
              Data Processing
AUTOPIC Automatic Personal Identification
          Code
          SF  *Computer Sciences
              Data Processing
AUTOPROMPT Automatic Programming of
              Machine Tools
          SF  *Computer Sciences
              Data Processing
AUV     Armoured Utility Vehicle
          SF  *Military Sciences
AV      Artificial Vagina
          SF  *Dairy Sciences
AVA     Aerodynamische Versuchsanstalt (Ger.)
          SF  *Aeronautics
              *Space Sciences
AVAS    Automatic VFR Advisory Service
          SF  *Aeronautics
              *Communication Systems
AVASI   Abbreviated Visual Approach Slope
            Indicator
          SF  *Aeronautics
              Approach and Landing
AVC     Automatic Voltage Compression
          SF  *Metallurgy and Metallography
              Metalworks
              Welding
AVC     Automatic Volume Control
          SF  *Aeronautics
              *Communication Systems
AVCS    Advanced Vidicon Camera System
          SF  *Aeronautics
              *Communication Systems
              *Photography
AVCS    Assistant Vice Chief of Staff
          SF  *Military Sciences
AVGAS   Aviation Gasoline
          SF  *Aeronautics
              Fuels
AVLB    Armoured Vehicle Launch Bridge
          SF  *Military Sciences
AVM     Air Vice Marshal
          SF  *Military Sciences
AVM     Airborne Vibration Monitoring
          SF  *Aeronautics
              Aircraft Noise
AVM     Automatic Vehicle Monitoring
          SF  Civil Engineering
              *Computer Sciences
              Data Processing
              *Engineering
AVS     Advanced Vertical Strike Fighter
          SF  *Aeronautics
              *Military Sciences
AW      Automatic Weapon
          SF  *Military Sciences
AWACS   Airborne Warning and Control System
          SF  *Aeronautics
              Air Traffic Control
```

```
              *Communication Systems
              *Electronics and Electrical
                Engineering
AWADS   Adverse Weather Aerial Delivery
          SF  *Aeronautics
              *Meteorology
AWC     Available Water Capacity
          SF  *Agricultural Sciences
AWCLS   All Weather Carrier Landing System
          SF  *Aeronautics
              Naval Aviation
AWCS    Air Weapons Control System
          SF  *Aeronautics
              *Military Sciences
AWG     American Wire Gage
          SF  *Aeronautics
              Aircraft
AWHC    Available Water Holding Capacity
          SF  *Agricultural Sciences
AWN     Automated Weather Network
          SF  *Meteorology
              Satellites
AWOP    All-Weather Operations Panel
          SF  *Aeronautics
              Air Traffic Control
              *Meteorology
AWP     Allied Weather Publication
          SF  *Meteorology
              *Military Sciences
AWRE    Atomic Weapons Research Establishment
          SF  *Biological and Medical Sciences
              *Military Sciences
AWS     Air Warning System
          SF  *Aeronautics
              Instruments
AWS     Air Weapon System
          SF  *Aeronautics
              *Military Sciences
AWS     Air Weather Service
          SF  *Aeronautics
              *Meteorology
AWS     American War Standards
          SF  *Military Sciences
              *Standards
AWS     American Welding Society
          SF  *Metallurgy and Metallography
              Metalworks
AZBN    Azobisisiobutyrnitrile
          SF  *Non-metallic Materials
              Polymers
AZCN    Azobiscyclohexane
          SF  *Non-metallic Materials
              Polymers
AZS     Automatic Zero Set
          SF  *Astronautics and Astrophysics
```

B

B   Boron
    SF   *Agricultural Sciences
B   Base
    SF   *Electronics and Electrical
        Engineering
B/A   Baron/Aluminium
    SF   Civil Engineering
        *Engineering
BA   Bentonite Agglutination
    SF   *Agricultural Sciences
BA   Benzanthracene
    SF   Biochemistry
        *Biological and Medical Sciences
BA   Buffer Amplifier
    SF   *Communication Systems
BAA   Breed Age Average
    SF   *Agricultural Sciences
        *Dairy Sciences
BAA   British Airports Authority
    SF   *Aeronautics
BAA   Broadband Antenna Amplifier
    SF   *Telecommunications
BABS   Blind Approach Beacon System
    SF   *Aeronautics
        Approach and Landing
BAC   Barometric Altitude Control
    SF   *Aeronautics
BAC   British Aircraft Corporation
    SF   *Aeronautics
BADGE   Base Air Defense Ground Environment
    SF   *Aeronautics
        *Military Sciences
BAEE   Benzoyl Arginine Ethyl-Ester
    SF   *Biological and Medical Sciences
BAI   Bentonite Agglutination Inhibition
    SF   *Agricultural Sciences
BAL   Basic Assembler Language
    SF   *Computer Sciences
        Data Processing
        *Information Retrieval Systems
BALMI   Ballistic Missile
    SF   *Military Sciences
BALPA   British Airline Pilots' Association
    SF   *Aeronautics
BALS   Blind Approach Landing System

    SF   *Aeronautics
        Approach and Landing
BAM   Bituminous Aggregate Mixtures
    SF   Civil Engineering
        Concretes
        *Engineering
BANS   Basic Air Navigation School
    SF   *Aeronautics
        Navigation
        *Training
BANS   Bright Alphanumeric Subsystem
    SF   *Aeronautics
        Radar Beacon System
BAP   Basic Assembler Program
    SF   *Computer Sciences
        Data Processing
BAR   Browning Automatic Rifle
    SF   *Military Sciences
BAR   Buffer Address Register
    SF   *Computer Sciences
        Data Processing
BARIG   Board of Airline Representatives
      in Germany
    SF   *Aeronautics
BART   Bay Area Rapid Transit
    SF   *Transportation
BAS   Basic Airspeed
    SF   *Aeronautics
BAS   Blind Approach System
    SF   *Aeronautics
        Approach and Landing
BASEC   British Approval Service for Electric
      Cables
    SF   *Standards
BASEEFA   British Approvals Service for
        Electrical Equipment in Flammable
        Atmospheres (UK)
    SF *Information Retrieval Systems
BASIC   Beginner's All Purpose Symbolic
      Instruction Code
    SF   *Computer Sciences
        Data Processing
        *Electronics and Electrical
        Engineering
BATRECON   Battle Reconnaissance

	SF *Military Sciences	
BATS	Basic Additional Teleprocessing Support	
	SF *Computer Sciences Data Processing	
BAUA	Business Aircraft Users' Association	
	SF *Aeronautics	
BB	Building Blocks	
	SF *Computer Sciences Data Processing	
BBB	Bisbenzimidazobenzophenanthrolines	
	SF *Geosciences	
BBC	British Broadcasting Corporation	
	SF *Communication Systems	
BBD	Bubble Bath Detector	
	SF *Biological and Medical Sciences Radiation X-ray	
BBN	Bolt Beranek and Newman	
	SF *Computer Sciences Data Processing	
BC	Benefit Cost	
	SF *General	
BC	Breeding Gain	
	SF *Nuclear Sciences Reactors	
BCA	Battery Control Area	
	SF *Aeronautics	
BCAA	Branched Chain Amino Acids	
	SF *Biological and Medical Sciences	
BCABP	Bureau of Competitive Assessment and Business Policy (US)	
	SF *Transportation	
BCAR	British Civil Airworthiness Requirements	
	SF *Aeronautics Inspection	
BCB	Brown Cupboard	
	SF *Dairy Sciences	
BCD	Binary Coded Decimal	
	SF *Computer Sciences Data Processing *Electronics and Electrical Engineering	
BCDC	Binary Code Decimal Counters	
	SF *Computer Sciences Electronics and Electrical Engineering	
BCE	Base Civil Engineering	
	SF Civil Engineering *Engineering *Military Sciences	
BCF	Bromochlorofluoromethane	
	SF *Aeronautics Airports Ground Equipment	
BCI	Interference to Broadcast	
	SF *Communication Systems	
BCIRA	British Cast Iron Research Association	

	SF *Metallurgy and Metallography Metalworks
BCKA	Branched Chain a-Keto Acids
	SF *Biological and Medical Sciences
BCL	Burroughs Common Language
	SF *Computer Sciences *Electronics and Electrical Engineering
BCM	Bromochlomethane
	SF *Dairy Sciences
BCPC	British Crop Protector Council
	SF *Agricultural Sciences
BCRA	British Ceramic Research Association
	SF *Engineering *Information Retrieval Systems
BCRA	British Coke Research Association
	SF *Engineering *Information Retrieval Systems
BCRRA	British Commonwealth Radio Reception Award
	SF *Communication Systems
BCS	British Computing Society
	SF *Computer Sciences
BCSI	Biometric Computer Service Incorporation
	SF *Computer Sciences
BD	Blocker Deflector
	SF *Aeronautics Thrust Reserver Concepts
BD	Blocking Devices
	SF Fission Chambers *Nuclear Sciences
BD	Bottom Down
	SF *Metallurgy and Metallography Metalworks
BDC	Binary Decimal Counter
	SF *Computer Sciences Data Processing
BDC	Bureau of Domestic Commerce (US)
	SF *Transportation
BDI	Bearing Deviation Indicator
	SF *Aeronautics Instruments
BDM	Bomber Defense Missile
	SF *Aeronautics *Military Sciences
BDNA	Benzyldinonylame
	SF *Nuclear Sciences
BDS	Benzenediazothioethers
	SF *Photography
BDS	Bomb Disposal Squad
	SF *Military Sciences
BDSA	Business and Defense Services Administration
	SF *Transportation
BDU	Bomb Disposal Unit
	SF *Military Sciences
BE	Baron Epoxy
	SF *Metallic Materials
BEA	British European Airways

SF   *Aeronautics
        *Transportation
BEAB   British Electrochemical Approvals
         Board
       SF   *Standards
BEAMA British Electrical and Allied
         Manufacturers' Association
       SF   *Metallurgy and Metallography
            Welding
BEBC   Big European Bubble Chamber
       SF   *Communication Systems
            Data Processing
BEEF   Business and Engineering Enriched
         FORTRAN
       SF   *Computer Sciences
            Data Processing
BEF   Band Elimination Filter
       SF   *Electronics and Electrical
              Engineering
            Solid-state Circuits
BEF   Blunt End Forward
       SF   *Aeronautics
            Navigation
BEMA   Business Equipment Manufacturers'
         Association
       SF   *General
            *Standards
BEST   Ballastable Earthmoving Sectionized
         Tractor
       SF   *Engineering
            Mechanical Engineering
            Terramechanics
BETA   Business Equipment Trade Association
       SF   *Computer Sciences
            Data Processing
            *Management
BEU   Basic Encoding Unit
       SF   *Computer Sciences
            Data Processing
BEV   Bovine Enterovirus
       SF   *Dairy Sciences
BEX   Broadband Exchange
       SF   *Computer Sciences
            Data Processing
BFER   Base Field Effect Resister
       SF   *Electronics and Electrical
              Engineering
            Solid-state Circuits
BFMIRA British Food Manufacturing
         Industries Research
       SF   *Information Retrieval Systems
BFN   British Forces Network
       SF   *Military Sciences
BFO   Beat Frequency Oscillator
       SF   *Communication Systems
            *Electronics and Electrical
              Engineering
BG   Bottom Grille
       SF   *Metallurgy and Metallography
            Metalworks

BGA   Brilliant Green Agar
       SF   *Agricultural Sciences
            *Dairy Sciences
BGA   British Gliding Association
       SF   *Aeronautics
BGAV   Blue Green Algae Viruses
       SF   *Biological and Medical Sciences
BGIRA British Glass Industry Research
         Association
       SF   *Engineering
            *Information Retrieval Systems
BGS   Bombing and Gunnery School
       SF   *Aeronautics
            *Military Sciences
            *Training
BGY   Bright Greenish Yellow
       SF   *Agricultural Sciences
            Cereals
BHA   Butylated Hydroxy Anisole
       SF   *Biological and Medical Sciences
            *Dairy Sciences
BHC   Benzene Hexachloride
       SF   *Agricultural Sciences
BHET   Bishydroxyethyl Terephthalate
       SF   *Non-metallic Materials
            Polymers
BHIA   Brain Heart Infusion Agar
       SF   *Agricultural Sciences
            Dairy Sciences
BHIB   Brain Heart Infusion Broth
       SF   *Agricultural Sciences
            Dairy Sciences
BHP   Brake Horsepower
       SF   *Mathematics
BHRA   British Hydromechanics Research
         Association
       SF   *Engineering
            *Information Retrieval Systems
BHT   Blowdown Heat Transfer
       SF   *Nuclear Sciences
            Reactors
BHT   Butylated Hydroxytoluene
       SF   *Biological and Medical Sciences
BI   Black Iron
       SF   *Metallurgy and Metallography
            Metalworks
BIATA British Independent Air Transport
         Association
       SF   *Aeronautics
BIBRA British Industrial Biological
         Research
       SF   *Information Retrieval Systems
BIEE   British Institute of Electrical
         Engineers (see IEE)
       SF   *Computer Sciences
            Data Processing
BIG   Bureau of International Commerce
       SF   *Transportation
BIM   Branch If Multiplexer
       SF   *Computer Sciences

Data Processing

BIM   British Institute of Management
       SF *Computer Sciences
           *Management
BIP   Binary Image Processor
       SF *Computer Sciences
           Data Processing
BIRPI International Bureaux for the
          Property of Intellectual Property
       SF *Copyright
           Industrial Properties
BIS   Business Information Systems
       SF *Communication Systems
BIT   Built In Test
       SF *Aeronautics
           *Computer Sciences
           Data Processing
BITE   Built-In Test Equipment
       SF *Aeronautics
           Navigation
BIT/S Bits Per Second
       SF *Computer Sciences
           Data Processing
BJ   Bar Joist
       SF *Metallurgy and Metallography
           Metalworks
BL   Building Line
       SF *Metallurgy and Metallography
           Metalworks
BL   Burkitt Lymphona
       SF *Biological and Medical Sciences
BLAC   British Light Aviation Centre
       SF *Aeronautics
BLC   Beef Liver Catalase
       SF *Biological and Medical Sciences
           Cytochemistry
BLC   Boundary Layer Control
       SF *Aeronautics
bldg   building
       SF *Metallurgy and Metallography
           Metalworks
BLEU   Blind Landing Experimental Unit
       SF *Aeronautics
           Approach and Landing
           Navigation
BLF   Band Limiting Filter
       SF *Electronics and Electrical
               Engineering
           Solid-state Circuits
BLG   Benzyl-L-Glutamate
       SF *Non-metallic Materials
           Polymers
BLG   Breech Loading Gun
       SF *Aeronautics
           Military Sciences
BLL   British Library Lending
       SF *Information Retrieval Systems
BLM   Basic Language Machine
       SF *Computer Sciences
           Data Processing

BLMRA British Leather Manufacturers'
          Research Association
       SF *Information Retrieval Systems
BLR   Breech Loading Rifle
       SF *Military Sciences
BLRA   British Launderers' Research
          Association
       SF *Information Retrieval Systems
BLTC   Bottom Loading Transfer Cast
       SF *Nuclear Sciences
           Reactors
BM   Boundary Marker
       SF *Aeronautics
BMCS   Bureau of Motor Carrier Safety
       SF *Engineering
           Mechanical Engineering
BMEP   Brake Mean Effective Pressure
       SF *Aeronautics
BMEWS Ballistic Missile Early Warning
          System
       SF *Military Sciences
           *Space Sciences
BML   Bovine Milk Lysozyme
       SF *Dairy Sciences
BMR   Bipolar Magnetic Regions
       SF *Lunar Sciences
BMS   Boeing Materials Specification
       SF *Aeronautics
BMS   Buttermilk Solids
       SF *Dairy Sciences
BMTT   Buffered Magnetic Tape Transport
       SF *Computer Sciences
           Data Processing
BNFL   British Nuclear Fuels Limited
       SF *Nuclear Sciences
           Fuels
BNFMRA British Non-Ferrous Metals Research
          Association
       SF *Information Retrieval Systems
BNL   Brookhaven National Laboratory (US)
       SF *Biological and Medical Sciences
BNRL   British Nuclear Reactor Limited
       SF *Nuclear Sciences
           Reactors
BNW   Battelle Northwest
       SF *Nuclear Sciences
           Reactors
BOAC   British Overseas Airways Corporation
       SF *Aeronautics
           *Transportation
BOC   British Oxygen Company
       SF *General
BOCCA Board for Co-ordination of Civil
          Aviation
       SF *Aeronautics
BOCM   British Oil and Cake Mills
       SF *Milling
BOD   Base Ordnance Depot
       SF *Military Sciences
BOD   Biochemical Oxygen Demand

SF   *Agricultural Sciences
    *Biological and Medical Sciences
    *Photography
BOD   Biological Oxygen Demand
    SF   *Biological and Medical Sciences
        *Brewery
BOD   Bottom Of Duct
    SF   *Metallurgy and Metallography
        Metalworks
BOF   Basic Oxygen Furnace
    SF   Civil Engineering
        *Engineering
BOMEX Barbados Oceanographic Meteorological
    Experiment
    SF   *Geosciences
        *Meteorology
BORAM Block Oriented Random Access Memory
    SF   *Aeronautics
        *Computer Sciences
        Data Processing
BOS   Back Of Slip
    SF   *Metallurgy and Metallography
        Metalworks
BOS   Basic Operating System
    SF   *Computer Sciences
        Data Processing
BOSOR Buckling Of Shells Of Revolution
    SF   *Aeronautics
        Aircraft
BOT   Beginning Of Tape
    SF   *Computer Sciences
        Data Processing
BP   Bandpass
    SF   *Electronics and Electrical
        Engineering
BPAM   Basic Partitioned Access Method
    SF   *Computer Sciences
        Data Processing
BPB   Bromophenol Blue
    SF   Biochemistry
        *Biological and Medical Sciences
BPD   Bean Positioning Device
    SF   *Nuclear Sciences
        Reactors
        Wire Chamber Spectrometer
BPF   Band Pass Filter
    SF   *Electronics and Electrical
        Engineering
        Solid-state Circuits
BPI   Bits per Inch
    SF   *Computer Sciences
        Data Processing
BPR-Thm Bureau of Public Roads - Transport
    Highway Mobilization (Can.)
    SF   *Transportation
BPS   Basic Programming Support
    SF   *Computer Sciences
        Data Processing
BPS   Basic Programming System
    SF   *Computer Sciences

Data Processing
BPS   Batch Processing System
    SF   *Computer Sciences
        Data Processing
BPT   Blade Passage Tone
    SF   *Aeronautics
        Aircraft Noise
BQL   Basic Query Language
    SF   *Computer Sciences
        Data Processing
BR   Bottom Register
    SF   *Metallurgy and Metallography
        Metalworks
BRC   Branch Conditional
    SF   *Computer Sciences
        *Electronics and Electrical
        Engineering
BRD   Binary Rate Divider
    SF   *Computer Sciences
        *Engineering
        Instruments
BRE   Building Research Establishment (UK)
    SF   *Building
BREL   Boeing Radiation Effect Laboratory
    SF   *Aeronautics
        *Space Sciences
        Space Simulation
BRG   Beacon Reply Group
    SF   *Aeronautics
        Radar
BRGW   Brake Release Gross Weight
    SF   *Aeronautics
        Aircraft
BRL   Ballistics Research Laboratory (US)
    SF   *Aeronautics
        *Space Sciences
BRL   Behavioural Research Laboratories
    SF   Education
        Microteaching
        Programmed Learning
        *Training
BRR   Battelle Research Reactor
    SF   Fuels
        *Nuclear Sciences
        Reactors
BRT   Brucella Ring Test
    SF   *Dairy Sciences
BRU   Branch Unconditional
    SF   *Computer Sciences
        *Electronics and Electrical
        Engineering
BS   Backspace
    SF   *Computer Sciences
        Data Processing
BS   Below Slab
    SF   *Metallurgy and Metallography
        Metalworks
BS   Beth Salpeter
    SF   Nuclear Physics
        *Nuclear Sciences

BS   Bismuth Sulphite
        SF   *Agricultural Sciences
             *Dairy Sciences
BSA   Bimetal Steel Aluminium
        SF   *Engineering
             Radio Engineering
             *Telecommunications
BSA   Bis-trimethylsilyl-acetamide
        SF   *Chemistry
             Organic Chemistry
BSA   Bovine Serum Albumin
        SF   *Biological and Medical Sciences
             *Dairy Sciences
BSAA   British South American Airways
        SF   *Aeronautics
             *Transportation
BSAM   Basic Sequential Access Method
        SF   *Computer Sciences
             Data Processing
BSC   Binary Synchronous Communication
        SF   *Communication Systems
             *Computer Sciences
             Data Processing
BSD   Ballistic System Division
        SF   *Military Sciences
             *Space Sciences
BSD   Base Supply Depot
        SF   *Military Sciences
BSI   British Standards Institution
        SF   *Standards
BSLT   Blankenbecler and Sugar and Logunov
        and Tarkkelidze
        SF   Nuclear Physics
             *Nuclear Sciences
BSO   Blue Stellar Objects
        SF   *Lunar Sciences
BSRA   British Ship Research Association
        SF   *Information Retrieval Systems
BSS   Basiocliocarp-inducing Substance(s)
        SF   *Agricultural Sciences
BSTFA   Bistrimethylsilyl Trifluoroacetamide
        SF   Biochemistry
             *Biological and Medical Sciences
BT   Bathythermograph
        SF   *Agricultural Sciences
             Fisheries
             Navigation
BTAM   Basic Telecommunications Access Method
        SF   *Computer Sciences
             Data Processing
             *Electronics and Electrical
             Engineering
BTB   Bus Tie Breakers
        SF   *Electronics and Electrical
             Engineering
BTCC   Berzothiazolocarbon-Cyanine
        SF   *Photography
BTDA   Benzophenone Tetracarboxylic Dianhydride
        SF   *Non-metallic Materials
             Polymers

BTDU   Benzylthiodihydrouracil
        SF   Biochemistry
             *Biological and Medical Sciences
BTE   Baldwin-Tate-Emery
        SF   *Nuclear Sciences
BTM   Batch Time-Sharing Monitor
        SF   *Computer Sciences
             Data Processing
BTMF   Block Type Manipulation Facility
        SF   *Computer Sciences
             Data Processing
BTO   Bombing Through Overcast
        SF   *Military Sciences
BTSS   Basic Time Sharing System
        SF   *Communication Systems
BU   Bottom Up
        SF   *Metallurgy and Metallography
             Metalworks
BUCLASP Buckling of Laminated Stiffened
        Plates
        SF   *Aeronautics
             Aircraft
BUDWSR Brown University Display for Working
        Set References
        SF   *Computer Sciences
             Data Processing
BUEC   Back-Up Emergency Communications
        SF   *Aeronautics
             Navigation
BUGS   Brown University Graphic System
        SF   *Computer Sciences
             *Electronics and Electrical
             Engineering
BUIC   Back Up Interceptor Control
        SF   *Electronics and Electrical
             Engineering
BUM   Back Up Mode
        SF   *Aeronautics
             Radar
BUN   Blood Urea Nitrogen
        SF   Biochemistry
             *Biological and Medical Sciences
             Pharmacology
BUT   Broadband Unbalanced Transformer
        SF   *Engineering
             Radio Engineering
             *Telecommunications
BUV   Backscatter Ultraviolet
        SF   Environmental Monitoring
             *Geosciences
BV   Benzyl Viologen
        SF   *Agricultural Sciences
BVD   Bovine Viral Diarrhoea
        SF   *Dairy Sciences
BW   Biological Warfare
        SF   *Biological and Medical Sciences
             *Military Sciences
BW   Body Weight
        SF   *Agricultural Sciences
BWP   Brown Wrapping Paper

```
  —        SF   *Agricultural Sciences
                *Dairy Sciences
BWR      Boiling Water Reactors
           SF   *Nuclear Sciences
                 Reactors
BYP      Bypass
           SF   *Computer Sciences
```

C

C   Coulombmeter
    SF *Electronics and Electrical
        Engineering
        Meters

C-A   Conventional Alloy
    SF *Nuclear Sciences
        Thermocouples

Ca   Calcium
    SF *General

CA   Cellulose Acetate
    SF *Biological and Medical Sciences

CA   Chromic Acid
    SF *Biological and Medical Sciences
        Cytochemistry

CA   Cinnamic Acid
    SF *Non-metallic Materials
        Polymers

CA   Controlled Atmosphere
    SF *General

CAA   Civil Aeronautics Administration (US)
    SF *Aeronautics
        *Transportation

CAA   Civil Aviation Authority (UK)
    SF *Aeronautics
        *Transportation

CAAC Civil Aviation Administration of China
    SF *Aeronautics
        *Transportation

CAADRP Civil Aircraft Airworthiness Data
       Recording
    SF *Aeronautics
        Inspection

CAARC Commonwealth Advisory Aeronautical
       Research Council
    SF *Aeronautics

CAAS Computer Aided Approach Sequencing
    SF *Aeronautics
        Navigation

CAAS Computer Assisted Approach Sequencing
    SF *Aeronautics
        Approach and Landing

CAB   Civil Aeronautics Board (US)
    SF *Aeronautics
        *Transportation

CABATM Civil Aeronautics Board Air Transport
       Mobilization (US)
    SF *Aeronautics
        *Transportation

CaBP Calcium Binding Protein
    SF *Biological and Medical Sciences
        Physiology

CAC   Commonwealth Aircraft Corporation
       (Aust.)
    SF *Aeronautics

CACAC Civil Aircraft Control Advisory
       Committee (UK)
    SF *Aeronautics
        Air Traffic Control

CACAS Civil Aviation Council of Arab States
    SF *Aeronautics

CAD   Computer Aided Design
    SF *Computer Sciences
        Data Processing

CADA Cellulose Acetate Diethyl Aminoacetate
    SF *Photography

CADA Computer Aided Designer Analysis
    SF *Computer Sciences
        *Electronics and Electrical
          Engineering

CADAM Computer-graphic Augmented Design and
       Manufacturing
    SF *Computer Sciences

CADC Central Air Data Computer
    SF *Aeronautics
        *Computer Sciences
        Data Processing

CAE   Compare Alpha Equal
    SF *Computer Sciences
        *Electronic and Electrical
          Engineering

CaF   Calcium Free
    SF Dairy Sciences

CAFMNA Compound Animal Feeding Stuffs
       Manufacturers' Association
    SF *Agricultural Sciences
        Milling

CAG   Civil Aviation Groups
    SF *Aeronautics

CAI   Computer Aided Instruction
    SF *Computer Sciences

      *Electronics and Electrical
        Engineering
      *Training

CAI   Computer Assisted Instruction
    SF *Computer Sciences
       Microteaching
       Programmed Learning
       *Training

CAINS Carrier Aircraft Inertial Navigation
     System
    SF *Aeronautics
       Navigation

CAK   Command Access Keys
    SF *Computer Sciences

CAK   Command Acknowledge
    SF *Computer Sciences
       Data Processing

CAL   Computer Aided Learning
    SF *Computer Sciences

CAL   Confined Area Landing
    SF *Aeronautics
       Approach and Landing

CAL   Cornell Aeronautical Laboratory
    SF *Aeronautics
      *Engineering
       Mechanical Engineering
       Safety Engineering

calc calculated
    SF *Mathematics

CALC Cargo Acceptance and Load Control
    SF *Computer Sciences
       Data Processing
      *Transportation

CAM   Cellulose Acetate Methacrylate
    SF   Chemical Engineering
      *Engineering

CAM   Cement Aggregate Mixture
    SF   Civil Engineering
       Concrete
      *Engineering

CAM   Civil Aeronautics Manual
    SF *Aeronautics

CAM   Commercial Air Movement
    SF *Aeronautics

CAM   Computer Aided Manufacturing
    SF *Computer Sciences
       Data Processing

CAM   Computer Assisted Manufacturing
    SF *Computer Sciences
       Data Processing

CAM   Content Addressable Memory
    SF *Computer Sciences
       Data Processing

CAM   Crassulacean Acid Metabolism
    SF *Biological and Medical Sciences

CAMI Civil Aeromedical Institute (US)
    SF *Aeronautics
       Aviation Medicine

CAMI Civil Aviation Medical Institute
    SF *Aeronautics

      *Biological and Medical Sciences

CAMP Computer Assisted Menu Planning
    SF *Biological and Medical Sciences
      *Computer Sciences
       Data Processing

CAMP Cyclic Adenosine Monosine
     Monophosphate
    SF   Biochemistry
      *Biological and Medical Sciences

CAN   Cancel
    SF *Computer Sciences
       Data Processing

CANDU-BLW Canada Deuterium Uranium Boiling
     Light Water
    SF *Nuclear Sciences
       Reactors

CANS Civilian Air Navigation School
    SF *Aeronautics
       Navigation
      *Training

CANTRAN Cancel Transmission
    SF *Computer Sciences
       Data Processing

CAP   Chloramphenicol
    SF   Biochemistry
      *Biological and Medical Sciences

CAP   Civil Air Patrol
    SF *Aeronautics
      *Transportation

CAP   Civil Aviation Publication
    SF *Aeronautics

CAP   Combat Air Patrol
    SF *Aeronautics

CAP   Common Agricultural Policy
    SF *Agricultural Sciences

CAP   Computer Analysts and Programmers
    SF *Computer Sciences
       Data Processing

CAPC Civil Aviation Planning Committee
    SF *Aeronautics

CAPDAC Computer Aided Piping Design And
     Construction
    SF *Computer Sciences
       Data Processing

CAPE Communications Automatic Processing
     Equipment
    SF *Computer Sciences
      *Electronics and Electrical
        Engineering

CAPER Cost of Attaining Personnel
     Requirement
    SF *Management
      *Training

CAPI Computer Administered Programmed
     Instruction
    SF   Programmed Learning
      *Training

CAPR Catalog of Program
    SF *Computer Sciences
      *Electronics and Electrical
        Engineering

CAPRI   Coded Address Private Radio Intercom
    SF   *Aeronautics
       *Communication Systems
CAR   Channel Address Register
    SF   *Computer Sciences
       Data Processing
CAR   Civil Air Regulation
    SF   *Aeronautics
       Air Traffic Control
CARA   Cargo and Rescue Aircraft
    SF   *Aeronautics
CARA   Combat Aircrew Rescue Aircraft
    SF   *Aeronautics
       *Military Sciences
CARD   Compact Automatic Retrieval Display
    SF   Business System
       *Management
CARDE   Canadian Armament Research and
    Development Establishment
    SF   *Aeronautics
       *Military Sciences
CARF   Central Altitude Reservation Facility
    SF   *Aeronautics
       *Communication Systems
CARN   Conditional Analysis for Random
    Networks
    SF   Cybernetics
       *Electronics and Electrical
         Engineering
CARP   Computed Air Released Point
    SF   *Aeronautics
       *Computer Sciences
CAS   Calibrated Airspeed
    SF   *Aeronautics
       Avionics
CAS   Central Amplifier Stations
    SF   *Engineering
       Radio Engineering
       *Telecommunications
CAS   Close Air Support
    SF   *Aeronautics
       *Communication Systems
       *Military Sciences
CAS   Collision Avoidance System
    SF   *Aeronautics
       Air Traffic Control
       *Communication Systems
CAS   Control Augmentation System
    SF   *Aeronautics
       *Military Sciences
CAS   Controlled Airspace
    SF   *Aeronautics
       Air Traffic Control
CASDAC Computer Aided Ship Design and
    Construction
    SF   *Computer Sciences
       Data Processing
CASME   Commonwealth Association of Science
    and Mathematics Education
    SF   *Mathematics

CAST   Computerized Automatic System Tester
    SF   *Computer Sciences
CAST   Council for Agricultural Science and
    Technology
    SF   *Agricultural Sciences
CASWS   Close Air Support Weapon System
    SF   *Aeronautics
       *Military Sciences
CAT   Canon Auto Tuning
    SF   *Photography
CAT   Civil Air Transport
    SF   *Aeronautics
CAT   Clear Air Turbulence
    SF   *Aeronautics
CAT   Computer Aided Typesetting
    SF   *Printing
CAT   Computer Average Transients
    SF   *Computer Sciences
CATITB Civil Air Transport Industry
    Training Board
    SF   *Aeronautics
       *Training
CATV   Community Antenna Television
    SF   *Communication Systems
CAU   Compare Alpha Unequal
    SF   *Computer Sciences
       *Electronics and Electrical
         Engineering
CAV   Composite Analog Video
    SF   *Space Sciences
       Space Simulation
CAVU   Ceiling And Visibility Unlimited
    SF   *Aeronautics
       Instrument Flying
CAW   Channel Address Word
    SF   *Computer Sciences
       Data Processing
CAWS   Common Aviation Weather System
    SF   *Aeronautics
       Air Traffic Control
       *Meteorology
CAX   Community Automatic Exchange
    SF   *Computer Sciences
       *Electronics and Electrical
         Engineering
CB   Coated Back
    SF   *Printing
CB   Coupled Biquad
    SF   *Electronics and Electrical
         Engineering
CBC   Canadian Broadcasting Corporation
    SF   *Communication Systems
CBF   Cerebral Blood Flow
    SF   *Biological and Medical Sciences
CBOM   Current Break Off and Memory
    SF   *Noncrystalline Solids
CBOSS   Count Back Order and Sample Select
    SF   *Computer Sciences
       Data Processing
CBT   Core Block Table

SF   *Computer Sciences
    *Electronics and Electrical
     Engineering

CC   Camp Commandant
    SF   *Military Sciences

CC   Coliform Count
    SF   *Agricultural Sciences
        *Dairy Sciences

CC   Colour Compensating
    SF   *Photography

CC   Combat Commandant
    SF   *Military Sciences

CC   Comparison Circuit
    SF   *Telecommunications

CC   Conventional Colour
    SF   *Agricultural Sciences

CCA   Carrier Control Approach
    SF   *Aeronautics

CCA   Cement and Concrete Association (UK)
    SF   Civil Engineering
        *Engineering

CCA   Chromated Copper Arsenate
    SF   *Engineering
        *Metallurgy and Metallography

CCB   Command Control Block
    SF   *Computer Sciences
        Data Processing

CCB   Configuration Control Board
    SF   Civil Engineering
        *Engineering
        *Military Engineering

CCBS   Centre for Computer Based Behavioural
    Studies
    SF   *Behavioural Sciences

CCC   Central Computational Computer
    SF   *Computer Sciences
        Data Processing

CCC   Central Computer Complex
    SF   *Computer Sciences
        Data Processing

CCC   Channel Control Check

CCC   Chlorochline Chloride
    SF   *Dairy Sciences

CCC   Civilian Conservation Corps
    SF   *Training

CCC   Computer Central Complex
    SF   *Computer Sciences
        Data Processing

CCC   Computer Control Complex
    SF   *Computer Sciences
        Data Processing

CCC   Convert Character Code
    SF   *Communication Systems

CCD   Charged Coupled Device
    SF   *Computer Sciences
        Data Processing
        *Electronics and Electrical
         Engineering

CCD   Controlled Current Distribution
    SF   *Engineering
        Radio Engineering

        *Telecommunications

CCE   Chief Construction Engineer
    SF   Civil Engineering
        *Engineering

CCECA   Consultative Committee on Electronics
    for Civil Aviation
    SF   *Aeronautics

CCEEP   Canada Committee for Coordination of
    Emergency Economic Planning
    SF   *Transportation

CCF   Central Communications Facility
    SF   *Information Retrieval Systems

CCF   Cross-Correlation Function
    SF   *Engineering
        Radio Engineering
        *Telecommunications

CCGE   Cold Cathode Gauge Experiment
    SF   *Lunar Sciences

CCH   Channel Check Handler
    SF   *Computer Sciences
        Data Processing

CCI   Consolidated City of Indianapolis
    SF   *Transportation

CCIP   Continuous Computation of Impact
    Point
    SF   *Military Sciences
        Missile Systems

CCIR   International Radio Consultative
    Committee
    SF   *Engineering
        Radio Engineering
        *Telecommunications

CCITT   Comité Consultatif International
    Télégraphique et Téléphonique
    SF   *Communication Systems

CCITT   International Telegraph and Telephone
    Consultative Committee
    SF   *Communication Systems

CCK   Channel Control Check
    SF   *Computer Sciences
        *Electronics and Electrical
         Engineering

CCL   Core Current Layer
    SF   *Lunar Sciences

CCM   Chain Crossing Model
    SF   Armorphous Semiconductors
        Liquid Semiconductors
        *Noncrystalline Solids

CCMD   Continuous Current Monitoring Device
    SF   *Non-metallic Materials
        Plastics

CCP   Communication Control Package
    SF   *Communication Systems
        *Computer Sciences

CCP   Console Control Package
    SF   *Computer Sciences
        Data Processing

CCS   Central Computer Station
    SF   *Computer Sciences

CCS   Communication Control System

```
        SF  *Aeronautics
            *Communication Systems
CCS     Hundred Call Seconds
        SF  *Communication Systems
            *Computer Sciences
CCT     Continuous Cooling Transformation
        SF  *Metallurgy and Metallography
            Welding
CCTV    Closed Circuit Television
        SF  *Aeronautics
            *Communication Systems
CCU     Contaminant Collection Unit
        SF  *Space Sciences
CCV     Control Configured Vehicles
        SF  *Aeronautics
            Aircraft
            *Military Sciences
CCVS    COBOL Compiler Validation System
        SF  *Computer Sciences
            Data Processing
CCW     Channel Command Word
        SF  *Computer Sciences
            Data Processing
            *Electronics and Electrical
              Engineering
CCWBAD  Counterclockwise Bottom Angular Down
        SF  *Metallurgy and Metallography
            Metalworks
CCWBAU  Counterclockwise Bottom Angular Up
        SF  *Metallurgy and Metallography
            Metalworks
CCWBH   Counterclockwise Bottom Horizontal
        SF  *Metallurgy and Metallography
            Metalworks
CCWDB   Counterclockwise Down Blast
        SF  *Metallurgy and Metallography
            Metalworks
CCWTAD  Counterclockwise Top Angular Down
        SF  *Metallurgy and Metallography
            Metalworks
CCWTAU  Counterclockwise Top Angular Up
        SF  *Metallurgy and Metallography
            Metalworks
CCWTH   Counterclockwise Top Horizontal
        SF  *Metallurgy and Metallography
            Metalworks
CCWUB   Counterclockwise Up Blast
        SF  *Metallurgy and Metallography
            Metalworks
CD      Cage Dipole
        SF  *Electronics and Electrical
              Engineering
CD      Ceiling Diffuser
        SF  *Metallurgy and Metallography
            Metalworks
CD      Check Digit
        SF  *Computer Sciences
            *Electronics and Electrical
              Engineering
CD      Circular Dichroic
```

```
        SF  *Biological and Medical Sciences
            Metal Ions
CD      Circular Dichroism
        SF  *Agricultural Sciences
            Cereals
CD      Civil Defence
        SF  *Military Sciences
CD      Coherent Detector
        SF  *Engineering
            Instruments
CD      Common Digitizer
        SF  *Aeronautics
            Air Traffic Control
            Radar Beacon Systems
CD      Displaced Central (Trajectory)
        SF  Beam Transport System
            Measurements
            *Nuclear Sciences
CDA     Command and Data Acquisition
        SF  *Aeronautics
            *Computer Sciences
            *Military Sciences
CDA     Comprehensive Development Area
        SF  *Building
CDC     Call Direct Code
        SF  *Computer Sciences
            Data Processing
            *Electronics and Electrical
              Engineering
CDC     Career Development Courses
        SF  *Training
CDC     Code Directing Character
        SF  *Computer Sciences
            Data Processing
CDC     Computer Display Channel
        SF  *Aeronautics
            *Communication Systems
            *Computer Sciences
            Data Processing
CDC     Control Data Corporation
        SF  *Computer Sciences
CDE     Certified Data Educater
        SF  *Computer Sciences
            Data Processing
CDF     California Division of Forestry
        SF  *Agricultural Sciences
CDI     Control Deviation Indicator
        SF  *Aeronautics
            Navigation
CDI     Control Direction Indicator
        SF  *Aeronautics
            Navigation
CDI     Course Deviation Indicator
        SF  *Aeronautics
            Instrument Flying
CDI     Course Director Indicator
        SF  *Aeronautics
            Navigation
CDK     Channel Data Check
        SF  *Computer Sciences
```

           *Electronics and Electrical
           Engineering

CDL   Computer Design Language
    SF *Computer Sciences
        Data Processing

CDMA Code Division Multiple Access
    SF *Electronics and Electrical
        Engineering

CDMS COMRADE Data Management System
    SF *Computer Sciences
        Data Processing
        *Management

CDP   Certificate in Data Processing
    SF *Computer Sciences
        Data Processing

CDP   Communications Data Processor
    SF *Aeronautics
        *Communication Systems

CDP   Cytidine Diphosphate-Diacylglycerols
    SF Biochemistry
        *Biological and Medical Sciences
        Pharmacology

CDR   Chemtob Durso and Riska
    SF Nuclear Physics
        *Nuclear Sciences

CDR   Composit Damage Risk
    SF *Aeronautics
        Environmental Science
        Noise

CDSF COMRADE Data Storage Facility
    SF *Computer Sciences
        Data Processing

CdS   Cadmium Sulphide
    SF *Engineering
        Instruments

CDU   Control Display Unit
    SF *Aeronautics
        Navigation

CDX   Control Differential Transmitter
    SF *Communication Systems
        *Electronics and Electrical
        Engineering

CE   Channel End
    SF *Computer Sciences
        *Electronics and Electrical
        Engineering

CE   Coulomb Excitation
    SF *Nuclear Sciences
        Radiation

CEA   Carcinoembryonic Antigens
    SF *Biological and Medical Sciences

CEA   Commissariat a l'Energie Atomique
      (Fr.)
    SF *Nuclear Sciences

CEAC Central European Analysis Commission
    SF *Brewery

CEAC Committee for European Airspace
      Coordination
    SF *Aeronautics
        *Communication Systems

        *Military Sciences

CEADI Coloured Electronics Altitude
      Director Indicator
    SF *Electronics and Electrical
        Engineering

CEBMCO Corps Engineers Ballistic Missile
      Construction Office
    SF Civil Engineering
        *Engineering
        *Military Sciences

CEC   Cation Exchange Capacity
    SF *Agricultural Sciences

CEC   Consulting Engineers Council
    SF *Engineering

CEF   Critical Experiments Facility
    SF *Nuclear Sciences
        Reactors

CEFAC Civil Engineering Field Activities
      Center
    SF Civil Engineering
        *Engineering
        *Military Sciences

CEGB Central Electricity Generating Board
    SF *Electronics and Electrical
        Engineering
        *Nuclear Sciences

CEI   Council of Engineering Institutions
    SF *Engineering

CEIF Council of European Industrial
      Federation
    SF *Copyright
        Industrial Property

ceil ceiling
    SF *Metallurgy and Metallography
        Metalworks

CEL   Carbon Equivalent Liquids
    SF *Metallurgy and Metallography

CEM   Computer Education for Management
    SF *Computer Sciences
        *Training

CEMIRT Civil Engineering Maintenance
      Inspection, Repair and Training
    SF *Engineering
        *Military Sciences
        *Training

CEP   Civil Emergency Planning
    SF *Transportation

CEP   Command Executive Procedures
    SF *Computer Sciences
        Data Processing

CEP   Probable Circular Error
    SF *Aeronautics
        Navigation

CEPC Canada Civil Emergency Planning
      Committee
    SF *General
        *Transportation

CEPT European Conference of Posts and
      Telecommunications
    SF *Copyright

*Telecommunications

CER   Controlled Environment Rooms
      SF *Agricultural Sciences
CERD European Committee on Research and
         Development
      SF *General
CERN Organisation Européene pour la
         Recherche Nucléaire
      SF *Computer Sciences
            Data Processing
            *Nuclear Sciences
CES   Constant Elasticity of Substitution
      SF *Statistics
CES   Coordinated Evaluation System
      SF *Engineering
            Structural Engineering
CESA Canadian Engineering Standards
         Association
      SF *Standards
CESEMI Computer Evaluation of Scanning
         Electron Microscope Images
      SF *Lunar Sciences
CESI Centro Elettrotecnico Sperimentale
         Italiano
      SF *Communication Systems
            Power Systems
CEU   Communications Expansion Unit
      SF *Computer Sciences
            *Electronics and Electrical
               Engineering
CEX   Central Excitation
      SF   Elementary Particles
            *Physics
CF   Cathode Follower
      SF *Communication Systems
            *Engineering
            Radio Engineering
cf   Centripetal Force
      SF *Mathematics
CF   Coated Front
      SF *Printing
CF   Combined Function
      SF   Nuclear Sciences
cf   Contemporary Force
      SF *Mathematics
CF   Corn Flour
      SF *Agricultural Sciences
            *Dairy Sciences
CF   Correlation Function
      SF *Engineering
            Radio Engineering
            *Telecommunications
CF   Crude Fiber
      SF *Dairy Sciences
CFAE Contractor Furnished Aircraft Equipment
      SF *Aeronautics
CFANS Canadian Forces Air Navigation School
      SF *Aeronautics
            Navigation
            *Training

CFAP Copenhagen Frequency Allocation Plan
      SF *Engineering
            Radio Engineering
            *Telecommunications
CFAR Constant False Alarm Rate
      SF *Communication Systems
            Radar Technology
CFB   Coated Front and Back
      SF *Printing
CFC   Colony Forming Cells
      SF *Biological and Medical Sciences
            Cytochemistry
CFD   Constant Fraction Discriminator
      SF *Electronics and Electrical
               Engineering
CFER Collector Field Effect Register
      SF *Electronics and Electrical
               Engineering
            Solid-state Circuit
CFF   Critical Flicker Frequency
      SF *Aeronautics
            Aircraft Noise
CFL   Clear Flight Level
      SF *Aeronautics
            Air Traffic Control
CFM   Cubic Feet per Minute
      SF *Metallurgy and Metallography
            Metalworks
CFMS Chained File Management System
      SF *Computer Sciences
            Data Processing
            *Information Retrieval Systems
CFO   Critical Flashover
      SF *Communication Systems
            Transmission Lines
CFPA Chlorophenyl-trifluo vomethyl
         Phenoxyacetate
      SF   Biochemistry
            *Biological and Medical Sciences
            Pharmacology
CFPHT Constant Traction of Pulse Height
         Trigger
      SF *Engineering
            Instruments
CFPRA Campden Food Preservation Research
         Association (UK)
      SF *Information Retrieval Systems
CFR   Code of Federal Regulation
      SF *Aeronautics
CFR   Commercial Fast Reactor
      SF *Nuclear Sciences
            Reactors
CFR   Contact Flight Rules
      SF *Aeronautics
            Air Traffic Control
CFT   Complement Fixation Test
      SF *Agricultural Sciences
CFT   Constant Fraction Trigger
      SF   Instruments
            *Nuclear Sciences

CFTD	Constant Fraction Timing Discriminator	
	SF *Communication Systems	
CFU	Colony Forming Units	
	SF *Biological and Medical Sciences	
	Cytochemistry	
CFU	Current File User	
	SF *Computer Sciences	
	Data Processing	
cg	Centre of Gravity	
	SF *Mathematics	
CG	Computer Graphics	
	SF *Computer Sciences	
	Data Processing	
CGA	Compagnie Générale d'Automatisme (Fr.)	
	SF *Aeronautics	
	Navigation	
CGL	Chronic Granulocytic Leukaemia	
	SF *Biological and Medical Sciences	
	Cytochemistry	
CGLO	Commonwealth Geological Liaison Office (UK)	
	SF *Information Retrieval Systems	
CGN	Canadian General Electric	
	SF *Nuclear Sciences	
CGR	Crop Growth Rate	
	SF *Agricultural Sciences	
CGRAM	Clock Generator Random Access Memory	
	SF *Computer Sciences	
	Testing	
CGS	Control Guidance Subsystems	
	SF Automatic Test Systems	
	*Engineering	
	Testing	
CH	Calcium Hydroxid	
	SF *Ceramics	
CH	Ceiling Height	
	SF *Metallurgy and Metallography	
	Metalworks	
CHAG	Chain Arrester Gear	
	SF *Aeronautics	
	Airports	
char	character	
	SF *Computer Sciences	
	Data Processing	
CHC	Clearinghouse for Copyright	
	SF *Copyright	
	Patents	
CHCA	Cyclohexanecarboxylic Acid	
	SF *Agricultural Sciences	
CHD	Congenital Heart Disease	
	SF *Biological and Medical Sciences	
CHD	Coronary Heart Disease	
	SF *Aeronautics	
	Aviation Medicine	
	*Biological and Medical Sciences	
ChE	Cholinesterase	
	SF *Biological and Medical Sciences	
	Cytochemistry	
CHF	Critical Heat Flux	
	SF *Nuclear Sciences	

Reactors
CHKPT Checkpoint
SF *Computer Sciences
Data Processing
CHL Chain Home Low
SF *Aeronautics
CHO Carbohydrates
SF *Biological and Medical Sciences
*Dairy Sciences
CHP California Highway Patrol
SF *Transportation
ChPi Chelyabinisk Polytechnic Institute
SF *Metallurgy and Metallography
Welding
CHS Chediak Higashi Syndrome
SF *Biological and Medical Sciences
Cytochemistry
CHT Cycloheptatriene
SF Lasers
*Nuclear Sciences
Quantum Electronics
Chu Centigrade Heat Unit
SF *Mathematics
CHY Chymotrypsinogen
SF *Dairy Sciences
CI Call Indicator
SF *Computer Sciences
Data Processing
CI Cardiac Index
SF Biochemistry
*Biological and Medical Sciences
CI Colloidal Iron
SF *Biological and Medical Sciences
Cytochemistry
CIA Central Intelligence Agency
SF *Security
CIA Certified Internal Auditor
SF *Computer Sciences
Data Processing
CIA Chemiluminescence Immunoassay
SF *Biological and Medical Sciences
Microbiology
CIAP Climatic Impact Assessment Program
SF *Communication Systems
*Meteorology
*Space Sciences
CIAP Clinical Impact Assessment Program
SF *Geosciences
Atmospheric Pollution
CIAT International Center for Tropical Agriculture
SF *Agricultural Sciences
Cereals
CIBS CERN-IHEP Boston Spectrometer
SF Nuclear Physics
*Nuclear Sciences
CIC Combat Information Center
SF *Aeronautics
*Military Sciences
CIC Communication Intelligence Channel

       SF *Computer Sciences
           Data Processing
CIC   Counter Intelligence Corps
       SF *Military Sciences
           *Security
CICD   Computer Aided Circuit Design
       SF *Electronics and Electrical
           Engineering
           Solid-state Circuits
CICP   Committee to Investigate Copyright
           Problems
       SF *Copyright
           Patents
CICS   Customer Information Control System
       SF *Computer Sciences
           Data Processing
CIDA   Current Input Differential Amplifier
       SF *Electronics and Electrical
           Engineering
           Solid-state Circuits
CIDIN Common ICAO Data Interchange Network
       SF *Aeronautics
           Radar Equipment
CIDNP Chemically Induced Dynamic Nuclear
           Polarization
       SF   Instruments
           *Nuclear Sciences
CIDST Committee for Information and
           Documentation on Science and
           Technology (UK)
       SF *Information Retrieval Systems
CIE   Commission Internationale de
           l'Éclairage
       SF *Photography
CIFRR Common IFR Room
       SF *Aeronautics
           Air Traffic Control
           Instruments
CIG   Cryogenic In-Ground
       SF *Engineering
CINC   Commander-In-Chief
       SF *Military Sciences
CINCEUR Commander-In-Chief Europe
       SF *Military Sciences
CINCPAC Commander-In-Chief Pacific
       SF *Military Sciences
CIOCS Communications Input/Output Control
           System
       SF *Computer Sciences
           Data Processing
CIOM   Communications Input/Output
           Multiplexer
       SF *Aeronautics
           *Computer Sciences
           Data Processing
           Ground Communication Networks
CIOT   International Telegraph Operation
           Centre
       SF *Telecommunications
CIOU   Custom Input/Output Unit

       SF *Computer Sciences
           Data Processing
CIP   Civil Institution Program
       SF   Civil Engineering
           *Engineering
           *Military Sciences
CIP   Cleaned-In-Place
       SF *Agricultural Sciences
           *Dairy Sciences
Cir   Circulate
       SF *Computer Sciences
CIR   Characteristic Instants of
           Restitution
       SF *Engineering
           Radio Engineering
           *Telecommunications
circ   Circumference
       SF *Metallurgy and Metallography
           Metalworks
CIRF   Corn Industries Research Foundation
       SF *Agricultural Sciences
           Cereals
CIRIA Construction Industry Research and
           Information (UK)
       SF *Engineering
           *Information Retrieval Systems
CIRIS Complete Integrated Reference
           Instrumentation System
       SF *Aeronautics
           Instruments
CISAC International Confederation of
           Societies of Authors and Composers
       SF   Industrial Property
           *Patents
CISCO Construction Information System,
           Cost and Operation
       SF   Civil Engineering
           *Engineering
           *Military Sciences
CIT   Cranfield Institute of Technology
           (UK)
       SF *Aeronautics
CIU   Control Indicator Unit
       SF *Aeronautics
           Testing
CK   Cleatine Kinase
       SF *Biological and Medical Sciences
           Medical Ions
CKRS   Corn Kennel Red Steak
       SF *Agricultural Sciences
CL   Cable Links
       SF *Engineering
           Radio Engineering
           *Telecommunications
CL   Chemiluminescence
       SF   Civil Engineering
           *Engineering
CL   Connecting Lines
       SF *Engineering
           Radio Engineering

```
              *Telecommunications
CL     Control Leader
       SF  *Computer Sciences
           Data Processing
CL     Current Layer
       SF  *Lunar Sciences
CLAM   Chemical Low Altitude Missile
       SF  *Military Sciences
CLC    Central Logic Control
       SF  *Computer Sciences
           Data Processing
CLC    Constant Light Compensating
       SF  *Photography
CLC    Course Line Computer
       SF  *Computer Sciences
CLCOLL Clinch Collar
       SF  *Metallurgy and Metallography
           Metalworks
CLD    Constant Level Discriminator
       SF  *Electronics and Electrical
             Engineering
CLD    Constant Level Descriptor
       SF   Instruments
            *Nuclear Sciences
CLEM   Closed Loop Ex-vessel Machine
       SF  *Nuclear Sciences
           Reactors
CLI    Command Language Interpreter
       SF  *Computer Sciences
           Data Processing
CLIRA  Closed Loop In-Reactor Assemblies
       SF  *Nuclear Sciences
           Reactors
CLK    Clock
       SF  *Computer Sciences
CLL    Central Light Loss
       SF  *Biological and Medical Sciences
CLL    Chronic Lymphocytic Leukaemia
       SF  *Biological and Medical Sciences
           Cytochemistry
CLR    Constant Load Rupture
       SF  *Metallurgy and Metallography
           Welding
CLS    Control and Launch Subsystems
       SF  *Computer Sciences
           Data Processing
CM     Carboxymethyl
       SF  *Brewery
cm     centimetre
       SF  *Mathematics
CM     Command Module
       SF  *Lunar Sciences
CM     Common Mode
       SF  *Electronics and Electrical
             Engineering
           Solid-state Circuits
CM     Communication Multiplexer
       SF  *Computer Sciences
           Data Processing
CM     Cross Modulation
```

```
       SF  *Electronics and Electrical
             Engineering
           Solid-state Circuits
CMA    Contact-Making Ammeter
       SF  *Electronics and Electrical
             Engineering
           Meters
CMACL  Composite Mode Adjective Checklist
       SF  *Aeronautics
           Air Traffic Control
CMB    Concrete Median Barrier
       SF  *Engineering
           Structural Engineering
CMC    Canadian Meteorological Centre
       SF  *Meteorology
CMC    Carboxymethylcellulose
       SF  *Brewery
CMC    Command Module Computer
       SF  *Astronautics and Astrophysics
           Navigation
CMC    Computer Machinery Company
       SF  *Computer Sciences
           *Management
CMC    Contact-Making Clock
       SF  *Electronics and Electrical
             Engineering
           Meters
CMC    Coordinal Manual Controls
       SF  *Electronics and Electrical
             Engineering
CMD    Contract Management District
       SF  *Engineering
CMD    Coupled Mobility Devices
       SF  *Engineering
           Mechanical Engineering
           Terramechanics
CMG    Computer Management Group
       SF   Business Systems
            *Management
CMHC   Community Mental Health Centres
       SF  *Biological and Medical Sciences
           Physiology
CMI    Cell Medicated Immunity
       SF  *Biological and Medical Sciences
CMI    Computer Managed Instruction
       SF  *Computer Sciences
           Data Processing
CML    Chronic Myelogenous Leukaemia
       SF  *Biological and Medical Sciences
CML    Current Mode Logic
       SF  *Electronics and Electrical
             Engineering
           Integrated Circuits
           Solid-state Circuits
CMM    Computerized Modular Monitoring
       SF  *Aeronautics
           Air Traffic Control
           *Computer Sciences
CMM    Coordinate Measuring Machines
       SF  *Engineering
```

Instruments
CMOS   Contemporary Metal Oxide
          Semiconductor
       SF *Electronics and Electrical
              Engineering
           Solid-state Circuits
CMR   Carbon Magnetic Resonance
       SF *Biological and Medical Sciences
CMR   Common Mode Rejection
       SF *Electronics and Electrical
              Engineering
           Solid-state Circuits
CMRR   Common Mode Rejection Ratio
       SF *Nuclear Sciences
CMS   Ca-Mg-Silicate
       SF *Ceramics
CMS   Cambridge Monitor System
       SF *Computer Sciences
           Data Processing
CMS   Coincidence Mössbauer Spectroscopy
       SF *Nuclear Sciences
           Spectroscopy
CMT   California Mastitis Test
       SF *Agricultural Sciences
           *Dairy Sciences
CMTC   Coupled Monostable Trigger Circuit
       SF *Electronics and Electrical
              Engineering
           Solid-state Circuits
CMU   Computer Memory Unit
       SF *Computer Sciences
           Navigation
CMV   Common Mode Voltage
       SF *Electronics and Electrical
              Engineering
CMV   Contact-Making Voltmeter
       SF *Electronics and Electrical
              Engineering
           Meters
CMV   Cytomegalovirus
       SF *Biological and Medical Sciences
CN   Cascade Nozzle
       SF *Aeronautics
           Thrust Vectoring Concepts
CN   Caudate Nucleus
       SF *Biological and Medical Sciences
CNBr   Cyanogen Bromide
       SF *Biological and Medical Sciences
CNC   Computer Numerical Control
       SF *Computer Sciences
           Data Processing
CN-CA Cellulose Nitrate-Cellulose Acetate
       SF Chemical Engineering
           *Engineering
CNCS   Central Navigation Control School
       SF *Aeronautics
           Navigation
           *Training
CNE   Compare Numeric Equal
       SF *Computer Sciences

           Electronics and Electrical
              Engineering
CNG   Compressed Natural Gas
       SF Explosives
           *Nuclear Sciences
           Reactors
CNI   Communication, Navigation and
          Information
       SF *Aeronautics
           Navigation
CNI   Communications, Navigation and
          Identification
       SF *Aeronautics
           *Communication Systems
           Navigation
CNI   Conservation Needs Inventory
       SF *Agricultural Sciences
CNO   Chief of Naval Operation
       SF *Military Sciences
CNP   Chief of Naval Personnel
       SF *Military Sciences
CNR   Composite Noise Rating
       SF *Aeronautics
           Aircraft Noise
CNS   Central Navigation School
       SF *Aeronautics
           *Training
CNS   Central Nervous System
       SF *Biological and Medical Sciences
CNU   Compare Numeric Unequal
       SF *Computer Sciences
           *Electronics and Electrical
              Engineering
CNV   Contingent Negative Variation
       SF *Biological and Medical Sciences
CO   Crystal Oscillator
       SF *Communication Systems
           *Engineering
           Radio Engineering
COA   Conversion Of Acetyl
       SF *Biological and Medical Sciences
           Pharmacology
COAM   Customer Owned And Maintained
       SF *Computer Sciences
           Data Processing
COAMP Cost Analysis of Maintenance
       SF Logistics
           *Military Sciences
COAT   Correct Outside Air Temperature
       SF *Aeronautics
COBOL Common Business Oriented Language
       SF *Computer Sciences
COD   Carrier Onboard Delivery
       SF *Aeronautics
           Navigation
COD   Chemical Oxygen Demand
       SF *Agricultural Sciences
           Biochemistry
           *Dairy Sciences
COD   Clean Out Door

```
          SF   *Metallurgy and Metallography
               Metalworks
COD     Crack Open Displacement
          SF   *Nonmetallic Materials
               Polymers
CODASYL Conference on Data Systems
          Languages
          SF   *Computer Sciences
               Data Processing
CODES   Computer Design and Evaluation System
          SF   *Computer Sciences
               Data Processing
CODIS   Controlled Digital Simulator
          SF   *Aeronautics
               *Computer Sciences
coeff   coefficient
          SF   *Mathematics
COF     Correct Operation Factor
          SF   *Engineering
               Radio Engineering
               *Telecommunications
COGD    Circulator Outlet Gas Duct
          SF   *Metallurgy and Metallography
               Welding
COGS    Continuous Orbital Guidance System
          SF   *Aeronautics
               *Space Sciences
col     column
          SF   *Metallurgy and Metallography
               Metalworks
COL     Computer Oriented Language
          SF   *Computer Sciences
               Data Processing
COM     Computer Output Microfilm
          SF   *Computer Sciences
               *Information Retrieval Systems
               *Photography
COMATS  Commander Military Air Transport
          Service
          SF   *Military Sciences
               *Transportation
COMCM   Communication Countermeasures
          SF   *Communication Systems
COMESA  Committee on the Meteorological
          Effects of Stratospheric Aircraft
          (UK)
          SF   *Aeronautics
               Air Pollution
               *Meteorology
COMLO   Compass Locator
          SF   *Aeronautics
               Navigation
COMPAC  Computer Program for Automatic
          Control
          SF   *Computer Sciences
               Data Processing
COMPACT Compatible Algebraic Compiler and
          Translator
          SF   *Computer Sciences
               Data Processing
```

```
COMPAY  Computer Payroll
          SF   *Computer Sciences
               Data Processing
COMRADE Computer Aided Design Environment
          SF   *Computer Sciences
COMSAT  Communication Satellite
          SF   *Communication Systems
COMT    Catechol-O-Methyltransferase
          SF   *Biological and Medical Sciences
               Neutrotransmitters
COMZ    Communication Zone
          SF   *Communication Systems
CONAD   Continental Air Defence
          SF   *Military Sciences
CONC    Concrete
          SF   *Engineering
               *Metallurgy and Metallography
               Metalworks
CONHAN  Contextual Harmonic Analysis
          SF   *Computer Sciences
               *Music
CONN    Connection
          SF   *Metallurgy and Metallography
               Metalworks
CONTRAN Control Translator
          SF   *Computer Sciences
COOP    Continuity of Operation Plan
          SF   *General
coord   Co-ordinate
          SF   *Mathematics
COP     Copper
          SF   *Metallurgy and Metallography
               Metalworks
COPA    Committee of Agricultural
          Organizations
          SF   *Agricultural Sciences
COPAG   Collision Prevention Advisory Group
          SF   *Aeronautics
COPD    Chronic Obstructive Pulmonary Disease
          SF   *Biological and Medical Sciences
COPEP   Committee of Public Engineering
          Policy (US)
          SF   *Engineering
               Mechanical Engineering
CORA    Coherent Radar Array
          SF   *Aeronautics
               Air Traffic Control
CORDS   Coherent-on-Receive Doppler System
          SF   *Aeronautics
               Air Traffic Control
CORF    Committee on Radio Frequency
          SF   *Communication Systems
               *Space Sciences
CORTEX  Communications Oriented Real Time
          Executive
          SF   *Communication Systems
               *Computer Sciences
COS     Chief of Staff
          SF   *Military Sciences
cos     cosine
```

            SF *Mathematics
COSATI Committee on Scientific and
        Technical Information
        SF   Microfilms
             *Photography
COSBA Computer Service and Bureaux
       Association
        SF   Business Systems
             *Computer Sciences
             Data Processing
             *Management
cosec cosecant
        SF *Mathematics
COSEC Culham One-line Single Experimental
       Consol
        SF *Computer Sciences
            Data Processing
COSMIC Computer Software and Management
        Information Center
        SF *Information Retrieval Systems
COSPAR Committee on Space Research
        SF *Astronautics and Astrophysics
            *Space Sciences
COSY Compiler System
        SF *Computer Sciences
            Data Processing
COSY Correction System
        SF *Computer Sciences
            Data Processing
COT   Cycleoctatetraene
        SF *Electronics and Electrical
            Engineering
            Lasers
            Quantum Electronics
COTC Canadian Overseas Telecommunication
       Corporation
        SF *Telecommunications
cP   Centipose
        SF *Mathematics
CP   Central Processor
        SF *Computer Sciences
            Data Processing
CP   Chemical Preparation
        SF *Ceramics
            *Chemistry
CP   Clock Pulse
        SF *Computer Sciences
            Data Processing
CP   Coherent Potential
        SF   Liquid Semiconductors
             *Non-crystalline Solids
CP   Collision Probability
        SF *Nuclear Sciences
            Reactors
CP   Colour Printing
        SF *Photography
CP   Command Processor
        SF *Computer Sciences
            Data Processing
CP   Continuous Phase

        SF   Bioengineering
             *Biological and Medical Sciences
CP   Control Panel
        SF *Aeronautics
CP   Crude Protein
        SF *Agricultural Sciences
CPA   Certified Public Account
        SF *Computer Sciences
            Data Processing
CPA   Closest Point of Approach
        SF *Aeronautics
            Navigation
CPA   Coherent Potential Approximation
        SF   Liquid Semiconductors
             *Non-crystalline Solids
CPA   Concurrent Photon Amplification
        SF *Photography
CPB   Channel Program Block
        SF *Computer Sciences
            Data Processing
CPB   Competitive Protein Binding
        SF *Agricultural Sciences
CPC   Channel Program Command
        SF *Computer Sciences
            Data Processing
CPC   Controlled Potential Coulometry
        SF   Nuclear Measurements
             *Nuclear Sciences
CPCS Cheque Processing Control System
        SF *Computer Sciences
            Data Processing
CPD   Carboxypeptidase
        SF *Biological and Medical Sciences
            Metal Ions
CPD   Citrate Phosphate Dextrose
        SF *Biological and Medical Sciences
            Blood Preservation
CPE   Circular Probable Error
        SF *Aeronautics
            Navigation
CPED Continuous Particle Electrophoresis
       Device
        SF   Bioengineering
             *Biological and Medical Sciences
CPF   Colloidal Phosphate Free
        SF *Dairy Sciences
CPFMS COMRADE Permanent File Management
       System
        SF *Computer Sciences
            Data Processing
CPG   Clock-Pulse Generator
        SF *Engineering
            Radio Engineering
            *Telecommunications
CPI   Character Per Inch
        SF *Computer Sciences
            Data Processing
CPI   Crash Position Indicator
        SF *Aeronautics
CPIB Chlorophenoxisobutyrate

	SF *Biological and Medical Sciences
	Cytochemistry
CPIP	Chlorophenoxyisophate
	SF Biochemistry
	*Biological and Medical Sciences
CPID	Computer Program Integrated Document
	SF *Computer Sciences
CPILS	Correlation Protected Instrument
	Landing System
	SF *Aeronautics
	Approach and Landing
	Instruments
CPK	Creatine Phosphokinase
	SF *Chemistry
	Organic Chemistry
CPL	CAST Programming Language
	SF *Computer Sciences
CPL	Computer Projects Limited
	SF *Computer Sciences
	Data Processing
CPLEE	Changed Particle Lunar Environment
	Experiment
	SF *Lunar Sciences
CPM	Central Processor Modules
	SF *Aeronautics
	*Communication Systems
	*Computer Sciences
	Data Processing
CPM	Critical Path Method
	SF *Computer Sciences
	*Electronics and Electrical
	Engineering
	*General
CPO	Compulsory Purchase Order
	SF *Building
CPO	Concurrent Peripheral Operations
	SF *Computer Sciences
	Data Processing
CPR	Canadian Pacific Railway
	SF *Transportation
CPS	CERN Proton Synchrotron
	SF Elementary Particles
	*Nuclear Sciences
CPS	Character Per Second
	SF *Computer Sciences
	Data Processing
CPS	Conversational Programming System
	SF *Computer Sciences
	*Information Retrieval Systems
CPS	Cycles Per Second
	SF *Communication Systems
	*Computer Sciences
	*Electronics and Electrical
	Engineering
CPSM	Critical Path Scheduling Method
	SF *Computer Sciences
	Data Processing
	Operational Research
CPU	Central Processor Unit
	SF *Aeronautics

	Air Traffic Control
	*Computer Sciences
CPU	Computer Processor Unit
	SF *Computer Sciences
CPW	Cooked Potato Weight
	SF *Agricultural Sciences
CPW	Coplanar Waveguide
	SF *Electronics and Electrical
	Engineering
CR	Card Reader
	SF *Computer Sciences
CR	Carriage Return
	SF *Computer Sciences
	Data Processing
CR	Ceiling Register
	SF *Metallurgy and Metallography
	Metalworks
CR	Communications Register
	SF *Computer Sciences
	Data Processing
CR	Constant Rate
	SF *Biological and Medical Sciences
CR	Control Routine
	SF *Computer Sciences
	Data Processing
CRAAM	Centre of Radio Astronomy and
	Astrophysics, Mackenzie University
	(Sao Paulo)
	SF Communication Systems
	*Telecommunications
CRAF	Civil Reserve Air Fleet
	SF *Aeronautics
	*Military Sciences
	*Transportation
CRAM	Card Random Access Memory
	SF *Computer Sciences
	Data Processing
CRC	Communications Research Centre
	SF *Communication Systems
CRS	Control and Reporting Center
	SF *Aeronautics
	*Communication Systems
	*Military Sciences
CRC	Cyclic Redundancy Checksum
	SF *Computer Sciences
	Data Processing
CRCC	Cyclic Redundancy Check Character
	SF *Computer Sciences
	Data Processing
CRCP	Continuously Reinforced Concrete
	Pavements
	SF Civil Engineering
	*Engineering
CRD	Card Read
	SF *Computer Sciences
	Data Processing
CRETC	Combined Radiating Effects Test
	Chamber
	SF *Space Sciences
	Space Simulation

CRF   Corticotropin Releasing Factor
        SF   *Biological and Medical Sciences
CRJE   Conversational Remote Job Entry
        SF   *Computer Sciences
             Data Processing
CRLB   Cramer Rao Lower Bound
        SF   Ordnance
             Rockets
CRN   Continuous Random Network
        SF   Liquid Semiconductors
             *Non-crystalline Solids
CRNL   Chalk River Nuclear Laboratories
        (Can.)
        SF   *Nuclear Sciences
CRO   Cathode Ray Oscillograph
        SF   *Electronics and Electrical
             Engineering
             Meters
CRO   Cathode Ray Oscilloscope
        SF   *Biological and Medical Sciences
             *Electronics and Electrical
             Engineering
CRP   Constant Rate of Penetration
        SF   Civil Engineering
             Construction
             *Engineering
CRP   Control and Reporting Post
        SF   *Aeronautics
             *Communication Systems
             *Military Sciences
CRSMP   Calcium Reduced Skim Milk Power
        SF   *Dairy Sciences
CRT   Cathode Ray Tube
        SF   *Aeronautics
             *Communication Systems
             *Computer Sciences
             *Electronics and Electrical
             Engineering
             *General
CRU   Gyro Reference Unit
        SF   *Aeronautics
             Navigation
cS   Centistokes
        SF   *Mathematics
CS   Citrate Synthase
        SF   Biochemistry
             *Biological and Medical Sciences
CS   Coal Store
        SF   *Building
CS   Communications Satellites
        SF   *Telecommunications
CS   Concrete Slab
        SF   *Metallurgy and Metallography
             Metalworks
CS   Cycles per Second
        SF   *Mathematics
CS   Cyclo-Stationary
        SF   *Computer Sciences
             *Electronics and Electrical
             Engineering

CSA   Central Supply Agency
        SF   *Transportation
CSC   Chief Sector Controller
        SF   *Aeronautics
             Air Traffic Control
CSC   Civil Service Commission
        SF   *General
CSC   Common Signalling Channel
        SF   *Telecommunications
CSC   Communications Satellite Corporation
        SF   *Communication Systems
             *Space Sciences
CSC   Computer Sciences Corporation
        SF   *Computer Sciences
             Data Processing
CSC   Course and Speed Computer
        SF   *Computer Sciences
CSD   Computer Sciences Division
        SF   *Computer Sciences
             Data Processing
CSD   Constant Simulus Differences
        SF   *Aeronautics
             Aircraft Noise
CSD   Constant Speed Drive
        SF   *Aeronautics
             Aircraft
CSE   Containment Systems Experiment
        SF   *Nuclear Sciences
             Radiators
CSECT   Control Section
        SF   *Computer Sciences
             *Electronics and Electrical
                Engineering
CSEF   Current Switch Emitter Follower
        SF   *Communication Systems
CSF   Cerebrospinal Fluid
        SF   *Biological and Medical Sciences
             Stress
CSG   Combat Support Group
        SF   *Military Sciences
CSI   Computer Systems International
        SF   *Computer Sciences
             Data Processing
CSI   Construction Specification Institute
        (US)
        SF   *Engineering
             Mechanical Engineering
CSIRO   Commonwealth Scientific and Industrial
        Research Organization (Aust.)
        SF   *General
CSL   Computer Simulation Language
        SF   *Computer Sciences
CSL   Constant Scattering Length
        SF   *Nuclear Sciences
CSL   Control and Simulation Language
        SF   *Computer Sciences
             Data Processing
CSM   Command Service Module
        SF   *Astronautics and Astrophysics
             *Lunar Sciences

```
                *Space Sciences
                 Telecommunications
CSM     Corn-Soy-Milk
        SF   *Agricultural Sciences
              Cereals
CSMFRA  Cotton, Silk and Man-made Fibres
          Research Association (UK)
        SF   *Information Retrieval Systems
CSML    Continuous Self Mode Locking
        SF   *Electronics and Electrical
                 Engineering
              Lasers
              Quantum Electronics
CSMP    Continuous System Modelling Program
        SF   *Computer Sciences
              Data Processing
CSO     Cotton Seed Oil
        SF   *Agricultural Sciences
CSP     Concentrated Super-Phosphate
        SF   *Agricultural Sciences
CSP     Control Switching Point
        SF   *Computer Sciences
              Data Processing
CSS     Computer Sale and Services
        SF    Business Systems
              *Management
CSS     Computer Subsystem
        SF   *Computer Sciences
              Data Processing
CSS     Computer System Simulator
        SF   *Computer Sciences
              Data Processing
CSTF    Continuous Stirred Tank Fermentator
        SF    Bioengineering
              *Biological and Medical Sciences
CSTR    Committee on Solar Terrestrial
          Research
        SF   *Meteorology
              *Space Sciences
CSTR    Continuous Stirred Tank Reactor
        SF    Bioengineering
              *Biological and Medical Sciences
CSW     Channel Status Word
        SF   *Computer Sciences
              Data Processing
ct      Centre Tap
        SF   *Communication Systems
CT      Charge Transfer
        SF   *Photography
CT      Colloidal Thorium
        SF   *Biological and Medical Sciences
              Cytochemistry
CT      Control Transformer
        SF   *Communications Systems
              *Electronics and Electrical
                 Engineering
CT      Cooling Tower
        SF   *Metallurgy and Metallography
              Metalworks
CT      Current Transformer
```

```
        SF   *Aeronautics
              *Electronics and Electrical
                 Engineering
CTA     Cystine Trypticase Agar
        SF   *Biological and Medical Sciences
              Microbiology
CTAB    Cetyl Trimethylammonium Bromide
        SF   *Agricultural Sciences
              Cereals
CTAB    Commerce Technical Advisory Board
          (US)
        SF   *Geosciences
              *Transportation
CTB     Computer Time Bookers
        SF   *Computer Sciences
              Data Processing
CTC     Carbon Tetrachloride
        SF   *Agricultural Sciences
              Fumigation
              Milling
CTC     Communications Transistor Corporation
          (US)
        SF   *Communication Systems
              Electronics and Electrical
                 Engineering
CTC     Compact Transpiration Cooling
        SF   *Military Sciences
              Missiles
CTD     Cross Track Distance
        SF   *Aeronautics
              Instruments
CTF     Controlled Thermonuclear Fission
        SF   *Nuclear Sciences
CTF     Cottonseed Flour
        SF   *Agricultural Sciences
              *Dairy Sciences
CTFM    Continuous Transmission Frequency
          Modulated
        SF   *Communication Systems
              *Fisheries
CTIO    Cerro Tololo Inter-American
          Observatory (Chile)
        SF   *Astronautics and Astrophysics
              Observatories
              *Space Sciences
CTO     Chloxtetracycline
        SF    Biochemistry
              *Biological and Medical Sciences
CTOL    Conventional Takeoff and Landing
        SF   *Aeronautics
              Aircraft
CTP     Cholinephosphate Cytidyltransferase
        SF    Biochemistry
              *Biological and Medical Sciences
              Pharmacology
CTP     Cytidine Triphosphate
        SF   *Biological and Medical Sciences
              Biophysics
CTR     Certified Test Requirements
        SF   *Space Sciences
```

Space Simulation

CTR   Collective Television Reception
SF   *Engineering
Radio Engineering
*Telecommunications

CTR   Controlled Thermonuclear Reactor
SF   *Engineering
Mechanical Engineering
*Nuclear Sciences

CTRA   Coal Tar Research Association (UK)
SF   *Information Retrieval Systems

CTS   Cleveland Transit System
SF   *Transportation

CTS   Common Test Subroutines
SF   *Computer Sciences
Data Processing

CTS   Communications Technology Satellite
SF   *Communication Systems
*Space Sciences

CTS   Computerized Training System
SF   *Training

CTS   Contralateral Threshold Shift
SF   *Aeronautics
Environmental Sciences
Noise

CTS   Controlled Thermal Severity
SF   *Metallurgy and Metallography
Welding

CTS   Cooke Troughton and Simms
SF   *Photography

CTS/RTS Clear-to-Send/Request-to-Send
SF   *Computer Sciences
Data Processing

CTTL   Complementary Transistor-Transistor
Logic
SF   *Electronics and Electrical
Engineering
Solid-state Circuits

CTU   Channel Testing Unit
SF   *Telecommunications

CTV   Control Test Vehicle
SF   *Aeronautics
*Military Sciences

Cu   Copper
SF   *General
*Metallurgy and Metallography

CU   Consolidated Undrained
SF   Civil Engineering
*Engineering
Testing

CU   Control Unit
SF   *Computer Sciences
*General
*Telecommunications

CUE   Computer Up-date Equipment
SF   *Aeronautics
*Computer Sciences
Data Processing

CUE   Control Unit End
SF   *Computer Sciences

*Electronics and Electrical
Engineering

CUEA   Coastal Upwelling Ecosystems Analysis
SF   *Computer Sciences
Data Processing

CUED   Cambridge University Engineering
Development
SF   *Engineering

CuLPCN Copper Leucophalocyanine
SF   *Photography

C-V   Capacitance-Voltage
SF   *Physics

CV   Coefficient of Variation
SF   *Agricultural Sciences
*General

CV   Condensing Vacuole
SF   *Biological and Medical Sciences
Cytochemistry

CVC   Consolidated Vacuum Corporation (US)
SF   *Space Sciences
Space Simulation

CVC   Current Voltage Characteristics
SF   *Telecommunications

CVD   Chemical Vapor Deposition
SF   *Nuclear Sciences
X-ray Techniques

CVD   Creative Visual Dynamics
SF   *Photography

CVF   Controlled Visual Flight
SF   *Aeronautics

CVIS   Computerized Vocational Information
System
SF   *Computer Sciences
*Information Retrieval Systems

CVM   Cervico Vaginal
SF   *Dairy Sciences

CVP   Central Venous Pressure
SF   Biochemistry
*Biological and Medical Sciences
Pharmacology

CVR   Cockpit Voice Recorder
SF   *Aeronautics
*Communication Systems

CVS   Constant Volume Sampling
SF   Civil Engineering
*Engineering

CVT   Crystal Violet Tetrazolium
SF   *Agricultural Sciences
*Dairy Sciences

CVTR   Carolians-Virginia Tube Reactors
SF   *Nuclear Sciences
Reactors

CW   Call Waiting
SF   *Computer Sciences
Data Processing

CW   Carrier Wave
SF   *Communication Systems

CW   Chemical Warfare
SF   *Military Sciences

CW   Clipping Weight

```
         SF   *Agricultural Sciences
CW     Continuous Wave
         SF   *Aeronautics
              *Computer Sciences
               Data Processing
               Navigation
CWBAD  Clockwise Bottom Angular Down
         SF   *Metallurgy and Metallography
               Metalworks
CWBAU  Clockwise Bottom Angular Up
         SF   *Metallurgy and Metallography
               Metalworks
CWDB   Clockwise Down Blast
         SF   *Metallurgy and Metallography
               Metalworks
CWC    Cell Wall Constituents
         SF   *Agricultural Sciences
CWED   Cold Weld Evaluation Device
         SF   *Metallurgy and Metallography
              *Space Sciences
               Space Simulation
               Welding
CWO    Chief Warrant Officer
         SF   *Military Sciences
CWP    Chorleywood Process
         SF   *Milling
CWT    Critical Water Temperature
         SF   *Biological and Medical Sciences
cwt    Hundredweight
         SF   *Mathematics
CWTAD  Clockwise Top Angular Down
         SF   *Metallurgy and Metallography
               Metalworks
CWTAU  Clockwise Top Angular Up
         SF   *Metallurgy and Metallography
               Metalworks
CWTG   Computer World Trade Group (UK)
         SF   *Computer Sciences
CWTH   Clockwise Top Horizontal
         SF   *Metallurgy and Metallography
               Metalworks
CWUB   Clockwise Up Blast
         SF   *Metallurgy and Metallography
               Metalworks
CX     Control Transmitter
         SF   *Communication Systems
              *Electronics and Electrical
               Engineering
CY     Cubic Yard
         SF   *Mathematics
CZC    Chromated Zinc Chloride
         SF   *Engineering
              *Metallurgy and Metallography
CZE    Compare Zone Equal
         SF   *Computer Sciences
              *Electronics and Electrical
               Engineering
CZR    Center for Zoonoses Research (US)
         SF   *Agricultural Sciences
```

```
CZU    Compare Zone Unequal
         SF   *Computer Sciences
              *Electronics and Electrical
               Engineering
```

D

d   Diode
     SF   *Electronics and Electrical
         Engineering
         Semiconductor Devices

d   Drain
     SF   *Electronics and Electrical
         Engineering
         Semiconductor Devices

DA   Define Area
     SF   *Computer Sciences
         Data Processing

DA   Delay Amplifier
     SF   *Electronics and Electrical
         Engineering

D-A   Digital-to-Analog
     SF   *Computer Sciences

DA   Direct Access
     SF   *Computer Sciences
         Data Processing

DA   Discrete Address
     SF   *Computer Sciences
         Data Processing

DA   Dopamine
     SF   Biochemistry
         *Biological and Medical Sciences

DAA   Data Access Arrangement
     SF   *Computer Sciences
         Data Processing

DAAM   Diacetone Acrylamide
     SF   *Nonmetallic Materials
         Polymers

DAB   Diaminobenzidine
     SF   *Biological and Medical Sciences
         Cytochemistry

DAB   Dimethylaminoazobenzene
     SF   Biochemistry
         *Biological and Medical Sciences

DABS   Discrete Address Beacon System
     SF   *Aeronautics
         Air Traffic Control
         Communication Systems
         Radar Beacon Systems

DA/C   Data Acquisition
     SF   *Computer Sciences

DAC   Digital-to-Analog Converter
     SF   *Computer Sciences

DAC   Distance Amplitude Correction
     SF   *Nuclear Sciences
         Pressure Boundaries

DACOM   Data Communication
     SF   *Communication Systems
         *Computer Sciences

DACOS   Deputy Assistant Chief of Staff
     SF   *Military Sciences

DACU   Digitizing and Control Unit
     SF   *Computer Sciences

DADB   Data Analysis Data Base
     SF   *Computer Sciences
         Data Processing

DADPS   Diaminodiphenylsulphone
     SF   *Non-metallic Materials
         Plastics
         Polymers

DADS   Data Acquisition and Display
       Subsystem
     SF   *Computer Sciences
         Data Processing

DADS   Digital Air Data System
     SF   *Aeronautics
         Data Processing

DAFT   Digital Analogue Function Table
     SF   *Computer Sciences
         Data Processing

DAG   Deputy Adjutant General
     SF   *Military Sciences

DAIR   Driver Aid Information and Routing
     SF   Cybernetics
         *Information Retrieval Systems
         *Transportation

DAIR   Dynamic Allocation Interface Routine
     SF   *Computer Sciences
         Data Processing

DAIS   Digital Avionics Information System
     SF   *Aeronautics

DAK   Decision Acknowledge
     SF   *Computer Sciences
         Data Processing

DAM   Dual Absorption Model
     SF   Nuclear Physics
         *Nuclear Sciences

DAMP Downrange Anti-Missile Measurement
      Program
      SF   *Military Sciences
           *Space Sciences
DAMS Defense Analyst Missile Systems
      SF   *Military Sciences
           *Space Sciences
DAPA Diaminopimelic Acid
      SF   *Agricultural Sciences
DAPP Data Acquisition and Processing
      Program
      SF   *Information Retrieval Systems
DAR   Damage Assessment Routine
      SF   *Computer Sciences
           Data Processing
DARC Direct Access Radar Channel
      SF   *Aeronautics
           *Communication Systems
DARMS Digital Alternate Representation
      of Music Symbols
      SF   *Computer Sciences
           *Music
DARPA Defence Advanced Research Project
      Agency
      SF   *Aeronautics
           Aircraft
DART Daily Automatic Rescheduling
      Technique
      SF   *Computer Sciences
           *Electronics and Electrical
             Engineering
DAS   Data Acquisition Subsystem
      SF   *Aeronautics
           Air Traffic Control
           *Computer Sciences
           Data Processing
DAS   Data Acquisition System
      SF   *Computer Sciences
           *General
DAS   Data Acquisitioning System
      SF   *Computer Sciences
           *Space Sciences
           Space Simulation
DAS   Data Analysis System
      SF   *Computer Sciences
           Data Processing
DASA Defense Atomic Support Agency (US)
      SF   *Military Sciences
DASD Direct Access Storage Device
      SF   *Computer Sciences
           Data Processing
DASH Drone Anti-Submarine Helicopter
      SF   *Military Sciences
DASS Demand Assigned Signalling and
      Switching
      SF   *Telecommunications
DAT   Dynamic Address Translator
      SF   *Computer Sciences
           *Electronics and Electrical
             Engineering

DATICO Digital Automatic Tape Intelligence
      Checkout
      SF   *Computer Sciences
           Data Processing
DAVIE Digital Alpha-Numeric Video Insertion
      Equipment
      SF   *Aeronautics
           Radar
DAWNS Design of Aircraft Wing Structures
      SF   *Aeronautics
DB   Double Biased
      SF   *Electronics and Electrical
             Engineering
DBA   Data Base Administrator
      SF   *Computer Sciences
           Data Processing
DBA   Design Basic Accident
      SF   *Nuclear Sciences
           Reactors
DBA   Dibenzathracene
      SF   *Biological and Medical Sciences
DBDA Dibenzyldodecylamine
      SF   *Nuclear Sciences
           Radiation
DBH   Dopamine Beta Hydroxylase
      SF   *Biological and Medical Sciences
           Neurotransmitters
DBHI Dopamine B Hydroxylase Inhibitors
      SF   Biochemistry
           *Biological and Medical Sciences
           Pharmacology
DBM   Decibels Meter
      SF   *Electronics and Electrical
             Engineering
           Meters
DBMS Data Base Management Software
      SF   *Computer Sciences
           Data Processing
DBMS Data Base Management Systems
      SF   *Computer Sciences
           Data Processing
DBMSPSM Data Base Management System Problem
      Specification Model
      SF   *Computer Sciences
           Data Processing
DBP   Diastolic Blood Pressure
      SF   *Aeronautics
           Aviation Medicine
           *Biological and Medical Sciences
DBP   Dibutyl Phthalate
      SF   *Biological and Medical Sciences
           Forensic Sciences
DBRN Decibels Based Reference Noise
      SF   *Computer Sciences
           *Electronics and Electrical
             Engineering
DBS   Direct Broadcast Satellite
      SF   *Space Sciences
DBTG Data Base Task Group
      SF   *Computer Sciences

Electronics and Electrical
Engineering
DBU   Digital Buffer Unit
SF   Automatic Test System
*Computer Sciences
DBV   Doppler Broadening Velocity
SF   Astronomy and Astrophysics
*Lunar Sciences
DC   Despatcher Console
SF   *Engineering
Radio Engineering
*Telecommunications
DC   Device Control
SF   *Computer Sciences
Data Processing
DC   Digestibility Coefficients
SF   *Agricultural Sciences
Cereals
DC   Direct Connections
SF   *Communication Systems
Radio Engineering
*Telecommunications
DC   Direct Current
SF   *Communication Systems
*Computer Sciences
Data Processing
*Electronics and Electrical
Engineering
DCA   Dichloroacetic
SF   *Nonmetallic Materials
Polymers
DCA   Direct Calorimetric Analysis
SF   *Biological and Medical Sciences
Liquid Semiconductors
*Noncrystalline Solids
DCA   Driver Control Area
SF   *Computer Sciences
Data Processing
DCB   Data Control Block
SF   *Computer Sciences
Data Processing
DCB   Define Control Block
SF   *Computer Sciences
Data Processing
DCB   Drawout Circuit Breakers
SF   *Electronics and Electrical
Engineering
DCBD   Define Control Block Dummy
SF   *Computer Sciences
Data Processing
DCC   Digital Cross Correct
SF   *Computer Sciences
Data Processing
DCC   Direct Computer Control
SF   *Computer Sciences
*Communication Systems
DCC   Display Channel Complex
SF   *Aeronautics
Air Traffic Control
*Communication Systems

dcc   Double Cotton Covered
SF   *Communication Systems
*Engineering
Radio Engineering
DCC-MSF   Direct Contract Condensation
Multistage Flash
SF   Chemical Engineering
*Engineering
DCCU   Data Communication Control Units
SF   *Aeronautics
*Communication Systems
*Computer Sciences
Data Processing
DCD   Digital Coherent Detector
SF   Instruments
*Nuclear Sciences
DCE-FPC   Dichloroethane Extracted Fish
Protein Concentrate
SF   *Dairy Sciences
DCI   Data Communication Interrogate
SF   *Computer Sciences
Data Processing
DCL   Dual Current Lager
SF   Astronomy and Astrophysics
*Lunar Sciences
DCM   Defence Combat Maneuvering
SF   *Aeronautics
*Military Sciences
DCP   Data Collection Platform
SF   *Geosciences
*Oceanography
DCP   Dicalcium Phosphate
SF   *Agricultural Sciences
DCP   Dicumyl Peronide
SF   *Non-metallic Materials
Polymers
DCPA   Defense Civil Preparedness Agency
(US)
SF   *Military Sciences
*Transportation
DCPIP   Dichlorophenolindophenol
SF   *Biological and Medical Sciences
Cytochemistry
DCR   Data Communication Read
SF   *Computer Sciences
Data Processing
DCS   Data Communications System
SF   *Information Retrieval Systems
DCS   Defence Communications System
SF   *Military Sciences
DCS   Direct Coupled System
SF   *Computer Sciences
Data Processing
DCS   Distributed Computer System
SF   *Computer Sciences
DCS/O   Deputy Chief of Staff, Operations
SF   *Military Sciences
DCSS   Damage Control Suit System
SF   *Biological and Medical Sciences
DCTL   Direct Coupled Transistor Logic

SF *Computer Sciences
    *Electronics and Electrical
      Engineering
    Integrated Circuits

DCU Device Control Unit
    SF *Computer Sciences
      Data Processing

DCW Data Communication Write
    SF *Computer Sciences
      Data Processing

DD Data Definition
    SF *Computer Sciences
      Data Processing

dd Density Dependent
    SF *Nuclear Sciences

DDA Data Differential Analyzer
    SF *Computer Sciences
      Data Processing

DDC Defense Documentation Center
    SF *Information Retrieval Systems
      *Military Sciences

DDC Direct Digital Control
    SF *Computer Sciences
      Data Processing

DDD Direct Distance Dialing
    SF *Communication Systems
      *Computer Sciences
      Data Processing

DDI Direct Dial In
    SF *Computer Sciences
      Data Processing

DDL Data Description Language
    SF *Computer Sciences
      *Electronics and Electrical
        Engineering

DDPL Demand Deposit Program Library
    SF *Computer Sciences
      Data Processing

DDR Dynamic Device Reconfiguration
    SF *Computer Sciences
      Data Processing

DDS Digital Data Service
    SF *Computer Sciences
      Data Processing

DDS Digital Spectrum Stabilizer
    SF *Electronics and Electrical
      Engineering

DDS Distillers Dried Solubles
    SF Bioengineering
      *Biological and Medical Sciences

DDT Dichlorodiphenyl Trichloroethane
    SF *Biological and Medical Sciences

DDTV Dry Driver Transport Vehicle
    SF *Transportation

DE Device End
    SF *Computer Sciences
      Data Processing

DE Differential Equation
    SF *Mathematics

DE Digestible Energy

SF *Agricultural Sciences
    *Dairy Sciences

DEAE Diethylaminoethyl
    SF *Dairy Science

DEB Data Extension Block
    SF *Computer Sciences
      Data Processing

DEC Digital Equipment Corporation
    SF *Computer Sciences
      Data Processing

DECB Data Event Control Block
    SF *Computer Sciences
      Data Processing

DECLAB Digital Equipment Company
      Laboratory
    SF *Computer Sciences

DECM Defense Electronic Countermeasures
      System
    SF *Electronics and Electrical
        Engineering
      *Military Sciences

DECOM Delay Cost Model
    SF *General
      *Transportation

DECOR Digital Electronic Continuous Ranging
    SF *Electronics and Electrical
        Engineering
      *Military Sciences

DECTRA Decca Tracking and Ranging
    SF *Electronics and Electrical
        Engineering
      *Military Sciences
      Navigation

DEDS Data Entry and Display Subsystem
    SF *Aeronautics
      Air Traffic Control
      *Communication Systems

DEFCON Defense Readiness Condition
    SF *Military Sciences
      *Transportation

DEFT Dynamic Error Free Transmission
    SF *Electronics and Electrical
        Engineering
      *Military Sciences

DEL Delate
    SF *Computer Sciences
      Data Processing
      *General

DELRAC Decca Long Range Area Coverage
    SF *Electronics and Electrical
        Engineering
      *Military Sciences
      Navigation

DELTIC Delay-Line Time Compression
    SF *Electronics and Electrical
        Engineering
      Solid-state Circuits

DEM Demodulator
    SF *Computer Sciences
      Data Processing

DEN   Di-Ethyl Nitrosamine
       SF *Biological and Medical Sciences
DEPA   Defense Electric Power Administration
          (US)
       SF *Transportation
DEPC   Diethylpyrocarbonate
       SF *Agricultural Sciences
           *Dairy Sciences
DEPE   Double Escape Peak Efficiency
       SF   Gamma-rays
            *Nuclear Sciences
DES   Desoxycholate
       SF *Agricultural Sciences
           *Dairy Sciences
DES   Diethylsliboestrol
       SF *Biological and Medical Sciences
           Drugs
DES   Dynamic Environment Simulator
       SF   Aviation Medicine
            *Biological and Medical Sciences
DESC   Defense Electronic Supply Center
       SF *Electronics and Electrical
            Engineering
           *Military Sciences
DETA   Diethylenetriamine
       SF *Non-metallic Materials
           Polymers
DEU   Data Entry Unit
       SF *Computer Sciences
           Data Processing
DEUCE Digital Electronic Universal
          Calculating Engine
       SF *Computer Sciences
           *Electronics and Electrical
            Engineering
DEW   Distant Early Warning
       SF *Military Sciences
DEWIZ Distant Early Warning Identification
          Zone
       SF *Military Sciences
DEX   Deferred Execution
       SF *Computer Sciences
           Data Processing
DEXAN Digital Experimental Airborne
          Navigator
       SF *Aeronautics
           Navigation
DF   Direction Finding
       SF *Aeronautics
           Instrument Flying
DF   Disk File
       SF *Computer Sciences
           Data Processing
DF   Distribution Feeders
       SF *Engineering
           Radio Engineering
           *Telecommunications
DFB   Distribution Feeders Branch
       SF *Engineering
           Radio Engineering

           *Telecommunications
DFC   Disk File Check
       SF *Computer Sciences
           Data Processing
DFCU   Disk File Control Unit
       SF *Computer Sciences
           Data Processing
DFDR   Digital Flight Data Recorder
       SF *Aeronautics
           Airborne Recording Systems
DFI   Disk File Interrogate
       SF *Computer Sciences
           Data Processing
DFR   Disk File Read
       SF *Computer Sciences
           Data Processing
DFR   Dounreay Fast Reactor
       SF *Nuclear Sciences
DFRA   Drop Forging Research Association (UK)
       SF *Information Retrieval Systems
DFSU   Disk File Storage Unit
       SF *Computer Sciences
           Data Processing
DFT   Diagnostic Function Test
       SF *Computer Sciences
           Data Processing
DFW   Disk File Write
       SF *Computer Sciences
           Data Processing
DG   Diacylglycerols
       SF   Biochemistry
            *Biological and Medical Sciences
DG   Directional Gyroscope
       SF *Aeronautics
           Navigation
DGBC   Digital Geoballistic Computer System
       SF *Computer Sciences
           *Space Sciences
DH   Decision Height
       SF *Aeronautics
           Instrument Flying
DHA   Dehydrated Humulinic Acid
       SF *Brewery
DHE   Dump Heat Exchangers
       SF *Nuclear Sciences
           Reactors
DHI   Dairy Herd Improvement
       SF *Dairy Sciences
DHIA   Dairy Herd Improvement Association
          (US)
       SF *Agricultural Sciences
           *Dairy Sciences
DHS   Data Handling System
       SF *Electronics and Electrical
            Engineering
DHS   Dual Hardness Steel
       SF *Metallic Materials
           *Metallurgy and Metallography
DHUD   Department of Housing and Urban
          Development (US)

SF *General

DHX Dump Heat Exchangers
  SF *Nuclear Sciences
      Reactors

dia Diameter
  SF *Mathematics

DIAL Defense Industry Advisory Council
  SF *Military Sciences

DIAM Data Independent Architecture Model
  SF *Computer Sciences
      Data Processing

DIAN Decca Integrated Airborne Navigation
  SF *Aeronautics
      *Electronics and Electrical
          Engineering
      Navigation

DIANE Digital Integrated Attack Navigation
      System
  SF *Aeronautics
      *Military Sciences
      Navigation

DICBM Defense Intercontinental Ballistic
      Missile
  SF *Military Sciences
      *Space Sciences

DICON Digital Communication Through Orbiting
      Needles
  SF *Communication Systems
      *Space Sciences

DICORAP Directional Controlled Rocket
      Assisted Projectile
  SF *Space Sciences

DID Distant Dependent
  SF *Computer Sciences
      Data Processing

DIDS Digital Information Display System
  SF *Computer Sciences
      Data Processing
      *Information Retrieval Systems

DIFKIN Diffusion Kinetics
  SF Civil Engineering
      *Engineering

DIG Digital Input Gate
  SF *Computer Sciences
      Data Processing

DILS Doppler Inertial Loran System
  SF *Aeronautics
      Navigation

DIM Device Interface Module
  SF *Computer Sciences
      Data Processing

DIO Direct Input Output
  SF *Computer Sciences
      Data Processing

DIOS Distribution Information and
      Optimizing System
  SF *Computer Sciences
      *Transportation

DIP Dual Inline Package
  SF *Computer Sciences

Data Processing

DIPD Double Inverse Pinch Device
  SF *Physics

DIPEC Defense Industrial Plant Equipment
      Center
  SF Military Sciences

DIR Development Inhibitator Releasing
  SF *Photography

DISC Differential Isochronous
      Self-collimating
  SF *Nuclear Sciences
      Particle Identification

DISCOS Disturbance Compensation Systems
  SF *Communication Systems
      *Space Sciences

DISS Digital Interface Switching System
  SF *Computer Sciences
      Data Processing

DISTRO Distribution Rotation
  SF *Computer Sciences

DKI Data Key Idle
  SF *Computer Sciences
      Data Processing

DL Delay Line
  SF Fission Chamber
      *Nuclear Sciences

DL Difference Limen
  SF *Engineering
      Instruments
      Photogrametic Engineering

DL Dynamic Loader
  SF *Computer Sciences
      Data Processing

DLA Distributed Lumped Active
  SF *Electronic and Electrical
          Engineering
      Solid-state Circuits

DLC Direct Lift Control
  SF *Aeronautics

DLCS Data Line Concentrator System
  SF *Computer Sciences
      Data Processing

DLE Data Link Escape
  SF *Computer Sciences
      Data Processing

dLO Longitudinal Difference
  SF *Aeronautics
      Navigation

DLSC Defense Logistics Service Center
  SF *Military Sciences

DLT Data Loop Transceiver
  SF *Computer Sciences
      Data Processing

DLT Dorsolateral Tract
  SF *Biological and Medical Sciences

DLU Data Line Unit
  SF *Computer Sciences
      Data Processing

DLVL Diverted (into) Low Velocity Layer
  SF *Biological and Medical Sciences

dm   Decimetre
         SF   *Mathematics
DM   Demand Meter
         SF   *Electronics and Electrical
                Engineering
                Meters
DM   Differential Mode
         SF   *Electronics and Electrical
                Engineering
                Solid-state Circuits
DM   Digital Monolithic
         SF   *Electronics and Electrical
                Engineering
DM   Dry Matter
         SF   *Dairy Sciences
DMA   Dimethyl Acetamide
         SF   *Non-metallic Materials
                Polymers
DMA   Direct Memory Access
         SF   *Computer Sciences
                Data Processing
DMA   Dry Matter Accumulation
         SF   *Agricultural Sciences
DMBA   Dimethylbenzanthracene
         SF   *Biological and Medical Sciences
DMC   Dichloromethyl Carbinol
         SF   *Agricultural Sciences
DMC   Direct Multiplexed Control
         SF   *Computer Sciences
DMD   Dimethyl Oxozolidinedione
         SF   Biochemistry
                *Biological and Medical Sciences
DMD   Dry Matter Disappearance
         SF   *Agricultural Sciences
                *Dairy Sciences
DME   Dimethyl Ethanolamine
         SF   *Non-metallic Materials
                Polymers
DME   Distance Measuring Equipment
         SF   *Aeronautics
                Air Traffic Control
                Instrument Flying
                Navigation
DMET   Distance Measuring Equipment TACAN
         SF   *Aeronautics
                Air Traffic Control
                Military Sciences
                Navigation
DMF   Digital Matched Filter
         SF   *Engineering
                Radio Engineering
                *Telecommunications
DMF   Dimethylformanide
         SF   Biochemistry
                *Biological and Medical Sciences
                *Photography
DMI   Desmethylimipramine
         SF   Biochemistry
                *Biological and Medical Sciences
DML   Data Manipulation Language

         SF   *Computer Sciences
                Data Processing
DMLS   Doppler Microwave Landing Guidance
           System
         SF   *Aeronautics
                Air Traffic Control
                Navigation
DMM   Data Manipulation Mode
         SF   *Computer Sciences
                Data Processing
DMM   Dimethylmercury
         SF   *Chemistry
                Physical Chemistry
DMN   Di-Methyl Nitrosamine
         SF   *Biological and Medical Sciences
DMO   Defense Mobilization Order (US)
         SF   *Military Sciences
                *Transportation
DM/PRT   Dual-Mode Personal Rapid Transit
         SF   *Transportation
DMS   Database Management System
         SF   *Computer Sciences
                Data Processing
                *Management
DMS   Defense Management Simulation (US)
         SF   Logistics
                *Military Sciences
DMS   Differential Maneuvering Simulator
         SF   *Aeronautics
                Simulators
DMS   Display Management System
         SF   *Computer Sciences
                Data Processing
DMSCC   Direct Microscopic Somatic Cell
           Count
         SF   *Agricultural Sciences
                *Dairy Sciences
DMSO   Dimethyl Sulphoxide
         SF   *Agricultural Sciences
                *Biological and Medical Sciences
                *Photography
DMT   Dimethyl Terephthatate
         SF   *Non-metallic Materials
                Polymers
DMV   Department of Motor Vehicles (US)
         SF   *Engineering
                Safety Engineering
                *Transportation
DNA   Deoxyribonucleic Acid
         SF   *Agricultural Sciences
                *Biological and Medical Sciences
DNA   Dinolylaniline
         SF   *Nuclear Sciences
                Radiation
DNC   Direct Numerical Control
         SF   *Computer Sciences
                Data Processing
DNE   Dinitroethane
         SF   *Chemistry

Physical Chemistry
DNL   Differential Non Linearity
      SF   Measurement
            *Nuclear Sciences
DNMRT Duncan's New Multiple Range Test
      SF   *Agricultural Sciences
            *Dairy Sciences
DNP   Deoxyribonucleoproteins
      SF   *Agricultural Sciences
            *Biological and Medical Sciences
            Cytochemistry
DNP   Dinitrophenol
      SF   Biochemistry
            *Biological and Medical Sciences
DNPH Dinitrophenylthydrazin
      SF   *Agricultural Sciences
            Cereals
DNT   Desmethylnortriptyline
      SF   Biochemistry
            *Biological and Medical Sciences
DO   Dissolved Oxygen
      SF   Bioengineering
            *Biological and Medical Sciences
DOA   Department of Agriculture
      SF   *Agricultural Sciences
DOA   Differential Operational Amplifiers
      SF   *Engineering
            Radio Engineering
            *Telecommunications
DOA   Dominant Obstacle Allowance
      SF   *Aeronautics
            Approach and Landing
DOC   Department of Commerce (US)
      SF   *Transportation
DOC   Direct Operating Cost
      SF   *General
            *Management
DOCA Deoxycorticosterone Acetate
      SF   Biochemistry
            *Biological and Medical Sciences
DOCSYS Display of Chromosome Statistics
            (System)
      SF   *Computer Sciences
            Data Processing
DOI   Department of Interior (US)
      SF   *General
DOL   Department of Labor (US)
      SF   *General
DOMD Digestible Organic Matter in Dry
      SF   *Agricultural Sciences
DOPA Dihydroxyphenylalanine
      SF   *Biological and Medical Sciences
            Cytochemistry
DOR   Digital Output Relay
      SF   *Computer Sciences
            Data Processing
DORA Directorate of Operational Analysis
      SF   *Aeronautics
DORF Diamond Ordinance Radiation Facility
      SF   *Biological and Medical Sciences
            Non-crystalline Solids
DORIS Direct Order Recording and Invoicing

System
      SF   *General
DOS   Decision Outstanding
      SF   *Computer Sciences
            Data Processing
            *General
DOS   Disc Operating System
      SF   *Computer Sciences
            Data Processing
DOT   Deep Ocean Transponder
      SF   *Naval Sciences
            Navigation
DOT   Department of Transportation
      SF   *Aeronautics
            *Transportation
DOT   Dictionary of Occupational Titles
      SF   *Training
DOT   Discrete Ordinate Transport
      SF   *Nuclear Sciences
            Radiation
DOTCOOP Department of Transportation
            Continuity of Operations Plan
      SF   *Transportation
DP   Data Processing
      SF   *Computer Sciences
            Data Processing
DP   Degree of Polymerization
      SF   *Photography
DP   Differential Pressure
      SF   *Nuclear Sciences
            Thermal Generating Units
DP   Dispersed Phase
      SF   Bioengineering
            *Biological and Medical Sciences
DP   Display Package
      SF   *Aeronautics
            *General
DPC   Data Processing Control
      SF   *Computer Sciences
            Data Processing
DPC   Defense Planning Committee
      SF   *Military Sciences
            *Transportation
DPC   Display Processor Code
      SF   *Computer Sciences
            Data Processing
DCPM Differential Pulse Code Modulation
      SF   *Biological and Medical Sciences
            *Electronics and Electrical
            Engineering
DPCT Differential Protection Current
         Transformer
      SF   *Aeronautics
            Aircraft
DPDT Double Pole Double Throw
      SF   *Communication Systems
            *Computer Sciences
            *Electronics and Electrical
            Engineering
DPG   Diphosphoglycerate
      SF   *Biological and Medical Sciences
DPH   Diphenylhydantoin

DPH   Diamond Pyramid Hardness
      SF   *Nuclear Sciences
           Reactors
DPH   Diphenylhydantoin
      SF   *Biological and Medical Sciences
DPM   Digital Panel Meters
      SF   *Electronics and Electrical
             Engineering
           Instruments
DPMA Data Processing Management Association
      SF   *Computer Sciences
DPNH Diphosphopyridine Nucleotide
      SF   *Biological and Medical Sciences
           Cytochemistry
DPolT Differential Polarization Telegraphy
      SF   *Engineering
           Radio Engineering
           *Telecommunications
DPS   Data Processing Subsystem
      SF   *Aeronautics
           *Communication Systems
           *Computer Sciences
           Data Processing
DPS   Defense Printing Service (US)
      SF   *Military Sciences
           *Printing
DPSA Data Processing Supplies Association
      SF   *Computer Sciences
           Data Processing
DPSA Deep Penetration Strike Aircraft
      SF   *Aeronautics
           *Miltary Sciences
           Military Aircraft
DPSK Differential Phase Shift Keying
      SF   *Engineering
           Radio Engineering
           *Telecommunications
DPST Double Pole Single Throw
      SF   *Computer Sciences
           *Electronics and Electrical
             Engineering
DPT   Diamond Pyramid Hardnesses
      SF   *Nuclear Sciences
           Reactors
DPTH Diphenylthiohydantoin
      SF   *Biological and Medical Sciences
DPWM Double-Sided Pulse Width Modulation
      SF   *Engineering
           Radio Engineering
           *Telecommunications
DQE   Detective Quantum Efficiency
      SF   *Photography
DR   Dead Reckoning
      SF   *Naval Sciences
           Navigation
DR   Deduced Reckoning
      SF   *Naval Sciences
           Navigation
DR   Defined Readout
      SF   *Engineering
           Radio Engineering
           Telecommunications

DRAI Dead Reckoning Analyzer Indicator
      SF   *Naval Sciences
           Navigation
DRC   Damage Risk Contours
      SF   *Aeronautics
           Noise
DRDTO Detection Radar Data Take-Off
      SF   *Aeronautics
           Navigation
DRE   Data Recording Equipment
      SF   *Computer Sciences
           Data Processing
DRI   Descent Rate Indicator
      SF   *Aeronautics
           Instruments
           *Space Sciences
DRIC Defence Research Information Centre
      SF   *Information Retrieval Systems
DRID Direct Readout Image Dissector
      SF   *Telecommunications
DRIDAC Drum Input to Digital Automatic
           Computer
      SF   *Computer Sciences
           Data Processing
DRIFT Diversity Receiving Instrumentation
           for Telemetry
      SF   *Aeronautics
           *Communication Systems
           *Space Sciences
DRIR Direct Readout Infrared
      SF   *Aeronautics
           *Communication Systems
DRL   Defense Research Laboratories (US)
      SF   *Military Sciences
DRM   Direction of Relative Movement
      SF   *Naval Sciences
           Navigation
DRP   Dense Random Packed
      SF   Liquid Semiconductors
           *Non-crystalline Solids
DRS   Detection Ranging Set
      SF   *Aeronautics
           Military Aircraft
           *Military Sciences
DRT   Dead Reckoning Tracer
      SF   *Naval Sciences
           Navigation
DRTE Defence Research Telecommunications
           Establishment
      SF   *Telecommunications
DRW   Defensive Radio Warfare
      SF   *Communication Systems
           *Military Sciences
DS   Data Set
      SF   *Computer Sciences
           Data Processing
DS   Descent Stage
      SF   *Space Sciences
           Spacecraft
DS   Digit Select
      SF   *Computer Sciences
           Data Processing

DS   Digital Signal
        SF   *Engineering
               Radio Engineering
             *Telecommunications
DS   Double Stranded
        SF   *Biological and Medical Sciences
DSA   Defence Shipping Agency
        SF   *Military Sciences
             *Transportation
DSA   Defence Supply Agency (US)
        SF   *Military Sciences
DSA   Dynamic Spring Analysis
        SF   *Geosciences
DSAP   Defence Systems Application Program
        SF   *Communication Systems
             *Space Sciences
DSARC   Defense Systems Acquisition Review
          Council (US)
        SF   Logistics
             *Military Sciences
DSB   Demand Scheduled Bus
        SF   *Transportation
DSB   Double Side Band
        SF   *Aeronautics
             *Communication Systems
DSC   Defense Shipping Council
        SF   *Military Sciences
             *Transportation
DSC   Differential Scanning Calorimetry
        SF   *Biological and Medical Sciences
             Liquid Semiconductors
             Non-crystalline Solids
DSCB   Data Set Control Block
        SF   *Computer Sciences
             Data Processing
DSCS   Defense Satellite Communications
          System
        SF   *Aeronautics
             *Communication Systems
             *Military Sciences
             *Space Sciences
DSDP   Deep Sea Drilling Projects
        SF   *Oceanography
DSE   Data Set Extension
        SF   *Computer Sciences
             Data Processing
DSEB   Defense Shipping Executive Board (US)
        SF   *Military Sciences
             *Transportation
DSF   Defatted Soy Flour
        SF   *Agricultural Sciences
             *Dairy Sciences
DSFT   Detection Scheme with Fixed
          Thresholds
        SF   *Communication Systems
             Navigation
DSI   Dairy Society International
        SF   *Agricultural Sciences
             *Dairy Sciences
DSIR   Department of Science and Industrial

        Research (UK)
        SF   *General
DSL   Data Set Label
        SF   *Computer Sciences
             Data Processing
DSLT   Detection Scheme with Learning of
          Thresholds
        SF   *Communication Systems
             Navigation
DSN   Deep Space Network
        SF   *Space Sciences
DSP   Dextran Sulphate Precipitable
        SF   *Dairy Sciences
DSR   Danish State Railways
        SF   *Transportation
DSRV   Deep Submergence Rescue Vehicle
        SF   *Naval Sciences
             Navigation
DSS   Digital Sub-system
        SF   *Computer Sciences
DSS   Discrete Syne System
        SF   *Engineering
             Radio Engineering
             *Telecommunications
DSSM   Dynamic Sequencing and Segregation
          Model
        SF   *Computer Sciences
             Data Processing
DSSP   Deep Submergence Systems Project
        SF   *Military Sciences
DSSV   Deep Submergence Search Vehicle
        SF   *Naval Sciences
             Navigation
DST   Data Summary Tape
        SF   Data Recording
             *Electronics and Electrical
               Engineering
DST   Data Systems Test
        SF   *Aeronautics
             *Space Sciences
             Testing
DSU   Data Selector Units
        SF   *Computer Sciences
             Data Processing
DSU   Data Storage Unit
        SF   *Aeronautics
             Airborne Recording Systems
DSV   Deep Submergence Vehicle
        SF   *Military Sciences
             *Naval Sciences
             Navigation
DT   Data Transmission
        SF   *Engineering
             Radio Engineering
             *Telecommunications
DT   Deuterium and Tritium
        SF   *Electronics and Electrical
               Engineering
             Lasers and Masers
DT   Doubling Time

	SF *Nuclear Sciences
	Reactors
DT	Drop Top
	SF *Metallurgy and Metallography
	Metalworks
DT	Dummy Target
	SF Nuclear Physics
	*Nuclear Sciences
DT	Dust Turn
	SF *Metallurgy and Metallography
	Metalworks
DT	Dynamic Tear
	SF *Metallurgy and Metallography
DTA	Dental Therapy Assistant
	SF *Training
DTA	Differential Thermal Analysis
	SF *Biological and Medical Sciences
	*Dairy Sciences
	*Nuclear Sciences
DTAS	Data Transmission and Switching System
	SF *Communication Systems
	*Electronics and Electrical
	Engineering
DTCP	Diode Transistor Compound Pair
	SF *Electronics and Electrical
	Engineering
	Solid-state Circuits
DTCU	Data Transmission Control Unit
	SF *Computer Sciences
	Data Processing
DTD	Data Transfer Done
	SF *Computer Sciences
	Data Processing
DTD	Dimethyl Tin Difluoride
	SF *Nuclear Sciences
	Spectroscopy
DTE	Development Test and Evaluation
	SF *Aeronautics
DTF	Definite Tape File
	SF *Computer Sciences
	Data Processing
DTL	Diode Transistor Logic
	SF *Communication Systems
	*Computer Sciences
	*Electronics and Electrical
	Engineering
dTMP	Thymidine Monophosphate
	SF Biochemistry
	*Biological and Medical Sciences
DTR	Demand Totalizing Relay
	SF *Electronics and Electrical
	Engineering
	Meters
DTR	Diffusion Transfer
	SF *Photography
DTR	Disposable Tape Reel
	SF *Computer Sciences
	Data Processing
DTR	Distribution Tape Reel
	SF *Computer Sciences

	Data Processing
DTS	Double Thermostat and Safety
	SF *Nuclear Sciences
	Reactors
DTSS	Dartmouth Time Sharing System
	SF *Computer Sciences
	Data Processing
	*Management
DTT	Dithiotheitol
	SF Biochemistry
	*Biological and Medical Sciences
	*Dairy Sciences
dTTP	Thymidine Triphosphate
	SF Biochemistry
	*Biological and Medical Sciences
DTTU	Data Transmission Terminal Unit
	SF *Computer Sciences
	Data Processing
DTU	Data Transfer Unit
	SF *Computer Sciences
	Data Processing
DTU	Data Transmission Unit
	SF *Computer Sciences
	Data Processing
DU	Delay Unit
	SF *Nuclear Sciences
DU	Display Unit
	SF *Aeronautics
	Navigation
DUP	Disk Utility Programme
	SF *Computer Sciences
	*Nuclear Sciences
DUT	Devices Under Test
	SF *Computer Sciences
	Data Processing
DVARS	Doppler Velocity Altimeter Radar Set
	SF *Aeronautics
	Navigation
DVM	Digital Voltmeters
	SF *Electronics and Electrical
	Engineering
DWB	Development Workbook
	SF *Computer Sciences
	Data Processing
DWBA	Distorted Wave Born Approximation
	SF *Nuclear Sciences
DWCM	Dried Weight of Cell Mass
	SF *Dairy Sciences
DWD	District Works Department
	SF *Building
DWL	Downwind Localizer
	SF *Astronautics
	Approach and Landing
DWT	Deadweight Tonnage
	SF *Transportation
DX	Distance
	SF *Computer Sciences
	Data Processing
DX	Duplex
	SF *Computer Sciences

```
            Data Processing
DY     Dairy Yield
       SF  *Agricultural Sciences
DZA    Doppler Zeeman Analyzer
       SF   *Lunar Sciences
            *Space Sciences
```

E

E   Emitter
    SF *Electronics and Electrical
        Engineering
        Semiconductor Devices

EA   Effective Address
    SF *Computer Sciences
        Data Processing

EA   Enemy Aircraft
    SF *Aeronautics
        *Military Sciences
        Military Aircraft

EA   Exhaust Air
    SF *Metallurgy and Metallography
        Metalworks

EAAFRO East African Agriculture and Forest
      Research Organization
    SF *Agricultural Sciences

EAC Error Alert Control
    SF *Computer Sciences
        Data Processing
        *Nuclear Sciences
        Reactors

EAC Except Approach Clearance
    SF *Aeronautics
        Instrument Flying

EACS Electronic Automatic Chart System
    SF *Aeronautics
        Data Processing

EADI Electronic Altitude Director Indicator
    SF *Aeronautics
        *Electronics and Electrical
        Engineering
        Navigation

EAGLE Elevation Angle Guidance Landing
      Equipment
    SF *Aeronautics
        Approach and Landing

EAIR Extended Area Instrumentation Radar
    SF *Aeronautics

EAL Electronics Associates Limited
    SF *Computer Sciences
        *Electronics and Electrical
        Engineering

EAM Electronic Accounting Machine
    SF *Computer Sciences

        *Electronics and Electrical
        Engineering

EANS Empire Air Navigation School
    SF *Aeronautics
        Navigation
        *Training

EAR Employee Appraisal Record
    SF *Aeronautics
        Aviation Medicine

EARB European Airline Research Bureau
    SF *Aeronautics
        *Transportation

EAROM Electrically Alterable Read Only
      Memories
    SF *Computer Sciences
        Data Processing

EAS Equivalent Air Speed
    SF *Aeronautics
        Approach and Landing

EASAMS E-A Space and Advanced Military
      Systems
    SF *Aeronautics
        Military Sciences

EASCON Electronics and Aerospace Systems
      Conference
    SF *Aeronautics
        *Electronics and Electrical
        Engineering

EASY Efficient Assembly System
    SF *Computer Sciences
        Data Processing

EAT Ehrlich Ascites Tumour
    SF *Biological and Medical Sciences

EAT Expected Approach Time
    SF *Aeronautics

EATC Ehrlich Ascites Tumour Cells
    SF *Biological and Medical Sciences
        Cytochemistry

EATS Empire Air Training Scheme
    SF *Aeronautics
        Navigation

EAX Electronic Automatic Exchange
    SF *Computer Sciences
        *Electronics and Electrical
        Engineering

EB   Electron Beam
        SF   *Metallurgy and Metallography
             Welding
EB   Equal Brake
        SF   *Metallurgy and Metallography
             Metalworks
EBAM   Electron Beam Addresses Memory
        SF   *Computer Sciences
EBC   European Brewery Convention
        SF   *Brewery
EBCDIC Extended Binary Coded Decimal
             Information Code
        SF   *Computer Sciences
             Data Processing
EBCDIC Extended Binary Coded Decimal
             Interchange Code
        SF   *Computer Sciences
             Data Processing
EBF   Externally Blown Flap
        SF   *Aeronautics
             Aircraft Noise
EBM   Electronic Bearing Marker
        SF   *Aeronautics
             Navigation
EBOR   Experimental Beryllium Oxide Reactors
        SF   *Nuclear Sciences
             Reactors
EBR   Experimental Breeder Reactor
        SF   *Nuclear Sciences
             Reactors
EBU   European Broadcasting Union
        SF   *Communication Systems
             Copyright
             *Telecommunications
EBV   Epstein-Barr Virus
        SF   *Biological and Medical Sciences
EBW   Empty Body Weight
        SF   *Agricultural Sciences
EC   Electrical Conductivities
        SF   *Agricultural Sciences
             *Electronics and Electrical
                 Engineering
EC   Enterochromaffin Cells
        SF   *Biological and Medical Sciences
             Cytochemistry
EC   Error Counter
        SF   Radio Engineering
             *Telecommunications
EC   Esterified Cholesterol
        SF   Biochemistry
             *Biological and Medical Sciences
             Pharmacology
EC   Ethyl Centralite
        SF   *Fuels
             Propellants and Fuels
ECAC   Electromagnetic Compatibility
             Analysis Center
        SF   *Aeronautics
             *Electronics and Electrical
                 Engineering

ECAC   European Civil Aviation Conference
        SF   *Aeronautics
             *Transportation
ECAP   Electronic Circuit Analysis Program
        SF   *Computer Sciences
             *Electronics and Electrical
                 Engineering
             Solid-state Circuits
ECAR   East Central Area Reliability
        SF   *Electronics and Electrical
                 Engineering
             Power Systems
ECB   Event Control Block
        SF   *Computer Sciences
             Data Processing
ECCM   Electronic Counter-Counter Measure
        SF   *Aeronautics
             *Electronics and Electrical
                 Engineering
             *Military Sciences
ECCS   Emergency Core Cooling System
        SF   *Nuclear Sciences
             Reactors
ECD   Energy Conversion Devices
        SF   *Non-crystalline Solids
ECE   Economic Commission for Europe
        SF   Industrial Property
             *Patents
ECF   Emmission Contribution Fraction
        SF   *Aeronautics
             Aircraft
ECF   Extracellular Fluid
        SF   Biochemistry
             *Biological and Medical Sciences
ECG   Electrocardiogram
        SF   *Space Sciences
             Space Simulation
ECG   Electrocardiograph
        SF   *Aeronautics
             Aviation Medicine
             *Biological and Medical Sciences
ECL   Emitter Coupled Logic
        SF   *Computer Sciences
             *Electronics and Electrical
                 Engineering
ECM   Electro-Chemical Machining
        SF   Non-destructive Evaluation
             *Nuclear Sciences
ECM   Electronic Countermeasures
        SF   *Aeronautics
             *Electronics and Electrical
                 Engineering
             *Military Sciences
             Navigation
ECM   Extended Core Memory
        SF   *Computer Sciences
             Data Processing
ECMA   European Computer Manufacturers'
             Association
        SF   *Computer Sciences

ECNG   East Central Nuclear Group (US)
       SF   *Nuclear Sciences
            Reactors
ECO   Ektachrome Commercial
       SF   *Photography
ECO   Electron Coupled Oscillator
       SF   *Communication Systems
            *Engineering
            Radio Engineering
ECR   External Control Registers
       SF   *Nuclear Sciences
ECS   Environmental Control System
       SF   *Aeronautics
            Air Pollution
ECS   Environmental Control Subsystem
       SF   *Space Sciences
            Space Simulation
ECS   European Communication Satellite
       SF   *Communication Systems
ECT   Electro-Convulsive (Shock) Therapy
       SF   *Biological and Medical Sciences
ECT   Environment Control Table
       SF   *Computer Sciences
            Data Processing
ECT   Evans Clean Tunnel
       SF   *Aeronautics
ED   External Deflector
       SF   *Aeronautics
            Thrust Vectoring Concepts
EDA   Electronic Differential Analyser
       SF   *Computer Sciences
            *Electronics and Electrical
            Engineering
EDAC   Error Detection and Correction
       SF   *Computer Sciences
            *Electronics and Electrical
            Engineering
EDB   Ethylene Dibromide
       SF   *Agricultural Sciences
            Fumigation
            *Milling
EDC   Energy Distribution Curves
       SF   *Biological and Medical Sciences
            Non-crystalline Solids
EDC   Ethylene Dichlorine
       SF   *Agricultural Sciences
            *Milling
EDCL   Electrical Discharge Convection Lasers
       SF   *Electronics and Electrical
            Engineering
            Instruments
EDD   Electronic Data Display
       SF   *Aeronautics
            Airports
EDGE   Electronic Data Gathering Equipment
       SF   *Computer Sciences
            *Electronics and Electrical
            Engineering
EDITAR Electronic Digital Tracking and
       Ranging

       SF   *Electronics and Electrical
            Engineering
            *Space Sciences
EDM   Electrical Discharge Machining
       SF   Non-destructive Evaluation
            *Nuclear Sciences
EDP   Electronic Data Processing
       SF   *Computer Sciences
            *Electronics and Electrical
            Engineering
EDP   Experimental Development
       SF   *General
EDPS   Electronic Data Processing System
       SF   *Computer Sciences
            Data Processing
EDRL   Effective Damage Risk Level
       SF   *Aeronautics
            Noise
EDS   Environmental Data Service
       SF   *Geosciences
EDS   Estimated Daughter Superiority
       SF   *Dairy Sciences
EDTA   Ethylenediamine Tetra Acetate
       SF   *Biological and Medical Sciences
            Cytochemistry
EDTA   Ethylenediaminetetraacete
       SF   *Agricultural Sciences
            *Dairy Sciences
EDTA   Ethylenediane Tatra Acetic
       SF   *Brewery
EDTA   Ethylenediaminetetraacetic Acid
       SF   *Agricultural Sciences
            Dairy Sciences
            *Nuclear Sciences
            *Printing
EEC   Eurocontrol Experimental Centre
       SF   *Aeronautics
            Air Traffic Control
EEC   European Economic Community
       SF   *General
EEG   Electroncephalographic
       SF   *Aeronautics
            Aviation Medicine
            *Biological and Medical Sciences
            *Electronics and Electrical
            Engineering
EEM   Earth Entry Module
       SF   Satellites
            *Space Sciences
EEMTIC Electrical and Electronic Measurement
       and Test Instruments Conference
       SF   *Electronics and Electrical
            Engineering
EEPNL Estimated Effective Perceived Noise
       Level
       SF   *Aeronautics
            Environmental Sciences
            Noise
EERL   Earthquake Engineering Research
       Laboratory (US)

        SF   *Oceanography
EFAS   Electronic Flash Approach System
        SF   *Electronics and Electrical
               Engineering
             *Space Sciences
EFATCA European Federation of Air Traffic
          Controllers' Association
        SF   *Aeronautics
             Air Traffic Control
EFC   Expect Further Clearance
        SF   *Aeronautics
             Instruments Flying
EFFE   European Federation of Flight
          Engineers
        SF   *Aeronautics
EFL   Emitter Follower Logic
        SF   *Electronics and Electrical
               Engineering
             Solid-state Circuits
EFPD   Equivalent Full Power Days
        SF   *Nuclear Sciences
             Reactors
EFR   Emerging Flux Regions
        SF   *Astronautics and Astrophysics
             Solar Physics
EG   Electron Gun
        SF   *Electronics and Electrical
               Engineering
EG   Ethylene Glycol
        SF   *Non-metallic Materials
             Polymers
EGD   Electrogas Dynamics
        SF   *Engineering
EGIF   Equipment Group Interface
        SF   *Computer Sciences
             Data Processing
EGT   Exhaust Gas Temperature
        SF   *Aeronautics
             Aircraft Noise
EHD   Electrohydrodynamic
        SF   *Engineering
             Mechanical Engineering
EHF   Extremely High Frequency
        SF   *Communication Systems
             *Space Sciences
EHP   Effective Horsepower
        SF   *Mathematics
EHTR   Emergency Highway Transport Regulation
        SF   *Transportation
EHV   Extra High Voltage
        SF   *Computer Sciences
             *Electronics and Electrical
               Engineering
EIA   Electronic Industries Association
        SF   *Electronics and Electrical
               Engineering
EIA   Endotoxin Inactivating Agent
        SF   *Agricultural Sciences
EIDLT   Emergency Identification Light
        SF   *Aeronautics

EIRMA   European Industrial Research
          Management Association
        SF   Industrial Property
             *Patents
EIRP   Equivalent Isotropical Radiated
          Power
        SF   *Aeronautics
             *Communication Systems
EIT   Engineer In Training
             Civil Engineering
             *Engineering
             *Training
EJC   Engineers Joint Council
        SF   *Engineering
EKG   Electrocardiography
        SF   *Biological and Medical Sciences
             *Computer Sciences
             Data Processing
EKS   Energetic Komprimierendes System
        SF   *Nuclear Sciences
EL   Electroluminescent
        SF   *Naval Sciences
             Navigation
EL   Elevation
        SF   *Metallurgy and Metallography
             Metalworks
EL   External Lamina
        SF   *Biological and Medical Sciences
             Cytochemistry
ELD   Edge Lit Display
        SF   *Computer Sciences
             Data Processing
ELD   Embryos Lethal Dose
        SF   *Biological and Medical Sciences
ELDO   European Launcher Development
          Organization
        SF   *Aeronautics
             *Space Sciences
ELE   Equivalent Logic Element
        SF   *Engineering
             Radio Engineering
             *Telecommunications
ELF   Electroluminescent Ferroelectric
        SF   *Photography
             Photoelectric Devices
ELF   Extremely Low Frequency
        SF   *Biological and Medical Sciences
             Radiobiology
ELINT   Electronic Intelligent

ELMS   Elastic Loop Mobility System
        SF   *Engineering
             Mechanical Engineering
ELS   External Lamina Substance
        SF   *Biological and Medical Sciences
             Cytochemistry
ELSIE   Electronic Letter Sorting and
          Indicating Equipment
        SF   *Computer Sciences
             *Electronics and Electrical
               Engineering

ELSS   Extravehicular Life Support System
       SF   *Space Sciences
            Space Simulation
ELT   Emergency Location Transmitters
       SF   *Aeronautics
            Air Traffic Control
ELTAD Emergency Locator Transmitters
          Automatic Deployable
       SF   *Aeronautics
            *Electronics and Electrical
             Engineering
ELTAF Energy Locator Transmitters Automatic
          Fixed
       SF   *Aeronautics
            *Communication Systems
ELTAP Emergency Locator Transmitters
          Automatic Portable
       SF   *Aeronautics
            *Electronics and Electrical
             Engineering
ELTR   Emergency Locator Transmitter
          Receiver
       SF   *Aeronautics
            Air Traffic Control
            *Communication Systems
EM   Electron Microscopy
       SF   *Non-metallic Materials
            Polymers
EM   End of Medium
       SF   *Computer Sciences
            Data Processing
EM   Ethoxylated Monoglycerides
       SF   *Agricultural Sciences
            *Cereals
EMA   Emergency Minerals Administration (US)
       SF   *General
EMB   Eosine Methylene Blue
       SF   *Agricultural Sciences
            *Dairy Sciences
EMBERS Emergency Bed Request System
       SF   *Computer Sciences
            *Management
EMBO   European Molecular Biological
          Organization
       SF   *Biological and Medical Sciences
            Physiology
EMC   Electromagnetic Compatibility
       SF   *Aeronautics
            *Electronics and Electrical
             Engineering
            *Space Sciences
EMC   Excess Minority Carriers
       SF   *Electronics and Electrical
             Engineers
            Solid-state Circuits
EMCCC European Military Communication
          Coordinating Committee
       SF   *Military Sciences
EMCRO Experimental Medical Care Review
          Organization

       SF   *Biological and Medical Sciences
            Clinical Medicine
EMD   Electronic Map Display
       SF   *Aeronautics
            Navigation
emf   Electromotive Force
       SF   *Aeronautics
            *Communication Systems
            *Mathematics
EMF   Evolving Magnetic Features
       SF   *Astronautics and Astrophysics
            *Physics
            Solar Physics
EMG   Electromyographic
       SF   *Aeronautics
            Air Traffic Control
EMI   Ernst-Mach Institut (FR Germ.)
       SF   *Aeronautics
            Hypersonic Facilities
EMLC   Experimental Manpower Laboratory for
          Correction
       SF   *Management
            *Training
EMM   Ebers Moll Model
       SF   *Electronics and Electrical
             Engineering
            Solid-state Circuits
EMMA   Electron Manual Metal Arch
       SF   *Metallurgy and Metallography
            Welding
EMP   Electromagnetic Pulse
       SF   *Aeronautics
            Avionics
EMPCO Electronic Mechanical Products
          Company
       SF   *Printing
ENQ   Enquiry
       SF   *Computer Sciences
            Data Processing
EMR   Engine Mixture Ratio
       SF   *Fuels
            *Space Sciences
            Space Simulation
EMS   Ethyl Methane Sulphorate
       SF   *Biological and Medical Sciences
            Physiology
emu   Electromagnetic Unit
       SF   *Mathematics
EMU   Expanded Memory Unit
       SF   *Computer Sciences
            Data Processing
EMU   Extravehicular Mobility Unit
       SF   *Space Sciences
            Space Simulation
            *Telecommunications
ENC   Equivalent Noise Charge
       SF   *Aeronautics
END   Equivalent Neutral Density
       SF   *Photography
ENDOR Electron Nuclear Double Resonance

	SF	*Biological and Medical Sciences Medical Ions
ENE	Estimated Net Energy	
	SF	*Dairy Sciences
ENEA	European Nuclear Energy Agency	
	SF	*Nuclear Sciences
ENG	Engineer	
	SF	*Metallurgy and Metallography Metalworks
ENIAC	Electronic Numerical Integrator and Calculator	
	SF	*Computer Sciences *Electronics and Electrical Engineer
EOA	End of Address	
	SF	*Computer Sciences Data Processing
EOAP	Earth Observations Aircraft Program	
	SF	*Aeronautics *Communication Systems *Space Sciences
EOB	End of Block	
	SF	*Computer Sciences Data Processing
EOC	Emergency Operating Center (US)	
	SF	*General *Transportation
EOD	Entry-on-Duty	
	SF	*Aeronautics Aviation Medicine
EOE	Error and Omission Excepted	
	SF	*Computer Sciences Data Processing
EOF	Emergency Operating Facility (US)	
	SF	*Transportation
EOF	End of File	
	SF	*Computer Sciences Data Processing
EOJ	End of Job	
	SF	*Computer Sciences Data Processing
EOL	End of Line	
	SF	*Computer Sciences Data Processing
EOLM	Electro-Optic Light-Modulator	
	SF	Biochemistry *Biological and Medical Sciences
EOM	End of Message	
	SF	*Computer Sciences Data Processing
EOP	Executive Office of the President (US)	
	SF	*General
EOPAP	Earth and Ocean Physics Program	
	SF	*Aeronautics *Space Sciences
EOR	End of Reel	
	SF	*Computer Sciences Data Processing
EORTC	European Organization for Research on the Treatment of Cancer	

	SF	*Biological and Medical Sciences
EOT	End of Tape	
	SF	*Computer Sciences Data Processing
EOT	End of Task	
	SF	*Computer Sciences
EOT	End of Transmission	
	SF	*Computer Sciences Data Processing
EOT	Engine Order Telegraph	
	SF	*Naval Sciences Navigation
EOV	End of Volume	
	SF	*Computer Sciences Data Processing
EOW	Engine Over the Wing	
	SF	*Aeronautics Aircraft
EP	Electrically Polarized	
	SF	*Electronics and Electrical Engineering Switches
EPA	Environmental Protection Agency	
	SF	*Aeronautics Air Pollution Aircraft Noise
EPD	Electronic Proximity Detector	
	SF	*Electronics and Electrical Engineering *Space Sciences
EPDT	Estimated Project Duration Time	
	SF	*Computer Sciences Data Processing Operational Research
EPG	Electrostatic Particle Guide	
	SF	*Nuclear Sciences
EPGA	Emergency Petroleum and Gas Administration	
	SF	*Fuels
EPIC	Earth Pointing Instrument Carrier	
	SF	*Space Sciences
EPIRB	Energy Position Indicating Radio Beacon	
	SF	*Telecommunications
EPM	Economic Performance Monitoring	
	SF	*Nuclear Sciences Reactors
EPMA	Electron Probe Microanalysis	
	SF	*Metallurgy and Metallography Welding
EPN	External Priority Number	
	SF	*Computer Sciences Data Processing
EPNdB	Equivalent Perceived Noise Level, Decibels	
	SF	*Aeronautics Noise
EPNG	El Paso Natural Gas	
	SF	*Nuclear Sciences Reactors

EPNL   Effective Perceived Noise Level
       SF *Aeronautics
           Aircraft Noise
EPOs   Examination Procedure Outlines
       SF *Engineering
           Test Equipment
EPP   End Plate Potential
       SF *Biological and Medical Sciences
EPR   Electron Paramagnetic Resonance
       SF *Biological and Medical Sciences
           Medical Ions
           *Nuclear Sciences
EPR   Engine Pressure Radio
       SF *Aeronautics
           Aircraft
           *Communication Systems
EPR   Engine Pressure Ration
       SF *Aeronautics
           *Engineering
           Equipment
EPS   Electromagnetic Position Sensor
       SF *Aeronautics
           Instruments
EPSPs Excitatory Post Synaptic Potentials
       SF Cybernetics
           *Electronics and Electrical
           Engineering
EPTC   Ethyl Dipropylthiocarbamate
       SF *Agricultural Sciences
EPU   Emergency Power Unit
       SF *Aeronautics
           Aircraft
           *Electronics and Electrical
           Engineering
Eq   Equal
       SF *Computer Sciences
EQ   Equalizer
       SF *Electronics and Electrical
           Engineering
equ   Equation
       SF *Mathematics
EQUATE Electronic Quality Assurance Test
       Equipment
       SF *Electronics and Electrical
           Engineering
           Testing
equiv Equivalent
       SF *Mathematics
ER   Electronic Ram
       SF *Electronics and Electrical
           Engineering
           Instruments
ER   Endoplastic Recticulum
       SF *Biological and Medical Sciences
           Cytochemistry
ER   Error Recovery
       SF *Computer Sciences
           Data Processing
ERA   Electrical Research Association (UK)
       SF *Electronics and Electrical

           Engineering
           *Information Retrieval Systems
ERC   Electronic Research Center (US)
       SF *Electronics and Electrical
           Engineering
           Navigation
ERE   Edison Responsive Environment
       SF Microteaching
           *Programmed Learning
           *Training
EREP   Earth Resources Experimental Package
       SF *Aeronautics
           *Communication Systems
EREP   Environmental Recording Editing and
       Printing
       SF *Computer Sciences
           Data Processing
ERG   Electroretinogram
       SF *Oceanography
ERGS   Electronic Route Guidance System
       SF *Transportation
ERIC   Educational Resources Information
       Center
       SF *Computer Sciences
           *Information Retrieval Systems
EROS   Earth Resources Observation Satellite
       SF *Space Sciences
EROS   Earth Resources Observation System
       SF *Aeronautics
           *Space Sciences
ERP   Effective Radiated Power
       SF *Aeronautics
           *Communication Systems
ERS   Electrical Resistance Strain
       SF Civil Engineering
           *Engineering
ERSOS Earth Resources Survey Operational
       Satellites
       SF *Telecommunications
ERTS   Earth Resources Technology Satellite
       SF *Aeronautics
           *Communication Systems
           *Space Sciences
           *Telecommunications
ES   Earth Spring
       SF *Agricultural Sciences
ES   Electronic Switch
       SF *Computer Sciences
           *Electronics and Electrical
           Engineering
ES   Exchangeable Sodium
       SF *Agricultural Sciences
ESA   Economic Stabilization Administration
       (US)
       SF *General
ESC   Escape Character
       SF *Computer Sciences
           Data Processing
ESC   European Space Conference
       SF *Communication Systems

```
                *Space Sciences
ESCA   Electron Spectroscopy for Chemical
          Analysis
       SF   *Biological and Medical Sciences
            *Nuclear Sciences
ESCES  Experimental Satellite Communication
          Earth Station
       SF   *Telecommunications
ESD    Electronics Systems Division
       SF    Civil Engineering
            *Engineering
            *Military Sciences
ESD    Ending Sequence Done
       SF   *Computer Sciences
            Data Processing
ESFA   Emergency Solid Fuel Administration
       SF   *Fuels
ESH    Electric Strip Heater
       SF   *Metallurgy and Metallography
            Metalworks
ESME   Excited State Mass Energy
       SF   *Aeronautics
            Instruments
ESO-FHWA Federal Highway Administration
          Emergency Standby Order (US)
       SF   *Transportation
ESP    Electron Spin Polarization
       SF   *Physics
            Solid Mechanics
ESPI   Electronic Speckle Pattern Interometer
       SF   *Biological and Medical Sciences
ESPOL  Executive Systems Problem Oriented
          Language
       SF   *Management
ESR    Electron Spin Resonance
       SF   *Lunar Sciences
            *Space Sciences
ESR    Erythrocyte Sedimentation Rate
       SF   *Biological and Medical Sciences
ESRO   European Space Research Organization
       SF   *Aeronautics
            *Communication Systems
            Space Sciences
            *Telecommunications
ESS    Earle's Salt Solution
       SF   *Biological and Medical Sciences
            Cytochemistry
ESS    Electronic Switching System
       SF   *Computer Sciences
            *Electronics and Electrical
            Engineering
ESSA   Environmental Science Services
          Administration
       SF   *Military Sciences
            *Telecommunications
ESSA   Environmental Survey Satellite
       SF   *Geosciences
            *Meteorology
ESSCO  Electronic Space Structure Corporation
       SF   *Space Sciences
```

```
                *Telecommunications
ESTEC  European Space Technology Center
       SF   *Space Sciences
esu    Electrostatic Unit
       SF   *Mathematics
ET     Emf-Temperature
       SF   *Nuclear Sciences
            Thermocouples
ET     Ephemerics Time
       SF   *Naval Sciences
            Navigation
ET     Equal Taper
       SF   *Metallurgy and Metallography
            Metalworks
ET     Evapotranspiration
       SF   *Agricultural Sciences
ETA    Estimated Time of Arrival
       SF   *Aeronautics
            Air Traffic Control
            *Transportation
ETB    End of Transmission Block
       SF   *Computer Sciences
            Data Processing
ETC    Electrothermal Integrated Circuits
       SF   *Electronics and Electrical
            Engineering
            Solid-state Circuits
ETC    European Traffic Committee
       SF   *Aeronautics
            Air Traffic Control
ETD    Equivalent Transmission Density
       SF   *Photography
ETD    Estimated Time of Departure
       SF   *Aeronautics
            Air Traffic Control
            *Transportation
ETE    Estimated Time Enroute
       SF   *Aeronautics
            Instrument Flying
ETF    Engine Test Facility
       SF   *Aeronautics
            Aircraft
ETIM   Elapsed Time
       SF   *Computer Sciences
            Data Processing
ETM    Electronic Test and Measurement
       SF   *Electronics and Electrical
            Engineering
EtNC   Ethyl Isocyanide
       SF    Biochemistry
            *Biological and Medical Sciences
ETO 25 Esso Turbo Oil 25
       SF   *Aeronautics
            *Fuels
ETR    Eastern Test Range (US)
       SF   *Space Sciences
ETR    Experimental Test Reactor
       SF   *Nuclear Sciences
            Reactors
ETS    Electronic Test Set
```

```
       SF  *Aeronautics
           *Communication Systems
ETSL   Estimated Total Shelf Life
       SF  *Agricultural Sciences
           *Dairy Sciences
ETX    End of Text
       SF  *Computer Sciences
           Data Processing
EU     Electronic Unit
       SF  *Electronics and Electrical
              Engineering
EUCOM  European Command
       SF  *Military Sciences
EUROCAE European Organization for Civil
           Aviation Electronics
       SF  *Aeronautics
           Air Traffic Control
           *Communication Systems
EUROCONTROL European Organization for the
              Safety of Air Navigation
       SF  *Aeronautics
           Air Traffic Control
EUV    Extreme Ultra Violet
       SF   Lunar Sciences
            Radiation
           *Space Sciences
           *Telecommunications
eV     Electronvolt
       SF  *Electronics and Electrical
              Engineering
           *Mathematics
EVA    Ethylene Vinyl Acetate
       SF  *Agricultural Sciences
           *Non-metallic Materials
           Polymers
EVA    Extra Vehicular Activity
       SF  *Lunar Sciences
           *Space Sciences
EVCS   Extravehicular Communication System
       SF  *Communication Systems
           *Space Sciences
           Space Simulation
EVR    Electronic Video Recording
       SF  *Photography
EVTCM  Expected Value Terminal Capacity
       SF  *Mathematics
EWI    Education With Industry
       SF   Air Force
           *Engineering
           *Military Sciences
EWL    Egg White Lysozyme
       SF  *Dairy Sciences
EWTR   Electronic Warfare Test Range
       SF  *Aeronautics
           Military Sciences
           *Military Sciences
EXCP   Executive Channel Program
       SF  *Computer Sciences
           Data Processing
EXD    Exchange Degeneracy
```

```
       SF  *Nuclear Sciences
EXEC   Executive
       SF  *Computer Sciences
           Data Processing
           *General
EXH    Exhaust
       SF  *Metallurgy and Metallography
           Metalworks
EXR    Execute and Repeat
       SF  *Communication Systems
           *Computer Sciences
EXTRN  External Reference
       SF  *Computer Sciences
           Data Processing
```

F

f   Filament
        SF   *Electronics and Electrical
             Engineering
             Semiconductor Devices
f-   Filament Negative
        SF   *Electronics and Electrical
             Engineering
             Semiconductor Devices
f   Frequency
        SF   *Electronics and Electrical
             Engineering
             Semiconductor Devices
FA   Free Area
        SF   *Metallurgy and Metallography
             Metalworks
FA   Fresh Air
        SF   *Metallurgy and Metallography
             Metalworks
FAA   Federal Aviation Administration
        SF   *Aeronautics
             Civil Aviation
             *Transportation
FAA   Federal Aviation Agency
        SF   *Aeronautics
FAAP   Federal Aid Airport Program
        SF   *Aeronautics
FAAR   Forward Area Alerting Radar
        SF   *Aeronautics
             Air Traffic Control
FABMDS Field Army Ballistic Missile Defence
             System
        SF   *Military Sciences
             *Space Sciences
FAC   Forward Air Control
        SF   *Aeronautics
             Air Traffic Control
FAC   Forward Air Controller
        SF   *Aeronautics
             Air Traffic Control
FACE   Field Artillery Computer Equipment
        SF   *Computer Sciences
             *Military Sciences
FAD   Flavine Adenine Dinucleotide
        SF   *Agricultural Sciences
FADAC   Field Artillery Digital Automatic

        Computer
        SF   *Computer Sciences
             *Military Sciences
FADES   Fuselage Analysis and Design
             Synthesis
        SF   *Aeronautics
             Aircraft
FAF   Final Approach Fix
        SF   *Aeronautics
             Approach and Landing
             Instruments
FAGS   Federation of Astronomical and
             Geophysical Service
        SF   *Geosciences
FAI   Fresh Air Intake
        SF   *Metallurgy and Metallography
             Metalworks
FAKS   File Access Keys
        SF   *Computer Sciences
             Data Processing
FAMOS   Floating Gate Avalanch-Injection
             Metal Oxide Semiconductor
        SF   *Electronics and Electrical
             Engineering
             Solid-state Circuits
FAP   Financial Analysis Program
        SF   *Computer Sciences
             Data Processing
FAR   Federal Airworthiness Regulations (US)
        SF   *Aeronautics
             Aircraft
FAR   Federal Aviation Regulation
        SF   *Aeronautics
FARR   Forward Area Refuelling and Rearing
        SF   *Aeronautics
             Logistics
             *Military Sciences
FASEB   Federation of American Societies for
             Experimental Biology
        SF   *Agricultural Sciences
             *Biological and Medical Sciences
FAT   Fluorescent Antibody Test
        SF   *Agricultural Sciences
             Dairy Sciences
FAV   Fast Acting Value

70

SF   *Electronics and Electrical
          Engineering
FAWS Flight Advisory Weather Service
      SF   *Aeronautics
           *Meteorology
FAX   Facsimile
      SF   *Computer Sciences
           Data Processing
FB   Flat Bottom
      SF   *Metallurgy and Metallography
           Metalworks
FBO   Fixed Base Operator
      SF   *Space Sciences
FBRL Final Bomb Release Line
      SF   *Aeronautics
           *Military Sciences
FC   Flexible Connection
      SF   *Metallurgy and Metallography
           Metalworks
FC   Free Cholesterol
      SF   Biochemistry
           *Biological and Medical Sciences
FC   Full Corners
      SF   *Metallurgy and Metallography
           Metalworks
FCA   Faraday Cup Array
      SF   *Electronics and Electrical
               Engineering
           Instruments
FCA   Fluidized Combustor Ash
      SF   *Agricultural Sciences
FCA   Frequency Control and Analysis
      SF   *Aeronautics
FCAP Fluor Chrome Arsenate Pheonol
      SF   *Engineering
           *Metallurgy and Metallography
FCC   Federal Communications Commission
      SF   *Communication Systems
FCC   Flat Conductor Cable
      SF   *Aeronautics
           Aircraft
FCC   Flight Control Center
      SF   *Aeronautics
           Air Traffic Control
FCC   Food Contaminants Commission (US)
      SF   *Agricultural Sciences
           *Dairy Sciences
FCCTS Federal COBOL Compiler Testing Service
      SF   *Computer Sciences
           Data Processing
FCG   Federal Coordination Group (US)
      SF   *General
FCIA Foreign Credit Insurance Association
      SF   *Engineering
           Engineering Consultancy
FCLP Field Carrier Landing Practice
      SF   *Aeronautics
FCM   Fat Corrected Milk
      SF   *Dairy Sciences
FCO   Flight Clearance Office

SF   *Aeronautics
          Airports
FCP   Fatigue Crack Propagation
      SF   *Metallurgy and Metallography
FCP   File Control Procedure
      SF   *Computer Sciences
           Data Processing
FCR   Facility Change Request
      SF   Air Force
           *Military Sciences
FCR   Fire Control Radar
      SF   *Aeronautics
FCS   Fire Control System
      SF   *Aeronautics
FCSS Fire Control Sight System
      SF   *Aeronautics
           Avionics
fct   Filament Centre Tap
      SF   *Electronics and Electrical
               Engineering
           Semiconductor Devices
FCTC Fuel Centerline Thermocouples
      SF   Fuels
           *Nuclear Sciences
FCU   Fares Calculating Units
      SF   *Aeronautics
           Air Transport
FCVS Free Calf Vaccination Service
      SF   *Agricultural Sciences
FD   File Directory
      SF   *Computer Sciences
           Data Processing
FD   Fire Damper
      SF   *Metallurgy and Metallography
           Metalworks
FD   Flight Director
      SF   *Aeronautics
FD   Floppy Disc
      SF   *Computer Sciences
           Data Processing
FD   Frequency Demodulator
      SF   Radio Engineering
           *Telecommunications
FD   Frequency Diversity
      SF   *Aeronautics
           Air Traffic Control
           *Communication Systems
fd   Frequency Doubler
      SF   *Communication Systems
           Radio Engineering
FD   Full Duplex
      SF   *Computer Sciences
           Data Processing
FDA   Food and Drug Administration (US)
      SF   *Agricultural Sciences
           *Biological and Medical Sciences
FDAA Federal Disaster Assistance
          Administration (US)
      SF   *General
FDAA Fluorenyldiacetamide

```
          SF    Biochemistry                        SF   *Aeronautics
                *Biological and Medical Sciences  FDS   Fallout Decay Simulator
FDAU   Flight Data Acquisition Unit                   SF   *Biological and Medical Sciences
          SF   *Aeronautics                       FDS   Field Separator
FDC    Flight Director Computer                       SF   *Computer Sciences
          SF   *Aeronautics                                 *Electronics and Electrical
               Data Processing                               Engineering
FDDS   Flight Data Distribution System           FDS   Frequency Division Separator
          SF   *Aeronautics                           SF   *Computer Sciences
               Communication Systems                        *Electronics and Electrical
               *Computer Sciences                            Engineering
               Data Processing                    FDSU  Flight Data Storage Unit
FDEP   Flight Data Entry Panel                        SF   *Aeronautics
          SF   *Aeronautics                       FDT   Formated Data Tapes
               Airborne Recording Systems             SF   *Computer Sciences
FDI    Field Director Indicator                             Data Processing
          SF   *Aeronautics                       FDV   Fault Detect Verification
               Navigation                             SF   *Computer Sciences
FDI    Flight Director Indicator                            Data Processing
          SF   *Aeronautics                       FDX   Full Duplex
               Space Sciences                         SF   *Computer Sciences
FDL    Fast Development Logistics                           Data Processing
          SF   *Military Sciences                 FE    Flash Evaporation
FDM    Frequency Division Multiplexer                 SF   *Biological and Medical Sciences
          SF   *Computer Sciences                           Non-crystalline Solids
               Data Processing                    FE    Format Effector
FDM    Frequency Division Multiplexing                SF   *Computer Sciences
          SF   *Electronics and Electrical                  Data Processing
               Engineering                        Fe    Iron
FDMA   Frequency Division Multiple Access             SF   *Agricultural Sciences
          SF   *Aeronautics                                 *General
               *Communication Systems             FEA   Federal Energy Administration (US)
               *Electronics and Electrical            SF   *General
               Engineering                        FeAA  Ferric Acetylacetonate
FDNB   Fluorodinitrobenzene                           SF   *Non-metallic Materials
          SF   *Agricultural Sciences                       Polymers
               Cereals                            FEBA  Forward Edge of Battle Area
FDNR   Frequency Dependent Negative Register         SF    Logistics
          SF   *Electronics and Electrical                 *Military Sciences
               Engineering                        FECPs Facility Engineering Change Proposals
               *Engineering                            SF    Air Force
               Solid-state Circuits                         *Engineering
FDNR   Frequency Dependent Negative                        *Military Sciences
       Resistance                                 FED   Front End Processors
          SF   *Electronics and Electrical            SF   *Computer Sciences
               Engineering                                  Data Processing
FDP    Fast Digital Processor                     FEP   Financial Evaluation Program
          SF   *Aeronautics                           SF   *Computer Sciences
               Air Traffic Control                          Data Processing
               *Computer Sciences                          *Management
               Data Processing                    FEP   Front End Packages
FDP    Field Developed Program                        SF   *Aeronautics
          SF   *Computer Sciences                           Wind Tunnel
               Data Processing                     FEP   Front End Processors
FDP    Flight Data Processing                         SF   *Aeronautics
          SF   *Aeronautics                                 *Computer Sciences
               Air Traffic Control                          Data Processing
               *Computer Sciences                           Transponders
               Data Processing                    FEPE  Full Energy Peak Efficiency
FDR    Flight Data Recorder                           SF    Gamma Rays
```

*Nuclear Sciences
FES   Family Expenditure Survey
      SF *Statistics
FES   Florida Engineering Society
      SF *Engineering
FET   Field Effect Transistor
      SF *Communication Systems
          *Computer Sciences
          *Electronics and Electrical
              Engineering
          Instruments
          Solid-state Circuits
FETT Field Effect Tetrode Transistor
      SF *Communication Systems
          *Electronics and Electrical
              Engineering
FF   Filtration Faction
      SF Biochemistry
          *Biological and Medical Sciences
FF   Flip Flops
      SF *Computer Sciences
          Data Processing
FF   Form Feed
      SF *Computer Sciences
          Data Processing
FF   Fuel Flow
      SF *Aeronautics
          Aircraft Fuels
          Propellants and Fuels
FFA   Free Fatty Acids
      SF *Agricultural Sciences
          Biochemistry
          *Biological and Medical Sciences
          *Dairy Sciences
FFL   Finished Floor
      SF *Metallurgy and Metallography
          Metalworks
FFS   Flory Fox Schaefgen
      SF *Non-metallic Materials
          Polymers
FFSF Full Fat Soy Flour
      SF *Agricultural Sciences
          *Dairy Sciences
FFT   Fast Fourier Transform
      SF *Aeronautics
          *Communication Systems
          *Computer Sciences
          *Electronics and Electrical
              Engineering
          Radar Detection
FFTF Fast Flux Test Facility
      SF *Nuclear Sciences
          Reactors
FFTR Fast Flux Test Reactors
      SF *Nuclear Sciences
          Reactors
FGCS Flight Guidance and Control Systems
      SF *Aeronautics
          Instruments
FHS   Framingham Heart Study

      SF *Aeronautics
          Aviation Medicine
          *Biological and Medical Sciences
FHWA Federal Highway Administration (US)
      SF Civil Engineering
          *Engineering
          *Transportation
FIA   International Federation of Actors
      SF *Copyright
FIC   Flight Information Center
      SF *Aeronautics
FICPI International Federation of Patent
      Agents
      SF *Copyright
          Industrial Property
FID   Fédération Internationale de
      Documentation
      SF *Computer Sciences
          Data Processing
          *Information Retrieval Systems
FIDAC Film Input to Digital Automatic
      Computer
      SF *Computer Sciences
          Data Processing
FIDACSYS FIDAC System
      SF *Computer Sciences
          Data Processing
FIDO Fog Investigation and Dispersal
      Operation
      SF *Aeronautics
          *Meteorology
FIGS Figures Shift
      SF *Computer Sciences
          Data Processing
FIILS Full Integrity Instrument Landing
      System
      SF *Aeronautics
          Approach and Landing
FIM   Field Ion Microscope
      SF *Chemistry
          Physical Chemistry
FIM   International Federation of
      Musicians
      SF *Copyright
          *Music
FINAC Fast Interline Non Active Automatic
      Control
      SF *Computer Sciences
          Data Processing
FIND File Interrogation of Nineteen
      Hundred Data
      SF *Computer Sciences
          Data Processing
FIND Forecasting Institutional Needs for
      Dartmouth
      SF *Computer Sciences
          Data Processing
          *Management
FIOT Flags and Input-Output Transfer
      SF Measurement Systems

              *Nuclear Sciences
FIPS Federal Information Processing
       Standards
      SF *Aeronautics
          *Computer Sciences
          Data Processing
          Ground Communication Networks
FIR   Flight Information Region
      SF *Aeronautics
          *Information Retrieval Systems
FIRA Furniture Industry Research
       Association (UK)
      SF *Information Retrieval Systems
          Reports Acquisition
FIS   Flight Information Service
      SF *Aeronautics
          Airports
FIT   File Information Table
      SF *Computer Sciences
          Data Processing
FITC Fluorescein Isothiocyanate
      SF *Biological and Medical Sciences
          Cytochemistry
FITH Fire In The Hole
      SF *Space Sciences
          Space Simulation
FJCC Fall Joint Computer Conference
      SF *Computer Sciences
          Data Processing
FKG   Fortuin Kasteleyn and Ginibre
      SF *Physics
FL   Flight Level
      SF *Aeronautics
          Instrument Flying
FLAR Forward Looking Airborne Radar
      SF *Aeronautics
FL-BE Filter Band Elimination
      SF *Communication Systems
          *Electronics and Electrical
            Engineering
FL-BP Filter Bandpass
      SF *Electronics and Electrical
            Engineering
FLBR Fusible Link Bottom Register
      SF *Metallurgy and Metallography
          Metalworks
FLECHT Full Length Emergency Cooling Heat
       Transfer
      SF *Nuclear Sciences
          Reactors
FLF   Follow the Leader Feedback
      SF *Electronics and Electrical
            Engineering
FL-HP Filter High Pass
      SF *Electronics and Electrical
            Engineering
FLIP Floating Instrument Platform
      SF *Astronautics and Astrophysics
          *Geosciences
          Instruments

FLIR Forward Looking Infrared
      SF *Aeronautics
          *Computer Sciences
          *Electronics and Electrical
            Engineering
FL-LP Filter Low Pass
      SF *Electronics and Electrical
            Engineering
FLOP Floating Point
      SF *Computer Sciences
          Data Processing
FLPC Federal Local Port Controller (US)
      SF *Transportation
FLTR Fusible Link Top Register
      SF *Metallurgy and Metallography
          Metalworks
FLTSATCOM Fleet Satellite Communication
      SF *Aeronautics
          *Communication Systems
          *Space Sciences
FM   Flour Milling
      SF *Agricultural Sciences
          *Milling
FM   Frequency Modulation
      SF *Communication Systems
          *Computer Sciences
          Data Processing
          *Electronics and Electrical
            Engineering
          Instruments
FM   Frequency Multiplier
      SF *Electronics and Electrical
            Engineering
FMA   Facilities Management Analysis
      SF   Air Force
          Civil Engineering
          *Engineering
          *Military Sciences
FMA   Flight Manual Allowance
      SF *Aeronautics
          Instruments
FMBRA Flour Milling and Baking Research
       Association (UK)
      SF *Information Retrieval Systems
          *Milling
FMC   Flutter Mode Control
      SF   Aerodynamics
          *Aeronautics
FMICW Frequency Modulated Intermittent
       Continuous Wave
      SF *Electronics and Electrical
            Engineering
FMIS Fiscal Management Information
       System
      SF *Computer Sciences
          Data Processing
          *Information Retrieval Systems
FMS   Force Measurement System
      SF *Space Sciences
          Space Simulation

FMSO (Naval) Fleet Material Supply Office
    SF   Logistics
       *Military Sciences
FMSR Finite Mass Sum Rules
    SF   Nuclear Physics
       *Nuclear Sciences
FMT   Flour Milling Technology
    SF   *Agricultural Sciences
       *Milling
FNS   File Nesting Store
    SF   *Computer Sciences
       Data Processing
FNWC Fleet Numerical Weather Central (US)
    SF   *Agricultural Sciences
       *Meteorology
FOAMS Forecasting, Order Administration, and
    Master Scheming
    SF   *Management
FOBS Fractional Orbital Bombardment System
    SF   *Military Sciences
FOD   Flies-Odors-Ducts
    SF   *Agricultural Sciences
       *Dairy Sciences
FOI   Follow-on Intercepter
    SF   *Aeronautics
       *Military Sciences
FORTRAN Formula Translation
    SF   *Computer Sciences
       Data Processing
FOSDIC Film Optical Sensing Device for
    Input to Computers
    SF   *Computer Sciences
       Data Processing
       *Photography
FOV   Field Of View
    SF   *Astronautics and Astrophysics
       *Lunar Sciences
FP   Fire Proofing
    SF   *Metallurgy and Metallography
       Metalworks
FPC   Federal Power Commission (US)
    SF   *General
FPC   Fish Protein Concentrate
    SF   *Agricultural Sciences
       *Biological and Medical Sciences
       *Dairy Sciences
FPCE Fission Product Conversion
    Encapsulation
    SF   *Nuclear Sciences
FPH   Floating Point Hardware
    SF   *Computer Sciences
       Data Processing
FPL   Field Flight Plan
    SF   *Aeronautics
       Airports
FPL   Foxbro Programming Language
    SF   *Computer Sciences
       Data Processing
FPL   Functional Problem Log
    SF   *Computer Sciences

       Data Processing
FPM   Feet Per Minute
    SF   *Metallurgy and Metallography
       Metalworks
FPN   Fixed Pattern Noise
    SF   *Electronics and Electrical
         Engineering
       Solid-state Circuits
FPP   Floating Point Processor
    SF   *Computer Sciences
       Data Processing
FPPS Flight Plan Progressing System
    SF   *Aeronautics
FPQA Fixed Portion Queue Area
    SF   *Computer Sciences
       Data Processing
FPRL Forest Products Research Laboratory
    (UK)
    SF   *Information Retrieval Systems
       Reports Acquisition
FPSK Frequency and Phase Shift Keying
    SF   *Engineering
       Radio Engineering
       *Telecommunications
FRA   Federal Railroad Administration (US)
    SF   *Transportation
FRC   Federal Radio Commission
    SF   *Aeronautics
       Air Traffic Control
       *Communication Systems
FRC   Flight Research Center
    SF   *Aeronautics
       Aircraft Noise
FRD   Fibre Resin Developments (UK)
    SF   Moulding
       *Non-metallic Materials
FRED Fractionally Rapid Electronic Device
    SF   *Computer Sciences
       Data Processing
FRP   Fibre Reinforced Polyester
    SF   *Engineering
       Mechanical Engineering
       *Non-metallic Materials
       Polymers
FRP   Fibreglass Reinforced Plastics
    SF   *Non-metallic Materials
       Polymers
FRSB Frequency Referenced Scanning Beam
    SF   *Aeronautics
       Approach and Landing
FRU   Field Replacement Unit
    SF   *Computer Sciences
       Data Processing
FRWI Framingham Relative Weight Index
    SF   *Aeronautics
       Aviation Medicine
       *Biological and Medical Sciences
FS   Field Separator
    SF   *Computer Sciences
       Data Processing

FS	File Separation
	SF *Computer Sciences
	Data Processing
FS	Flat Slip
	SF *Metallurgy and Metallography
	Metalworks
FS	Free Sterols
	SF Biochemistry
	*Biological and Medical Sciences
	Pharmacology
FS	Freeze Substitution
	SF *Biological and Medical Sciences
	Cytochemistry
FS	Frequency Synthesizer
	SF *Telecommunications
FSAA	Flat Slips All Around
	SF *Metallurgy and Metallography
	Metalworks
FSAA	Flight Simulator for Advanced Aircraft
	SF *Aeronautics
	Airworthiness
FSB	Flat Slip on Bottom
	SF *Metallurgy and Metallography
	Metalworks
FSC	Free Secretory Component
	SF *Dairy Sciences
fsd	Full Scale Deflection
	SF *Communication Systems
	Radio Engineering
FSF	Flight Safety Foundation
	SF *Aeronautics
FSH	Follicle Stimulating Hormone
	SF *Biological and Medical Sciences
	Cytochemistry
FSK	Frequency Shift Keying
	SF *Computer Sciences
	Data Processing
	Radio Engineering
	*Telecommunications
FSR	Forward Space Record
	SF *Computer Sciences
	Data Processing
FSS	Flight Service Station
	SF *Aeronautics
	Instrument Flying
FSS	Flight Standards Service
	SF *Aeronautics
FST	Flat Slip On Top
	SF *Metallurgy and Metallography
	Metalworks
FSTC	Foreign Science and Technology Center (US)
	SF *Biological and Medical Sciences
FSU	Field Select Unit
	SF *Computer Sciences
	Data Processing
ft	Filament Positive
	SF *Electronics and Electrical Engineering
	Semiconductor Devices

FT	Flat Top
	SF *Metallurgy and Metallography
	Metalworks
fT	Transistor Frequency
	SF *Electronics and Electrical Engineering
	Semiconductor Devices
FTC	Fast Time Constant
	SF *Aeronautics
	*Communication Systems
	Radar Technology
FTC	Federal Trade Commission
	SF *Engineering
	Instruments
FTD	Folded Triangular Dipole
	SF *Electronics and Electrical Engineering
FTE	Fracture Transition Elastic
	SF Materials
	*Nuclear Sciences
FTFET	Four Terminal Field Effect Transistor
	SF *Electronics and Electrical Engineering
	Solid-state Circuits
FTHMA	Frequency Time Hopping Multiple Access
	SF *Aeronautics
	*Electronics and Electrical Engineering
ftIbf	Foot Pound Force
	SF *Mathematics
FTM	Folded Triangular Monopole
	SF *Electronics and Electrical Engineering
FTMT	Final Thermomechanical Treatment
	SF *Engineering
	Mechanical Engineering
	*Metallurgy and Metallography
FTP	Federal Test Procedure
	SF Civil Engineering
	*Engineering
FTS	Federal Telecommunication System
	SF *Telecommunications
FTS	Flying Training School
	SF *Aeronautics
	*Training
FTU	Formazin Turbidity Units
	SF *Agricultural Sciences
	*Dairy Sciences
FU	Fumarate Concentration
	SF Bioengineering
	*Biological and Medical Sciences
FUB	Facilities Utilization Board
	SF Air Force
	Civil Engineering
	*Engineering
	*Military Sciences
FVD	Friction Volume Damper
	SF *Metallurgy and Metallography
	Metalworks

FVN   Failed Vector Numbers
          SF   *Computer Sciences
                  Testing
FVRDE Fighting Vehicle Research and
          Development Establishment
          SF   *Aeronautics
                  *Military Sciences
FWHM   Full Width Half Maximum
          SF   *Astronautics and Astrophysics
                  *Lunar Sciences
                  *Nuclear Sciences
                  Quantum Electronics
                  Spectroscopy
FWTT   Fixed Wing Tactical Transport
          SF   *Aeronautics
                  *Military Sciences

G

G   Graph
      SF *Mathematics
g   Grid, Gate
      SF *Electronics and Electrical
            Engineering
            Semiconductor Devices
GA   Gibberellic Acid
      SF *Agricultural Sciences
            Biochemistry
            *Biological and Medical Sciences
            *Brewery
GA   Glyoxylic Acid
      SF *Biological and Medical Sciences
            Cytochemistry
GABA Gamma Aminobutyric Acid
      SF *Biological and Medical Sciences
GAD   Glutamic Acid Decarboxylase
      SF *Agricultural Sciences
            *Cereals
GADO General Aviation District Organization
      SF *Aeronautics
GAELIC Grumman Aerospace Engineering
            Language for Instructional Checkout
      SF *Computer Sciences
            Data Processing
GAFAWG General Aviation Fuel Allocation
            Working Group (UK)
      SF *Aeronautics
            Fuels
GAI   Generalized Area of Intersection
      SF *Nuclear Sciences
            Reactors
GAM   Graphic Access Method
      SF *Computer Sciences
            Data Processing
GAM   Ground-to-Air Missile
      SF *Aeronautics
            *Military Sciences
GAMA General Aviation Manufacturers'
      Association
      SF *Aeronautics
GAO   General Accounting Office
      SF *General
GaP   Gallium Phosphide
      SF *Computer Sciences

            Data Processing
GAP   General Assembly Program
      SF *Computer Sciences
            Data Processing
GAPA Ground-to-Air Pilotless Aircraft
      SF *Aeronautics
GAPAN Guild of Air Pilots and Air
            Navigators
      SF *Aeronautics
            Navigation
GARD General Address Reading Device
      SF *Communication Systems
GAREX Ground Aviation Radio Exchange System
      SF *Aeronautics
            *Communication Systems
GARP Global Atmospheric Research Program
      SF *Aeronautics
            *Biological and Medical Sciences
            *Communication Systems
            *Meteorology
            *Space Sciences
GAT   General Air Traffic
      SF *Aeronautics
            Air Traffic Control
GATD Graphic Analysis of Three-dimensional
      Data
      SF *Computer Sciences
            Data Processing
GATE GARP Atlantic Tropical Experiment
      SF *Communication Systems
            *Geosciences
            *Meteorology
GATE Global Atlantic Tropical Experiment
      SF *Aeronautics
            *Communication Systems
            *Space Sciences
GATF Graphic Arts Technical Foundation
      SF *Printing
GATR Ground Air Transmitter Receiver
      SF   Air Force
            *Communication Systems
            *Military Sciences
GATV Gemini Agena Target Vehicle
      SF *Space Sciences
gb   Grid Bias

	SF *Communication Systems		SF Lasers and Masers
	Radio Engineering		*Physics
GB	Gun Branch	GDMS	Generalized Data Management System
	SF *Electronics and Electrical		SF *Computer Sciences
	Engineering		Data Processing
GBC	General Binding Corporation		*Management
	SF Binding	GDO	Gun Direction Officer
	*Printing		SF *Aeronautics
GBM	Glomerular Basement Membrane		*Military Sciences
	SF Biochemistry	GDOP	Geometric Dilution of Precision
	*Biological and Medical Sciences		SF *Aeronautics
	Pharmacology		*Communication Systems
GC	Gas Chromatography		Navigation
	SF *Biological and Medical Sciences	GDP	Guanosine Disphosphate
	*Chemistry		SF *Biological and Medical Sciences
	*Space Sciences		Cytochemistry
GC	General Contractor	GDR	General Design Requirements
	SF *Metallurgy and Metallography		SF *Electronics and Electrical
	Metalworks		Engineering
GCA	Ground Control Approach		Solid-state Circuits
	SF *Aeronautics	GDR	Ground Delay Response
	Approach and Landing		SF *Engineering
	Instruments		Radio Engineering
GCB	Generator Circuit Breaker		*Telecommunications
	SF *Electronics and Electrical	GDTA	Ground for Development of Aerospace
	Engineering		Teledection
GCC	Ground Control Centre		SF *Telecommunications
	SF *Aeronautics	GE	Gaussian Elimination
	Air Traffic Control		SF *Electronics and Electrical
GCFR	Gas Control Fast Reactor		Engineering
	SF *Nuclear Sciences	GE	Greater Than/Equal To
	Nucleonics		SF *Computer Sciences
	Reactors		Data Processing
GCI	Ground Controlled Interception	GEC	General Electric Company
	SF *Aeronautics		SF *Electronics and Electrical
	Air Traffic Control		Engineering
GC-MS	Gas Chromatography Mass Spectrometry	GEC	Generalized Equivalent Cylinder
	SF *Biological and Medical Sciences		SF *Nuclear Sciences
	*Chemistry	GECOS	General Comprehensive Operating
	*Space Sciences		Supervisory
GCR	Generator Control Relay		SF *Computer Sciences
	SF *Electronics and Electrical		Data Processing
	Engineering	GEG	Generalized Euclidean Geometry
GCU	Generator Control Unit		SF *Electronics and Electrical
	SF *Aeronautics		Engineering
	Aircraft		*Mathematics
GCVS	General Catalog of Variable Stars	GEGB	General Electricity Generating Board
	SF *Astronautics and Astrophysics		SF *Electronics and Electrical
	*Lunar Sciences		Engineering
GD	Ground Detector	GEIS	General Electric Information Service
	SF *Electronics and Electrical		SF *Computer Sciences
	Engineering		Data Processing
	Meters	GEMM	Generalized Electronics Maintenance
GDG	General Data Group		Model
	SF *Computer Sciences		SF Logistics
	Data Processing		*Military Sciences
GDH	Glutamate Dehydrogenase	GENOT	General Notices
	SF Biochemistry		SF *Aeronautics
	*Biological and Medical Sciences		Ground Communication
GDL	Gas Dynamic Laser	GEON	Gyro Erected Optical Navigation

SF   *Aeronautics
     *Naval Sciences
     Navigation

GEORGE General Organisational Experiment
     SF   *Computer Sciences
          Data Processing

GESO Geodetic Earth Orbiting Satellite
     SF   *Geosciences
          *Space Sciences

GET Ground Elapsed Time
     SF   *Astronautics and Astrophysics
          *Lunar Sciences
          Navigation

GETOL Ground Effect Take-Off and Landing
     SF   *Aeronautics
          Approach and Landing

GFAE Government Furnished Aeronautical
          Equipment
     SF   *Aeronautics

GFM Government Furnished Materials
     SF   Logistics
          *Military Sciences

GFR Glomerular Filtration Rate
     SF   Biochemistry
          *Biological and Medical Sciences
          Pharmacology

GGA Gulf General Atomic
     SF   *Nuclear Sciences
          Neutrons

GGRT Goddard Goldstone Rebbi and Thorn
     SF   Nuclear Physics
          *Nuclear Sciences

GH   Growth Hormone
     SF   Biochemistry
          *Biological and Medical Sciences
          *Dairy Sciences

GHA Greenwich Hour Angle
     SF   *Aeronautics
          *Naval Sciences

GI   Galvanized Iron
     SF   *Metallurgy and Metallography
          Metalworks

GI   Gastrointestinal
     SF   Biochemistry
          *Biological and Medical Sciences
          Pharmacology

GIC Generalized Immittance Converter
     SF   *Electronics and Electrical
          Engineering

GIDEP Government Industry Data Exchange
          Program
     SF   *Engineering

GIGO Garbage In Garbage Out
     SF   *Computer Sciences
          Data Processing

GIS Generalised Information System
     SF   *Computer Sciences
          Data Processing

GJE Gauss Jordon Elimination
     SF   *Electronics and Electrical

          Engineering

GJP Graphic Job Processor
     SF   *Computer Sciences
          Data Processing

GLA Gross Leasable Area
     SF   *Engineering
          Engineering Consultancy

GLC Gas Liquid Chromatography
     SF   *Agricultural Sciences
          *Dairy Sciences
          *Nuclear Sciences
          Nucleonics

GLLD Ground Laser Locator Designator
     SF   *Aeronautics
          *Military Sciences

GM   Group Mark
     SF   *Computer Sciences
          Data Processing

GM   Guided Missile
     SF   *Aeronautics
          *Military Sciences

GMA Glycol Methacrylate
     SF   *Biological and Medical Sciences
          Cytochemistry

GMC Ground Movement Control
     SF   *Aeronautics

GMM General Matrix Manipulator
     SF   *Management

GMN LeGuillou Morel Navelet
     SF   Elementary Particles
          *Nuclear Sciences

GMP Ground Movement Planner
     SF   *Aeronautics

GMS Geostationary Meteorological Satellite
     SF   *Telecommunications

GMT Greenwich Mean Time
     SF   *General
          Navigation

GMWM Group Mark/Word Mark
     SF   *Computer Sciences
          Data Processing

GNC Global Navigation Chart
     SF   *Aeronautics
          Navigation

GNC Graphic Numerical Control
     SF   *Computer Sciences
          Data Processing

GOES Geostationary Operational Environmental
          Satellite
     SF   *Telecommunications

GOT Glutamic Oxalacetic Transaminase
     SF   Biochemistry
          *Biological and Medical Sciences

GPA Grade Point Average
     SF   Programmed Learning
          *Training

GPABP Guinea Pig Anti-Bovine Protection
     SF   *Dairy Sciences

GPAS General Purpose Airborne Simulator
     SF   *Aeronautics

Aircraft
GPB   Ground Power Breaker
       SF   *Electronics and Electrical
            Engineering
GPC   Gel Permeation Chromatography
       SF   *Agricultural Sciences
            Cereals
            *Dairy Sciences
            *Non-metallic Materials
GPC   Gross Profit Contribution
       SF   *General
GPCS   Guinea Pig Control Serum
       SF   *Dairy Sciences
GPDC   General Purpose Digital Computer
       SF   *Computer Sciences
GPH   Gallons Per Hour
       SF   *General
GPI   Glucose Phosphate Isomerase
       SF   *Biological and Medical Sciences
GPI   Ground Position Indicator
       SF   *Aeronautics
GPLAN Generalized Data Base Planning System
       SF   *Computer Sciences
            Data Processing
GPM   Gallons Per Minute
       SF   *Aeronautics
            Aircraft
            *Metallurgy and Metallography
            Sheet-work
GPMTD Greater Pretoria Mass Transit
       District
       SF   *Transportation
GPO   General Post Office
       SF   *Communication Systems
            *General
GPO   Government Printing Office
       SF   *General
            *Printing
GPOS   General Purpose Operating System
       SF   Business Systems
            *Computer Sciences
            Data Processing
            *Management
GPR   General Purpose Radar
       SF   *Aeronautics
            Radar Detection
GPS   Global Positioning System
       SF   *Astronautics and Astrophysics
            *Communication Systems
            Navigation
            *Space Sciences
GPSS   General Purpose Simulation Program
       SF   *Engineering
            Engineering Consultancy
GPT-C Glutamic Pyruvic Tranminase-C
       SF   *Biological and Medical Sciences
GPWS   Ground Proximity Warning System
       SF   *Aeronautics
            Avionics
GQE   Generalized Queue Entry

       SF   *Computer Sciences
            Data Processing
GR   Gypsum Requirement
       SF   *Agricultural Sciences
GRA   Government Reports Announcement
       SF   *General
            *Information Retrieval Systems
GRAN   Global Rescue Alarm Net
       SF   *Communication Systems
GREMEX Goddard Research and Engineering
       Management Exercise
       SF   *Management
GRID   Graphical Interactive
       SF   *Computer Sciences
            Data Processing
GRIP   Grandmet Information Processing
       SF   *Computer Sciences
GRP   Glass Reinforced Polyester
       SF   *Non-metallic Materials
            Plastics
GS   General Schedule
       SF   *Aeronautics
            Air Traffic Control
GS   General Solution
       SF   *Mathematics
GS   Group Separator
       SF   *Computer Sciences
            Data Processing
GSA   General Services Administration
       SF   *Computer Sciences
            Data Processing
GSCG   Ground Systems Coordination Group
       SF   Civil Engineering
            *Engineering
            *Military Sciences
GSD   Generator Starter Drive
       SF   *Aeronautics
            Aircraft
GSE   Ground Support Equipment
       SF   *Aeronautics
            *Communication Systems
            *Space Sciences
GSFC   Goddard Space Flight Center (US)
       SF   *Communication Systems
            *Space Sciences
GSP   General Syntactic Processor
       SF   *Computer Sciences
            Data Processing
G6PDH Glucose-6-Phosphate Dehydrogenase
       SF   *Agricultural Sciences
GSU   Guaranteed Supply Unit
       SF   *Engineering
            Radio Engineering
            *Telecommunications
GT   Greater Than
       SF   *Computer Sciences
            Data Processing
GTA   Gas Tungston Arc
       SF   *Metallurgy and Metallography
            *Nuclear Sciences

GTC   Gain Time Control
        SF   *Aeronautics
GTD   Geometrical Theory of Diffraction
        SF   *Electronics and Electrical
                  Engineering
             *Mathematics
GTE   General Telephone and Electronics
        SF   *Computer Sciences
             Data Processing
GTP   Guanosine Triphosphate
        SF   *Biological and Medical Sciences
             Cytochemistry
GTS   Geostationary Technology Satellites
        SF   *Astronautics and Astrophysics
GTS   Global Telecommunications System
        SF   *Aeronautics
             *Telecommunications
GVH   Graft Versus Host
        SF   *Biological and Medical Sciences
             Drugs
GYFM   General Yielding Fracture Mechanics
        SF   *Metallurgy and Metallography
             Welding

h   Heater
        SF   *Electronics and Electrical
                Engineering
                Semiconductor Devices

h   Heplode
        SF   *Electronics and Electrical
                Engineering
                Semiconductor Devices

H   Hexapole
        SF   *Nuclear Sciences

h   Hexode
        SF   *Electronics and Electrical
                Engineering
                Semiconductor Devices

HA   Half Add
        SF   *Computer Sciences
                Data Processing

HA   Hemagglutinin
        SF   Biochemistry
                *Biological and Medical Sciences

HA   Hyaluronic
        SF   Biochemistry
                *Biological and Medical Sciences

HAA   Height Above Aerodrome
        SF   *Aeronautics
                Approach and Landing

HAA   Height Above Airport
        SF   *Aeronautics
                Approach and Landing

HAC   High Alumina Cement
        SF   *Building

HAES   High Altitude Effects Simulation
        SF   *Astronautics and Astrophysics
                *Geosciences

HAQO   Hydroxyaminoquinoline Oxide
        SF   Biochemistry
                *Biological and Medical Sciences

HAS   Hardened Aircraft Shelters
        SF   *Aeronautics

HAS   Heading Attitude System
        SF   *Aeronautics

HAS   Houston Automatic Spooling-Priority
        (System)
        SF   *Computer Sciences
                Data Processing

HASP   High Level Automatic Scheduling
        Program
        SF   *Computer Sciences
                Data Processing

HAT   Height Above Touchdown
        SF   *Aeronautics
                Approach and Landing

HAT   Hypoxanthine, Aminopterin and
        Thymidine
        SF   *Biological and Medical Sciences

HATRA   Hosiery and Allied Trades Research
        Association (UK)
        SF   *Information Retrieval Systems

HAZ   Heat Affected Zone
        SF   *Metallurgy and Metallography
                Welding

HBAg   Hepatitis B Antigen
        SF   *Biological and Medical Sciences
                Microbiology

HBFP   Hematoxylin-Basic Fuchsin-Picric
        SF   *Biological and Medical Sciences

HBSS   Hanks Balanced Salt Solution
        SF   *Biological and Medical Sciences

HBWR   Halden Boiling Heavy Water Reactor
        SF   *Nuclear Sciences
                Reactors

HC   Hanging Ceiling
        SF   *Metallurgy and Metallography
                Metalworks

HC   Heating Coil
        SF   *Metallurgy and Metallography
                Metalworks

HCB   Hexachlorobenzene
        SF   *Biological and Medical Sciences

HCEX   Hypercharge Exchange
        SF   Nuclear Physics
                *Nuclear Sciences

HCG   Hardware Character Generator
        SF   *Computer Sciences
                Data Processing

HCG   Human Chorionic Gonadotrophin
        SF   *Agricultural Sciences
                *Biological and Medical Sciences
                Cytochemistry

HCHP   Harvard Community Health Plan (US)

SF   *Biological and Medical Sciences
HCL   Hydrogen Chloride
      SF   *Biological and Medical Sciences
hct   Heater Centre Tap
      SF   *Electronics and Electrical
              Engineering
           Semiconductor Devices
HD   Half Duplex
      SF   *Computer Sciences
           Data Processing
HD   Hepatosis Diaetetica
      SF   *Agricultural Sciences
HD   High Density
      SF   *Computer Sciences
           Data Processing
HD   Horizontal Distance
      SF   *Photography
HDC   Hydrogen Depolarized CO2 Concentrator
      SF   *Aeronautics
           Aviation Medicine
           *Biological and Medical Sciences
HDL   High Density Lipoprotein
      SF   Biochemistry
           *Biological and Medical Sciences
           Pharmacology
HDM   Hidrodensimeter
      SF   *Nuclear Sciences
           Reactors
HDX   Half Duplex
      SF   *Computer Sciences
           Data Processing
HE   Hall Effect
      SF   Armorphus Semiconductors
           Liquid Semiconductors
           *Non-crystalline Solids
HEAMF Hydroxyethylated Acid Modified Flour
      SF   *Agricultural Sciences
           Cereals
HEAO High Energy Astronomy Observatories
      SF   *Space Sciences
HEF   High Expansion Foam
      SF   *Aeronautics
           Airports
           Ground Equipment
HELMS Helicopter Multifunction System
      SF   *Aeronautics
           Radar Detection
HELOS Highly Eccentric Lunar Occultation
           Satellite
      SF   *Astronautics and Astrophysics
           Lunar Sciences
HEMAC Hybrid Electro Magnetic Antenna
           Couplers
      SF   *Communication Systems
           Navigation
HEPA High Efficiency Particulate Air
      SF   *Space Sciences
           Space Simulation
HET   Health Education Telecommunications
      SF   *Communication Systems

         *Telecommunications
HEW   Health Education and Welfare (US)
      SF   *Biological and Medical Sciences
           *General
HF   High Frequency
      SF   *Aeronautics
           *Communication Systems
           Navigation
HF   Hyperfine
      SF   *Biological and Medical Sciences
           Medical Ions
HFIR High Flux Isotope Reactor
      SF   *Nuclear Sciences
           Reactors
HEPS High Frequency Phase Shifter
      SF   Radio Engineering
           *Telecommunications
HFS   Hyperfine Structure
      SF   *Nuclear Sciences
           Radiation
HF-SCF Hartree-Fock Self-Consistent Field
      SF   *Nuclear Sciences
           Spectroscopy
HG   Horizon Grow
      SF   *Lunar Sciences
HGCA Home Grown Cereals Authority (US)
      SF   *Agricultural Sciences
           Cereals
HGLF High Grain Low Fibre
      SF   Cereals
           *Dairy Sciences
HGPRT Hypoxanthine Guanine Phosphoribosyl
           Transferase
      SF   *Biological and Medical Sciences
           Cytochemistry
HGT   Hypergeometric Group Testing
      SF   *Computer Sciences
           Data Processing
HGV   Heavy Goods Vehicle
      SF   *Transportation
HHMU Handheld Maneuvering Unit
      SF   *Space Sciences
           Space Simulation
HIC   Hybrid Integrated Circuits
      SF   *Telecommunications
HIP   Hot Isostatic Pressing
      SF   *Engineering
           Mechanical Engineering
HIPS High Impact Polystyrene
      SF   *Non-metallic Materials
           Polymers
HIR   Halden Internal Reports
      SF   *Computer Sciences
           *Nuclear Sciences
HIRF High Intensity Reciprocity Failure
      SF   *Photography
HIRIS High Resolution Interferometer
           Spectrometer
      SF   *Astronautics and Astrophysics
           *Geosciences

HIRL	High Intensity Runway Lights SF *Aeronautics Approach and Landing
HIRS	High Resolution Infrared Radiation Sounder SF *Photography

HIS	Honeywell Information System
	SF *Computer Sciences
	    Data Processing
	    *Information Retrieval Systems

HITS	Holloman Infrared Target Simulator SF *Aeronautics Testing
HK	Hexokinase SF *Biological and Medical Sciences Cytochemistry
HL	Hearing Level SF *Aeronautics Noise
HLA	Human Lymphocyte Antigens SF *Dairy Sciences
HLAD	Hearing Lookout Assist Device SF *Naval Sciences Navigation
HLH	Heavy Lift Helicopters SF *Aeronautics *Military Sciences
HLH	High Level Heating SF *Nuclear Sciences Reactors
HLL	High Level Language SF *Computer Sciences Data Processing
HLU	House Logic Unit SF *Computer Sciences Data Processing
HM	Higher Melting SF *Non-metallic Materials Polymers
HMC	High Moisture (Shelled) Corn SF *Dairy Sciences

HMC	Horizontal Motion Carriage
	SF *Engineering
	    Mechanical Engineering
	    Terramechanics

HMDS	Hexamethydisilazane SF *Chemistry Organic Chemistry
HMF	Hydroxymethylfuraldehyde SF *Agricultural Sciences Cereals
HML	Human Milk Lysozyme SF *Dairy Sciences
HMO	Hiickel-approximation Molecular Orbital SF *Photography

HMP	Hexose Monophosphate
	SF Biochemistry
	    *Biological and Medical Sciences
	    Pharmacology

HNED	Horizontal Null External Distance SF *Mathematics
HNTD	Highest Non-Toxic Dose SF *Biological and Medical Sciences Drugs
HO	High Order SF *Computer Sciences Data Processing
HOBOS	Homing Bomb System SF *Military Sciences
HOE	Height Of Eye SF *Naval Sciences Navigation

hp	High Pass
	SF *Communication Systems
	    Radio Engineering
	    *Electronics and Electrical
	    Engineering

HP	High Pressure SF *Metallurgy and Metallography Metalworks

HP	Horsepower
	SF *Electronics and Electrical
	    Engineering
	    *Mathematics

HP	Hydroxyproline SF *Agricultural Sciences *Dairy Sciences
HPA	High Power Amplifiers SF *Telecommunications
HPBW	Half Power Beamwidths SF *Astronautics and Astrophysics *Lunar Sciences
HPCS	High Pressure Core Spray System SF *Nuclear Sciences Reactors
HPD	Highest Posterior Density SF *Statistics
HPD	Horizontal Polar Diagram SF *Aeronautics Radar Beacon Systems
HPNS	High Pressure Nervous Syndrome SF *Biological and Medical Sciences

HPR	Halden Project Report
	SF *Computer Sciences
	    Data Processing
	    *Nuclear Sciences

HQ	Hydro-Quinone SF *Photography
HQO	Hydroxyquinoline Oxide SF Biochemistry *Biological and Medical Sciences

HR	Heart Rates
	SF *Aeronautics
	    Aviation Medicine
	    *Biological and Medical Sciences

HR	Hypersensitive SF *Agricultural Sciences
HRP	Horseradish Peroxidase SF *Biological and Medical Sciences

Cytochemistry

HRS   Hard Red Spring
    SF   *Agricultural Sciences
        Cereals

HRS   Host Resident Software
    SF   *Computer Sciences
        Data Processing

HRSEM High Resolution Scanning Electron
       Microscope
    SF   *Biological and Medical Sciences
        Cytochemistry

HRW   Hard Red Winter
    SF   *Agricultural Sciences
        Cereals

HS   Hard Stripping
    SF   *Agricultural Sciences

HS   Holographic Stereogram
    SF   *Photography

HSD   Horizontal Situation Display
    SF   *Aeronautics
        Navigation

HSG   Horizontal Sweep Generator
    SF   Radio Engineering
        *Telecommunications

HSGTC High Speed Ground Test Center
    SF   *Aeronautics
        *Communication Systems

HSI   Horizontal Situation Indicator
    SF   *Aeronautics
        Navigation

HSP   High Speed Printer
    SF   *Computer Sciences
        Data Processing

HSR   High Speed Reader
    SF   *Computer Sciences
        Data Processing

HSR   High Stocking Rate
    SF   *Agricultural Sciences

HSRI   Highway Safety Research Institute
    SF   *Engineering
        Safety Engineering
        *Transportation

HSST   Heavy Section Steel Technology
    SF   *Nuclear Sciences
        Pressure Boundaries

HST   Hypervelocity Shock Tunnel
    SF   *Aeronautics
        Dynamic Calibrators

HSTCO High Stability Temperature Compensated
       Crystal Oscillator
    SF   *Electronics and Electrical
        Engineering

HT   Homing Transponders
    SF   *Aeronautics
        Navigation

HT   Horizontal Tab
    SF   *Computer Sciences
        Data Processing

HT   HydroxyTryplamine
    SF   *Biological and Medical Sciences

Cytochemistry

HTA   Hypophysiotropic Area
    SF   *Biological and Medical Sciences

htap   Heat Tap
    SF   *Electronics and Electrical
        Engineering

HTC   Hematocrit
    SF   *Biological and Medical Sciences

HTGR   High Temperature Gas Cooled Reactor
    SF   *Engineering
        Mechanical Engineering
        *Nuclear Sciences

HTL   High Threshold Logic
    SF   *Electronics and Electrical
        Engineering
        Integrated Circuits

HTPB   Hydroxy Terminated Polybutadiene
    SF   *Non-metallic Materials

HTR   High Temperature Reactors
    SF   *Engineering
        Mechanical Engineering
        *Nuclear Sciences
        Reactors

HTSM   High Temperature Skim Milk
    SF   *Dairy Sciences

HUO   Head-Up-Display
    SF   *Aeronautics
        Avionics
        Displays

HV   Hardware Virtualizer
    SF   *Computer Sciences
        Data Processing

HV   Heating and Ventilating
    SF   *Metallurgy and Metallography
        Metalworks

HVAC   Heating Ventilating and Air
       Conditioning
    SF   *Metallurgy and Metallography
        Metalworks

HVAC   High Voltage Alternative Current
    SF   *Electronics and Electrical
        Engineering

HVC   High Velocity Clouds
    SF   *Astronautics and Astrophysics
        Lunar Sciences

HVD   High Velocity Detonation
    SF   *Chemistry
        *Military Sciences
        Physical Chemistry

HVE   Horizontal Vertex Error
    SF   *Nuclear Sciences
        Wire Chamber Spectrometer

HVG   High Voltage Generator
    SF   *Engineering
        *Telecommunications

HVIS   Hypervelocity Impact Symposium
    SF   *Aeronautics

HVOSM Highway Vehicle Object Simulation
       Model
    SF   *Engineering

```
            Structural Engineering
            *Transportation
HVRA   Heating and Ventilating Research
          Association
       SF   *Information Retrieval Systems
HVTS   Hypervelocity Techniques Symposium
       SF   *Aeronautics
HYLO   Hybrid Loran
       SF   *Aeronautics
            Navigation
```

I

IA   Intermediate Amplifier
    SF   *Aeronautics
       *Communication Systems
IAA   Indole Acetic Acid
    SF   *Agricultural Sciences
       Biochemistry
       *Biological and Medical Sciences
IABSE International Association of Bridge
       and Structural Engineering
    SF   Civil Engineering
       *Engineering
IADB   Inter American Development Bank
    SF   Banking
       *General
IAEA   International Atomic Energy Agency
    SF   *Engineering
       *Nuclear Sciences
IAEE   International Association of
       Earthquake Engineers
    SF   *Building
       Civil Engineering
       *Engineering
IAF   Initial Approach Fix
    SF   *Aeronautics
       Air Traffic Control
IAF   Instrument Approach Fix
    SF   *Aeronautics
       Navigation
IAF   International Astronautical Federation
    SF   *Nuclear Sciences
       *Space Sciences
IAL   International Aeradio Limited
    SF   *Aeronautics
IAMS   International Association of
       Microbiological Societies
    SF   *Agricultural Sciences
       *Biological and Medical Sciences
IANAP Interagency Noise Abatement Program
    SF   *Aeronautics
       Noise
IAOPA International Aircraft Owners'
       and Pilots' Associations
    SF   *Aeronautics
       Air Transport
IAR   Instruction Address Register

    SF   *Computer Sciences
IAS   Indicated Air Speed
    SF   *Aeronautics
       Approach and Landing
IAT   International Automatic Time
    SF   *Aeronautics
       Navigation
IATA   International Air Transport
       Association
    SF   *Aeronautics
       Air Transport
IAU   International Aeronautical Union
    SF   *Aeronautics
IBA   Indole Butyric Acid
    SF   *Agricultural Sciences
IBB   International Brotherhood of
       Bookbinders
    SF   Binding
       *Printing
IBM   International Business Machines
    SF   *Computer Sciences
       Data Processing
IBR   Infectious Bovine Rhinotracheitis
    SF   *Dairy Sciences
IBRD   International Bank for Reconstruction
       and Development
    SF   Banking
       Consultancy
       *General
IBTE   Imperial Board of Telecommunications
       of Ethiopia
    SF   *Telecommunications
IBY   International Book Year
    SF   *Copyright
IC   Input Circuit
    SF   Radio Engineering
       *Telecommunications
IC   Instrument Correction
    SF   *Aeronautics
       *Naval Sciences
       Navigation
IC   Integrated Circuits
    SF   *Communication Systems
       *Computer Sciences
       *Electronics and Electrical
       Engineering

IC   Internal Connection
        SF   *Electronics and Electrical
             Engineering
             Semiconductor Devices
IC   Internal Conversion
        SF   Electrons
             *Nuclear Sciences
ICA   Initial Cruise Altitude
        SF   *Aeronautics
ICA   Institute of Chartered Accountants
        SF   *Computer Sciences
             Data Processing
ICA   International Cartographic Association
        SF   Cartography
             *Photography
ICA   International Communication
        Association
        SF   *Computer Sciences
             Data Processing
ICAF   International Committee on
        Aeronautical Fatigue
        SF   *Aeronautics
ICAMRS International Civil Aviation Message
        Routing System
        SF   *Aeronautics
             *Communication Systems
ICAN   International Commission for Air
        Navigation
        SF   *Aeronautics
             Air Traffic Control
             Navigation
ICAO   International Civil Aviation
        Organization
        SF   *Aeronautics
             *Transportation
I-CAS   Independent Collision Avoidance
        System
        SF   *Aeronautics
             Avionics
ICBM   Inter Continental Ballistic Missiles
        SF   Air Force
             *Engineering
             *Military Sciences
ICC   Internal Conversion Coefficients
        SF   *Nuclear Sciences
             Radioactivity
ICC   International-Association of Cereal
        Chemistry
        SF   *Agricultural Sciences
             Cereals
ICC   International Chamber of Commerce
        SF   Industrial Property
             *Patents
ICC   International Computation Center
        (Rome)
        SF   *Computer Sciences
             Data Processing
ICC   Interstate Commerce Commission
        SF   *Transportation
ICCAIA International Coordinating Council

        of Aerospace Industries Association
        SF   *Space Sciences
ICCP   Institute for Certification of
        Computer Professionals
        SF   *Computer Sciences
ICCTM   Interstate Commerce Commission
        Transport Mobilization (US)
        SF   *Transportation
ICDH   Isocitrate Dehydrogenase
        SF   *Biological and Medical Sciences
             Medical Ions
ICE   Institution of Civil Engineers (UK)
        SF   *Engineering
ICES   Integrated Civil Engineering System
        SF   *Computer Sciences
             Data Processing
             *Engineering
ICF   International Contract Furnishings,
        Inc.
        SF   Industrial Property
             *Patents
ICFC   Industrial and Commercial Finance
        Corporation
        SF   *Computer Sciences
             Data Processing
ICG   Interactive Computer Graphics
        SF   *Computer Sciences
             Data Processing
ICHCA   International Cargo Handling
        Coordination Association
        SF   *Transportation
ICHTF   Low Cycle High Temperature Fatigue
        SF   *Aeronautics
             *Materials
ICIASF Instrumentation in Aerospace
        Simulation Facilities
        SF   *Astronautics and Astrophysics
             Systems
ICIP   International Conference on
        Information Processing
        SF   *Computer Sciences
             Data Processing
ICIREPAT International Cooperation in
        Information Retrieval Among
        Patent Officers
        SF   Industrial Properties
             *Patents
ICIS   Interdepartmental Committee on
        Internal Security
        SF   *General
ICL   International Computer Limited
        SF   *Computer Sciences
             Data Processing
             *Printing
ICM   Integral Charge-control Model
        SF   *Electronics and Electrical
             Engineering
             Solid-state Circuits
ICMSF   International Commission on
        Microbiological Specifications

for Foods
    SF *Agricultural Sciences
       *Dairy Sciences

ICO   Intercity Coin Offices
    SF   Radio Engineering
       *Telecommunications

ICP   Indicator Control Panel
    SF *Aeronautics
       Instruments

ICP   Inter-Connected Processing
    SF *Astronautics and Astrophysics

ICRP International Commission on
    Radiological Protection
    SF *Biological and Medical Sciences
       Radiopharmaceutics

ICS   Input Control Subsystem
    SF *Computer Sciences
       Data Processing

ICSC Interim Communications Committee
    Satellite
    SF *Communication Systems
       Telecommunications

ICSID International Council of Society of
    Industrial Design
    SF *Engineering

ICSMP International Continuous Systems
    Modeling Program
    SF *Computer Sciences

ICSU International Council of Scientific
    Unions
    SF *Biological and Medical Sciences

ICT   Interactive Control Table
    SF *Computer Sciences
       Data Processing

ICTP International Centre for Theoretical
    Physics
    SF *Physics

ID   Inner Diameter
    SF *General

ID   Inside Diameter
    SF *Mathematics

ID   Inside Dimension
    SF *Metallurgy and Metallography
       Metalworks

ID   Isotope Dilution-mass
    SF   Nuclear Measurements
       *Nuclear Sciences

IDA   Integrated Digital Avionics
    SF *Aeronautics
       Avionics

IDCAS Industrial Development Centre for
    Arab States
    SF *Copyright
       Patents

IDF   Intermediate Distribution Frame
    SF *Computer Sciences
       Data Processing

IDG   Integrated Drive Generator
    SF *Aeronautics
       *Electronics and Electrical

       Engineering

IDH   Isocitrate Dehydrogenase
    SF *Biological and Medical Sciences
       Cytochemistry

IDIIOM Information Display Incorporation
    Input Output Machine
    SF *Aeronautics
       Air Traffic Control
       Screen Display

IDIOT Instrumentation Digital On-line
    Transcriber
    SF *Computer Sciences
       Data Processing

IDM   Integral and Differential Monitoring
    SF   Radio Engineering
       *Telecommunications

IDOE International Decade of Ocean
    Exploration
    SF *Oceanography

IDP   Ionside Diphosphate
    SF *Biological and Medical Sciences
       Cytochemistry

IDP   Integrated Data Processing
    SF *Computer Sciences
       Data Processing

IDS   Integrated Data Store
    SF *Computer Sciences
       Data Processing

IDS   Interim Decay Storage
    SF *Nuclear Sciences
       Reactors

IDSCS Initial Defense Satellite
    Communications Systems
    SF *Aeronautics
       *Military Sciences
       *Space Sciences

IDW   Institut für Dokumentationswesen
    SF *Information Retrieval Systems

IEC   International Electrotechnical
    Commission
    SF *Electronics and Electrical
       Engineering
       *Engineering

IECG Interagency Emergency Coordinating
    Group
    SF *Transportation

IEE   Institution of Electrical Engineers
    SF *Communication Systems
       *Electronics and Electrical
       Engineering
       *Telecommunications

IEEE Institute of Electrical and Electronics
    Engineers
    SF *Communication Systems
       *Electronics and Electrical
       Engineering

IEIS Integrated Engine Instrument System
    SF *Aeronautics
       *Electronics and Electrical
       Engineering

IEP   Image Edge Profile
       SF   *Photography
IEP   Instrument for Evaluation of
          Pictures
       SF   *Photography
IEP   Isoelectric Point
       SF   Bioengineering
            *Biological and Medical Sciences
IEPB   Interagency Emergency Planning Board
       SF   *General
IEPC   Interagency Emergency Planning
          Committee
       SF   *General
IES   Internal Environmental Simulator
       SF   *Space Sciences
IETC   Interagency Emergency Transportation
          Committee
       SF   *Transportation
IF   Information Feedback
       SF   Radio Engineering
            *Telecommunications
IF   Intermediate Frequency
       SF   Radio Engineering
            *Telecommunications
IFALPA International Federation of Air Line
          Pilots' Association
IFATCA International Federation of Air
          Traffic Controllers' Association
       SF   *Aeronautics
            Air Traffic Control
IFF   Identification Friend or Foe
       SF   *Aeronautics
            Air Traffic Control
            Radar Beacon Systems
IFIA   International Federation of Inventors
          Association
       SF   Industrial Sciences
            *Patents
IFILE Interface File
       SF   *Computer Sciences
            Data Processing
IFIP   International Federation of
          Information Processing
       SF   *Computer Sciences
            Data Processing
IFL   Initial Flight Level
       SF   *Aeronautics
            Air Traffic Control
IFPI   International Federation of
          Photographic Industry
       SF   *Copyright
            *Photography
IFR   Instrument Flight Rules
       SF   *Aeronautics
            Instrument Flying
IFRB   International Frequency Registration
          Board
       SF   *Telecommunications
IFS   Interchange File Separator
       SF   *Computer Sciences

           Data Processing
IFT   Intermediate Frequency Transformer
       SF   *Communication Systems
            Radio Engineering
IFTC   International Film and Television
          Council
       SF   *Copyright
            Patents
IFYGL International Field Year for the
          Great Lakes
       SF   *Geosciences
            Environmental Monitoring
IGFET Insulated Gate Field Effect
          Transistor
       SF   *Electronics and Electrical
               Engineering
            Solid-state Circuits
IGIA   Interagency Group for International
          Aviation
       SF   *Aeronautics
            Air Traffic Control
            *Communication Systems
IGM   Intergalactic Medium
       SF   *Astronautics and Astrophysics
            *Lunar Sciences
IGN   National Geographic Institute
       SF   *Meteorology
            *Telecommunications
IGS   Information Generator System
       SF   *Engineering
            Instruments
IGS   Integrated Graphic System
       SF   *Computer Sciences
            *Electronics and Electrical
               Engineering
IGS   Interchange Group Separator
       SF   *Computer Sciences
            Data Processing
IGY   International Geophysical Year
       SF   *Astronautics and Astrophysics
            *Lunar Sciences
IH   Interaction Handler
       SF   *Computer Sciences
            Data Processing
IHD   International Hydrological Decade
       SF   Earthscience
            *Geosciences
IHP   Indicated Horsepower
       SF   *Mathematics
IHX   Intermediate Heat Exchanger
       SF   *Nuclear Sciences
            Reactors
IIB   International Patent Institute
       SF   Industrial Property
            *Patents
IID   Intermittently Integrated Doppler
       SF   *Oceanography
IIP   Instantaneous Impact Point
       SF   *Naval Sciences
            Navigation

IIRC Interrogation and Information
        Reception Circuits
      SF   Radio Engineering
           *Telecommunications
           Telephone Networks
IISLS Improved Interrogator Sidelobe
        Suppression
      SF   *Aeronautics
           Air Traffic Control
           Radar Beacon Systems
IITY Image Intensified Television
      SF   *Astronautics and Astrophysics
           *Biological and Medical Sciences
IL   Indication Lamps
      SF   *Electronics and Electrical
             Engineering
ILAAS Integrated Light Attack Avionics
        System
      SF   *Aeronautics
           Displays
ILAI International Literary and Artistic
        Association
      SF   *Copyright
ILC   Instruction Length Counter
      SF   *Computer Sciences
           Data Processing
ILF   Integrated Lift Fan
      SF   *Aeronautics
ILO   Injection Locked Oscillators
      SF   *Electronics and Electrical
             Engineering
ILP   International Logistics Program
      SF   Logistics
           *Military Sciences
ILS   Instrument Landing Systems
      SF   *Aeronautics
           Approach and Landing
           Instruments
ILS   Integrated Logistic Support
      SF   Automatic Support Systems
           *Engineering
           Testing
ILS-LOC Instrument Landing System Localizer
      SF   *Aeronautics
           *Communication Systems
IM   Inner Marker
      SF   *Aeronautics
           Instrument Flying
IM   Intermodulation
      SF   *Electronics and Electrical
             Engineering
           Solid-state Circuits
IM   Item Mark
      SF   *Computer Sciences
           Data Processing
IMC   Instrument Meteorological Conditions
      SF   *Aeronautics
           Human Factors
           Instruments
IMCO Intergovernmental Maritime

        Consultative Organization
      SF   *Naval Sciences
           Navigation
           *Telecommunications
IMD   Intermodulation Distortion
      SF   *Electronics and Electrical
             Engineering
           Solid-state Circuits
IME   International Magnetosphere Explorer
      SF   *Aeronautics
           *Space Sciences
IMF   Intermediate Moisture Food
      SF   *Agricultural Sciences
           Cereals
IMI   Improved Manned Intercepter
      SF   *Aeronautics
           *Military Sciences
IMP   Interface Message Processor
      SF   *Computer Sciences
           *Electronics and Electrical
             Engineering
IMP   Interplanetary Monitoring Platform
      SF   *Aeronautics
           *Communication Systems
           *Space Sciences
IMPATT IMPact Avalanche Transit Time
      SF   *Nuclear Sciences
           Microwave Oscillators
IMRAP Infrared Monochromatic Radiation
        Pyrometer
      SF   *Nuclear Sciences
IMS   Information Management System
      SF   *Computer Sciences
           Data Processing
IMS   International Magnetospheric Study
      SF   *Aeronautics
           *Electronics and Electrical
             Engineering
           *Space Sciences
IMU   Inertial Measurement Units
      SF   *Aeronautics
           Navigation
           Testing
in   Inch
      SF   *Mathematics
IN   Intranasally
      SF   *Dairy Sciences
INAA Instrumental Neutron Activation
        Analysis
      SF   *Lunar Sciences
INDOR Internuclear Double Resonance
      SF   *Biological and Medical Sciences
INS   Inertial Navigation System
      SF   *Aeronautics
           Navigation
           *Communication Systems
INS   Initial Water Solubles
      SF   *Agricultural Sciences
           Cereals
INTELSAT International Telecommunications

```
                Satellite
        SF  *Aeronautics
            *Communication Systems
            *Space Sciences
            *Telecommunications
INTERALIS International Advanced Life
            Information System
        SF  *Computer Sciences
            Data Processing
INTIPS Integrated Information Processing
        System
        SF  *Computer Sciences
            Data Processing
            *Information Retrieval Systems
INU     Inertial Navigation Unit
        SF  *Aeronautics
            Navigation
I/O     Input/Output
        SF  *Computer Sciences
            Data Processing
IOBS    Input Output Buffering System
        SF  *Computer Sciences
            Data Processing
IOC     Indirect Operating Cost
        SF  *General
IOC     Input Output Controller
        SF  *Computer Sciences
            Data Processing
IOC     Intergovernmental Oceanographic
            Commission
        SF  *Oceanography
IOCE    Input Output Control Elements
        SF  *Aeronautics
            Radar Equipment
            Transponders
IOCS    Input Output Control System
        SF  *Computer Sciences
            Data Processing
IOFC    Income Over Feed Cost
        SF  *Dairy Sciences
IOLS    Input Output Label System
        SF  *Computer Sciences
            Data Processing
IOM     Institute of Office Management
        SF  *Computer Sciences
            Data Processing
IOOP    Input Output Operation
        SF  *Computer Sciences
            Data Processing
IOP     Input Output Processor
        SF  *Aeronautics
            *Communication Systems
            *Computer Sciences
            Data Processing
IORB    Input Output Record Block
        SF  *Computer Sciences
            Data Processing
IOREQ   Input Output Request
        SF  *Computer Sciences
            Data Processing
```

```
IOS     International Organization of
            Standards
        SF  *Engineering
            Mechanical Engineering
            *Standards
IP      Imaginary Part
        SF  *Mathematics
IP      Imipramine
        SF  Biochemistry
            *Biological and Medical Sciences
IP      Inorganic Phosphorus
        SF  *Agricultural Sciences
IPA     International Publishers' Association
        SF  *Copyright
IPAD    Integrated Programs for Aerospace-
            Vehicle Design
        SF  *Aeronautics
            *Space Sciences
IPC     Intermittent Positive Control
        SF  *Aeronautics
            Air Traffic Control
            *Communication Systems
IPL     International Classification of
            Patents
        SF  *Copyright
IPF     Indicative Planning Figures
        SF  *Engineering
IPL     Information Processing Language
        SF  *Computer Sciences
            Data Processing
IPL     Initial Program Load
        SF  *Computer Sciences
            Data Processing
IPLA    Interstate Producers' Livestock
            Association (US)
        SF  *Agricultural Sciences
IPM     Input Position Map
        SF  *Computer Sciences
            Data Processing
IPMA    In-Plant Printing Management
            Association
        SF  *Printing
IPN     Initial Priority Number
        SF  *Computer Sciences
            Data Processing
IPNL    Integrated Perceived Noisiness Level
        SF  *Aeronautics
            Environmental Sciences
            Noise
IPO-A   Indolephenoloxidase
        SF  Biochemistry
            *Biological and Medical Sciences
IPQC    In Process Quality Control
        SF  *Engineering
            Instruments
IPS     Impact Polystyrene
        SF  *Non-metallic Materials
            Polymers
IPS     Inches Per Second
        SF  *Computer Sciences
```

Data Processing
IPSPS Inhibitory Post Synaptic Potentials
    SF   Cybernetics
        *Electronics and Electrical
          Engineering
        *Management
IPTM Interval Pulse Time Modulations
    SF   Radio Engineering
        *Telecommunications
IPTS International Practical Temperature
      Scale
    SF   *Physics
        Thermocouples
IPU Instruction Processing Unit
    SF   *Computer Sciences
        Data Processing
IR Infra Red
    SF   *Metallurgy and Metallography
        Welding
IR Intermediate Register
    SF   Radio Engineering
        *Telecommunications
        Telephone Network
IR Intraruminal
    SF   *Dairy Sciences
IRATE Interim Remote Area Terminal Equipment
    SF   *Aeronautics
        Approach and Landing
        Instruments
IRB Infinitely Rigid Beam
    SF   *Engineering
        Mechanical Engineering
IRHS Intact Reentry Heat Source
    SF   *Nuclear Sciences
        Reactors
IRIG Inter Range Instrument Group
    SF   *Aeronautics
        Instruments
        *Space Sciences
IRM Image Rejection Mixer
    SF   *Electronics and Electrical
          Engineering
IRM Isothermal Remnant Magnetization
    SF   *Lunar Sciences
IROS Increase Reliability Operational
      System
    SF   Logistics
        *Military Sciences
IRR-2 Israel Research Reactor-2
    SF   *Nuclear Sciences
        Reactors
IRS Infinitely Rigid System
    SF   *Engineering
        Mechanical Engineering
IRS Infrared Spectroscope
    SF   *Nuclear Sciences
IRS Infrared Spectroscopy
    SF   *Space Sciences
IRS Interchange Record Separator
    SF   *Computer Sciences

Data Processing
IS Information Separator
    SF   *Computer Sciences
        Data Processing
IS Isomer Shifts
    SF   *Nuclear Sciences
        Spectroscopy
ISA Interrupt Storage Area
    SF   *Computer Sciences
        Data Processing
ISAM Indexed Sequential Access Method
    SF   *Computer Sciences
        Data Processing
ISAT Interrupt Storage Area Table
    SF   *Computer Sciences
        Data Processing
ISC Initial Slope Circuit
    SF   Radio Engineering
        *Telecommunications
ISCC Inter Society Colour Council
    SF   *Photography
ISD Initial Selection Done
    SF   *Computer Sciences
        Data Processing
ISD Internal Symbol Dictionary
    SF   *Computer Sciences
        Data Processing
ISDS Integrated Ship Design System
    SF   *Computer Sciences
        Data Processing
ISEPS International Sun Earth Physics
      Programme
    SF   *Astronautics and Astrophysics
        Satellites
        *Space Sciences
ISETU International Secretariat of
      Entertainment Trade Unions
    SF   *Copyright
ISIS International Satellites for
      Ionospheric Studies
    SF   *Telecommunications
ISLS Improved Sidelobe Suppression
    SF   *Aeronautics
        Air Traffic Control
ISLS Interrogator Sidelobe Suppression
    SF   *Aeronautics
        Air Traffic Control
        Radar Beacon Systems
ISM Insulation System Modules
    SF   *Engineering
        Mechanical Engineering
ISO International Society for
      Photogrammetry
    SF   *Photography
ISO International Standards Organization
    SF   *Aeronautics
        *General
        *Standards
ISP Isolated Soy Flour
    SF   *Agricultural Sciences

```
                *Dairy Sciences
ISR    Image Storage Retrieval
       SF  *Computer Sciences
           *Information Retrieval Systems
ISR    Intersecting Storage Rings
       SF  *Biological and Medical Sciences
           *Nuclear Sciences
ISRO   Indian Space Research Organization
       SF  *Telecommunications
ISS    Image Sharpness Scale
       SF  *Photography
ISS    Ionosphere Sounding Satellite
       SF   Satellites
           *Telecommunications
ISTS   International Shock Tube Symposium
       SF  *Aeronautics
ISTVS  International Society for Terrain
         Vehicle Systems
       SF  *Engineering
           Mechanical Engineering
           Terramechanics
ISU    Inertial Sensor Unit
       SF  *Aeronautics
ISVD   Information System for Vocational
         Decisions
       SF  *Computer Sciences
           *Information Retrieval Systems
IT     Intratracheal
       SF  *Biological and Medical Sciences
ITA    Institut du Transport Aérien
       SF  *Aeronautics
           *Transportation
ITACS  Integrated Tactical Air Control
         System
       SF  *Aeronautics
           *Communication Systems
ITC    Interval Timer Control
       SF  *Computer Sciences
           Data Processing
ITE    Institute of Telecommunications
         Engineers
       SF  *Computer Sciences
           Data Processing
           *Telecommunications
ITE    Intercity Transportation Efficiency
       SF  *Transportation
ITF    Interactive Terminal Facility
       SF  *Computer Sciences
           Data Processing
ITL    Intergrate Transfer Launch
       SF   Air Force
           Civil Engineering
           *Engineering
           *Military Sciences
ITMJ   Incoming Trunk Message Junction
       SF   Radio Engineering
           *Telecommunications
           Telephone Networks
ITMT   Intermediate Thermomechanical
         Treatments
```

```
       SF  *Engineering
           Mechanical Engineering
           Metallic Materials
           *Metallurgy and Metallography
ITNS   Integrated Tactical Navigation
         System
       SF  *Aeronautics
           *Communication Systems
           Navigation
ITOS   Improved Tiros Operational Satellite
       SF  *Telecommunications
ITPR   Infrared Temperature Profile
         Radiometer
       SF  *Aeronautics
           *Communication Systems
ITR    In-core Thermionic Reactor
       SF  *Nuclear Sciences
           Reactors
ITRM   Inverse Thermoremnant Magnetization
       SF  *Astronautics and Astrophysics
           *Lunar Sciences
ITS    Invitation To Send
       SF  *Computer Sciences
           Data Processing
ITT    International Telephone and Telegraph
       SF  *Computer Sciences
           *Communication Systems
ITU    International Telecommunication Unit
       SF  *Aeronautics
           *Computer Sciences
           Data Processing
           *Telecommunications
IU     International Units
       SF  *General
IUCAF  Inter-Union Commission on Allocation
         of Frequency
       SF  *Telecommunications
IUCSTP Inter-Union Commission on Solar
         Terrestrial Physics
       SF  *Meteorology
           *Space Sciences
IUE    International Ultraviolet Explorer
       SF  *Space Sciences
           Spacecraft
IUPAC  International Union of Pure and
         Applied Chemistry
       SF  *Nuclear Sciences
IUS    Initial Upper Stage
       SF  *Aeronautics
           *Space Sciences
           Spacecraft
IUS    Interchange Unit Separator
       SF  *Computer Sciences
           Data Processing
IUV    Iata Unit of Value
       SF  *Aeronautics
           Air Transport
           Fares
IV     Intravascular Volume
       SF  *Biological and Medical Sciences
```

IVC   Intermediate Velocity Clouds
        SF *Astronautics and Astrophysics
            *Lunar Sciences
IVD   In Vitro Digestability
        SF *Agricultural Sciences
IVDMD   In Vitro Dry Matter Digestability
        SF *Agricultural Sciences
IVHM   In-Vessel Handling Machine
        SF *Nuclear Sciences
            Reactors
IVM   Initial Virtual Memory
        SF *Computer Sciences
            Data Processing
IVOMD   In Vitro Organic Matter Digestion
        SF *Agricultural Sciences
IW   Index Word
        SF *Computer Sciences
            Data Processing
IWG   International Writers Guild
        SF *Copyright

J

JANAIR Joint Army-Navy Aircraft
      Instrumentation Research (US)
    SF *Aeronautics
      Instruments
      *Military Sciences
JARC Joint Avionics Research Committee
    SF *Aeronautics
      Air Traffic Control
      Avionics
JATCRUs Joint Air Traffic Control Radar
      Units
    SF *Aeronautics
      Air Traffic Control
JATO Jet Assisted Take Off
    SF *Aeronautics
JCAE Joint Committee on Atomic Energy
    SF *Nuclear Sciences
      Nucleonics
JCASR Joint Committee on Avionics Systems
    Research
    SF *Aeronautics
      Avionics
JCC   Joint Communications Centre
    SF *Communication Systems
      *Computer Sciences
      Data Processing
JCC   Joint Control Centers
    SF *Aeronautics
      Air Traffic Control
      *Communication Systems
JCII Japan Camera Inspection Institute
    SF *Photography
JCL   Job Control Language
    SF *Computer Sciences
      Data Processing
      *Electronics and Electrical
        Engineering
JCS   Joint Chief of Staff
    SF *Military Sciences
JDES Joint Density of Electronic States
    SF Armorphous Semiconductors
      Liquid Semiconductors
      *Non-crystalline Solids
JDL   Job Descriptor Language
    SF *Computer Sciences

      Data Processing
JE   Junction Exchanges
    SF Radio Engineering
      *Telecommunications
JEN   Junta de Energia Nuclear (Sp.)
    SF *Nuclear Sciences
      Reactors
JEQ   Jump Equal
    SF *Computer Sciences
      Testing
JES   Job Entry Subsystem
    SF *Computer Sciences
      Data Processing
JFET Junction Field Effect Transistors
    SF *Computer Sciences
      *Electronics and Electrical
        Engineering
      Solid-state Circuits
JGA   Juxtaglomerular Apparatuses
    SF *Biological and Medical Sciences
JHD   Joint Hypocenter Determination
    SF *Geosciences
      *Oceanography
JNACC Joint Nuclear Accident Coordinating
    Center
    SF *Nuclear Sciences
      Radiation
JNE   Jump Not Equal
    SF *Computer Sciences
      Testing
JO   Junction Office
    SF Radio Engineering
      *Telecommunications
JOBS Job Opportunities in the Business
    Sector
    SF *Training
JOVIAL Jules Own Version of the
      International Algorithmic Language
    SF *Computer Sciences
      Data Processing
JPG   Job Proficiency Guide
    SF *General
JPL   Jet Propulsion Laboratory (US)
    SF *Space Sciences
      Space Simulation

JPNL   Judged Perceived Noise Level
        SF   *Aeronautics
             Environmental Sciences
             Noise
JSC   Johnson Space Center
        SF   *Space Sciences
JSL   Job Specification Language
        SF   *Computer Sciences
             Data Processing
JW   Junction Wide
        SF   Radio Engineering
             *Telecommunications

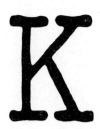

K

K	Kilo		SF	*Mathematics
	SF *Computer Sciences		KM	Kirchhoff Method
KA	Kynurenic Acid			SF *Communication Systems
	SF Biochemistry		KMER	Kodak Metal Etch Resist
	*Biological and Medical Sciences			SF *Photography
KB	Keyboard		KRP	Krebs Ringer Phosphate
	SF *Computer Sciences			SF *Agricultural Sciences
	*General		KSR	Keyboard Sent Receive
KB	Kilobits			SF *Computer Sciences
	SF *Computer Sciences			Data Processing
KB	Kilobytes		KTFR	Kodak Thin Film Resist
	SF *Computer Sciences			SF *Photography
kcal	Kilocalorie		KTSP	Knots True Air Speed
	SF *Mathematics			SF *Aeronautics
kc/s	Kilocycle per Second			Aircraft Noise
	SF *Communication Systems		KUR	Kyoto University Reactor
	Radio Engineering			SF *Nuclear Sciences
KD	Knocked Down		kv	Kilovolts
	SF *Metallurgy and Metallography			SF *Communication Systems
	Metalworks			Radio Engineering
KDS	Keydata Station		kW	Kilowatt
	SF *Computer Sciences			SF *Communication Systems
	Data Processing			Mathematics
KE	Kitchen Exhaust		KWAC	Keyword And Context
	SF *Metallurgy and Metallography			SF *Computer Sciences
	Metalworks		KWIC	Keyword In Context
KEAS	Knots Equivalent Air Speed			SF *Computer Sciences
	SF *Aeronautics			Data Processing
	Aircraft		KWIT	Keyword In Title
KeV	Kilovolts			SF *Computer Sciences
	SF *Electronics and Electrical			Data Processing
	Engineering		KWOC	Keyword Out of Context
	Lasers and Masers			SF *Computer Sciences
kg	Kilogramme			Data Processing
	SF *Mathematics			
KHN	Knoop Hardness Number			
	SF *Ceramics			
KIAS	Knots Indicated Air Speed			
	SF *Aeronautics			
	Aircraft Noise			
kl	Kilolitre			
	SF *Mathematics			
KLH	Keyhole Limpet Haemocyanin			
	SF *Biological and Medical Sciences			
km	Kilometre			

L

La   Lactic Acid
      SF *Agricultural Sciences
LAC   Lunar Aeronautical Charts
      SF *Aeronautics
          Navigation
LACES London Airport Cargo EDP System
      SF *Computer Sciences
          Data Processing
LAD   Leaf Area Duration
      SF *Agricultural Sciences
LAD   Lookout Assist Device
      SF *Aeronautics
          Navigation
LAFTA Latin American Free Trade Association
      SF *Copyright
          Marks
          Patents
LAHS Low Altitude High-Speed
      SF *Aeronautics
          Navigation
LAI   Leaf Area Index
      SF *Agricultural Sciences
LAMA Locomotive and Allied Manufacturers
          Association
      SF *Metallurgy and Metallography
          Welding
LAMS Load Alleviation and Mode
          Stabilization
      SF   Aerodynamics
          *Aeronautics
LAMSAC Local Authorities Management Services
          and Computer Committee
      SF *Computer Sciences
          Data Processing
LAREC Los Alamos Reactor Economics Code
      SF *Nuclear Sciences
          Reactors
LARS London Airways Radar Station
      SF *Aeronautics
          Radar Beacon Systems
LAS   Li Aluminosilicate
      SF *Ceramics
LAS   Line Apparatus Shops
      SF   Radio Engineering
          *Telecommunications

LASA Large Aperture Seismic Array
      SF *Oceanography
          Radar
          Seismic Detection
LASER Light Amplification by Stimulated
          Emission of Radiation
      SF *Computer Sciences
          Data Processing
LAT   Laser Acquisition and Tracking
      SF *Aeronautics
          *Communication Systems
LATCC London Air Traffic Control Centre
      SF *Aeronautics
          Air Traffic Control
LAW   Light Antitank Weapon
      SF   Explosives
          *Military Sciences
LAWDS Loran-inertial Aided Weapon Delivery
          System
      SF *Geosciences
          Navigation
LB   Line Buffer
      SF *Computer Sciences
          Data Processing
lb   Pound
      SF *Mathematics
LBCM Locator at the Back Course Marker
      SF *Aeronautics
          Instrument Flying
LBG   Locust Bean Gum
      SF *Dairy Sciences
LBNP Lower Body Negative Pressure
      SF   Aviation Medicine
          *Biological and Medical Sciences
LBTS Land Based Test Site
      SF *Computer Sciences
          Data Processing
LC   Lower Case
      SF *Computer Sciences
          Data Processing
LC   Lyman Continuum
      SF *Astronautics and Astrophysics
          *Biological and Medical Sciences
LCAO Linear Combination of Atomic Orbitals
      SF *Physics

LCB   Line Control Block
       SF   *Computer Sciences
            Data Processing
LCC   Lead Coated Copper
       SF   *Metallurgy and Metallography
            Metalworks
LCE   Land Covered Earth
       SF   *Geosciences
            *Meteorology
LCF   Low Cycle Fatigue
       SF   *Aeronautics
            *Materials
LCL   Library Control Language
       SF   *Aeronautics
            Avionics
LCL   Low Capacity Link
       SF   *Communication Systems
            Radio Engineering
lcl   Lowest Car Load
       SF   *Transportation
LCLU   Land Control and Logic Units
       SF   *Aeronautics
            Air Traffic Control
LCRU   Landing Craft Retriever Unit
       SF   Logistics
            *Military Sciences
LCRU   Lunar Communications Relay Unit
       SF   *Lunar Sciences
            *Telecommunications
LCS   Laboratory Computer Silence
       SF   *Computer Sciences
            Data Processing
LCS   Large Capacity Store
       SF   *Computer Sciences
            Data Processing
LCS   Large Core Storage
       SF   *Computer Sciences
            *Information Retrieval Systems
LCT   Linear Combination Technique
       SF   Gamma-ray Analysis
            *Nuclear Sciences
LCW   Line Control Word
       SF   *Computer Sciences
            Data Processing
LD   Lethal Dose
       SF   *Biological and Medical Sciences
            Drugs
LD   Liftover Drag
       SF   *Aeronautics
            Soaring
LD   Low Density
       SF   *Computer Sciences
            Data Processing
LDA   Localizer Directional Aid
       SF   *Aeronautics
            Instrument Flying
LDF   Linear Discriminate Function
       SF   *Nuclear Sciences
            Reactors
LDH   Lactate Dehydrogenase

       SF   *Agricultural Sciences
            *Biological and Medical Sciences
LDH   Lactic Dehydrogenase
       SF   Biochemistry
            *Biological and Medical Sciences
            Cytochemistry
LDH-A Lactate Dehydrogenase A
       SF   *Biological and Medical Sciences
LDH-B Lactate Dehydrogenase B
       SF   *Biological and Medical Sciences
LDL   Low Density Lipoprotein
       SF   Biochemistry
            *Biological and Medical Sciences
            Pharmacology
LDPE   Low Density Polyethylene
       SF   *Non-metallic Materials
            Polymers
LE   Large End
       SF   *Metallurgy and Metallography
            Metalworks
LE   Leading Edge
       SF   *Computer Sciences
            Data Processing
LE   Logic Element
       SF   Radio Engineering
            *Telecommunications
LED   Light Emitting Diodes
       SF   *Computer Sciences
            *Electronics and Electrical
              Engineering
            Instruments
LEED   Low Energy Electron Diffraction
       SF   Nuclear Instruments
            *Nuclear Sciences
            *Physics
LEFM   Linear Elastic Fracture Mechanics
       SF   *Metallurgy and Metallography
            Welding
LEM   Laser Exhaust Measurement
       SF   Civil Engineering
            *Engineering
LEM   Lunar Excursion Module
       SF   *Astronautics and Astrophysics
            Navigation
LES   Launch Escape System
       SF   *Space Sciences
            Spacecraft
LES   Light Emitting Switch
       SF   *Electronics and Electrical
              Engineering
            Solid-state Circuits
LES   Light Exposure Speed
       SF   *Photography
LESC   Light Emitting Switch Control
       SF   *Electronics and Electrical
              Engineering
            Solid-state Circuits
LEST   Low Energy Speed Transmission
       SF   *Aeronautics
            Navigation

LET　Launch Escape Tower
　　　SF　*Space Sciences
　　　　　　Spacecraft
LET　Leading Edge Trigger
　　　SF　Gamma Rays
　　　　　　*Nuclear Sciences
LET　Linear Energy Transfer
　　　SF　*Space Sciences
LF　Limiting Fragmentation
　　　SF　Elementary Particles
　　　　　　*Physics
LF　Line Feed
　　　SF　*Computer Sciences
　　　　　　Data Processing
LF　Logic Function
　　　SF　Radio Engineering
　　　　　　*Telecommunications
LF　Low Frequency
　　　SF　*Aeronautics
　　　　　　*Communication Systems
　　　　　　Navigation
LFCM　Low Frequency Cross Modulation
　　　SF　*Electronics and Electrical
　　　　　　　　Engineering
　　　　　　Solid-state Circuits
LFFET　Low Frequency Field Effect Transistors
　　　SF　*Electronics and Electrical
　　　　　　　　Engineering
　　　　　　Solid-state Circuits
LFM　Limited-area Fine-mesh Model
　　　SF　*Meteorology
LFPS　Low Frequency Phase Shifter
　　　SF　Radio Engineering
　　　　　　*Telecommunications
LFS　Logical File Structure
　　　SF　*Computer Sciences
　　　　　　Data Processing
LG　Line Graph
　　　SF　*Mathematics
LG　Linear Gate
　　　SF　*Electronics and Electrical
　　　　　　　　Engineering
LG　Linkage Groups
　　　SF　*Biological and Medical Sciences
　　　　　　Cytochemistry
LGS　Landing Guidance System
　　　SF　*Aeronautics
　　　　　　Approach and Landing
　　　　　　Avionics
LGV　Large Granular Vesicles
　　　SF　*Biological and Medical Sciences
　　　　　　Cytochemistry
LGV　Lymphogranuloma Venereu
　　　SF　*Biological and Medical Sciences
　　　　　　Clinical Medicine
LH　Left Hand
　　　SF　*Metallurgy and Metallography
　　　　　　Metalworks
LH　Linear Hybrid
　　　SF　*Electronics and Electrical

　　　　　　Engineering
LH　Locating Head
　　　SF　Civil Engineering
　　　　　　Construction Engineering
　　　　　　*Engineering
LH　Luteal Hormone
　　　SF　*Dairy Sciences
LH　Luteinizing Hormone
　　　SF　*Biological and Medical Sciences
　　　　　　*Dairy Sciences
LHA　Local Hour Angle
　　　SF　*Aeronautics
　　　　　　Navigation
LHC　Left Hand Circular
　　　SF　*Aeronautics
　　　　　　*Communication Systems
LHSV　Liquid Hourly Space Velocity
　　　SF　Chemical Engineering
　　　　　　*Engineering
LIA　Lysine Iron Agar
　　　SF　*Dairy Sciences
LIC　Linear Integrated Circuit
　　　SF　*Communication Systems
　　　　　　*Electronics and Electrical
　　　　　　　　Engineering
　　　　　　Radio Engineering
LICCD　International League Against Unfair
　　　　　Competition
　　　SF　Industrial Property
　　　　　　*Patents
LiF　Lithium Fluoride
　　　SF　*Electronics and Electrical
　　　　　　　　Engineering
LIFE　League for International Food
　　　　　Education
　　　SF　*Agricultural Sciences
LIFO　Last In First Out
　　　SF　*Computer Sciences
　　　　　　Data Processing
LIL　Large Ionic Lithophile
　　　SF　*Biological and Medical Sciences
　　　　　　*Lunar Sciences
LIOD　Laser Inflight Obstacle Detector
　　　SF　*Aeronautics
　　　　　　Lasers
LIRF　Low-Intensity Reciprocity Failure
　　　SF　*Photography
LISP　List Processor
　　　SF　*Computer Sciences
　　　　　　Data Processing
LLD　Low Level Discriminator
　　　SF　*Electronics and Electrical
　　　　　　　　Engineering
　　　　　　Photomultipliers
LLFM　Low Level Flux Monitors
　　　SF　*Nuclear Sciences
　　　　　　Reactors
LLH　Low Level Heating
　　　SF　*Nuclear Sciences
　　　　　　Reactors

LLLTV Low Light Level Television
    SF   *Aeronautics
LM   Light Microscope
    SF   *Biological and Medical Sciences
        Cytochemistry
LM   Linear Monolithic
    SF   *Electronics and Electrical
        Engineering
LM   Lower Melting
    SF   *Non-metallic Materials
        Polymers
LM   Lunar Module
    SF   *Lunar Sciences
       *Space Sciences
       Space Simulation
LMC Large Megallanic Cloud
    SF   *Astronautics and Astrophysics
       *Lunar Sciences
LME Light Mitochondrial Extract
    SF   *Biological and Medical Sciences
LMEC Liquid Metal Engineering Center (US)
    SF   *Engineering
       *Nuclear Sciences
       Reactors
LMFBR Liquid Metal-cooled Fast Breeder
    Reactor
    SF   Fuels
       *Nuclear Sciences
       Reactors
LMP Lunar Module Pilot
    SF   *Astronautics and Astrophysics
       Navigation
LNF Liposoluble Neutral Fraction
    SF   *Biological and Medical Sciences
LNFB Linear Negative Feedback
    SF   Radio Engineering
       *Telecommunications
LNG Liquefied Natural Gas
    SF   *Aeronautics
       *Engineering
       Fuels
       *Nuclear Sciences
       Reactors
       *Transportation
LNPK Limestone Nitrogen Phosphorus and
    Potassium
    SF   *Agricultural Sciences
LNR Low Noise Receivers
    SF   *Telecommunications
LO   Local Oscillator
    SF   *Nuclear Sciences
       Proton Target
LO   Low Order
    SF   *Computer Sciences
       Data Processing
LOBAT Lunar Orbiter Block Triangulation
    SF   *Engineering
       Photometric Engineering
LOC Localizer
    SF   *Aeronautics

       Approach and Landing
       Navigation
LOCA Loss of Coolant Accident
    SF   *Nuclear Sciences
       Reactors
LOD Locally One Dimensional
    SF   Civil Engineering
       *Engineering
LOD Location Dependent
    SF   *Computer Sciences
       Data Processing
LOM Locator at the Outer Marker
    SF   *Aeronautics
       Instrument Flying
LOP Line of Position
    SF   *Aeronautics
       Navigation
LOS Loss Of Signal
    SF   *Computer Sciences
       Data Processing
LOSAT Lunar Orbiter Satellite
    SF   *Engineering
       *Lunar Sciences
       Photogrametric Engineering
LOW Low [Core Threshold]
    SF   *Computer Sciences
       Data Processing
LP   Line Printer
    SF   *Computer Sciences
       Data Processing
LP   Linear Programming
    SF   *Computer Sciences
       Data Processing
LP   Low Pass
    SF   *Computer Sciences
       *Electronics and Electrical
         Engineering
       Radio Engineering
LP   Low Pressure
    SF   *Metallurgy and Metallography
       Metalworks
LPA Linear Pulse Amplifier
    SF   *Communication Systems
LPA Link Pack Area
    SF   *Computer Sciences
       Data Processing
LPA Log Periodic Antennas
    SF   *Telecommunications
LPC Laboratory Pasteurized Count
    SF   *Agricultural Sciences
       *Dairy Sciences
LPC Least Preferred Coworker
    SF   *Behavioural Sciences
       Psychology
LPCI Low Pressure Coolant Injection
    System
    SF   *Nuclear Sciences
       Reactors
LPD Landing Point Designator
    SF   *Aeronautics

Navigation

LPD   Linear Phasing Device
       SF   Radio Engineering
              *Telecommunications
LPE   Loop Preparation Equipment
       SF   *Nuclear Sciences
              Reactors
LPF   Low Pass Filter
       SF   Radio Engineering
              *Telecommunications
LPG   Liquified Petroleum Gas
       SF   *Transportation
LPIU Lithographers and Photoengravers
       International Union
       SF   *Printing
LPL   Lipoprotein Lipase
       SF   *Dairy Sciences
LPL   Lipoprotein Lipid
       SF   Biochemistry
              *Biological and Medical Sciences
              Pharmacology
LPL   List Processing Language
       SF   *Computer Sciences
              *Information Retrieval Systems
LPM   Lines Per Minute
       SF   *Computer Sciences
              Data Processing
LPM   Lunar Portable Magnetometer
       SF   *Astronautics and Astrophysics
              Lunar Sciences
LPRE Liquid Propellant Rocket Engines
       SF   *Engineering
              Mechanical Engineering
LPS   Line Per Second
       SF   *Computer Sciences
              Data Processing
LPS   Linear Pulse Sector
       SF   *Communication Systems
              Data Recording
LPTB London Passenger Transport Board
       SF   *Transportation
LR   Landing Radar
       SF   *Aeronautics
              Navigation
LR   Living Room
       SF   *Building
LRBA Laboratoire de Recherches Balistiques
       et Aerodynamiques (Fr.)
       SF   *Aeronautics
              Hypersonic Facilities
LRC   Longitudinal Redundancy Check
       SF   *Computer Sciences
              Data Processing
LRC   Long Range Cruise Speed
       SF   *Aeronautics
              Aircraft
LRL   Lawrence Radiation Laboratory (US)
       SF   *Nuclear Sciences
              Reactors
LRL   Lunar Receiving Laboratory

       SF   *Astronautics and Astrophysics
              *Lunar Sciences
LRMTS Laser Rangefinder and Marked Target
       Seeker
       SF   *Aeronautics
              Avionics
              *Military Sciences
LRPA Long Range Patrol Aircraft
       SF   *Aeronautics
              Navigation
LRRS Long Range Radar Site
       SF   *Aeronautics
              Navigation
              Radar
LRS   Laser Raman Scattering
       SF   *Chemistry
              Physical Chemistry
LRS   Log and Reporting System
       SF   *Computer Sciences
              Data Processing
LRU   Least Recently Used
       SF   *Computer Sciences
              Data Processing
LRU   Line Replacement Union
       SF   *Aeronautics
              Aircraft
LRV   Lunar Roving Vehicle
       SF   *Astronautics and Astrophysics
              *Engineering
              Mechanical Engineering
LSAI Leaf Stem Area Index
       SF   *Agricultural Sciences
LSB   Least Significant Bit
       SF   *Computer Sciences
              Data Processing
lsb   Lower Side-Band
       SF   *Communication Systems
              Radio Engineering
LSD   Language for Systems Development
       SF   *Computer Sciences
LSD   Large Screen Display
       SF   *Aeronautics
              Air Traffic Control
LSD   Last Significant Digit
       SF   *Computer Sciences
              Data Processing
LSD   Lysergic Acid Diethylamide
       SF   *Biological and Medical Sciences
LSD   Lysergic Acid Diethylamine
       SF   *Biological and Medical Sciences
              Neutrotransmitters
LSE   Longitudinal Section Electric
       SF   *Electronics and Electrical
              Engineering
LSF   Lumped Selection Filters
       SF   Radio Engineering
              *Telecommunications
LSFO Logistics Support Field Office
       SF   *Military Sciences
              *Transportation

LSI   Large Scale Integration
        SF *Computer Sciences
            Data Processing
            *Electronics and Electrical
             Engineering
LSIC   Large Scale Integrated Circuits
        SF *Electronics and Electrical
             Engineering
LSIG   Line Scan Image Generator
        SF *Photography
LSI-MOS Large Scale Integration of Metal
            Oxide Silicon
        SF *Aeronautics
            Navigation
LSL   Ladder Static Logic
        SF *Electronics and Electrical
             Engineering
            *Engineering
            Mechanical Engineering
LSM   Longitudinal Section Magnetic
        SF *Electronics and Electrical
             Engineering
LSM   Lunar Surface Magnetometer
        SF *Astronautics and Astrophysics
            *Lunar Sciences
LSPET   Lunar Sample Preliminary Examination
            Team
        SF *Lunar Sciences
LSQA   Local System Queue Area
        SF *Computer Sciences
            Data Processing
LSR   Low Stocking Rate
        SF *Agricultural Sciences
LSS   Lunar Soil Simulator
        SF *Astronautics and Astrophysics
            *Engineering
            *Lunar Sciences
            Terramechanics
LST   Large Space Telescopes
        SF *Astronautics and Astrophysics
            *Communication Systems
            *Space Sciences
LT   Less Than
        SF *Computer Sciences
            Data Processing
lt   Lower Tension
        SF *Communication Systems
            Radio Engineering
LTA   Lighter Than Air
        SF Logistics
            *Military Sciences
LTE   Local Thermodynamic Equilibrium
        SF *Astronautics and Astrophysics
            *Lunar Sciences
LTH   Low Temperature Herschel
        SF *Photography
LTMR   Laser Target Marker Ranger
        SF *Aeronautics
            Avionics
LTP   Long Tailed Pair

        SF *Electronics and Electrical
             Engineering
            Solid-state Circuits
LTR   Long Term Revitalization
        SF *Building
LTRS   Letters Shift
        SF *Computer Sciences
            Data Processing
LTU   Line Termination Units
        SF *Computer Sciences
            Data Processing
luf   Lower Usable Frequency
        SF *Communication Systems
            Radio Engineering
luhf   Lower Usable High Frequency
        SF *Communication Systems
            Radio Engineering
LUNR   Land Use and Natural Resources
        SF Civil Engineering
            *Engineering
LUT   Launcher Umbilical Tower
        SF *Astronautics and Astrophysics
            *Space Sciences
LVD   Low Velocity Detonation
        SF *Chemistry
            Physical Chemistry
LVDT   Linear Variable Differential
            Transformer
        SF *Agricultural Sciences
            *Electronics and Electrical
             Engineering
            *Lunar Sciences
            *Nuclear Sciences
            Reactors
LVDT   Linear Voltage Differential
            Transformer
        SF Non-destructive Evaluation
            *Nuclear Sciences
LVL   Low Velocity Layer
        SF *Biological and Medical Sciences
LVRJ   Low Volume Ram Jet
        SF *Aeronautics
            Aircraft
            *Military Sciences
            *Naval Sciences
LWF   Light Weight Fighter
        SF *Aeronautics
            *Military Sciences
LWR   Light Water Reactor
        SF *Nuclear Sciences
            Reactors
LY   Lysosomes
        SF *Biological and Medical Sciences
LZT   Lead Zirconate Titanate
        SF *Metallurgy and Metallography
            Welding

M

M Magnetron
 SF *Electronics and Electrical
   Engineering
M Mega
 SF *Computer Sciences
   Data Processing
M Milli
 SF *Computer Sciences
   Data Processing
M Millimeter
 SF *Computer Sciences
   Data Processing
M Mira
 SF *Astronautics and Astrophysics
   *Lunar Sciences
MA Main Amplifier
 SF *Communication Systems
MA Matched Angles
 SF *Metallurgy and Metallography
   *Metalworks
MA Mass Analyzer
 SF *Astronautics and Astrophysics
   *Lunar Sciences
MA Methyl Acrylate
 SF *Non-metallic Materials
   Polymers
MA Milliammeter
 SF *Electronics and Electrical
   Engineering
   Meters
MA Moving Average
 SF *Mathematics
MA Multi-channel Analyser
 SF *Electronics and Electrical
   Engineering
MAA Macroaggregates
 SF *Biological and Medical Sciences
   Radiopharmaceutical
MAACS Multi-Address Asynchronous
   Communication System
 SF Radio Engineering
   *Telecommunications
MAB Monomethylaminoazobenzene
 SF Biochemistry
   *Biological and Medical Sciences

MABS Maritime Application Bridge System
 SF *Naval Sciences
   Navigation
   Radar
MAC Mean Aerodynamic Chord
 SF Aerodynamics
   *Aeronautics
   Aircraft
MAC Military Aircraft Command
 SF *Aeronautics
   *Military Sciences
   *Transportation
MAC Multi Access Computer
 SF *Aeronautics
   *Computer Sciences
   Data Processing
MACDAC Machine Communication with Digital
   Automatic Computer
 SF *Computer Sciences
   Data Processing
MACDACSYS MACDAC System
 SF *Computer Sciences
   Data Processing
MACS Multi-purpose Acquisition Control
   System
 SF *Engineering
   Instruments
MAD Machine ANSI Data
 SF *Computer Sciences
   Data Processing
MAD Magnetic Azimuth Detector
 SF *Aeronautics
   Navigation
MAD Mass Analyzer Detector
 SF *Astronautics and Astrophysics
   *Lunar Sciences
MADGE Microwave Aircraft Digital Guided
   Equipment
 SF *Aeronautics
MAFWPB Minimum Acceptable Flour for White
   Pan-Bread Production
 SF *Agricultural Sciences
   Cereals
MALS Minimum Intensity Approach Light
   System

```
        SF   *Aeronautics
             Approach and Landing
MAM    Methylazoxymethanol
        SF   *Biological and Medical Sciences
MAMAc  Methylazoxymethanol Acetate
        SF   Biochemistry
             *Biological and Medical Sciences
MANOVA Multivariate Analysis of Variance
        SF   *Mathematics
MAO    Manoamine Oxidase
        SF   *Biological and Medical Sciences
             Neutrotransmitters
MAP    Macro Assembly Program
        SF   *Computer Sciences
             Data Processing
MAP    Message Acceptance Pulse
        SF   *Computer Sciences
             Data Processing
MAP    Military Assistance Program
        SF   Civil Engineering
             *Engineering
             *Military Sciences
MAP    Minimum Audible Pressure
        SF   *Aeronautics
             Noise
MAP    Missed Approach Point
        SF   *Aeronautics
             Approach and Landing
MAP    Monoammonium Phosphate
        SF   *Agricultural Sciences
MAR    Memory Address Register
        SF   *Computer Sciences
             Data Processing
MAR    Minimal Angle of Resolution
        SF   *Aeronautics
             Navigation
MARAD  Maritime Administration
        SF   *Naval Sciences
             *Transportation
MARK   Management Ability and Reprographic
             Know-how
        SF   *Printing
MARR   Marine Accidents Requiring Rescue
        SF   *Naval Sciences
             Navigation
MARS   Market Analysis Research System
        SF   *Management
MARS   Multi Access Retrieval System
        SF   Business Systems
             *Management
MARSAT Maritime Satellite
        SF   *Astronautics and Astrophysics
             Satellites
MARV   Multi-element Articulated Research
             Vehicle
        SF   *Engineering
             Mechanical Engineering
             Terramechanics
MAS    Metal Aluminium Oxide
        SF   *Electronics and Electrical
```

```
             Engineering
             Solid-state Circuits
MAS    Middle Airspace
        SF   *Aeronautics
             Air Traffic Control
MAS    Military Alert System
        SF   *Military Sciences
             *Transportation
MASSTER Mobile Army Sensor Systems Test
             Evaluation and Review
        SF   *Aeronautics
             *Military Sciences
             Navigation
MAST   Military Assistance for Safety and
             Traffic
        SF   *Military Sciences
             *Transportation
MAT    Micro Alloy Transistor
        SF   *Computer Sciences
             Data Processing
MAT    Mobile Assistance Team
        SF   *Transportation
MA-TPM Maritime Administration Transportation
             Planning Mobilization (US)
        SF   *Transportation
MATS   Military Air Transport Service
        SF   *Aeronautics
             *Military Sciences
             *Transportation
MATZ   Military Aerodrome Traffic Zone
        SF   *Aeronautics
             *Military Sciences
MAU    Marine Amphibious Unit
        SF   *Aeronautics
             *Naval Sciences
MAWS   Mobile Aircraft Weighing System
        SF   *Aeronautics
             Instruments
max    Maximum
        SF   *Mathematics
MB     Magnetron Branch
        SF   *Electronics and Electrical
             Engineering
MB     Mixing Box
        SF   *Metallurgy and Metallography
             Metalworks
MBF    Molecular Beam Facility
        SF   *Astronautics and Astrophysics
             *Lunar Sciences
MBFR   Mutual and Balanced Force Reduction
        SF   *Military Sciences
MBO    Management By Objective
        SF   *Management
MBP    Mechanical Balance Package
        SF   *Aeronautics
             Wind-tunnel
MBS    Multiple Batch Station
        SF   *Computer Sciences
             Data Processing
MBU    Memory Buffer Unit
```

SF   *Computer Sciences
    Data Processing

MC   Main Channel
    SF   *Engineering
      Radio Engineering
      *Telecommunications

MC   Mast Cells
    SF   *Biological and Medical Sciences
      Cytochemistry

MC-A   Modified Conventional - Alloy
    SF   *Nuclear Sciences
      Thermocouples

MCA   Multichannel Analyzer
    SF   *Electronics and Electrical
        Engineering

MCAR   Machine Check Analysis and Recording
    SF   *Computer Sciences
      Data Processing

MCC   Mini-channel Communications Control
    SF   *Computer Sciences
      Data Processing

MCC   Mixing Cross-bar Connectors
    SF   Radio Engineering
      *Telecommunications

MCC   Modern Cereal Chemistry
    SF   *Agricultural Sciences
      Milling

MCC-H   Mission Control Center - Houston
    SF   *Astronautics and Astrophysics
      Navigation

MCD   Magnetic Circular Dichroic
    SF   *Biological and Medical Sciences
      Metal Ions

MCD   Magnetic Circular Dichromism
    SF   Instruments
      Optics
      *Physics

MCF   Mutual Coherence Function
    SF   *Aeronautics
      Lasers and Masers

MCH   Machine Check Handler
    SF   *Computer Sciences
      Data Processing

MCI   Microwave Communications, Inc. (US)
    SF   *Communication Systems

MCL   Mathematics Computation Laboratory
    (US)
    SF   *Transportation

MCM   Moving Coil Motor
    SF   *Computer Sciences

MCP   Master Control Program
    SF   *Computer Sciences
      Data Processing

MCP   Message Control Program
    SF   *Computer Sciences
      Data Processing

MCP   Microchannel Plate
    SF   *Biological and Medical Sciences

MCP   Military Construction Program
    SF   Civil Engineering

      *Engineering
      *Military Sciences

MCPHA   Multichannel Pulse Height Analyzer
    SF   Measurements
      *Nuclear Sciences

MCR   Master Control Routing
    SF   *Computer Sciences
      Data Processing

MCRN   Moscow City Relay Network
    SF   *Engineering
      Radio Engineering
      *Telecommunications

MCRR   Machine Check Recording and Recovery
    SF   *Computer Sciences
      Data Processing

MCRT   Maximum Cruise Thrust
    SF   *Aeronautics
      Aircraft

MCS   Marine Casualty Statistics
    SF   *Naval Sciences

MCS   Master Control System
    SF   *Computer Sciences
      Data Processing

MCS   Multiple Compression Shear
    SF   *Agricultural Sciences
      Cereals

MCT   Maximum Continuous Thrust
    SF   *Aeronautics
      Aircraft

MCT   Mobile Communication Terminal
    SF   *Communication Systems
      *Computer Sciences
      Data Processing

MCU   Memory Control Unit
    SF   *Computer Sciences
      Data Processing

MCU   Microprogrammed Control Unit
    SF   *Computer Sciences
      Data Processing

MCU   Multiplexer Control Unit
    SF   *Computer Sciences
      Data Processing

MCW   Modulated Continuous Wave
    SF   *Communication Systems
      Radio Engineering

MD   Manual Damper
    SF   *Metallurgy and Metallography
      Metalworks

MDA   McDonnel Douglas Aeronautics
    SF   *Aeronautics

MDA   Methylenedianiline
    SF   *Non-metallic Materials
      Plastics
      Polymers

MDA   Minimum Descent Altitude
    SF   *Aeronautics
      Approach and Landing

MDA   Multi-Dimensional Access
    SF   *Computer Sciences
      Data Processing

MDA   Multi-Dimensional Array
      SF   *Computer Sciences
           Data Processing
MDA   Multiple Docking Adapter
      SF   *Astronautics and Astrophysics
           Spacecraft
MDAI Multidisciplinary Accident
      Investigation
      SF   *Engineering
           Safety Engineering
           *Transportation
MDAL McDonnell Douglas Astrophysics
      Laboratory
      SF   *Aeronautics
MDAP Machine and Display Application
      Program
      SF   *Engineering
           Mechanical Engineering
MDC   McDonnell Douglas Corporation (US)
      SF   *Aeronautics
           Navigation
MDC   Materials Distribution Center
      SF   *Computer Sciences
           *Information Retrieval Systems
MDCE Monitoring and Duplicate Control
      Equipment
      SF   *Engineering
           Radio Engineering
           *Telecommunications
MDD   Machine Dependent Data
      SF   *Computer Sciences
           Data Processing
MDF   Main Distribution Frame
      SF   *Computer Sciences
           Data Processing
MDH   Maximum Diameter Heat
      SF   *Nuclear Sciences
           Nucleonics
MDMS Methylene Dimethane-sulphonate
      SF   Biochemistry
           *Biological and Medical Sciences
MDP   Methylenedioxyphenyl
      SF   Biochemistry
           *Biological and Medical Sciences
MDP   Missile Data Processor
      SF   *Computer Sciences
           Data Processing
MDR   Mark-sense Document Reader
      SF   *Information Retrieval Systems
MDS   Mohawk Data System
      SF   *Computer Sciences
           Data Processing
MDT   Maximum Diameter of the Thorax
      SF   *Nuclear Sciences
           Nucleonics
MDT   Minimum Mean Downtime
      SF   *Aeronautics
           Air Traffic Control
           Radar Equipment
MDT   Mean Down Time

      SF   *Computer Sciences
           Data Processing
ME   Magnetic Estimation
      SF   *Aeronautics
           Noise
           Psychacoustic Tests
ME   Maleate Concentration
      SF   Bioengineering
           *Biological and Medical Sciences
ME   Mature Equivalent
      SF   *Dairy Sciences
ME   Mercaptoethanol
      SF   *Dairy Sciences
ME   Metabolizable Energy
      SF   *Agricultural Sciences
           *Dairy Sciences
ME   Mössbauer Effect
      SF   *Nuclear Sciences
MEA   Malt Extract Agar
      SF   *Brewery
MEA   Minimum Enroute Altitude
      SF   *Aeronautics
           Instrument Flying
MECA Molecular Emission Cavity Analysis
      SF   *Biological and Medical Sciences
MECU Master Engine Control Unit
      SF   Aeronautics
           *Military Sciences
MeDAB Methyl Dimethylaminoazobenzene
      SF   Biochemistry
           *Biological and Medical Sciences
MEDAC Medical Electronic Data Acquisition
      and Control
      SF   *Biological and Medical Sciences
           *Computer Sciences
           Data Processing
MED COM Mediterranean Communications
      SF   *Military Sciences
MEDLARS Medical Literature Analysis and
      Retrieval System
      SF   *Biological and Medical Sciences
MEECN Minimum Essential Emergency Network
      (US)
      SF   *Military Sciences
           *Transportation
MEFET Metal Semiconductor Field Effect
      Transistor
      SF   *Electronics and Electrical
           Engineering
           Solid-state Circuits
MEM   Maximum Entropy Method
      SF   *Communication Systems
MEM   Modified Eagle's Medium
      SF   *Biological and Medical Sciences
MEMAs Microelectronic Modular Assemblies
      SF   *Aeronautics
           Navigation
MEP   m-fluorophenylanine
      SF   *Agricultural Sciences
MEP   Motor Evoked Potentials

SF   *Biological and Medical Sciences
   Physiology
MERDC Mobile Equipment Research and
   Development
SF   *Engineering
   Mechanical Engineering
MES   Mössbauer Effect Spectroscopy
SF   *Nuclear Sciences
   Spectroscopy
MESA Marine Ecosystems Analysis
SF   *Communication Systems
   *Geosciences
METS Modular Engine Test System
SF   *Engineering
   Mechanical Engineering
   Testing
MeV   Million Electron Volts
SF   *Electronics and Electrical
    Engineering
   Lasers and Masers
MEW   Microwave Early Warning
SF   *Communication Systems
   Radar Equipment
MF   Medium Frequency
SF   *Aeronautics
   *Communication Systems
   Navigation
MFBS Multifrequency Binary Sequence
SF   *Nuclear Sciences
   Reactors
MFD   Multifunction Display
SF   *Aeronautics
   Instruments
   Navigation
MFM   Multistage Frequency Multiplier
SF   *Engineering
   Radio Engineering
   *Telecommunications
MFO   Mixed Function Oxidase
SF   Biochemistry
   *Biological and Medical Sciences
MFT   Monolayer Formation Time
SF   *Space Sciences
   Space Simulation
MFT   Multiposition Frequency Telegraphy
SF   *Engineering
   Radio Engineering
   *Telecommunications
MFT   Multiprogramming Fixed Task
SF   *Computer Sciences
   Data Processing
MFV   Military Flight Vehicle
SF   *Aeronautics
   *Military Sciences
Mg   Magnesium
SF   Agricultural Sciences
   *General
MG   Master Generator
SF   *Engineering
   Radio Engineering

   *Telecommunications
MGA   Melengestrol Acetate
SF   *Dairy Sciences
MGGB Modular Guided Glide Bomb
SF   Defence Weapons
   *Military Sciences
MGL   Malachite Green Leucocyanite
SF   *Biological and Medical Sciences
   Instruments
MH   Mulberry Heart
SF   *Agricultural Sciences
MHA   Methionine Hydroxy Analog
SF   *Dairy Sciences
MHA   Mueller Hinton Agar
SF   *Biological and Medical Sciences
   Microbiology
MHD   Magnetohydrodynamic
SF   *Aeronautics
   *Astronautics and Astrophysics
   *Biological and Medical Sciences
   *Electronics and Electrical
    Engineering
   *Geosciences
   *Lunar Sciences
MHW   Multihundred Watt
SF   Atomic Energy
   *Nuclear Sciences
MIACF Meander Inverted Autocorrelated
   Function
SF   *Engineering
   Radio Engineering
   *Telecommunications
MIACS Manufacturing Information and Control
   System
SF   *Computer Sciences
   Data Processing
MIBK Methyl Isobutyl Ketone
SF   *Brewery
MIC   Management Information Centers
SF   *Information Retrieval Systems
MIC   Master Interrupt Control
SF   *Computer Sciences
   Data Processing
MIC   Monolithic Integrated Circuits
SF   Radio Engineering
   *Telecommunications
MICR Magnetic Ink Character Recognition
SF   *Computer Sciences
   Data Processing
MICS Manufacturing Information and Control
   System
SF   *Computer Sciences
   *Information Retrieval Systems
MIF   Macrophage Inhibition Factors
SF   Biochemistry
   *Biological and Medical Sciences
MIG   Metal Inert Gas
SF   *Metallurgy and Metallography
min   Minimum
SF   *Mathematics

MIR   Music Information Retrieval
      SF *Computer Sciences
          *Information Retrieval Systems
          *Music
MIRA Motor Industry Research Association
      (UK)
      SF *Information Retrieval Systems
MIRD Medical Internal Radiation Dose
      SF *Nuclear Sciences
          Reactors
MIS   Management Information Systems
      SF *Information Retrieval Systems
MIS   Metal Insulation Semiconductor
      SF *Electronics and Electrical
             Engineering
             Solid-state Circuits
MIS   Metering Information System
      SF *Telecommunications
misc Miscellaneous
      SF *General
MISFETs Metal Insulator Semiconductor
          Field Effect Transistors
      SF *Electronics and Electrical
             Engineering
MISP Medical Information Systems Program
      SF *Computer Sciences
          Data Processing
MIT   Master Instruction Tape
      SF *Computer Sciences
          Data Processing
MITI Ministry of International Trade and
      Industry
      SF *Computer Sciences
          Data Processing
MIUS Modular Integrated Utility System
      SF *Aeronautics
          *Space Sciences
MIW   Milk Ingredient Water
      SF *Agricultural Sciences
          *Dairy Sciences
MIX   Master Index
      SF *Computer Sciences
          Data Processing
MJS   Marine Jupiter Saturn
      SF *Space Sciences
          Spacecraft
ml   Millilitre
      SF *Mathematics
ML   Machine Language
      SF *Computer Sciences
          Data Processing
ML   Magnetic Latching
      SF *Electronics and Electrical
             Engineering
             Switches
MLC   Manoeuvre Load Control
      SF *Aeronautics
          Aircraft
MLD   Masking Level Difference
      SF *Aeronautics

          Noise
MLD   Mixed Layer Depth
      SF *Agricultural Sciences
          *Fisheries
MLE   Maximum Likelihood Estimates
      SF *Mathematics
          *Statistics
MLF   Median Longitudinal Fasciculus
      SF *Biological and Medical Sciences
MLF   Multilateral Force
      SF *Nuclear Sciences
MLG   Methyl-L-Glutamate
      SF *Non-metallic Materials
          Polymers
MLGW Maximum Landing Gross Weight
      SF *Aeronautics
          Aircraft
MLOP Mid-Leth Overpressure
      SF *Military Sciences
          Missiles
MLS   Microwave Landing System
      SF *Aeronautics
          Approach and Landing
MLSS Mixed Liquid Suspended Solids
      SF *Bioengineering
          *Biological and Medical Sciences
MLV   Moloney Leukaemia Virus
      SF *Biological and Medical Sciences
MLW   Mean Low Water
      SF Geosciences
          *Oceanography
MM   Middle Marker
      SF *Aeronautics
          Instrument Flying
mm   Millimetre
      SF *Mathematics
MM   Monostable Multivibrator
      SF *Electronics and Electrical
             Engineering
MM   MOS Monolithic
      SF *Electronics and Electrical
             Engineering
MM   Multiple Myeloma
      SF *Biological and Medical Sciences
          Cytochemistry
MMA   Manual Metal Arc
      SF *Metallurgy and Metallography
          Welding
MMA   Methyl Methacrylate
      SF *Non-metallic Materials
          Polymers
MMC   Micro Meteroid Capsule
      SF *Naval Sciences
          Navigation
MMD   Mass Medium Diameter
      SF *Agricultural Sciences
          Cereals
MMD   Mean Maturity Dates
      SF *Agricultural Sciences
MMF   Magnetomotive Force

SF   *Mathematics
MMF   Micromation Microfilm
       SF   Microfilms
             *Photography
MMF   Moving Magnetic Features
       SF   *Astronautics and Astrophysics
             Solar Physics
MMH   Methylmercury Hydroxide
       SF   Biochemistry
             *Biological and Medical Sciences
MMN   Metallurgie et Mécanique Nucléaires
       (Belg.)
       SF   *Nuclear Sciences
MMP   Monitoring Metering Panel
       SF   Radio Engineering
             *Telecommunications
MMR   Multiple Match Resolver
       SF   *Computer Sciences
             Data Processing
MMS   Magnetic Median Surface
       SF   *Electronics and Electrical
             Engineering
MMS   Methyl Methanesulphonate
       SF   Biochemistry
             *Biological and Medical Sciences
MMS   Mobile Multiple-shopping Services
       SF   *Management
MMW   Main Magnetization Winding
       SF   Radio Engineering
             *Telecommunications
Mn   Manganese
       SF   *General
             *Metallurgy and Metallography
MN   Motor Number
       SF   *Computer Sciences
             Data Processing
MNC   Multinational Corporations
       SF   *General
             Business Aspects
MNNG   Methyl Nitro Nitrosoguanidine
       SF   Biochemistry
             *Biological and Medical Sciences
MNOS   Metal-Nitride Oxide Semiconductors
       SF   *Electronics and Electrical
             Engineering
MNOS   Metal Nitride Oxide Silicon
       SF   *Electronics and Electrical
             Engineering
             Solid-state Circuits
MNOSFET Metal Nitride Oxide Semiconductor
             Field Effect Transistors
       SF   *Electronics and Electrical
             Engineering
MNP   N-Methyl-2-Pyrollodone
       SF   *Photography
MNR   Minimum Noise Routes
       SF   *Aeronautics
             Aircraft Noise
MNS   Modernized Number Services
       SF   *General

MNU   Methyl Nitrosourea
       SF   Biochemistry
             *Biological and Medical Sciences
MO   Masonry Opening
       SF   *Metallurgy and Metallography
             Metalwork
MO   Master Oscillator
       SF   *Engineering
             Radio Engineering
             *Telecommunications
MO   Mixed Oxide
       SF   *Ceramics
MO   Mobile Object
       SF   Radio Objective
             *Telecommunications
MOC   Minimum Operational Characteristics
       SF   *Aeronautics
             *Communication Systems
             Navigation
MOCA   Minimum Obstruction Clearance Altitude
       SF   *Aeronautics
             Instrument Flying
Mod   Modulator
       SF   *Electronics and Electrical
             Engineering
MODCAT Modified Catamaran
       SF   *Military Sciences
             *Naval Sciences
MODIA Methods of Designing Instructional
             Alternatives
       SF   *Training
MODILS Modular Instrument Landing System
       SF   *Aeronautics
             Navigation
MOE   Measure of Effectiveness
       SF   *Computer Sciences
MOI   Multiplicities of Infection
       SF   Bioengineering
             *Biological and Medical Sciences
MOL   Machine Oriented Language
       SF   *Computer Sciences
             Data Processing
MOL   Manned Orbital Laboratory
       SF   *Astronautics and Astrophysics
mol-wt Molecular Weight
       SF   *Mathematics
MOP   Multiple On-Line Programming
       SF   *Computer Sciences
             Data Processing
MOR   Magnetic Optical Rotation
       SF   *Biological and Medical Sciences
             Metal Ions
MOR   Malate Oxidoreductase
       SF   *Biological and Medical Sciences
             Cytochemistry
MOR   Mandatory Occurrence Reporting
       SF   *Aeronautics
             Accidents and Safety
MOS   Metal Oxide Semiconductor
       SF   *Computer Sciences

```
           *Electronics and Electrical          MPM    Maximum Pionization Method
              Engineering                               SF   *Mathematics
           *Engineering                                       Scaling Methods
           *Telecommunications                     MPN    Most Probable Number
MOS     Metal Oxide Silicon                               SF   *General
        SF   *Computer Sciences                   MPO    Myeloperoxidase
             Data Processing                              SF   *Biological and Medical Sciences
             *Electronics and Electrical                       Cytochemistry
              Engineering                          MPP    Mission Planning Program
MOS     Military Occupational Speciality                  SF   *Communication Systems
        SF   *Management                                       *Space Sciences
             *Military Sciences                    MPP    Most Probable Position
MOSFET  Metal Oxide Semiconductor Field                   SF   *Aeronautics
        Effect Transistor                                      Navigation
        SF   *Communication Systems               MPPL   Multi-Purpose Programming Language
             *Electronics and Electrical                  SF   *Computer Sciences
              Engineering                                       Data Processing
             *Engineering                          MPS    Modular-Runtimelinkable Programming
             Radio Engineering                            System
MOS/LSI Metal Oxide Semiconductor/Large                   SF   *Computer Sciences
        Scale Integration                                      Data Processing
        SF   *Communication Systems               MPS    Mucopolysaccharides
             *Electronics and Electrical                  SF   Biochemistry
              Engineering                                       *Biological and Medical Sciences
             *Engineering                          MPS    Multiprogramming System
MOST    Metal Oxide Semiconductor Transistor              SF   *Computer Sciences
        SF   *Electronics and Electrical                        Data Processing
              Engineering                          MPSX   Mathematical Programming System
             Solid-state Circuits                        Extended
MOT     Ministry of Transport                             SF   *Computer Sciences
        SF   *General                                          Data Processing
             *Transportation                       MPT    Multiple Pure Tones
MOTMX   Methoxy Trimethylxanthine                         SF   *Aeronautics
        SF   Biochemistry                                      Aircraft Noise
             *Biological and Medical Sciences      MR     Memory Information Register
MOTNE   Meteorological Operational                        SF   *Computer Sciences
        Telecommunications Network Europe                       Data Processing
        SF   *Aeronautics                          MRA    Minimum Reception Altitude
             *Meteorology                                 SF   *Aeronautics
             *Telecommunications                               Navigation
MOUSE   Manager Owner User Systems Engineer        MRC    Mouse Erythrocytes
        SF   *Naval Sciences                              SF   *Biological and Medical Sciences
             Navigation                                        Physiology
MP      Measured Pragmetric                        MRCA   Multi-Role Combat Aircraft
        SF   *Computer Sciences                           SF   *Aeronautics
             Testing                                           *Military Sciences
MPD     Map Pictorial Display                      MRO    Maintenance Repair and Operations
        SF   *Aeronautics                                 SF   *Transportation
             Data Processing                       MRPPS  Maryland Refutation Proof Procedure
MPDA    Metaphenylene Diamine                             System
        SF   *Non-metallic Materials                      SF   *Electronics and Electrical
             Polymers                                           Engineering
MPI     Mannose Phosphate Isomerase               MRR    Mechanical Reliability Report
        SF   *Biological and Medical Sciences             SF   *Aeronautics
MPIO    Mission and Payload Integrated Office                   Ground Communication
        SF   *Space Sciences                       MRS    Manned Repeater Station
             Spacecraft                                   SF   *Engineering
Mpip    Miniature Precision Inertial Platform                  Radio Engineering
        SF   *Aeronautics                                      *Telecommunications
             Navigation                            MRSA   Mandatory Radar Service Areas
```

```
          SF  *Aeronautics                      *Lunar Sciences
              Air Traffic Control        MSGs  Models Simulations and Games
MRSL  Marconi Radar Systems Limited            SF  *Mathematics
          SF  *Aeronautics              MSH   Melanocyte Stimulating Hormone
              Radar                              SF  *Biological and Medical Sciences
MRT   Modified Rhyme Test               MSI   Medium Scale Integrated
          SF  *Aeronautics                      SF  *Electronics and Electrical
              Noise                                    Engineering
MRV   Maximum Relative Variation                       Solid-state Circuits
          SF   Bioengineering           MSL   Mean Sea Level
              *Biological and Medical Sciences    SF  *Aeronautics
MS    Machine Stripping                              Instruments
          SF  *Agricultural Sciences    MSMLCS Mass Service Main Line Cable Systems
MS    Mobile System                             SF  *Engineering
          SF  *Engineering                           Radio Engineering
              Radio Engineering                      *Telecommunications
              *Telecommunications       MSPLT Master Source Program Library Tape
MS    Multispectral                             SF  *Computer Sciences
          SF  *Photography                           Data Processing
MSA   Mannitol Salt Agar                MSR   Machine Status Register
          SF  *Agricultural Sciences            SF  *Computer Sciences
              *Dairy Sciences                        Data Processing
MSA   Minimum Sector Altitude           MSR   Medium Stocking Rate
          SF  *Aeronautics                      SF  *Agricultural Sciences
              Instrument Flying         MSRE  Molten Salt Reactor Experiment
MSAM  Multiple Sequential Access Method         SF  *Nuclear Sciences
          SF  *Computer Sciences                     Reactors
              Data Processing           MSRS  Multiple Stylus Recording System
MSAR  Mine Safety Appliance Research            SF  *Agricultural Sciences
          SF   Electron Temperature                  *Fisheries
              *Nuclear Sciences         MSS   Multiple Selling Service
MSB   Most Significant Bit                      SF  *Management
          SF  *Computer Sciences        MSS   Multispectral Scaling
              Data Processing                   SF  *Electronics and Electrical
MSC   Manned Spacecraft Center (US)                    Engineering
          SF  *Space Sciences                        Modules
              Space Simulation          MSS   Multispectral Scanner
MSC   Military Sealift Command                   SF  *Biological and Medical Sciences
          SF  *Military Sciences                     *Communication Systems
              *Transportation                        *Photography
MSD   Most Significant Digit            MST   Minimum Spanning Tree
          SF  *Computer Sciences                SF  *Statistics
              Data Processing           MST   Mountain Standard Time
MSDS  Marconi Space and Defence Systems          SF  *Aeronautics
          SF  *Military Sciences                     Radar
              Navigation                MSU   Modern Sharing Unit
MSE   Modern Ship Equipment                     SF  *Computer Sciences
          SF  *Transportation                        Data Processing
MSF   Master Source File                MSUD  Maple Syrup Urine Disease
          SF  *Computer Sciences                SF  *Biological and Medical Sciences
              Data Processing           MSV   Murine Sarcoma Virus
MSF   Multi Stage Flash                         SF  *Biological and Medical Sciences
          SF  *Nuclear Sciences         MT    Magnetic Tape
              Reactors                          SF  *Computer Sciences
MSFC  Marshall Space Flight Center                   Data Processing
          SF  *Aeronautics              MT    Master Time
              *Astronautics and Astrophysics     SF  *Electronics and Electrical
              *Space Sciences                          Engineering
MSFN  Manned Space Flight Network       MT    Message Table
          SF  *Astronautics and Astrophysics     SF  *Computer Sciences
```

Data Processing
MTA   Milko Tester Automatic
      SF *Dairy Sciences
MTBCF Mean Time Between Confirmed Failures
      SF   Aerodynamics
           *Aeronautics
MTBF Mean Time Between Failure
      SF *Aeronautics
           Navigation
           *Computer Sciences
           Data Processing
MTBFC Mean Time Between Flight Cancellation
      SF *Aeronautics
           Navigation
MTBMA Mean Time Between Maintenance Actions
      SF *Aeronautics
MTC   Modulation Transfer Curves
      SF *Photography
MTCA Multiple Terminal Communications
        Adapter
      SF *Computer Sciences
           Data Processing
MTD   Moving Target Detector
      SF *Aeronautics
           Air Traffic Control
MTDS Marine Tactical Data System
      SF *Aeronautics
           *Naval Sciences
MTF   Mean Time to Failure
      SF *Electronics and Electrical
             Engineering
           Solid-state Circuits
MTF   Modulation Transfer Function
      SF *Photography
           *Space Sciences
           Space Simulation
MTFA Modulation Transfer Function Analyser
      SF *Aeronautics
           Testing
MTI   Moving Target Indicator
      SF *Aeronautics
           *Communication Systems
           Navigation
           Radar
MTIL Maximum Tolerable Insecurity Level
      SF *Communication Systems
           Thermal Generating Units
MTIRA Machine Tool Industry Research
        Association (UK)
      SF *Engineering
           *Information Retrieval Systems
MTL   Merged Transistor Logic
      SF *Electronics and Electrical
             Engineering
MTMTS Military Traffic Management and
        Terminal Service (US)
      SF *Military Sciences
           *Transportation
MToGW Maximum Takeoff Gross Weight
      SF *Aeronautics

Aircraft
MTP   Minimum Time Path
      SF *Aeronautics
           Navigation
MTPT Minimal Total Processing Time
      SF *Computer Sciences
           *Electronics and Electrical
             Engineering
MTR   Material Testing Reactor
      SF *Nuclear Sciences
           Reactors
MTR   Migration Traffic Rate
      SF *Aeronautics
           Radar
MTS   Michigan Terminal System
      SF *Computer Sciences
           *Information Retrieval Systems
MT/SC Magnetic Tape Composer Selectric
      SF *Printing
MT/ST Magnetic Tape Selectric Typewriter
      SF *Computer Sciences
           *Printing
MTTR Mean Time To Repair
      SF *Computer Sciences
MTU   Magnetic Tape Unit
      SF *Computer Sciences
           Data Processing
MTV   Mammary Tumour Virus
      SF *Biological and Medical Sciences
MU   Methylene Unit
      SF   Biochemistry
           *Biological and Medical Sciences
MUCHA Multiple Channel Analysis
      SF *Nuclear Sciences
           Reactors
MUF   Maximum Usable Frequency
      SF *Communication Systems
           *Engineering
           Radio Engineering
MUF   Milk Ultrafiltrate
      SF *Dairy Sciences
MUI   Module Interface Unit
      SF *Computer Sciences
           Data Processing
MUT   Minimum Mean Uptime
      SF *Aeronautics
           Air Traffic Control
           Radar Equipment
MUX   Multiplexer Channel
      SF *Aeronautics
           Radar Equipment
           Transponders
mv   Mean Value
      SF *Mathematics
MV   Measured Vectors
      SF *Computer Sciences
           Testing
MV   Microvillus
      SF *Biological and Medical Sciences
           Cytochemistry

MVA   Modern Volunteer Army
       SF *Military Sciences
            Training
MVB   Multivesicular Bodies
       SF *Biological and Medical Sciences
            Cytochemistry
MVE   Multivariate Exponential (Distribution)
       SF *Mathematics
MVLUE Minimum Variance Linear Unbiased
        Estimator
       SF *Statistics
MVM   Mariner Versus Mercury
       SF *Space Sciences
            Spacecraft
MVM   Minimum Virtual Memory
       SF *Computer Sciences
            Data Processing
MVT   Multi-programming Variable Tasks
       SF *Computer Sciences
            Data Processing
MVU   Minimum Variance Unbiased
       SF *Statistics
MW   Molecular Weight
       SF *Biological and Medical Sciences
            *General
MWB   Multiprogram Wire Broadcasting
       SF   Radio Engineering
            *Telecommunications
MWD   Molecular Weight Distribution
       SF *General
            *Non-metallic Materials
            Polymers
MWHGL Multiple Wheel Heavy Gear Load
       SF *Aeronautics
            Aircraft
MWPC   Moorepark Whey Protein Concentrates
       SF *Agricultural Sciences
MWR   Magnetic Tape Write Memory
       SF *Computer Sciences
            Data Processing
MY   Machine Yield
       SF *Agricultural Sciences
MYP   Mannito-egg Yolk Polymyxin
       SF *Agricultural Sciences
            *Dairy Sciences

N

N   Nitrogen
     SF *Agricultural Sciences
         *General
NA   Nautical Almanac
     SF *Naval Sciences
         Navigation
NA   Not Assigned
     SF *Computer Sciences
         Data Processing
NA   Not Available
     SF *Computer Sciences
         Data Processing
NA   Numerical Aperture
     SF *Photography
Na   Sodium
     SF *Agricultural Sciences
         *General
NAC North Atlantic Council
     SF *Military Sciences
NACA National Advisory Committee for
     Aeronautics
     SF *Aeronautics
NACAM National Association of Corn and
     Agricultural Merchants
     SF *Agricultural Sciences
         *Milling
NAD Nicotinamide Adenine Dinucleotide
     SF Biochemistry
         *Biological and Medical Sciences
NADC National Air Development Center
     SF *Aeronautics
         Aircraft
NADH Nicotin-amide Adenine Dinucleotide
     SF *Biological and Medical Sciences
         Cytochemistry
NADP Nicotinamide Adenine Dinucleotide
     Phosphate
     SF Biochemistry
         *Biological and Medical Sciences
NAE National Academy of Engineering (US)
     SF *Astronautics and Astrophysics
         *Engineering
         *Space Sciences
NAFEC National Aviation Facilities
     Experimental Center

     SF *Aeronautics
NAK Negative Acknowledgment
     SF *Computer Sciences
         Data Processing
NAL National Accelerator Laboratory (US)
     SF *Engineering
         Mechanical Engineering
NAM Nautical Air Miles
     SF *Aeronautics
NAMA National Automatic Merchandising
     Association
     SF *Dairy Sciences
NAM/Lb Nautical Air Mile per Pound
     SF Aerodynamics
         *Aeronautics
         Aircraft
NAMSA NATO Maintenance and Supply Agency
     SF *Military Sciences
         *Transportation
NAN Neutron Activation Analysis
     SF *Nuclear Sciences
NAN Naphthalene Acetic Acid
     SF *Agricultural Sciences
NAPL National Association of Photo-
     Lithographers
     SF *Printing
NAR Net Assimilation Rate
     SF *Agricultural Sciences
NAS National Academy of Science
     SF *Space Sciences
NAS National Airspace System
     SF *Aeronautics
         *Communication Systems
         Navigation
         *Space Sciences
NASA National Aeronautics and Space
     Administration
     SF *Aeronautics
         *Space Sciences
NASCO National Academy of Sciences
     Committee on Oceanography (US)
     SF *Naval Sciences
         Navigation
NASM National Air and Space Museum
     SF *Aeronautics

NASP   National Airport System Plan
    SF   *Aeronautics
       Airports
NASTRAN NASA Structural Analysis Program
    SF   *Aeronautics
       *Space Sciences
NATSPG North Atlantic Systems Planning
    Group
    SF   *Aeronautics
       Air Traffic Control
NAUS   National Airspace Utilization Study
    SF   *Aeronautics
       *Communication Systems
       Radar Beacon Systems
NAVELECSYSCOM Naval Electronic Systems
       Command
    SF   *Military Sciences
       *Naval Sciences
       Navigation
NAVFEC Naval Facilities Engineering Command
    SF   Civil Engineering
       *Engineering
       *Military Sciences
NAVORD Naval Ordnance
    SF   Logistics
       *Military Sciences
NAVSAT Navigation Satellite
    SF   *Naval Sciences
       Navigation
NAVSEC Naval Ship Engineering Center
    SF   *Military Sciences
       *Transportation
NAVSUP Naval Supply
    SF   Logistics
       *Military Sciences
NAWAS National Warning System (US)
    SF   *General
NB   No Bias
    SF   *Electronics and Electrical
       Engineering
       Switches
nbfm   Narrow Band Frequency Modulation
    SF   *Communication Systems
       *Engineering
       Radio Engineering
NBFU   National Board of Fire Underwriters
    SF   Civil Engineering
       *Engineering
NBS   National Bureau of Standards
    SF   *Standards
NBT   Narrow Beam Transducer
    SF   *Aeronautics
       *Naval Sciences
       Navigation
NBT   Nitrobule Tetrazolin
    SF   *Agricultural Sciences
NC   No Connection
    SF   *Electronics and Electrical
       Engineering
       Semiconductor Devices

NC   Non-crystalline
    SF   *Non-crystalline Solids
NC   Normally Closed
    SF   *Metallurgy and Metallography
       Metalworks
NC   Numerical Control
    SF   *Computer Sciences
       Data Processing
NC   Numbering Counter
    SF   *Computer Sciences
       Data Processing
NCA   National Command Authorities (US)
    SF   *Military Sciences
       *Transportation
NCAR   National Center for Atmospheric
    Research
    SF   *Astronautics and Astrophysics
       *Geosciences
       *Space Sciences
NCB   National Coal Board (UK)
    SF   *Fuels
NCC   National Computing Centre
    SF   *Computer Sciences
       Data Processing
NCC   Network Computer Center
    SF   *Computer Sciences
NCLT   Night Carrier Landing Trainer
    SF   *Aeronautics
       *Naval Sciences
NCN   Non-Casein Nitrogen
    SF   *Agricultural Sciences
NCR   National Cash Register
    SF   *Computer Sciences
       Data Processing
NCRP   National Council on Radiation
    Protection (US)
    SF   *Nuclear Sciences
       Radiation
NCS   National Communication System
    SF   *Communication Systems
       *Transportation
NCS   Numerical Category Scaling
    SF   *Aeronautics
       Noise
       Physioacoustic Tests
NCSORG Naval Control of Shipping
    Organization
    SF   *Military Sciences
       *Naval Sciences
       *Transportation
NCTRU Naval Clothing and Textile Research
    Unit
    SF   *Biological and Medical Sciences
       *Naval Sciences
NCU   Navigation Computer Unit
    SF   *Aeronautics
       Data Processing
NCWA   NATO Civil Wartime Agency
    SF   *Military Sciences
       *Transportation

NCYC National Collection of Yeast
        Culture (UK)
      SF *Brewery
NDB   Non-Directional Radio Beacon
      SF *Aeronautics
            Approach and Landing
            Navigation
NDC   National Data Communication
      SF *Computer Sciences
            Data Processing
NDC   National Drug Code
      SF *Biological and Medical Sciences
            Drugs
            Pharmacology
NDC   Negative Differential Conductivity
      SF *Non-crystalline Solids
NDF   Nonlinear Distortion Factor
      SF *Engineering
            Radio Engineering
            *Telecommunications
NDIR Non-Dispersive Infrared (Analyzers)
      SF *Engineering
NDPase Nucleoside Diphosphalase
      SF *Biological and Medical Sciences
            Cytochemistry
NDPS National Data Processing Service
      SF *Computer Sciences
            Data Processing
NDRF National Defense Reserve Fleet (US)
      SF *Military Sciences
            *Transportation
NDRO Non-Destructive Readout
      SF *Aeronautics
            *Computer Sciences
            Data Processing
NDS   Nonparametric Detection Scheme
      SF *Communication Systems
            Navigation
NDT   Nil-Ductility Transmission
      SF *Materials
            *Nuclear Sciences
NDT   Non-destructive Testing
      SF *Aeronautics
            Aircraft
            *Biological and Medical Sciences
            *Metallurgy and Metallography
            *Nuclear Sciences
            Reactors
NDUV Non-Dispersive Ultraviolet (Analyzers)
      SF   Civil Engineering
            *Engineering
NDV   Newcastle Disease Virus
      SF *Biological and Medical Sciences
NE   Norepinephrine
      SF *Aeronautics
            Aviation Medicine
            *Biological and Medical Sciences
            Cytochemistry
NEACP National Emergency Airborne Command
        Post (US)

      SF *Aeronautics
            *Communication Systems
NEAT NCR Electronic Autocoding Technique
      SF *Computer Sciences
            Data Processing
NEC   Nippon Electric Company
      SF *Telecommunications
NEDN Naval Environmental Data Network (US)
      SF *Meteorology
NEF   Noise Exposure Forecast
      SF *Aeronautics
            Aircraft Noise
NEL   National Engineering Laboratory
      SF *Computer Sciences
            Data Processing
            *Engineering
NEL   Navy Electronic Laboratory (US)
      SF *Military Sciences
NEM   N-ethylmaleimide
      SF *Dairy Sciences
NEMA National Electrical Manufacturers'
        Association
      SF *Computer Sciences
            Data Processing
NEMS Nimbus E Microwave Spectrometer
      SF *Aeronautics
            *Communication Systems
NEP   Nerve Ending Particles
      SF   Biochemistry
            *Biological and Medical Sciences
NEPA National Environmental Policy Act (US)
      SF *Nuclear Sciences
NEPS National Printing Equipment Show
      SF *Printing
NERVA Nuclear Energy Rocket Vehicle
        Application
      SF *Nuclear Sciences
            Reactors
NESC National Electrical Safety Code
      SF *Electronics and Electrical
              Engineering
NESC National Environmental Satellite
        Centre
      SF *Photography
            Satellites
NESS National Environmental Satellite
        Service
      SF *Aeronautics
            *Communication Systems
NETC National Emergency Transportation
        Center (US)
      SF *Transportation
NFB   Node (of) First-fruiting Branch
      SF *Agricultural Sciences
NFDC National Flight Data Center
      SF *Aeronautics
            Ground Communication Networks
NFDM Non-Fat Dry Milk
      SF *Agricultural Sciences
            *Dairy Sciences

NFE   Nearly Free Electron
      SF *Biological and Medical Sciences
          Liquid Semiconductors
nfm   Narrow Frequency Modulation
      SF *Communication Systems
          *Engineering
          Radio Engineering
NFM   Non-Fat Milk
      SF *Dairy Sciences
NFMS Non-Fat Milk Solids
      SF *Agricultural Sciences
          *Dairy Sciences
NFO   Naval Flight Officer
      SF *Aeronautics
          *Naval Sciences
NFT   Niagara Frontier Transit
      SF *Transportation
NG-EGDN Nitroglycerin-Ethylene Glycol
          Dinitrate
      SF *Nuclear Sciences
          Reactors
          Thermal Processes
NGF   Nerve Growth Factor
      SF *Biochemistry
          *Biological and Medical Sciences
          Cytochemistry
NGS   Nominal Guidance Scheme
      SF *Aeronautics
          Navigation
NGSDS National Geophysical and Solar
          Terrestrial Data Center (US)
      SF *Geosciences
NHK   National Broadcasting Corporation
          (Jap.)
      SF *Engineering
          Radio Engineering
          *Telecommunications
NHP   Nominal Horsepower
      SF *Mathematics
NHS   National Health Survey
      SF *Biological and Medical Sciences
          Public Health
NHTSA National Highway Traffic Safety
          Administration (US)
      SF *Transportation
NI   Noisiness Index
      SF *Aeronautics
          Aircraft Noise
NIAB National Institute of Agricultural
          Botany
      SF *Agricultural Sciences
NIAG NATO Industrial Advisory Group
      SF *Aeronautics
          *Military Sciences
NIAMDD National Institute of Arthritis
          Metabolism and Digestive Diseases
      SF *Biological and Medical Sciences
          Cytochemistry
NIC   Negative Immitance Converters
      SF *Engineering

          Radio Engineering
          *Telecommunications
NIC   Network Information Center
      SF *Computer Sciences
          Data Processing
NIC   Nineteen-Hundred Indexing and
          Cataloguing
      SF *Computer Sciences
          Data Processing
NIC   Not in Contact
      SF *Metallurgy and Metallography
          Metalworks
NICOL Nineteen-Hundred Commercial Language
      SF *Computer Sciences
          Data Processing
NIH   National Institute of Health (US)
      SF *Biological and Medical Sciences
NIM   Nuclear Instrument Nodule
      SF *Nuclear Sciences
NIMH National Institute of Mental Health
      SF *Biological and Medical Sciences
NIMMS Nineteen-Hundred Integrated Modular
          Management System
      SF *Computer Sciences
          Data Processing
NINI Nidbus to Nine
      SF Measurement Systems
          *Nuclear Sciences
NIOC Iranian National Oil Company
      SF *Fuels
NIP   Nucleus Initialisation Procedure
      SF *Computer Sciences
          Data Processing
NIPS NMCS Information Processing System
      SF *Computer Sciences
          *Electronics and Electrical
             Engineering
          *Military Sciences
NIPTS Noise Induced Permanent Threshold
          Shift
      SF *Aeronautics
          Noise
NIT   Nonlinear Inertialess Three-pole
      SF *Engineering
          *Telecommunications
NJ   Network Junction
      SF *Engineering
          Radio Engineering
          *Telecommunications
NJCC National Joint Computer Committee
      SF *Computer Sciences
          Data Processing
NL   New Line
      SF *Computer Sciences
          Data Processing
NLECS National Law Enforcement Communications
          Systems
      SF *Information Retrieval Systems
NLH   Non-Locating Head
      SF Civil Engineering

*Engineering

NLL   National Lending Library (UK)
      SF *Information Retrieval Systems
NLP   Non-Linear Programming
      SF *Computer Sciences
          Data Processing
NLRB National Labor Relations Board (US)
      SF *General
NM   Nautical Miles
      SF *Naval Sciences
          Navigation
NM   Noise Margin
      SF *Electronics and Electrical
          Engineering
          Solid-state Circuits
NM   Noise Meter
      SF *Electronics and Electrical
          Engineering
          Meters
NMB   National Mediation Board (US)
      SF *General
          *Transportation
NMC   National Mastitis Council
      SF *Agricultural Sciences
          *Dairy Sciences
NMC   National Meteorological Center
      SF *Aeronautics
          *Communication Systems
NMC   Network Measurement Center
      SF *Computer Sciences
NMCC National Military Command Center (US)
      SF   Military Sciences
NMCS National Military Command System
      SF *Computer Sciences
          *Electronics and Electrical
          Engineering
          *Military Sciences
NMCSSC National Military Command System
          Support Center
      SF *Military Sciences
NMD   Nutritional Muscular Dystrophy
      SF *Agricultural Sciences
          *Milling
nmi   Nautical Miles
      SF *Aeronautics
          Navigation
NMJ   Neuromuscular Junctions
      SF *Biological and Medical Sciences
          Cytochemistry
NMNH National Museum of Natural History
      SF *Biological and Medical Sciences
          Observatories
NMR   Nuclear Magnetic Resonance
      SF *Biological and Medical Sciences
          *Chemistry
          *Lunar Sciences
          *Nuclear Sciences
          *Photography
NMSD Next Most Significant Digit
      SF *Computer Sciences

Data Processing
NNI   Noise Number Index
      SF *Aeronautics
          Environmental Sciences
          Noise
NNSS Navy Navigation Satellite System
      SF *Naval Sciences
          Navigation
NO   Normally Open
      SF *Metallurgy and Metallography
          Metalworks
NOAA National Oceanographic Atmospheric
          Administration (US)
      SF *Aeronautics
          *Communication Systems
          *Oceanography
          *Space Sciences
          *Transportation
NOEB-E NATO Oil Executive Board - East
      SF *Military Sciences
          *Transportation
NOEB-W NATO Oil Executive Board - West
      SF *Military Sciences
          *Transportation
NOESS National Operational Environmental
          Satellite System
      SF *Aeronautics
          *Meteorology
          *Space Sciences
NOL   Naval Ordnance Laboratory (US)
      SF *Military Sciences
          Radar Detection
NORAD North American Air Defense (US)
      SF *Military Sciences
NOS   National Ocean Survey (US)
      SF   Photogrametric Engineering
          *Photography
NOSHEB North of Scotland Hydro-Electric
          Board
      SF *Electronics and Electrical
          Engineering
          Nuclear Sciences
NOTAM Notice To Air Men
      SF *Aeronautics
          Instrument Flying
NOTAP Naval Occupational Task Analysis
          Program
      SF *Training
NP   Neutrino Parents
      SF   Instruments
          *Nuclear Sciences
NP   No Pin
      SF *Electronics and Electrical
          Engineering
          Semiconductor Devices
NP   Nucleoside Phosphorylase
      SF *Biological and Medical Sciences
NPA   National Pilots' Association
      SF *Aeronautics
          Air Traffic Control

NPC   Nasopharynged Carcinoma Tissue
       SF *Biological and Medical Sciences
NPE   Natural Parity Exchange
       SF   Elementary Particles
            *Physics
NPG   Normalized electron-Peak to Gamma-peak
       SF *Electronics and Electrical
            Engineering
NPL   New Programming Language
       SF *Computer Sciences
            Data Processing
NPL   Noise Pollution Level
       SF *Aeronautics
            Environmental Sciences
            Noise
NPN   Non-Protein Nitrogen
       SF *Agricultural Sciences
            Cereals
NPPase Nucleoside Phosphatase
       SF *Biological and Medical Sciences
            Cytochemistry
NPPS   Navy Publications and Printing
        Services
       SF *Printing
NPR   Noise Power Ratio
       SF *Communication Systems
NPR   Nozzle Pressure Ratio
       SF *Aeronautics
NPSD   Neutron Power Spectral Density
       SF *Nuclear Sciences
NPT   Non-Proliferation Treaty
       SF *Nuclear Sciences
NPTRL Naval Personnel and Training Research
        Laboratory
       SF *Training
NPV   Net Present Value
       SF *General
NQ   Nitroquinoline
       SF   Biochemistry
            *Biological and Medical Sciences
NQO   Nitroquinoline Oxide
       SF   Biochemistry
            *Biological and Medical Sciences
NQR   Nuclear Quadrupole Resonance
       SF *Nuclear Sciences
NR   Natural Rubber
       SF *Non-metallic Materials
            Polymers
NR   Non-Reactive
       SF *Electronics and Electrical
             Engineering
            Switches
NRAO   National Radio Astronomy Observatory
       SF *Astronautics and Astrophysics
            *Lunar Sciences
NRC   National Research Council
       SF *General
NRC   Noise Rating Curves
       SF *Aeronautics
            Aircraft Noise

NRC   Notch Root Contraction
       SF *Metallurgy and Metallography
            Welding
NRCd   National Reprographic Centre for
        Documentation
       SF *Information Retrieval Systems
NRL   Naval Research Laboratory
       SF *Military Sciences
            *Naval Sciences
NRM   Natural Remnant Magnetization
       SF *Astronautics and Astrophysics
            *Lunar Sciences
            *Oceanography
NRN   Negative Run Number
       SF *Computer Sciences
            Data Processing
            *Mathematics
NRS   Normal Rabit Serum
       SF *Biological and Medical Sciences
            Physiology
NRZ   Non Return to Zero
       SF *Computer Sciences
            Data Processing
NRZI   Non Return to Zero Inverted
       SF *Computer Sciences
            Data Processing
NS   Na Silicate
       SF *Ceramics
NS   Navigation Subsystem
       SF *Aeronautics
            Navigation
NSA   National Shipping Authority (US)
       SF *Transportation
NSAb   Nasal Secretion Antibody
       SF *Dairy Sciences
NSF   National Science Foundation (US)
       SF *Engineering
            *General
            Mechanical Engineering
NSIA   National Security Industrial
        Association
       SF *Naval Sciences
            Navigation
NSPE   National Society of Professional
        Engineers
       SF *Engineering
            Engineering Consultancy
NSPP   Nuclear Safety Pilot Point
       SF *Nuclear Sciences
            Reactors
NSPV   Number of Scans Per Vehicle
       SF *Photography
NSRDC Naval Ship Research and Development
        Center
       SF *Military Sciences
            *Transportation
NSSL   National Severe Storms Laboratory (US)
       SF *Geosciences
NSSS   Nuclear Steam Supply System
       SF *Nuclear Sciences

```
                    Reactors
NSTF   National Scholarship Trust Fund
       SF   *Management
            *Training
NSV    Net Sales Value
       SF   *Computer Sciences
            Data Processing
NT     Nortriptyline
       SF   *Biological and Medical Sciences
NTA    Nitrilotriacetic Acid
       SF   *Chemistry
            Physical Chemistry
NTDS   Naval Tactical Data Systems
       SF   *Aeronautics
            Air Traffic Control
            *Communication Systems
            *Naval Sciences
NTIS   National Technical Information Service
       SF   *Information Retrieval Systems
NTS    Nevada Test Site
       SF    Explosives
            *Nuclear Sciences
NTS    Not To Scale
       SF   *Metallurgy and Metallography
            Metalworks
NTS    Notch Tensile Strength
       SF   *Nuclear Sciences
            Nucleonics
NTSB   National Transportation Safety Board
       SF   *Aeronautics
            Aircraft Accidents
NTSK   Nordiska Tele-Satelit Kommitton
       SF   *Telecommunications
NTV    Network Television
       SF   *Telecommunications
NUDET  Nuclear Detonation
       SF    Military Sciences
NUKEM  Nuklear Chemie und Metallurgie (Ger.)
       SF   *Nuclear Sciences
            Reactors
NUMEC  Nuclear Material Equipment Corporation
       SF   *Nuclear Sciences
            Reactors
NUSC   Naval Underwater Systems Center
       SF   *Military Sciences
            Naval Personnel
NWEP   Nuclear Weapons Effects Panel
       SF   *Aeronautics
            Avionics
            *Military Sciences
NWP    Numerical Weather Prediction
       SF   *Meteorology
NWS    National Weather Service
       SF   *Geosciences
            *Meteorology
NYARTOC New York Air Route Traffic Control
            Center
       SF   *Aeronautics
            Air Traffic Control
```

O   Octopole
     SF *Nuclear Sciences
OA   Outside Air
     SF *Metallurgy and Metallography
         Metalworks
OAC   Optimally Adaptive Control
     SF   Bioengineering
         *Biological and Medical Sciences
OAFU Observers' Advanced Flying Unit
     SF *Aeronautics
         Navigation
         *Training
OAI   Outside Air Intake
     SF *Metallurgy and Metallography
         Metalworks
OAL   Overall Length
     SF *Metallurgy and Metallography
         Metalworks
OALS Observer Air Lock System
     SF *Space Sciences
OAO   Orbital Astronomical Observatories
     SF *Space Sciences
         Spaceraft
OAO   Orthogonalized Atomic Orbital
     SF   Liquid Semiconductors
         *Non-crystalline Solids
OAR   Office of Research Analysis
     SF *General
OAS   Organization of American States
     SF *General
OASPL Overall Sound Pressure Level
     SF *Aeronautics
         Aircraft Noise
OAT   Operational Air Traffic
     SF *Aeronautics
         Air Traffic Control
OBAWS On Board Aircraft Weighing System
     SF *Aeronautics
         Instruments
OBD   Open Blade Damper
     SF *Metallurgy and Metallography
         Metalworks
OBE   One-Boson Exchange
     SF *Nuclear Sciences
OBF   One-Bar-Functions

     SF *Photography
OBR   Outbound Recorder
     SF *Computer Sciences
         Data Processing
OBSPL Octave Band Sound Pressure Level
     SF *Aeronautics
         Aircraft Noise
OC   On Center
     SF *Metallurgy and Metallography
         Metalworks
OCA   Operational Control Authority
     SF *Military Sciences
         *Transportation
OCC   Oceanic Control Centers
     SF *Communication Systems
OCE   Ocean Covered Earth
     SF *Geosciences
         *Meteorology
OCI   Operator Control Interface
     SF *Aeronautics
         Wind Tunnel
OCI   Optically Coupled Isolator
     SF *Computer Sciences
         Data Processing
OCP   Obstacle Clearance Panel
     SF *Aeronautics
         Approach and Landing
OCR   Optical Character Reader
     SF *Computer Sciences
         Data Processing
         *Information Retrieval Systems
OCR   Optical Character Recognition
     SF *Computer Sciences
         Data Processing
OCR   Organic Cooled Reactor
     SF *Nuclear Sciences
         Reactors
OCR   Overconsolidated Ratio
     SF   Civil Engineering
         *Engineering
OCS   Optical Contact Sensor
     SF *Aeronautics
         *Communication Systems
OCS   Output Control Subsystem
     SF *Computer Sciences

Data Processing
OCT   Operational Cycle Time
SF   *Computer Sciences
Data Processing
OCU   Operational Control Unit
SF   *Computer Sciences
Data Processing
OCV   Open Circuit Voltage
SF   *Electronics and Electrical
Engineering
OD   Optical Density
SF   Bioengineering
*Biological and Medical Sciences
Dairy Sciences
Instruments
OD   Outside Diameter
SF   *Communication Systems
*Engineering
*Mathematics
*Nuclear Sciences
OD   Outside Dimension
SF   *Metallurgy and Metallography
ODIN   Optimal Design Integration
SF   *Aeronautics
Aircraft
*Space Sciences
ODP   Optical Data Processor
SF   Lasers and Masers
*Physics
ODPCS Oceanographic Data Processing and
Control System
SF   *Naval Sciences
Navigation
ODR   Office of Defense Resources (US)
SF   *Military Sciences
*Transportation
ODR   Oxygen Diffusion Rate
SF   *Agricultural Sciences
OECD   Organisation for Economic Cooperation
and Development
SF   *General
OED   Quantum Electrodynamics
SF   Nuclear Physics
*Nuclear Sciences
OEMI   Office Equipment Manufacturers'
Institute
SF   *Computer Sciences
Data Processing
OEO   Office of Economic Opportunity (US)
SF   *General
OEP   Office Emergency Preparedness (US)
SF   *Transportation
OES   Office of Emergency Service (US)
SF   *Military Sciences
OES   Order Entry System
SF   *Computer Sciences
Data Processing
OEW   Operating Empty Weight
SF   *Aeronautics
Aircraft

OFP   O-Fluorophenylalanine
SF   *Agricultural Sciences
OFT   Operational Flight Trainer
SF   *Aeronautics
Human Factors
OFZ   Obstacle Free Zone
SF   *Aeronautics
Instruments
OH   Opposite Hand
SF   *Metallurgy and Metallography
Metalworks
OHA   Oxygen-Haemoglobin Affinity
SF   *Biological and Medical Sciences
OHM   Ohmmeter
SF   *Electronics and Electrical
Engineering
OHT   Oxygen at High Temperature
SF   *Biological and Medical Sciences
OICC   Officer In-Charge of Construction
SF   Civil Engineering
*Engineering
OJT   On Job Training
SF   *Computer Sciences
Data Processing
*Engineering
*Training
OL   Overhead Links
SF   *Engineering
Radio Engineering
*Telecommunications
OLPARS On Line Pattern Analysis and
Recognition System
SF   *Computer Sciences
Data Processing
OLTEP On-Line Test Executive Program
SF   *Computer Sciences
Data Processing
OLTS   On-Line Test System
SF   *Computer Sciences
Data Processing
OM   Operation and Maintenance
SF   *Aeronautics
OM   Organic Matter
SF   *Agricultural Sciences
*Biological and Medical Sciences
OM   Outer Marker
SF   *Aeronautics
Instrument Flying
OMB   Office of Management and Budget (US)
SF   *General
*Management
OMJ   Outgoing Message Junction
SF   Radio Engineering
*Telecommunications
OMR   Optical Mark Reader
SF   *Computer Sciences
OMR   Optical Mark Recognition
SF   *Computer Sciences
OND   Own Number Dialling
SF   *Engineering

*Telecommunications

ONERA Office National d'Etudes et de
Recherches Aéronautiques (Fr.)
SF *Aeronautics
*Space Sciences

ONR Office of Naval Research (US)
SF *Military Sciences
Naval Sciences

ONWARD Organization of the North West
Authorities for Rationalized
Design (US)
SF *Nuclear Sciences
Reactors

OP Orthogonal Polynomials
SF *Mathematics

OPE One Pion Exchange
SF Elastic Scattering
*Nuclear Sciences

OPGENS Optical Pollution Surveillance
Schedule Generating System
SF *Computer Sciences
Data Processing

OPLE OMEGA Position Locating Equipment
SF *Aeronautics
*Naval Sciences
Navigation

OPM Operational Per Minute
SF *Computer Sciences
Data Processing

OPM Output Position Map
SF *Computer Sciences
Data Processing

OPMS Officer Personnel Management System
SF Logistics
*Military Sciences

OPSKS Optimum Phase Shift Keyed Signals
SF *Engineering
Radio Engineering
*Telecommunications

OPT Ophthaldialdehyde
SF *Biological and Medical Sciences
Cytochemistry

OPTIM Order Point Technique for Inventory
Management
SF *Computer Sciences
Data Processing

ORD Optical Rotatory Dispersion
SF *Agricultural Sciences
Cereals

ORGDP Oak Ridge Gaseous Diffusion Plant
SF *Nuclear Sciences
Reactors

ORNL Oak Ridge National Laboratory
SF *Nuclear Sciences
Radiation

ORP Oxidation Reduction Potential
SF Bioengineering
*Biological and Medical Sciences

ORR Oak Ridge Reactor
SF *Nuclear Sciences
Reactors

ORS Operational Research Society
SF *Computer Sciences
Data Processing

OS Oblique Sounding
SF *Engineering
Radio Engineering
*Telecommunications

OS Operating System
SF *Computer Sciences
Data Processing

OSC Optimally Sensitive Controller
SF Bioengineering
*Biological and Medical Sciences

OSHA Occupational Safety and Health Act
SF *Engineering
Engineering Consultancy

OSHA Occupational Safety and Health
Administration
SF *Engineering
Human Factors
Mechanical Engineering

OSIL Operating System Implementation
League
SF *Computer Sciences
Data Processing

OSM Option Select Mode
SF *Computer Sciences
Data Processing

OSO Orbiting Solar Observatory
SF *Astronautics and Astrophysics
*Lunar Sciences

OSR Optical Solar Reflector
SF *Space Sciences
Space Simulation

OSR Over-the-Shoulder Rating
SF *Aeronautics
Air Traffic Control

OST Office of Secretary of Transportation
(US)
SF *Transportation

OSTCOOP Office of the Secretary of
Transportation Continuity of
Operations Plan (US)
SF *Transportation

OSTI Office for Scientific and Technical
Information
SF *Computer Sciences
Data Processing
*Information Retrieval Systems

OSW Office of Saline Water (US)
SF *Engineering
Engineering Consultancy

OTC One-stop Tour Charter
SF *Aeronautics
Air Transport

OTC   Overseas Telecommunications Commission
      SF   *Telecommunications
OTC   Oxytetracycline
      SF   Biochemistry
           *Biological and Medical Sciences
OTD   Original Transmission Densities
      SF   *Photography
OTF   Optical Transfer Function
      SF   *Photography
OTH   Over-the-Horizon
      SF   *Aeronautics
OTIU Overseas Technical Information Unit
       (UK)
      SF   *Information Retrieval Systems
OTL   Order Trunk Lines
      SF   *Engineering
           Radio Engineering
           *Telecommunications
OTMJ Outgoing Trunk Message Junctions
      SF   *Engineering
           Radio Engineering
           *Telecommunications
           Telephone Networks
OTS   Out-Of Service
      SF   *General
OTSR Optimum Track Ship Routing
      SF   *Meteorology
           *Transportation
OTU   Operational Taxonomic Unit
      SF   *Computer Sciences
           Data Processing
OVA   Ovalbumin
      SF   *Dairy Sciences
OVX   Ovariectomized
      SF   *Agricultural Sciences
           *Dairy Sciences
OWE   Operating Weight Empty
      SF   *Aeronautics
           Aircraft
           *Military Sciences
OWF   Optimal Worked Frequency
      SF   *Engineering
           Radio Engineering
           *Telecommunications
OWS   Orbital Station
      SF   *Astronautics and Astrophysics
           Spacecraft

P

P   Pentode
    SF   *Electronics and Electrical
         Engineering
         Semiconductor Devices
P   Phosphorus
    SF   *Agricultural Sciences
P   Print
    SF   *Computer Sciences
pa   Power Amplifier
    SF   *Communication Systems
         Radio Engineering
PA   Preamplifier
    SF   *Electronics and Electrical
         Engineering
PA   Puromycin Aminonucleoside
    SF   Biochemistry
         *Biological and Medical Sciences
PAA   Phase Antenna Arrays
    SF   *Electronics and Electrical
         Engineering
         *Engineering
         Radio Engineering
         *Telecommunications
PAA   Polyacrylamide
    SF   *Biological and Medical Sciences
         Cytochemistry
PAA-PS Polyacrylic Acid-Polysulfone
    SF   *Chemistry
PAB   Pulse Adsorption Bed
    SF   Civil Engineering
         *Engineering
PABX   Private Automatic Branch Exchange
    SF   *Communication Systems
         *Computer Sciences
         Data Processing
PAC   Package Assembly Circuit
    SF   *Computer Sciences
         Data Processing
PAC   Polycyclic Aromatic Hydrocarbons
    SF   *Chemistry
PACA   Polyamide Carboxylic Acid
    SF   *Non-metallic Materials
         Polymers
PACAF Pacific Air Force
    SF   Civil Engineering

         *Engineering
         *Military Sciences
PACE   Package Cram Executive
    SF   *Computer Sciences
         Data Processing
PACF   Periodic Autocorrelation Function
    SF   *Engineering
         Radio Engineering
         *Telecommunications
PACOM Pacific Command
    SF   Air Force
         *Military Sciences
PACT   Project for the Advancement of
         Coding Techniques
    SF   *Computer Sciences
         Data Processing
PAD   Positioning Arm Disc
    SF   *Computer Sciences
         Data Processing
PAD   Public Assistance Director (US)
    SF   *Military Sciences
PADS   Performance Analysis and Design
         Synthesis
    SF   *Space Sciences
         Spacecraft Design
PAF   pFormaldehyde-Picric Acid
    SF   *Biological and Medical Sciences
         Cytochemistry
PAFC   Phase-locked Automatic Frequency
         Control
    SF   *Engineering
         Radio Engineering
         *Telecommunications
PAG   Pre-Albumin Globulin
    SF   Biochemistry
         *Biological and Medical Sciences
         Pharmacology
PAG   Protein Advisory Group (US)
    SF   *Biological and Medical Sciences
PAGE   Polyacrylamide Gel Electrophoresis
    SF   *Agricultural Sciences
         *Dairy Sciences
PAIT   Program for the Advancement of
         Industrial Technology
    SF   *Electronics and Electrical

Engineering
    *Engineering
PALM Precision Altitude and Landing Monitor
    SF *Aeronautics
      Air Traffic Control
PAM Pozzolanic Mixtures
    SF Civil Engineering
      Concretes
      *Engineering
PAM Peripheral Adapter Module
    SF *Aeronautics
      *Electronics and Electrical
        Engineering
      Radar
PAM Pozzolan Aggregate Mixture
    SF Civil Engineering
      *Engineering
PAM Process Automatic Monitor
    SF *Computer Sciences
      Data Processing
PAM Pulse Amplitude Modulation
    SF *Aeronautics
      *Communication Systems
      *Computer Sciences
      Data Processing
      *Electronics and Electrical
        Engineering
PAMD Periodic Acid Mixed Diamine
    SF *Biological and Medical Sciences
      Cytochemistry
PAN Polyacrylonitrile
    SF *Biological and Medical Sciences
PANS Procedures for Air Navigation Services
    SF *Aeronautics
      Navigation
PAP p-Amonophenylamine
    SF *Agricultural Sciences
PAP Peroxidase Antiperoxidase
    SF *Biological and Medical Sciences
      Cytochemistry
PAPD Periodate-Dimethyl-phenylenediamine
    SF *Biological and Medical Sciences
      Cytochemistry
PAPS Periodic Acid Phenylhydrazine Schiff
    SF *Biological and Medical Sciences
      Cytochemistry
PAR Precision Approach Radar
    SF *Aeronautics
      Approach and Landing
      Instruments
PAR Processor Address Register
    SF *Computer Sciences
      Data Processing
PARM Participating Manager
    SF Logistics
      *Military Sciences
PARP Partially Acidulated Rock Phosphate
    SF *Agricultural Sciences
PAS Periodic Acid Schiff
    SF *Agricultural Sciences

      *Biological and Medical Sciences
      Cytochemistry
PA-SM Periodic Acid-Silver Methenamine
    SF *Biological and Medical Sciences
      Cytochemistry
PASNY Power Authority of the State of
    New York
    SF Civil Engineering
      *Engineering
PAT Programmable Automatic Tester
    SF *Computer Sciences
PAT Programmer's Aptitude Test
    SF *Computer Sciences
      Data Processing
PATCA Phase-lock Automatic Tuned Circuit
    Adjustment
    SF *Engineering
      Radio Engineering
      *Telecommunications
PATSY Programmer's Automatic Testing
    System
    SF *Computer Sciences
      Data Processing
PAX Private Automatic Exchange
    SF *Computer Sciences
      Data Processing
PB Peripheral Buffer
    SF *Computer Sciences
      Data Processing
PB Phenobarbital
    SF Biochemistry
      *Biological and Medical Sciences
PB Piperonyl Butoxide
    SF Biochemistry
      *Biological and Medical Sciences
PBC Psychrotrophic Count
    SF *Agricultural Sciences
      *Dairy Sciences
PBD Parallel Blade Damper
    SF *Metallurgy and Metallography
      Metalworks
PBE Pulsed Bridge Element
    SF *Engineering
      Radio Engineering
      *Telecommunications
PBEIST Planning Board for European Inland
    Surface Transport
    SF *Military Sciences
      *Transportation
PBF Potential Benefit Factor
    SF *Aeronautics
      Aircraft
PBI Polybenzimidazole
    SF *Biological and Medical Sciences
PBI Protein Bound Iodine
    SF *Agricultural Sciences
      *Dairy Sciences
PBOS Planning Board for Ocean Shipping
    SF *Military Sciences
      *Transportation

PBRF	Plum Brook Reactor Facility
	SF *Nuclear Sciences
	Reactors
PBS	Phosphate Buffered Saline
	SF *Agricultural Sciences
	*Biological and Medical Sciences
	Cereals
PBX	Private Branch Exchange
	SF *Computer Sciences
	Data Processing
PC	Parametric Cubic
	SF *Computer Sciences
	Data Processing
PC	Palvicellar
	SF *Biological and Medical Sciences
PC	Personal Call
	SF *Engineering
	Radio Engineering
	*Telecommunications
PC	Polycarbonate
	SF *Non-metallic Materials
	Polymers
PC	Premphasis Circuits
	SF *Engineering
	Radio Engineering
	*Telecommunications
PC	Printed Circuit
	SF *Computer Sciences
	*Electronics and Electrical
	Engineering
P-C	Processor-Controller
	SF *Computer Sciences
	Data Processing
PC	Program Computer
	SF *Computer Sciences
	Data Processing
PC	Punch Card
	SF *Computer Sciences
	Data Processing
PC	Pyrurate Carboxylase
	SF Biochemistry
	*Biological and Medical Sciences
PCA	Polar Cap Absorption
	SF *Communication Systems
	*Geosciences
	Navigation
PCB	Polychlorinated Biphenyl
	SF *Agricultural Sciences
	*Dairy Sciences
PCB	Printed Circuit Board
	SF *Communication Systems
	*Computer Sciences
	Data Processing
	Radio Engineering
PCC	Peripheral Control Computer
	SF *Computer Sciences
PCC	Portland Cement Concrete
	SF *Building
	Civil Engineering
	*Engineering

PCC	Power Control Center
	SF *Computer Sciences
	Data Processing
PCD	Production Common Digitizer
	SF *Aeronautics
	Radar Equipment
	Transponders
PCE	Program Cost Estimates
	SF *Management
PCE	Pyrometric Cone Equivalent
	SF *Chemistry
PCG	Phonocardiogram
	SF *Biological and Medical Sciences
	*Space Sciences
PCI	Packet Communications Incorporated
	SF *Communication Systems
PCI	Patterson Candy International
	SF *Agricultural Sciences
PCI	Peripheral Command Indicator
	SF *Aeronautics
	Navigation
PCI	Plant Control Interface
	SF *Aeronautics
	Aerospace
PCI	Programmed Control Interrupt
	SF *Computer Sciences
	Data Processing
PCL	Process Control Language
	SF *Computer Sciences
	Data Processing
PCM	Penalty Cost Model
	SF Logistics
	*Military Sciences
PCM	Pulse Code Modulation
	SF *Aeronautics
	*Biological and Medical Sciences
	*Communication Systems
	*Computer Sciences
	*Engineering
	Radio Engineering
PCM	Punched Card Machine
	SF *Computer Sciences
	Data Processing
PCMB	p-Chloromercuribenzoate
	SF *Dairy Sciences
PCMI	Photochromic Microimage
	SF *Computer Sciences
	Data Processing
	*Photography
PCOS	Process Control Operating System
	SF *Computer Sciences
	Data Processing
PCP	Primary Control Program
	SF *Computer Sciences
	Data Processing
PCP	Programmable Communication Processors
	SF *Communication Systems
	*Computer Sciences
PCPA	Para Chlorophenylalanine
	SF *Biological and Medical Sciences

Drugs

PCR   Positively Control Routes
      SF   *Aeronautics
           Air Traffic Control
PCR   Program Control Register
      SF   *Computer Sciences
           Data Processing
PCS   Power Conditioning System
      SF   *Aeronautics
           *Communication Systems
           *Electronics and Electrical
            Engineering
PCS   Print Contrast System
      SF   *Computer Sciences
           Data Processing
PCS   Project Control System
      SF   *Computer Sciences
           Data Processing
PCT   Patent Cooperation Treaty
      SF   *Copyright
PCU   Program Control Unit
      SF   *Computer Sciences
           Data Processing
PCV   Packed Cell Volume
      SF   *Statistics
PCV   Positive Crankcase Ventilation
      SF   *Engineering
           Mechanical Engineering
           Motor Vehicle Engineering
pd   Potential Difference
      SF   *Mathematics
pd   Potential Difference/Power Doubler
      SF   *Communication Systems
           *Engineering
           Radio Engineering
PD   Performance Data
PD   Principal Distance
      SF   *Photography
PDA   Potato Dextrose Agar
      SF   *Agricultural Sciences
PDAID Problem Determination Aid
      SF   *Computer Sciences
           Data Processing
PDAPS Pollution Detection and Prevention
      System
      SF   *Computer Sciences
           Data Processing
PDD   Projected Data Display
      SF   *Aeronautics
           Navigation
PDD   Pulse Delay Device
      SF   *Aeronautics
           Instruments
PDF   Pair Distribution Function
      SF   *Biological and Medical Sciences
PDF   Probability Density Functions
      SF   *Engineering
           Instruments
           Photometric Engineering

*Photography
PDF   Protected Difference Fat
      SF   *Agricultural Sciences
           *Dairy Sciences
PDI   Perfect Digital Invariants
      SF   *Mathematics
PDL   Procedure Definition Language
      SF   *Computer Sciences
           Data Processing
PDM   Protected Difference Milk
      SF   *Agricultural Sciences
           *Dairy Sciences
PDM   Pulse Duration Modulation
      SF   *Computer Sciences
           Data Processing
PDR   Pilot's Display Recorder
      SF   *Aeronautics
           Avionics
PDU   Pilot's Display Unit
      SF   *Aeronautics
PDW   Partially Delactosed Whey
      SF   *Dairy Sciences
PDWP Partially Delactosed Whey Power
      SF   *Dairy Sciences
PE   Plant Extrusion
      SF   *Agricultural Sciences
PE   Processing Elements
      SF   *Computer Sciences
           Data Processing
PEA   Polyethyl Acrylate
      SF   *Non-metallic Materials
           Polymers
PEAD Presidential Emergency Action
      Document (US)
      SF   *General
PEBV Pea Early Browning Virus
      SF   *Agricultural Sciences
PEC   Platform Electron Cards
      SF   *Electronics and Electrical
            Engineering
           Testing
PED   Pulse Edge Discrimination
      SF   *Aeronautics
           *Electronics and Electrical
            Engineering
           Radar
PEE   Proof and Experimental Establishment
      (UK)
      SF   *Aeronautics
           Hypersonic Facilities
PEG   Polyethylene Glycol
      SF   *Agricultural Sciences
           *Dairy Sciences
           *Non-metallic Materials
           *Photography
PELSS Precision Emitter Location Strike
      System
      SF   Defence Weapons
           *Military Sciences

PEN   Penicillin
        SF   *Agricultural Sciences
             *Dairy Sciences
             Drugs
PEO   Polyethylene Oxide
        SF   *Non-metallic Materials
             *Photography
             Polymers
PEP   p-Fluorophenylalanine
        SF   *Agricultural Sciences
PEP   Phosphoenolpyruvate
        SF   *Biological and Medical Sciences
             Medical Ions
PEP   Primate Equilibrium Platform
        SF   *Biological and Medical Sciences
             Radiobiology
PEP   Programme Evaluation Procedure
        SF   *Computer Sciences
             Data Processing
             Operational Research
PEP   Propulsion and Energetics Panel
        SF   *Aeronautics
PEPCK   Phosphoenolpyruvate Carboxykinase
        SF   Biochemistry
             *Biological and Medical Sciences
             Pharmacology
PEPP   Professional Engineers in Private
          Practice
        SF   *Engineering
             Engineering Consultancy
PER   Protein Efficiency Ratio
        SF   *Agricultural Sciences
             Cereals
PERA   Planning and Engineering for Repair
          and Alterations (US)
        SF   Logistics
             *Military Sciences
PERA   Production Engineering Research
          Association
        SF   *Engineering
             Mechanical Engineering
PERT   Program Evaluation Review Technique
        SF   Civil Engineering
             *Computer Sciences
             Data Processing
             *Engineering
             *Management
             *Military Sciences
PERT   Programme Evaluation Research Task
        SF   *Computer Sciences
             Data Processing
             Operational Research
PES   Programmer Electronic Switch
        SF   *Electronics and Electrical
               Engineering
PET   Pentaerythrital
        SF   *Astronautics and Astrophysics
             *Lunar Sciences
PET   Polyethylene Terephthalate
        SF   *Non-metallic Materials

PETN   Pentaerythritol Tetranitrate
        SF   *Chemistry
             Organic Chemistry
PEX   Projectable Excitation
        SF   Elementary Particles
             *Physics
PF   Peanut Flour
        SF   *Agricultural Sciences
             *Dairy Sciences
PF   Phenol Formaldehyde
        SF   *Non-metallic Materials
             Plastics
PF   Power Factor
        SF   *Electronics and Electrical
               Engineers
             Meters
PF   Punch Off
        SF   *Computer Sciences
             Data Processing
PFA   Popular Flying Association
        SF   *Aeronautics
PFA   Pulverized Fuel Ash
        SF   *Agricultural Sciences
             *Building
             Civil Engineering
             *Engineering
PFC   Pack Feed and Converter
        SF   *Management
             *Printing
PFC   Phase Frequency Characteristics
        SF   *Engineering
             Radio Engineering
             *Telecommunications
PFC   Plaque Forming Cells
        SF   *Biological and Medical Sciences
             Smoking
PFCR   Plaque Forming Cell Response
        SF   *Biological and Medical Sciences
             Smoking
PFCS   Primary Flight Control System
        SF   *Aeronautics
             Air Traffic Control
PFD   Power Flux Density
        SF   *Electronics and Electrical
               Engineering
             Electromagnetics
PFIR   Part Fill In and Ram
        SF   *Building
PFK   Phosphofructokinase
        SF   *Biological and Medical Sciences
             Cytochemistry
PFM   Practice of Flour Milling
        SF   *Agricultural Sciences
             *Milling
PFN   Permanent File Name
        SF   *Computer Sciences
             Data Processing
PFN   Pulse Forming Network
        SF   *Electronics and Electrical
               Engineering

PFP   Post Flight Processor
     SF *Aeronautics
        Testing
PFR   Prototype Fast Reactor
     SF *Nuclear Sciences
PFSS Particles and Field Sub-Satellite
     SF *Telecommunications
PFT   Physical Fitness Test
     SF *Biological and Medical Sciences
PFTE Polytetrafluoroethylene
     SF *Electronics and Electrical
         Engineering
        *Engineering
PFU   Plaque Forming Unit
     SF   Bioengineering
        *Biological and Medical Sciences
PG   Photosphoglycollate
     SF *Biological and Medical Sciences
        Medical Ions
PG   Power Gate
     SF *Electronics and Electrical
         Engineering
        Solid-state Circuits
PG   Pulse Generator
     SF *Engineering
        Radio Engineering
        *Telecommunications
PG   Pyrolytic Graphite
     SF *Nuclear Sciences
        Radioisotopes
PGA   Pressure Garment Assembly
     SF *Space Sciences
        Space Simulation
PGE   Primary Group Equipment
     SF *Engineering
        Radio Engineering
        *Telecommunications
PGI   Phosphoglucoisomerase
     SF *Biological and Medical Sciences
        Cytochemistry
PGK   Phosphoglycerate Kinase
     SF *Biological and Medical Sciences
        Cytochemistry
PGLIN Page and Line
     SF *Computer Sciences
        Data Processing
PGRO Pea Growing Research Organization
     SF *Agricultural Sciences
PGT   Pilot Ground Trainer
     SF *Aeronautics
PGUE Polyacrylamide Gel Urea Electrophoresis
     SF *Agricultural Sciences
        Cereals
PH   Phasemeter
     SF *Electronics and Electrical
         Engineering
        Meters
PHA   Pulse Height Analysis
     SF *Astronautics and Astrophysics
        *Lunar Sciences

PHA   Pulse Height Analyzer
     SF *Nuclear Sciences
        Instruments
PHM   Patrol Hydrofoil Missile
     SF *Aeronautics
        Anti-ship Missile
        *Military Sciences
PHS   Paternal Half Sister
     SF *Dairy Sciences
PHS   Public Health Service
     SF *Biological and Medical Sciences
PHTC Pulse Height to Time Converter
     SF *Nuclear Sciences
PI   Particular Integral
     SF *Mathematics
PI   Pepsin Inhibitor
     SF *Biological and Medical Sciences
PI   Position Indicator
     SF *Electronics and Electrical
         Engineering
        Meters
PI   Preliminary Incubation
     SF *Agricultural Sciences
        *Dairy Sciences
PI   Programmed Instruction
     SF *Computer Sciences
        Data Processing
PI   Programmer's Interface
     SF *Computer Sciences
        Data Processing
PI   Proportional-plus Integral
     SF *Engineering
        Radio Engineering
        *Telecommunications
PI   Propyl Isome
     SF *Biological and Medical Sciences
PIA   Printing Industries of America
     SF *Printing
PIBAL Polytechnic Institute of Brooklyn
      Aerodynamics Laboratory (US)
     SF *Aeronautics
PIC   Particle-In-Cell
     SF *Physics
PIC   Polymer Impregnated Concrete
     SF   Civil Engineering
        *Engineering
PIC   Process Interface Control
     SF *Computer Sciences
        Data Processing
PICAO Provisional International Civil
      Aviation Organization
     SF *Aeronautics
PICLS Purdue Instructional and Computational
      Learning System
     SF   Programmed Learning
        *Training
PICS Production Information and Control
      System
     SF *Computer Sciences
        *Information Retrieval Systems

PID   Proportional Integral Derivative
        SF   *Electronics and Electrical
             Engineering
PID   Pseudo Interupt Device
        SF   *Computer Sciences
PIMISS Pennsylvania Interagency Management
        Information Support System
        SF   *Information Retrieval Systems
             *Management
PIOU   Parallel Input/Output Unit
        SF   *Computer Sciences
             Data Processing
PIP   Peripheral Interchange Program
        SF   *Computer Sciences
             Data Processing
PIRA   Paper Industries Research Association
        (UK)
        SF   *Information Retrieval Systems
PIV   Production Inspection Verification
        SF   Logistics
             *Military Sciences
PK   Pyruvate Kinase
        SF   Biochemistry
             *Biological and Medical Sciences
PL   Phospholipids
        SF   Biochemistry
             *Biological and Medical Sciences
PL   Programming Language
        SF   *Computer Sciences
             Data Processing
PL/1   Programming Language One
        SF   *Computer Sciences
             Data Processing
PL   Psittacosis Lymphogranuloma
        SF   *Agricultural Sciences
PLA   Polylactic Acid
        SF   *Biological and Medical Sciences
PLA   Poly Lalanine
        SF   *Non-metallic Materials
             Polymers
PLACE   Programming Language for Automatic
        Checkout Equipment
        SF   *Computer Sciences
             *Electronics and Electrical
              Engineering
PLAN   Programming Language Nineteen Hundred
        SF   *Computer Sciences
             Data Processing
PLL   Peripheral Light Loss
        SF   *Aeronautics
             Aviation Medicine
             *Biological and Medical Sciences
PLL   Phase Locked Loop
        SF   *Aeronautics
             Avionics
             *Electronics and Electrical
              Engineering
PLRACTA Position Location Reporting and
        Control Tactical Aircraft
        SF   *Aeronautics

             *Communication Systems
PLSS   Portable Life Support System
        SF   *Space Sciences
PLUTO   Parts Listing and Used on Techniques
        SF   *Computer Sciences
             Data Processing
PM   Permanent Magnet
        SF   *Communication Systems
             *Engineering
             Radio Engineering
PM   Photomultiplier
        SF   Alpha Particles
             *Electronics and Electrical
              Engineering
             *Nuclear Sciences
             *Photography
             Quantum Electrons
PM   Plasma Membrane
        SF   *Biological and Medical Sciences
             Cytochemistry
PM   Post Mortem
        SF   *Computer Sciences
             Data Processing
PMA   Phenylmercuric Acetate
        SF   *Agricultural Sciences
PMA   Phorbol Myristate Acetate
        SF   *Biological and Medical Sciences
             Enzymes
PMA   Polymethyl Acrylate
        SF   *Non-metallic Materials
             Polymers
PMB   Post Mortem Dump
        SF   *Computer Sciences
             Data Processing
PMC   Princeton Microfilm Corporation
        SF   *Photography
PMC   Program Management Control
        SF   *Engineering
             *Military Sciences
PMCM   Pulse Morse Code Modulation
        SF   *Astronautics and Astrophysics
             *Biological and Medical Sciences
PMD   Program Module Dictionary
        SF   *Computer Sciences
             Data Processing
PMDA   Pyromellitic Dianhydride
        SF   *Non-metallic Materials
             Polymers
PMDR   Phosphorescence Microwave Double
        Resonance
        SF   *Chemistry
PMGS   Predictable Model Guidance Scheme
        SF   *Aeronautics
             Navigation
PMIP   Postmaintenance Inspection Pilots
        SF   *Aeronautics
             *Military Sciences
             *Naval Sciences
PMIS   Patient Medical Information System
        SF   *Biological and Medical Sciences

*Information Retrieval Systems

PMMA Polymethyl Methracrylate
    SF *Non-metallic Materials
       Plastics

PMN Polymorphonuclear Leukocyte
    SF *Biological and Medical Sciences
       Enzymes

PMP Pressure Measurement Package
    SF *Aeronautics
       Wind Tunnel

PMR Proton Magnetic Resonance
    SF Biochemistry
       *Biological and Medical Sciences

PMS Project Management System
    SF *Computer Sciences
       Data Processing
       *Management

PMS Projected Map System
    SF *Aeronautics
       Avionics

PMS Pregnant Mare's Serum
    SF *Agricultural Sciences
       *Biological and Medical Sciences
       Cytochemistry

PMS Public Message Service
    SF *Computer Sciences
       Data Processing

PMSE Program Management Simulation Exercise
    SF Logistics
       *Military Sciences

PMSG Pregnant Mare Serum Gonadotrophin
    SF *Dairy Sciences

PMT Pheny Mercaptote Trazole
    SF *Photography

PMT Photochemical Transfer
    SF *Printing

PMTS Predetermined Motion Time System
    SF *General
       *Management

PN Punch On
    SF *Computer Sciences
       Data Processing

PND Pictorial Navigation Display
    SF *Aeronautics

PNdB Perceived Noise Decibels
    SF *Aeronautics
       Aircraft Noise

PNL Perceived Noise Level
    SF *Aeronautics
       Aircraft Noise

PNMT Phenylethanolamine N-methyltransferase
    SF *Biological and Medical Sciences
       Neurotransmitters

PNP Precision Navigation Processor
    SF *Aeronautics
       Navigation

PO Polymerizable Oligomers
    SF *Non-metallic Materials
       Plastics

POC Process Operator's Console

SF *Computer Sciences
    Data Processing

POGO Programmer Oriented Graphics Operation
    SF *Computer Sciences
       *Electronics and Electrical
         Engineering

POL Pacific Oceanographic Laboratory
    SF *Oceanography

POL Problem Oriented Language
    SF *Computer Sciences
       Data Processing
       *Engineering
       Engineering Consultancy
       *Statistics

POLANG Polarization Angle
    SF *Telecommunications

POMR Problem Oriented Medical Record
    SF *Biological and Medical Sciences

POP Practical Ordered Program
    SF Programmed Learning
       *Training

POS Partially Ordered Set
    SF Programmed Learning
       *Training

POS Point of Sale
    SF *Communication Systems

POS Product Of Sums
    SF *Computer Sciences
       Data Processing

POT Propeller Order Transmitter
    SF *Aeronautics
       *Naval Sciences
       Navigation

POTF Polychromatic Optical Thickness Fringes
    SF Instruments
       *Physics

POUT Power Output
    SF *Electronics and Electrical
         Engineering
       Semiconductor Devices

POWU Post Office Work Unit
    SF *Computer Sciences
       Data Processing

p-p Peak-to-Peak
    SF *Communication Systems
       Radio Engineering

pp Parallel Processor
    SF *Computer Sciences
       Data Processing

pp Peripheral Processor
    SF *Computer Sciences
       Data Processing

pp Plane Parallel
    SF *Astronautics and Astrophysics
       *Lunar Sciences

pp Polypropylene
    SF Chemical Engineering
       *Engineering

pp   Present Position
      SF   *General
pp   Push Pull
      SF   *Communication Systems
           *Engineering
           Radio Engineering
PPB   Parts Per Billion
      SF   *General
PPB   Pyrethrins Piperonyl Butoxide
      SF   *Agricultural Sciences
           Fumigation
           *Milling
PPC   Patrol Plane Commander
      SF   *Aeronautics
           *Military Sciences
PPC   Printer Pension Corporation
      SF   *Printing
PPD   Pulse-type Phase Detector
      SF   *Engineering
           Radio Engineering
           *Telecommunications
PPDC Programming Panels and Decoding
      Circuits
      SF   *Computer Sciences
           *Electronics and Electrical
           Engineering
PPDI Pluperfect Digital Invariants
      SF   *Mathematics
PPFRT Prototype Preliminary Flight Rating
      Test
      SF   *Aeronautics
           Instruments
PPI   Plan Position Indicator
      SF   *Aeronautics
           *Communication Systems
           *Naval Sciences
           Navigation
           *Photography
           Radar
PPI   Planar-Plug-In
      SF   *Computer Sciences
           Data Processing
PPL   Private Pilot Licences
      SF   *Aeronautics
           *Training
PPLO Pleuro Pneumonia-Like Organisms
      SF   *Agricultural Sciences
ppm   Parts Per Million
      SF   *Mathematics
PPM   Peak Programme Meters
      SF   *Photography
           Television
PPM   Pulse Position Modulation
      SF   *Computer Sciences
           Data Processing
           *Engineering
           Radio Engineering
           *Telecommunications
PPO   Polyphenol Oxidase
      SF   *Agricultural Sciences

           Cereals
           *Non-metallic Materials
           Polymers
PPO   Precedence Partition and Outdegree
      SF   *Computer Sciences
           Data Processing
PPP   Platelet Poor Plasma
      SF   *Biological and Medical Sciences
PPQ   Pterygopalaloquadrate
      SF   *Biological and Medical Sciences
PPQA Pageable Partition Queue Area
      SF   *Computer Sciences
           Data Processing
PPR   Precedence Partition and Random
      [Assignment]
      SF   *Computer Sciences
           Data Processing
PPS   Plant Protection System
      SF   *Nuclear Sciences
           Reactors
PPTP Poly-p-Phenylenetere-phtalamide
      SF   *Chemistry
           Organic Chemistry
PPV   Polarized Platen Viewer
      SF   *Engineering
           Photogrametric Engineering
           *Photography
PRA   Research Association of [British]
      Paints
      SF   *Information Retrieval Systems
PRBS Pseudorandom Binary Sequence
      SF   *Nuclear Sciences
           Reactors
PRE   Protein Relaxation Enhancement
      SF   *Biological and Medical Sciences
           Biophysics
PRF   Pulse Repetition Frequency
      SF   *Aeronautics
           Air Traffic Control
           *Communication Systems
           *Electronics and Electrical
           Engineering
           Radar
PRFD Pulse Recurrence Frequency
      Discrimination
      SF   *Aeronautics
           *Communication Systems
PRFS Pulse Recurrence Frequency Stagger
      SF   *Aeronautics
           *Communication Systems
PRI   Production Rate Indices
      SF   *Agricultural Sciences
PRI   Projection Readout Indicator
      SF   *Aeronautics
           Air Traffic Control
           Radar Equipment
PRL   Print Lister
      SF   *Computer Sciences
           Data Processing
PRM   Pressure Remnant Magnetization

SF   *Lunar Sciences
PROFIT Program for Financed Insurance
        Techniques
    SF   *Computer Sciences
        Data Processing
PROM   Programmable Read Only Memory
    SF   *Computer Sciences
        Data Processing
PROMPT Production Reviewing, Organising and
        Monitoring of Performance
        Techniques
    SF   *Computer Sciences
        Data Processing
PROP   Profit Rating Of Projects
    SF   *Computer Sciences
        Data Processing
PROSPER Profit Simulation Planning and
        Evaluation of Risk
    SF   *Computer Sciences
        Data Processing
PROSPRO Process Systems Program
    SF   *Computer Sciences
        Data Processing
PRP   Platelet Rich Plasma
    SF   *Biological and Medical Sciences
PRP   Pulse Repetition Period
    SF   *Aeronautics
        *Communication Systems
PRPP   Phosphorybosil Pyrophosphate
    SF   Biochemistry
        *Biological and Medical Sciences
PRR   Pennsylvanian Railroad
    SF   *Transportation
PRR   Pulse Repetition Rate
    SF   *Aeronautics
        *Naval Sciences
        Navigation
PRS   Performing Right Society
    SF   *Copyright
PRT   Personal Rapid Transit
    SF   *Engineering
        Mechanical Engineering
        *Transportation
PRT   Platinum Resistance Thermometer
    SF   *Nuclear Sciences
        Thermocouples
PRT   Primary Ranging Test
    SF   *Aeronautics
        *Communication Systems
PRT   Program Reference Table
    SF   *Computer Sciences
        Data Processing
PRT   Pulse Repetition Time
    SF   *Communication Systems
        Radio Noise
PRTR   Plutonium Recycle Test Reactor
    SF   Decontamination
        *Nuclear Sciences
        Reactors
PRTS   Pseudorandom Ternary Sequence

    SF   *Nuclear Sciences
        Reactors
PRVT   Production Reliability Verification
        Testing
    SF   *Engineering
        Instruments
PS   Paradoxical Sleep
    SF   *Biological and Medical Sciences
PS   Phasing System
    SF   *Engineering
        Radio Engineering
        *Telecommunications
PS   Problem Specification
    SF   *Computer Sciences
        Data Processing
PS   Program Stores
    SF   *Computer Sciences
        Data Processing
PS   Programming System
    SF   *Computer Sciences
        Data Processing
PSA   Parametric Semiconductor Amplifiers
    SF   Radio Engineering
        *Telecommunications
PSA   Prefix Storage Area
    SF   *Computer Sciences
        Data Processing
PSALI Permanent Supplementary Artificial
        Lighting Installation
    SF   *Aeronautics
        Air Traffic Control
PSAR   Preliminary Safety Analysis Report
    SF   *Nuclear Sciences
        Reactors
PSC   Power Supply Circuits
    SF   *Engineering
        Radio Engineering
        *Telecommunications
PSD   Paternal Sister Dam
    SF   *Dairy Sciences
PSD   Power Spectral Density
    SF   *Aeronautics
        Turbulence
PSD   Pulse Shape Discrimination
    SF   *Electronics and Electrical
        Engineering
PSECT Phototype Section
    SF   *Computer Sciences
        Data Processing
PSG   Phosphosilicate Glass
    SF   *Electronics and Electrical
        Engineering
        Solid-state Circuits
PSG   Programme Sequence Control
    SF   *Computer Sciences
        Data Processing
PSGC   Puget Sound Governmental Conferences
        (US)
    SF   Civil Engineering
        *Engineering

PSI   Present Serviceability Index
       SF   Civil Engineering
            *Engineering
PSK   Phase Shift Keyed
       SF   *Aeronautics
            *Computer Sciences
            *Electronics and Electrical
              Engineering
            Radio Engineering
            *Telecommunications
PSL   Problem Specification Language
       SF   *Computer Sciences
            Data Processing
PSM   Parallel Slit Map
       SF   *Mathematics
PSMLG Public Services Microfilm Liaison
         Group (UK)
       SF   *Information Retrieval Systems
PSN   Public Switched Network
       SF   *Computer Sciences
            Data Processing
PSNS   Programmable Sampling Network
         Switching
       SF   *Computer Sciences
            Data Processing
PSO   Performance Structure Oriented
       SF   *Training
PSP   Paper Tape Space
       SF   *Computer Sciences
            Data Processing
PSP   Planned Schedule Performance
       SF   *Engineering
            Radio Engineering
            *Telecommunications
PSP   Programmable Signal Processor
       SF   *Computer Sciences
            Data Processing
PSS   Power Supply System
       SF   *Engineering
            Radio Engineering
            *Telecommunications
PSU   Port Sharing Unit
       SF   *Computer Sciences
            Data Processing
PSU   Power Supply Unit
       SF   *Aeronautics
            Testing
PSW   Processor State Word
       SF   *Statistics
PSW   Program Status Word
       SF   *Computer Sciences
            Data Processing
PT   Paper Tape
       SF   *Computer Sciences
            Data Processing
PTA   Phosphotungstic Acid
       SF   *Biological and Medical Sciences
            Cytochemistry
PTAB   Photographic Technical Advisory Board
         (US)

       SF   *Photography
PTACV Prototype Tracked Air Cushion Vehicle
       SF   *Aeronautics
            *Communication Systems
PTAH   Phosphotungstic Acid Haematoxylin
       SF   *Biological and Medical Sciences
            Neuropathology
PTC   Passive Thermal Control
       SF   *Naval Sciences
            Navigation
PTCR   Positive Temperature Coefficient of
         Resistivity
       SF   *Ceramics
PTF   Phase Transfer Function
       SF   *Photography
PTFCE Polytrifluorochloroethylene
       SF   *Non-metallic Materials
            Polymers
PTFE   Polytetrafluoroethylene
       SF   *Non-metallic Materials
            Polymers
PTFS   Pilot to Forecast Service
       SF   *Aeronautics
            Air Traffic Control
PTH   Parathyroid Hormone
       SF   *Dairy Sciences
PTI   Programmed Time of Arrival
       SF   *Aeronautics
            Navigation
PTL   Power Transmission Line
       SF   *Engineering
            Radio Engineering
            *Telecommunications
PTL   Process and Test Language
       SF   *Computer Sciences
            *Communication Systems
PTM   Performance Test Model
       SF   *Space Sciences
            Space Simulation
PTMEG Polytetramethylene Oxide Glycol
       SF   *Non-metallic Materials
            Polymers
PTMO   Polytetramethylene Oxide
       SF   *Non-metallic Materials
            Polymers
PTMT   Polyterephalate
       SF   *Electronics and Electrical
              Engineering
            *Engineering
PTP   Paper Tape Punch
       SF   *Computer Sciences
            Data Processing
PTP   Point To Point
       SF   *Computer Sciences
            Data Processing
PTR   Paper Tape Reader
       SF   *Computer Sciences
            Data Processing
PTR   Part Throttle Reheat
       SF   *Aeronautics

	Aircraft Engines
PTRM	Partial Thermoremnant Magnetization
	SF *Lunar Sciences
PTT	Partial Thromboplastin Times
	SF *Biological and Medical Sciences
PTT	Push to Talk
	SF *Computer Sciences
	Data Processing
PTU	Propylthiouracil
	SF *Agricultural Sciences
PU	Processor Unit
	SF *Computer Sciences
	Data Processing
PU	Propellant Utilization
	SF *Space Sciences
	Space Simulation
PUI	Pilot Under Instruction
	SF *Aeronautics
	Approach and Landing
PUP	Plutonium Utilization Program
	SF *Nuclear Sciences
	Reactors
PV	Polycythemia Vera
	SF *Biological and Medical Sciences
	Cytochemistry
PVA	Polyvinyl Acetate
	SF *Photography
PVA	Polyvinyl Alcohol
	SF *Photography
PVC	Polyvinyl Chloride
	SF *Agricultural Sciences
	*Engineering
	*Non-metallic Materials
	Polymers
PVC	Pulse Voltage Converter
	SF *Engineering
	Radio Engineering
	*Telecommunications
PVD	Plan Video Display
	SF *Aeronautics
	*Computer Sciences
	Data Processing
PVD	Plan View Display
	SF *Aeronautics
	Navigation
PVDC	Polyvinylidine Chloride
	SF *Non-metallic Materials
	Polymers
PVDF	Polyvinylide Fluoride
	SF *Non-metallic Materials
	Polymers
PVF	Polyvinyl Fluoride
	SF *Non-metallic Materials
	Polymers
PVK	Poly-N-Vinylearbarbazole
	SF *Photography
PVK	Poly-N-Vinylcarbazole
	SF *Photography
PVN	Paraventricular Nuclei
	SF *Biological and Medical Sciences

PVOR	Precision VOR
	SF *Aeronautics
	Navigation
PVP	Polyvinylpyrrolidone
	SF *Biological and Medical Sciences
	Cytochemistry
	*Photography
PVRC	Pressure Vessel Research Committee
	SF *Engineering
	Mechanical Engineering
	*Nuclear Sciences
PWI	Pilot Warning Indicator
	SF *Aeronautics
	Instruments
PWL	Power Level
	SF *Aeronautics
	Aircraft Noise
PWR	Pressurized Water Reactor
	SF *Nuclear Sciences
	Reactors
PWR-FLECHT	Pressurized Water Reactor -
	Full Length Emergency Core
	Heat Transfer
	SF *Nuclear Sciences
	Reactors
PWT	Propulsion Wind Tunnel
	SF Aerodynamics
	*Aeronautics
	Aircraft
PZT	Photographic Zenith Tube
	SF *Astronautics and Astrophysics
	Astronomy
	*Photography
PZT	Piezoelectric Translator
	SF *Electronics and Electrical
	Engineering
	Quantum Electronics

QA   Quasi Algorithms
         SF   Programmed Learning
              *Training
QAM   Queued Access Method
         SF   *Computer Sciences
              Data Processing
QC   Quantum Count
         SF   *Computer Sciences
              Data Processing
QCB   Queued Control Block
         SF   *Computer Sciences
              Data Processing
QCE   Quality Control Evaluation
         SF   Civil Engineering
              *Engineering
              *Military Sciences
QCM   Quartz Crystal Microbalance
         SF   Radiation
              *Space Sciences
QCMB   Quartz Crystal Microbalance Gravimetry
         SF   Measurements
              *Space Sciences
QCSEE   Quiet Clean STOL Experimental Engine
         SF   *Aeronautics
              Aircraft Noise
QEAF   Qatar Emiri Air Force
         SF   *Aeronautics
              *Military Sciences
QED   Quick Test Editor
         SF   *Computer Sciences
              Data Processing
QISAM   Queued Indexed Sequential Access
         Method
         SF   *Computer Sciences
              Data Processing
QL   Query Language
         SF   *Computer Sciences
              Data Processing
QM   Quinacrine Mustard
         SF   *Biological and Medical Sciences
              Cytochemistry
QMR   Qualitative Materiel Requirement
         SF   *Aeronautics
              Air Facilities
QO   Quinoline Oxide

         SF   Biochemistry
              *Biological and Medical Sciences
QP   Quasi-Peak
         SF   *Communication Systems
              Radio Noise
QS   Quadrupole Splitting
         SF   *Nuclear Sciences
              Spectroscopy
QSAM   Queued Sequential Access Method
         SF   *Computer Sciences
              Data Processing
QSATS   Quiet Shorthaul Air Transportation
         System
         SF   *Aeronautics
              *Transportation
QSEE   Quiet STOL Experimental Engine
         SF   *Aeronautics
              Aircraft Noise
QSG   Quasi-Stellar Galaxy
         SF   *Astronautics and Astrophysics
              *Space Sciences
QSRS   Quasi Stellar Radio Sources
         SF   *Astronautics and Astrophysics
              *Lunar Sciences
QSS   Quasi Stellar Sources
         SF   *Astronautics and Astrophysics
              *Lunar Sciences
QTAM   Queued Telecommunications Access Method
         SF   *Computer Sciences
              Data Processing
QUESTOL Quiet Experimental STOL
         SF   *Aeronautics
              Aircraft Noise

R

RA   Replacement Algorithm
        SF *Computer Sciences
            Data Processing
RA   Return Air
        SF *Metallurgy and Metallography
            Metalworks
RA   Right Ascension
        SF *Astronautics and Astrophysics
            *Lunar Sciences
RAA   Random Access Array
        SF *Computer Sciences
            Data Processing
RAAP   Radford Army Ammunition Plant
        SF *Biological and Medical Sciences
            *Military Sciences
RAAP   Residue Arithmetic Associative
            Processor
        SF *Computer Sciences
            Data Processing
RAAP   Resource Allocation and Planning
        SF *Computer Sciences
            Data Processing
RAAR   RAM Address Register
        SF *Computer Sciences
            Data Processing
RACES   Radio Amateur Civil Emergency Services
        SF *Communication Systems
            *Military Sciences
RAD   Radio Analysis Diagram
        SF *General
            *Metallurgy and Metallography
RAD   Rapid Access Device
        SF *Computer Sciences
RAD   Rapid Access Disc
        SF *Computer Sciences
RAD   Relative Air Density
        SF *Communication Systems
            Transmission Lines
RADA   Random Access Discrete Address
        SF *Telecommunications
RADC   Rome Air Development Center
        SF *Aeronautics
            *Management
RAE   Radio Astronomy Explorer
        SF *Communication Systems

            *Space Sciences
RAE   Royal Aircraft Establishment (UK)
        SF *Aeronautics
            *Military Sciences
RAHTS   Rabbit Antihuman Thymocyte Serum
        SF *Biological and Medical Sciences
RAIL   Runway Alignment Indicator Lights
        SF *Aeronautics
            Approach and Landing
RAL   Radio Annoyance Level
        SF *Communication Systems
            *Engineering
            Radio Engineering
RAM   Radar Absorbing Material
        SF *Aeronautics
            Radar
RAM   Random Access Memory
        SF *Communication Systems
            *Computer Sciences
            Data Processing
RAMAC   Random Access Method of Accounting
            and Control
        SF *Computer Sciences
            Data Processing
RANN   Research Applied to National Needs (US)
        SF *Engineering
            Mechanical Engineering
RAOB   Radio Observations
        SF *Geosciences
            *Meteorology
RAPCON Radar Approach Control
        SF *Aeronautics
            Air Traffic Control
            *Communication Systems
RAPRA   Rubber and Plastics Research
            Association (UK)
        SF *Information Retrieval Systems
RARDE   Royal Armament Research and
            Development Establishment (UK)
        SF *Aeronautics
            Hypersonic Facilities
RAREP   Radar Reports
        SF *Aeronautics
            *Communication Systems
            Ground Communication Network

RAS   Rutgers Annihilation Spectrometer
     SF   *Nuclear Sciences
RASS   Rotating Acoustic Stereo Scanners
     SF   *Communication Systems
RATE   Rémote Automatic Telemetry Equipment
     SF   *Computer Sciences
        Data Processing
RB   Radio Beacon
     SF   *Aeronautics
        Approach and Landing
RBC   Red Blood Cells
     SF   *Biological and Medical Sciences
        Physiology
RBM   Real-Time Batch Monitor
     SF   *Computer Sciences
RBP   Registered Business Programmer
     SF   *Computer Sciences
        Data Processing
RBPT   Rose Bengal Plate Tests
     SF   *Agricultural Sciences
RBV   Return Beam Vidicon
     SF   *Electronics and Electrical
          Engineering
        Instruments
        Photogrametric Engineering
        *Photography
RC   Reinforced Concrete
     SF   *Building
        Civil Engineering
        *Engineering
RC   Remote Control
     SF   Radio Engineering
        *Telecommunications
RCA   Radio Corporation of America
     SF   *Communication Systems
RCA   Royal College of Art
     SF   *Printing
RCAG   Remote Controlled Air/Ground
     SF   *Aeronautics
        Air Traffic Control
        *Communication Systems
RCC   Rescue Coordination Center (US)
     SF   *Aeronautics
        *Transportation
rcc   Resistance Capacitance Coupling
     SF   *Communication Systems
        Radio Engineering
RCC   Resources Control Centre
     SF   Logistics
        *Military Sciences
RCG   Radioactivity Concentration Guide
     SF   *Nuclear Sciences
        Radiation
RCI   Rating Cone Index
     SF   *Engineering
        Mechanical Engineering
        Terramechanics
RCLS   Runway Centerline Light System
     SF   *Aeronautics
        Approach and Landing

RCM   Random Covalent Model
     SF   *Non-crystalline Solids
RCS   Radar Cross Section
     SF   *Aeronautics
RCS   Reaction Control System
     SF   *Space Sciences
        Space Simulation
RCS   Remote Control Station
     SF   *Computer Sciences
        Data Processing
RCT   Region Control Task
     SF   *Computer Sciences
        Data Processing
RCTL   Resistor Capacitor Transistor Logic
     SF   *Electronics and Electrical
          Engineering
        Integrated Circuits
RD   Radiation Damage
     SF   *Nuclear Sciences
RD   Read Direct
     SF   *Computer Sciences
        Data Processing
RD   Recording Demand
     SF   *Electronics and Electrical
          Engineering
        Meters
RD   Research and Development
     SF   *General
RDA   Recommended Dietary Allowances
     SF   *Dairy Sciences
RDC   Recording Doppler Comparator
     SF   *Astronautics and Astrophysics
        Solar Physics
RDF   Radial Distribution Function
     SF   *Non-crystalline Solids
RDF   Radio Direction Finder
     SF   *Aeronautics
        *Telecommunications
RDOS   Real Time Disc Operating System
     SF   *Computer Sciences
RDP   Radar Data Processing
     SF   *Aeronautics
        Air Traffic Control
        *Computer Sciences
        Radar Beacon Systems
RDS   Relational Data System
     SF   *Computer Sciences
        Data Processing
RDS   Robust Detection Scheme
     SF   *Aeronautics
        *Communication Systems
        Navigation
RDT   Reactor Development and Technology
     SF   *Engineering
        Mechanical Engineering
RDTE   Research, Development, Test and
       Evaluation
     SF   *Aeronautics
        *General
RDTR   Radiographic Dielectric Track

Registration
SF   *Biological and Medical Sciences
Cytochemistry

RE   Ram Effect
SF   *Engineering
Instruments

RE   Raw End
SF   *Metallurgy and Metallography
Metalworks

RE   Relative Efficiency
SF   *Statistics

REA   Radar Echoing Area
SF   *Aeronautics
Radar

REB   Relativistic Electron Beam
SF   *Nuclear Sciences
Plasma Physics

REBA   Relativistic Electron Beam Accelerator
SF   *Electronics and Electrical
Engineering
Instruments

REC   Recording
SF   *Electronics and Electrical
Engineering
Meters

RED   Reflection Electron Diffraction
SF   *Nuclear Sciences

REE   Rare Earth Elements
SF   *Lunar Sciences

REFSYST Reference System
SF   *Computer Sciences
Data Processing

REGS   Registers
SF   *Computer Sciences
Data Processing

REIL   Runway End Identifier Lights
SF   *Aeronautics
Approach and Landing

REM   Rapid Eye Movement
SF   *Aeronautics
Aviation Medicine

REM   Replacement Micrographs
SF   Non-destructive Evaluation
*Nuclear Sciences

RENM   Request for Next Message
SF   *Computer Sciences
Data Processing

RENOT   Request Notices
SF   *Aeronautics
Ground Communication Networks

RENT   Reentry Nose Tip
SF   *Chemistry
Physical Chemistry

REQWQ   Requisition Work Queue
SF   *Computer Sciences
*Information Retrieval Systems

RER   Rough Endoplastic Reticulum
SF   *Biological and Medical Sciences
Cytochemistry

RES   Remote Entry Service
SF   *Computer Sciences
Data Processing

RES   Restore
SF   *Computer Sciences
Data Processing

RES   Reticuloendothelial System
SF   *Biological and Medical Sciences

RESAR   Reference Safety Analysis Report
SF   *Nuclear Sciences
Reactors

RETC   Regional Emergency Transportation
Center (US)
SF   *Transportation

RETCO   Regional Emergency Transportation
Coordinator
SF   *Transportation

RETREP   Regional Emergency Transportation
Representation
SF   *Transportation

REV/MIN Revolution per Minute
SF   *Mathematics

rev/s   Revolution per Second
SF   *Mathematics

REW   Rewind
SF   *Computer Sciences
Data Processing

RF   Radio Frequency
SF   *Aeronautics
*Communication Systems
*Electronics and Electrical
Engineering

RF   Reactive Factor
SF   *Electronics and Electrical
Engineering
Meters

RF   Release Fraction
SF   *Nuclear Sciences
Reactors

RF   Rice Flour
SF   *Agricultural Sciences
*Dairy Sciences

RF   Roof Fan
SF   *Metallurgy and Metallography
Metalworks

rfc   Radio Frequency Choke
SF   *Communication Systems
*Engineering
Radio Engineering

RFC   Rosette Forming Cells
SF   *Biological and Medical Sciences

RFDU   Reconfiguration and Fault Detection
Unit
SF   *Aeronautics
*Communication Systems
*Computer Sciences
Radar

RFI   Radio Frequency Interface
SF   *Aeronautics
*Communication Systems
Navigation

RFL   Requested Flight Level
      SF   *Aeronautics
           Air Traffic Control
RFO   Radio Frequency Oscillator
      SF   *Aeronautics
           Instruments
RFP   Requests for Proposals
      SF   *Computer Sciences
           Data Processing
RFR   Reduced Frequency Responses
      SF   *Engineering
           Radio Engineering
           *Telecommunications
RFS   Regional Fisheries Survey
      SF   *Fisheries
RFU   Reference Frequency Unit
      SF   *Engineering
           Radio Engineering
           *Telecommunications
RGA   Residual Gas Analyzer
      SF   *Space Sciences
           Space Simulation
RGCS Revision of General Conception of
           Separation
      SF   *Aeronautics
           Air Traffic Control
RGLET Rise-time Gated Leading Edge Trigger
      SF   *Nuclear Sciences
RGR   Relative Growth Rates
      SF   *Agricultural Sciences
           *Biological and Medical Sciences
RH   Relative Humidity
      SF   *Dairy Sciences
RH   Right Hand
      SF   *Metallurgy and Metallography
           Metalworks
RHA   Road Haulage Association (UK)
      SF   *Transportation
RHC   Reheat Coil
      SF   *Metallurgy and Metallography
           Metalworks
RHC   Right Hand Circular
      SF   *Aeronautics
           *Communication Systems
RHEL Rutherford High Energy Laboratory
      SF   *Information Retrieval Systems
RI   Radio Influence
      SF   *Communication Systems
           Radio Engineering
RI   Read In
      SF   *Computer Sciences
           Data Processing
RI   Refractive Index
      SF   *Agricultural Sciences
RIA   Radioimmunoassay
      SF   *Agricultural Sciences
           *Biological and Medical Sciences
           Cytochemistry
RIC   Relocation Instruction Counter
      SF   *Computer Sciences

           Data Processing
RIETCOM Regional Interagency Emergency
           Transportation Committee (US)
      SF   *Transportation
RIMS Radiant Intensity Measuring System
      SF   *Space Sciences
           Space Simulation
RIP   Ring Index Pointer
      SF   *Computer Sciences
           Data Processing
RIS   Receipt Inspection Segment
      SF   *Civil Engineering
           *Engineering
           *Military Sciences
RITC Ramethylrhodamine Isothiocyanate
      SF   *Biological and Medical Sciences
           Cytochemistry
RJE   Remote Job Entry
      SF   *Computer Sciences
           Data Processing
RKHS Reducing Kernel Hilbert Space
      SF   *Electronics and Electrical
           Engineering
RL   Radio Links
      SF   *Engineering
           Radio Engineering
           *Telecommunications
RLC   Rotating Litter Chair
      SF   *Biological and Medical Sciences
RM   Record Mark
      SF   *Computer Sciences
           Data Processing
RMA   Reactive Modulation-type Amplifiers
      SF   *Engineering
           Radio Engineering
           *Telecommunications
RMC   Rod Memory Computer
      SF   *Computer Sciences
           Data Processing
RME   Reflex Milk Ejection
      SF   *Biological and Medical Sciences
RMI   Radio Magnetic Indicator
      SF   *Aeronautics
           Instrument Flying
RMS   Recovery Management Support
      SF   *Computer Sciences
           Data Processing
RMS   Root Mean Square
      SF   *Computer Sciences
           Data Processing
           *Mathematics
           *Photography
RNA   Ribonucleic Acid
      SF   Biochemistry
           *Biological and Medical Sciences
           Cytochemistry
RNase Ribonuclease
      SF   *Biological and Medical Sciences
           Cytochemistry
RO   Receive Only

	SF *Computer Sciences		*Biological and Medical Sciences
	Data Processing	RPG	Random Pulse Generator
RO	Reference Oscillator		SF Radio Engineering
	SF Radio Engineering		*Telecommunications
	*Telecommunications	RPG	Report Program Generator
RO	Reverse Osmosis		SF *Computer Sciences
	SF *Agricultural Sciences		Data Processing
	*Biological and Medical Sciences	RPG	Rocket Propelled Grenade
ROC	Receiver Operating Characteristic		SF *Military Sciences
	SF *Communication Systems	RPH	Relative Pulse Height
	*Photography		SF *Nuclear Sciences
ROC	Remote Operator's Console	RPIE	Real Property Installed Equipment
	SF *Computer Sciences		SF Civil Engineering
	Data Processing		*Engineering
ROC	Required Operational Capacity		*Military Sciences
	SF Logistics	RPM	Random Phase Model
	*Military Sciences		SF Liquid Semiconductors
ROC	Return On Capital		*Non-crystalline Solids
	SF Accounting	RPM	Revolutions Per Minute
	*Management		SF *Aeronautics
ROD	Rate of Descent		Approach and Landing
	SF *Aeronautics		*Metallurgy and Metallography
	Approach and Landing		Metalworks
ROI	Return On Investment	RPQ	Request for Price Quotation
	SF *General		SF *Computer Sciences
ROM	Read Only Memory		Data Processing
	SF *Engineering	RPS	Radar Plotting Sheet
	Engineering Consultancy		SF *Aeronautics
ROS	Read Only Storage		Navigation
	SF *Computer Sciences	RPS	Revolutions Per Second
	Data Processing		SF *Computer Sciences
ROT	Reusable Orbital Transport		Data Processing
	SF *Aeronautics	RPT	Recruit Performance Tests
	Navigation		SF *Training
TOTR	Receive Only Typing Reperforator	RPV	Remote Pilotless Vehicle
	SF *Computer Sciences		SF *Aeronautics
	Data Processing		*Communication Systems
RO/UF	Reverse Osmosis Ultrafiltaration	RQE	Relative Quantum Efficiencies
	SF *Agricultural Sciences		SF *Photography
ROVD	Remotely Operated Volume Damper	RQ	Respiratory Quotient
	SF *Metallurgy and Metallography		SF *Biological and Medical Sciences
	Metalworks	RR	Railroads
ROW	Right of Way		SF *Transportation
	SF *Communication Systems	RR	Rendezvour Radar
	Transmission Lines		SF *Aeronautics
rp	Real Part		*Naval Sciences
	SF *Mathematics		Navigation
RP	Record Processor	RR	Ruthenim Red
	SF *Computer Sciences		SF *Biological and Medical Sciences
	Data Processing		Cytochemistry
RPC	Regional Preparedness Committee(US)	RRB	Railroad Retirement Board (US)
	SF *Transportation		SF *Transportation
RPC	Reversed Phase Chromatography	RRB	Rapid Response Bibliography
	SF Bioengineering		SF Microfilms
	*Biological and Medical Sciences		*Photography
RPC	Rice Polishings Concentrate	RRL	Radio Relay Link
	SF *Agricultural Sciences		SF *Telecommunications
	Cereals	RRR	Range and Range Rate
RPF	Renal Plasma Flow		SF *Telecommunications
	SF Biochemistry	RRS	Radio Range/Range-Rate System

SF   *Communication Systems
     Radio Engineering

RRS   Radio Relay Stations
      SF   Radio Engineering
           *Telecommunications

RRTC   Retractable Replaceable Thermocouple
       SF   *Nuclear Sciences
            Reactors

RS   Reader Stop
     SF   *Computer Sciences
          Data Processing

RS   Recorder Separator
     SF   *Computer Sciences
          Data Processing

RS   Resolver
     SF   *Electronics and Electrical
          Engineering

RSB   Regional Shipping Board
      SF   *Military Sciences
           *Transportation

RSDP   Remote Site Data Processing
       SF   *Computer Sciences
            Data Processing

RSGB   Radio Society of Great Britain
       SF   *Communication Systems
            Radio Engineering

RSPI   Resident Shared Page Index
       SF   *Computer Sciences
            Data Processing

RSRA   Rotor Systems Research Aircraft
       SF   *Aeronautics
            Aircraft

RSS   Relaxed Static Stability
      SF   *Aeronautics
           Flight Control System

RSS   Ribbed Smoked Sheet
      SF   *Non-metallic Materials
           Polymers

RSV   Respiratory Syncytial Virus
      SF   *Biological and Medical Sciences

RT   Radio Telephony
     SF   *Communication Systems
          *Engineering
          Radio Engineering

RT   Raise Top
     SF   *Metallurgy and Metallography
          Metalworks

RT   Reperforator/Transmitter
     SF   *Computer Sciences
          Data Processing

RT   Room Temperature
     SF   *Photography

RTA   Renal Tubular Acidosis
      SF   Biochemistry
           *Biological and Medical Sciences
           Pharmacology

RTAM   Remote Terminal Access Method
       SF   *Computer Sciences
            Data Processing

RTC   Reference Transfer Calibrator

SF   *Space Sciences
     Space Simulation

RTCM   Radio Technical Commission for Marine
       Services
       SF   *Naval Sciences
            Navigation

RTD   Resistant Temperature Detectors
      SF   Instruments
           *Nuclear Sciences
           Reactors

RTE   Real Time Executive
      SF   *Computer Sciences
           Data Processing

RTG   Radioisotope Thermoelectric Generator
      SF   *Nuclear Sciences
           Reactors

RTI   Referred To Input
      SF   *Computer Sciences
           Data Processing

RTL   Resistor Transistor Logic
      SF   *Computer Sciences
           Data Processing
           *Electronics and Electrical
           Engineering
           *Telecommunications

RTM   Real Time Monitor
      SF   *Computer Sciences
           Data Processing

RTM   Response Time Module
      SF   *Computer Sciences
           Data Processing

RTNE   Radio Technical New Entrant
       SF   *Communication Systems

RTO   Referred To Output
      SF   *Computer Sciences
           Data Processing

RTOL   Reduced Takeoff and Landing
       SF   *Aeronautics
            Approach and Landing
            Noise

RTOS   Real Time Operating System
       SF   *Computer Sciences
            Data Processing

RTS   Real Time Subroutines
      SF   *Computer Sciences

RTS   Remote Testing System
      SF   *Computer Sciences
           Data Processing

RTS   Rural Telephone System
      SF   Radio Engineering
           *Telecommunications

RTT   Reservoir and Tube Tunnel
      SF   *Aeronautics

RTTY   Radio Teletypewriter
       SF   *Communication Systems
            *Computer Sciences
            Data Processing

RTU   Remote Terminal Unit
      SF   *Computer Sciences
           Data Processing

RTV   Remote Television
        SF *Telecommunications
RTX   Real Time Executive
        SF *Computer Sciences
            Data Processing
RUC   Riverine Utility Craft
        SF *Engineering
            Mechanical Engineering
            Terramechanics
RUDI   Restricted Use Digital Instrument
        SF *Nuclear Sciences
RUFAS   Remote Underwater Fishery Assessment
            System
        SF *Agricultural Sciences
            *Fisheries
RUN   Rewind and Unload
        SF *Computer Sciences
            Data Processing
RURLAM Replacement Unit Repair Level
            Analysis Model
        SF Logistics
            *Military Sciences
RVP   Reid Vapour Pressure
        SF *Aeronautics
RVP   Renal Venous Pressure
        SF Biochemistry
            *Biological and Medical Sciences
            Pharmacology
RVR   Runway Visual Range
        SF *Aeronautics
            Air Traffic Control
            Approach and Landing
RVV   Runway Visibility Value
        SF *Aeronautics
            Instrument Flying
R/W   Read Write
        SF *Computer Sciences
            Data Processing
RWC   Relative Water Content
        SF *Agricultural Sciences
RWI   Radio Wire Integration
        SF *Aeronautics
            *Communication Systems
RWS   Receiver Waveform Simulation
        SF *Aeronautics
            *Communication Systems
RY   Residual Yield
        SF *Agricultural Sciences

S

SA   Submerged Arc
        SF *Metallurgy and Metallography
            Welding
SAb   Serum Antibody
        SF *Dairy Sciences
SAB   Solar Alignment Bay
        SF *Space Sciences
            Space Simulation
SAC   Strategic Air Command (US)
        SF *Aeronautics
            *Communication Systems
            *Military Sciences
SAC   Sulphacetamide
        SF *Dairy Sciences
SACEUR Supreme Allied Command, Europe
        SF *Military Sciences
SACLANT Supreme Allied Command, Atlantic
        SF *Military Sciences
SAE   Society of Automotive Engineers
        SF *Engineering
            *Transportation
SAFE   San Andreas Fault Experiment
        SF *Space Sciences
SAFT   Shortest Access Time First
        SF *Computer Sciences
            Data Processing
SAGA   Short Arc Geodetic Adjustment
        SF *Oceanography
SAGE   Semi Automatic Ground Environment
        SF *Aeronautics
            Civil Engineering
            *Engineering
SAGPGG Sheep Anti-Guinea Pig Gamma Globulin
        SF *Dairy Sciences
SALORS Structural Analysis of Layered
            Orthotropic Ring-stiffened Shells
        SF *Aeronautics
            Aircraft
SALS   Short Approach Light System
        SF *Aeronautics
            Approach and Landing
SALT   Strategic Arms Limitation Talks
        SF   Armed Forces
            *Military Sciences
SAM   Sequential Access Method

        SF *Computer Sciences
            Data Processing
SAM   Strong Absorption Model
        SF   Nuclear Physics
            *Nuclear Sciences
SAM   Surface-to-Air Missiles
        SF *Aeronautics
            *Military Sciences
            Naval Sciences
SAME   Society of American Military Engineers
        SF *Military Sciences
SAMSO   Space and Missile System Organization
        SF *Astronautics and Astrophysics
            *Communication Systems
SAMTEC Space and Missile Test Center (US)
        SF *Space Sciences
SAN   School of Air Navigation
        SF *Aeronautics
            Navigation
            *Training
SAO   Smithsonian Astrophysical Observatory
        SF *Astronautics and Astrophysics
SAODAP Special Action Office for Drug
            Abuse Prevention
        SF *Biological and Medical Sciences
            Drugs
SAP   System Assurance Program
        SF *Computer Sciences
            Data Processing
SAR   Search and Rescue
        SF *Communication Systems
            *Transportation
SAR   Synthetic Aperture Radar
        SF *Aeronautics
            Radar
SARARC Stable Auroral Red Arc
        SF *Nuclear Sciences
SARCEN Search and Rescue Central
        SF *Communication Systems
SARCOM Search and Rescue Communicator
        SF *Communication Systems
SARDA   State and Regional Disaster Airlift
        SF *Aeronautics
            *Transportation
SAREX   Search and Rescue Exercise

        SF *Biological and Medical Sciences
            *Communication Systems
SARPS Standard and Recommended Tractices
        SF *Aeronautics
            *Telecommunications
SARSAT Search and Rescue Satellite
        SF *Communication Systems
SAS   Segment Arrival Storage
        SF   Civil Engineering
            *Engineering
            *Military Sciences
SAS   Small Angle Scattering
        SF   Liquid Semiconductors
            *Non-crystalline Solids
SAS   Small Astronomical Satellite
        SF *Space Sciences
             Spacecraft
SAS   Stability Augmentation System
        SF   Aerodynamics
            *Aeronautics
             Aircraft
SAS   Support Amplifier Station
        SF   Radio Engineering
            *Telecommunications
SASPL Saturated Ammonium Sulphate
        Precipitation Limit
        SF *Brewery
SAT   Serum Agglutination Test
        SF *Agricultural Sciences
SATAF Site Activation Task Force
        SF   Civil Engineering
            *Engineering
            *Military Sciences
SATRA Shoe and Allied Trade Research
        Association (UK)
        SF *Information Retrieval Systems
SARS Solar Alignment Test Site
        SF *Space Sciences
             Space Simulation
SAVES Sizing of Aerospace Vehicle Structures
        SF *Aeronautics
             Aircraft
            *Space Sciences
SAXS Small Angle X-ray Scattering
        SF *Non-metallic Materials
             Polymers
SBA   Small Business Administration (US)
        SF *General
SBA   Standard Beam Approach
        SF *Aeronautics
             Radar
SBCA Sensor Based Control Adapter
        SF *Computer Sciences
SBD   Scholtky Barrier Diode
        SF *Electronics and Electrical
             Engineering
SBLG Small Blast Load Generator
        SF *Engineering
             Structural Engineering
SBM   Soybean Meal

        SF *Agricultural Sciences
            *Dairy Sciences
SBP   Shore Based Prototype
        SF *Nuclear Sciences
             Reactors
SBP   Strain Gauge Package
        SF *Aeronautics
             Wind Tunnel
SBP   Systolic Blood Pressure
        SF *Aeronautics
             Aviation Medicine
            *Biological and Medical Sciences
SBPT Small-modular-weight Basic Protein
        Toxins
        SF   Biochemistry
            *Biological and Medical Sciences
SBT   Surface Barrier Transistor
        SF *Computer Sciences
             Data Processing
SBU   Station Buffer Unit
        SF *Computer Sciences
             Data Processing
SBX   Subsea Beacon Transponder
        SF *Naval Sciences
             Navigation
SC   Scullery
        SF *Building
SC   Set Clock
        SF *Computer Sciences
             Testing
SC   Shaping Circuit
        SF *Electronics and Electrical
             Engineering
SC   Special Conventional Alloy
        SF *Nuclear Sciences
SC   Specific Conductivity
        SF *Agricultural Sciences
SC   Splat Cooled
        SF *Non-crystalline Solids
SC   Subcutaneously
        SF *Biological and Medical Sciences
SCA   Single Channel Analyzer
        SF *Communication Systems
            *Electronics and Electrical
             Engineering
SCAM Spectrum Characteristics Analysis and
        Measurement
        SF *Electronics and Electrical
             Engineering
SCAN Stock Control And Analysis
        SF *Computer Sciences
             Data Processing
SCAN Supermarket Computer Answering
        Service
        SF *Computer Sciences
             Data Processing
SCARS Software Configuration Accounting and
        Reporting System
        SF *Computer Sciences
             Data Processing

SCATANA Security Control of Air Traffic
    and Air Navigation Aids
    SF   *Aeronautics
       Air Traffic Control
       *Communication Systems
SCATS Sequentially Controlled Automatic
    Transmitter Start
    SF   *Computer Sciences
       Data Processing
SCB   Segment Control Bits
    SF   *Computer Sciences
SCB   Selenite Cystine Broth
    SF   *Agricultural Sciences
       *Dairy Sciences
SCB   Site Control Block
    SF   *Computer Sciences
       Data Processing
SCBS System Control Blocks
    SF   *Computer Sciences
       Data Processing
SCC   Single Cotton Covered
    SF   *Communication Systems
       *Engineering
       Radio Engineering
SCC   Somatic Cell Concentration
    SF   *Agricultural Sciences
       *Dairy Sciences
SCC   Stress Corrosion Cracking
    SF   *Engineering
       Mechanical Engineering
SCE   Single Charge Exchange
    SF   *Nuclear Sciences
SCEO Station Construction Engineering
    Officer
    SF   Civil Engineering
       *Engineering
       *Military Sciences
SCEO Systems Civil Engineering Office
    SF   Civil Engineering
       *Engineering
       *Military Sciences
SCF   Satellite Control Facility
    SF   *Aeronautics
       *Communication Systems
SCFMO Self Consistent Field Molecular
    Orbital
    SF   *Biological and Medical Sciences
SCI   Short Circuit
    SF   *Electronics and Electrical
       Engineering
SCI   Switched Collector Impedance
    SF   *Electronics and Electrical
       Engineering
       Solid-state Circuits
SCICON Scientific Control
    SF   *Aeronautics
       Air Traffic Control
       *Computer Sciences
       Data Processing
SCIM Speech Communication Index Meter

    SF   *Aeronautics
       Noise
SCL   Serum Cholesterol Level
    SF   *Dairy Sciences
SCL   Systems Consultants
    SF   *Computer Sciences
       Data Processing
SCLB Southern Corn Leaf Bright
    SF   *Agricultural Sciences
       Cereals
SCM   Smith Corona Merchant
    SF   *Computer Sciences
       Data Processing
SCM   Software Configuration Management
    SF   *Computer Sciences
SCM   Solids Collected Milk
    SF   *Dairy Sciences
SCM   Staran Control Module
    SF   *Computer Sciences
       Data Processing
SCN   Shortest Connected Network
    SF   *Engineering
       Radio Engineering
       *Telecommunications
SCN   Soybean Cyst Nematode
    SF   *Agricultural Sciences
SCOOP Scientific Computation of Optimum
    Programs
    SF   *Computer Sciences
       Data Processing
SCOOP Student Controlled On-line Programming
    SF   Programmed Learning
       *Training
SCP   Serial Character Printer
    SF   *Photography
SCP   Surveillance Communication Processor
    SF   *Aeronautics
       Air Traffic Control
SCPC Single Channel Per Carrier
    SF   *Telecommunications
SCR   Selective Chopper Radiometer
    SF   *Aeronautics
       *Communication Systems
SCR   Silicon Controlled Rectifier
    SF   *Electronics and Electrical
       Engineering
       Integrated Circuits
SCRAMJET Supersonic Combustion Ramjet
    SF   *Aeronautics
SCRATA Steel Casting Research and Trade
    Association (UK)
    SF   *Information Retrieval Systems
SCR-DC Silicon Controlled Rectifier Direct
    Current
    SF   *Nuclear Sciences
       Reactors
SCRTD Southern California Rapid Transit
    District
    SF   *Transportation
SCS   Satellite Communication System

SF   Radio Engineering
      *Telecommunications

SCS   Soybean Corn Silage
       SF *Dairy Sciences

SCS   Stimulated Compton Scattering
       SF   Optics
             *Physics

SCT   Schottky Clamped Transistor
       SF *Electronics and Electrical
           Engineering
           Solid-state Circuits

SCT   Surface Charge Transistor
       SF *Electronics and Electrical
           Engineering
           Solid-state Circuits

SCT^{2}L Schottky Clamped Transistor Transistor
         Logic
         SF *Electronics and Electrical
             Engineering
             Solid-state Circuits

SCU   Station Control Unit
       SF *Computer Sciences
           Data Processing

SCU   Sulphur Coated Urea
       SF *Agricultural Sciences

SCV   Sub-Clutter Visibility
       SF *Aeronautics
           Radar Beacon Systems

SCW   Super-Critical Wing
       SF *Aeronautics
           Aircraft

SD   Second Difference
       SF *Statistics

SD   Splitter Damper
       SF *Metallurgy and Metallography
           Metalworks

SD   Square-law Detector
       SF   Radio Engineering
             *Telecommunications

SD   Standard Deviation
       SF *Aeronautics
           Air Traffic Control

SD   Synchronous Detector
       SF *Electronics and Electrical
           Engineering
           Instruments

SDA   Share Distribution Agency
       SF *Computer Sciences
           Data Processing

SDA   Source Data Automation
       SF *Computer Sciences
           Data Processing

SDA   Symbolic Device Address
       SF *Computer Sciences
           Data Processing

SDAT   Symbolic Device Allocation Table
       SF *Computer Sciences
           Data Processing

SDBP   Small Data Base Package
       SF *Computer Sciences

      *Electronics and Electrical
       Engineering

SDCR   Source Data Communication Retrieval
       SF *Computer Sciences
           *Information Retrieval Systems

SDD   Synthetic Dynamic Display
       SF *Aeronautics
           Air Traffic Control

SDDTTG Stored Data Definition and Translation
       Task Group
       SF *Computer Sciences
           Data Processing

SDF   Ship Design File
       SF *Computer Sciences
           Data Processing

SDF   Simplified Directional Facility
       SF *Aeronautics
           Instrument Flying

SDF   Standard Data Format
       SF *Computer Sciences
           Data Processing

SDH   Succinate Dehydrogenase
       SF *Agricultural Sciences

SDH   Succinic Dehydrogenase
       SF *Biological and Medical Sciences
           Cytochemistry

SDI   Select Dissemination of Information
       SF *Computer Sciences
           Data Processing

SDI   Selective Dissemination of Information
       SF   Microfilms
             *Photography

SDI   Situation Display Indicator
       SF *Aeronautics
           Naval Aviation

SDM   Schwarz Differential Medium
       SF *Brewery

SDM   Site Defence of Minuteman
       SF *Electronics and Electrical
           Engineering

SDM   Staran Debug Module
       SF *Computer Sciences
           Data Processing

SDMA   Space Division Multiple Access
       SF *Aeronautics
           *Communication Systems
           *Space Sciences

SDR   Special Drawing Rights
       SF *Aeronautics
           Air Transport

SDR   Statistical Data Recorder
       SF *Computer Sciences
           Data Processing

SDRT   Slot Dipole Ranging Tests
       SF *Aeronautics
           *Communication Systems

SDS   Satellite Data System
       SF *Communication Systems
           *Space Sciences

SDS   Shared Data Set

SF *Computer Sciences
Data Processing
SDS   Sodium Dodecyl Sulphate
SF *Agricultural Sciences
*Biological and Medical Sciences
Cereals
Cytochemistry
*Dairy Sciences
SDS-PAGE Sodium Dodecyl Sulphate-
Polyacrylamide Gel Electrophoresis
SF *Agricultural Sciences
Cereals
SDSW   Sense Device Status Word
SF *Computer Sciences
Data Processing
SE   Slip End
SF *Metallurgy and Metallography
Metalworks
SE   Small End
SF *Metallurgy and Metallography
Metalworks
SE   Spherical Eyeball
SF *Aeronautics
Thrust Vector Concepts
SE   Starch Equivalent
SF *Agricultural Sciences
SEA   Spherical Electrostatic Analyzer
SF *Computer Sciences
*Electronics and Electrical
Engineering
SEA   Statistical Energy Analysis
SF *Physics
SEAL   Signal Evaluation Airborne Laboratory
SF *Aeronautics
Navigation
SEARCH   System for Electronic Analysis and
Retrieval of Criminal Histories
SF *Information Retrieval Systems
sec   Secant
SF *Mathematics
SEC   Studio Equipment Complex
SF   Radio Engineering
*Telecommunications
SECAL   Selective Calling
SF *Aeronautics
Air Traffic Control
*Communication Systems
SECAR   Structural Efficiency Cones with
Arbitrary Rings
SF *Aeronautics
Aircraft
SED   Strong Exchange Degeneracy
SF   Elementary Particles
*Physics
SEF   Small End Forward
SF *Aeronautics
*Naval Sciences
Navigation
SEFOR   Southern Experimental Fast Oxide
Reactor

SF *Nuclear Sciences
Reactors
SEM   Scanning Electron Micrograph
SF *Biological and Medical Sciences
Non-destructive Evaluation
*Nuclear Sciences
SEM   Scanning Electron Microscope
SF *Astronautics and Astrophysics
*Biological and Medical Sciences
*Lunar Sciences
SEME   School of Electrical and Mechanical
Engineering
SF *Metallurgy and Metallography
Welding
SEN   Single Edge Notch
SF *General
SEP   Separation Parameter
SF *Aeronautics
*Computer Sciences
Data Processing
SEP   System Engineering Process
SF *Training
SEPE   Single Escape Peak Efficiency
SF *Nuclear Sciences
SEPS   Solar Electric Propulsion System
SF *Space Sciences
SER   Sebum Excretion Rates
SF *Biological and Medical Sciences
SER   Single Electron Response
SF *Electronics and Electrical
Engineering
SER   Smooth Endoplasmic Reticulum
SF *Biological and Medical Sciences
Cytochemistry
SERV   Surface Effect Rescue Vehicle
SF   Accidents and Safety
*Biological and Medical Sciences
SES   Socio Economic Status
SF   Programmed Learning
*Training
SES   Superexcited Electronic States
SF *Chemistry
Radiation Chemistry
SES   Surface Effect Ship
SF *Military Sciences
*Naval Sciences
SESG   Southern European Shipping Group
SF *Military Sciences
*Transportation
SESL   Space Environment Simulation
Laboratory (US)
SF *Space Sciences
Space Simulation
SETE   Secretariat Electronics Test Equipment
SF *Electronics and Electrical
Engineering
Testing
SETF   STARAN Evaluation and Training
Facility
SF *Computer Sciences

SETM Sociéte d'Etudes et de Travaux
     Mécanographiques
    SF *Computer Sciences
SEV Sekundarelektronen Vervielfachern
    SF *Nuclear Sciences
SEZ Sulphaethoxypiridazine
    SF *Dairy Sciences
SF Separate Function
    SF   Multipole Admixture
      *Nuclear Sciences
      Quadnipole Fields
SF Stepping Factor
    SF *Computer Sciences
      Data Processing
SF Subject Field
    SF *General
SFC Specific Fuel Consumption
    SF Aerodynamics
      *Aeronautics
      Aircraft
SFD Sudden Frequency Deviation
    SF *Astronautics and Astrophysics
      *Lunar Sciences
SFG Signal Frequency Generator
    SF *Engineering
      Radio Engineering
      *Telecommunications
SFM Switching-mode Frequency Multipliers
    SF *Engineering
      Radio Engineering
      *Telecommunications
SFP Slack Frame Program
    SF *Computer Sciences
      Data Processing
SFR Signal Frequency Receiver
    SF *Engineering
      Radio Engineering
      *Telecommunications
SFSCL Shunt Feedback Schottky Clamped Logic
    SF *Electronics and Electrical
       Engineering
      Solid-state Circuits
SFSS Satellite Field Service Stations
    SF *Aeronautics
      *Communication Systems
SFV Semliki Forest Virus
    SF *Biological and Medical Sciences
sg Screen Grid
    SF *Communication Systems
      *Engineering
      Radio Engineering
SG Secretary Granule
    SF *Biological and Medical Sciences
      Cytochemistry
SG Solutions of Glucose
    SF *Brewery
SG Stream Generator
    SF *Engineering
      Mechanical Engineering
SG Sueroglyceride

    SF *Dairy Sciences
SG Supergranule
    SF *Astronautics and Astrophysics
      Solar Physics
SGE Secondary Group Equipment
    SF *Engineering
      Radio Engineering
      *Telecommunications
SGE Starch Gel Electrophoresis
    SF *Agricultural Sciences
SGHWR Stream Generating Heavy Water Reactors
    SF Atomic Energy
      *Nuclear Sciences
      Reactors
SGJP Satellite Graphic Job Processor
    SF *Computer Sciences
      Data Processing
SGOT SBPT Glutamin Oxalacetic Transaminase
    SF Biochemistry
      *Biological and Medical Sciences
SGOT Serum Glutamic Oxalic Transaminase
    SF *Dairy Sciences
SGR Short Growth Rate
    SF *Agricultural Sciences
SGV Small Granular Vesicles
    SF *Biological and Medical Sciences
      Cytochemistry
SGZ Surface Ground Zero
    SF Explosives
      *Nuclear Sciences
      Plowshare Detonation
SH Scratch Hardness
    SF *Lunar Sciences
SHA Software House Association
    SF Business Systems
      *Management
SHADCOM Shipping Advisory Committee
    SF *Military Sciences
      *Transportation
SHAPE Supreme Headquarters Allied Power,
    Europe
    SF *Military Sciences
      *Transportation
SHAS Shared Hospital Accounting System
    SF *Computer Sciences
      Data Processing
SHD Slant Hole Distance
    SF *Nuclear Sciences
      Reactors
SHF Super Hyperfine
    SF *Biological and Medical Sciences
      Medical Ions
SHG Second Harmonic Generation
    SF *Electronics and Electrical
       Engineering
      Quantum Electronics
shm Simple Harmonic Motion
    SF *Mathematics
SHP Shaft Horsepower
    SF *Mathematics

SHREAD Share Register and Dividend Warrants
    SF *Computer Sciences
        Data Processing
Si   Silicon
    SF *Agricultural Sciences
        *General
SI   Sample Interval
    SF *Computer Sciences
        Data Processing
SI   Shift In
    SF *Computer Sciences
        Data Processing
S/I   Signal-to-Interference
    SF *Aeronautics
        *Communication Systems
SI   Specific Inventory
    SF *Nuclear Sciences
        Nucleonics
        Reactors
SIA   Service Informatics Analysis
    SF *Computer Sciences
        Data Processing
SIA   Standard Instrument Approach
    SF *Aeronautics
        Approach and Landing
SIA   Stereoimage Alternator
    SF   Instruments
        Photogrametric Engineering
        *Photography
sic   Semiconductor Integrated Circuit
    SF *Communication Systems
        *Electronics and Electrical
           Engineering
SICA Schizont Infected Cell Agglutin
    SF *Biological and Medical Sciences
SID   Solubilization by Incipient Development
    SF *Photography
SID   Standard Instrument Departure
    SF *Aeronautics
        Instrument Flying
SID   Sudden Ionospheric Disturbance
    SF *Astronautics and Astrophysics
        Lunar Sciences
SID   Syntax Improving Device
    SF *Computer Sciences
SIDA Swedish International Development
    Agency
    SF *General
SIDE Superthermal Ion Detector Experiment
    SF   Astronomy
        *Lunar Sciences
SIE   Science Information Exchange
    SF *Information Retrieval Systems
SIF   Selective Identification Feature
    SF *Aeronautics
        Air Traffic Control
        Radar
SIGI System for Interactive Guidance and
    Information
    SF *Computer Sciences

        Information Retrieval Systems
SIGOP Signal Operation
    SF *Communication Systems
        Telecommunications
SIL   Speech Interference Level
    SF *Aeronautics
        Aircraft Noise
SIM   Scientific Instrument Module
    SF *Astronautics and Astrophysics
        *Lunar Sciences
SIMNS Simulated Navigation Systems
    SF *Aeronautics
sin   Sine
    SF *Mathematics
SINK Simulated Interactive Naval Kriegspiel
    SF *Military Sciences
SINS Ship's Inertial Navigation System
    SF *Naval Sciences
        Navigation
SIP   Standard Information Package
    SF *General
        *Nuclear Sciences
        Reactors
SIP   Stay-In-Place
    SF   Civil Engineering
        *Engineering
SIR   Selective Information Retrieval
    SF *Computer Sciences
        Data Processing
        *Information Retrieval Systems
SIRA Scientific Instruments Research
    Association
    SF *Engineering
SIRS Satellite Infrared Spectrometer
    SF *Telecommunications
SISTM Simulation Incremental Stochastic
    Transition Matrices
    SF *Mathematics
SITA Société Internationale de
    Télécommunications Aéronatiques
    SF *Aeronautics
        *Telecommunications
SITE Satellite Instructional Television
    Experiment
    SF *Aeronautics
        *Communication Systems
        *Space Sciences
SJCC Spring Joint Computer Conference
    SF *Computer Sciences
        Data Processing
SKL   Skip Lister
    SF *Computer Sciences
        Data Processing
SKP   Skip Line Printer
    SF *Computer Sciences
        Data Processing
SKT   Skill Knowledge Tests
    SF   Civil Engineering
        *Engineering
        *Military Sciences

SL   Source Level
      SF *Fisheries
SL   Subscriber's Lines
      SF *Engineering
          Radio Engineering
          *Telecommunications
SLAC Stanford Linear Accelerator Center
      SF *Nuclear Sciences
SLANG Systems Language
      SF *Computer Sciences
          Data Processing
SLAR Side Looking Airborne Radar
      SF *Aeronautics
          *Photography
          Radar
SLBM Submarine Launched Ballistic Missile
      SF *Military Sciences
          Missiles
SLC   Simulated Linguistic Computer
      SF *Computer Sciences
          Data Processing
SLCM Sea Launched Cruise Missile
      SF *Aeronautics
          *Military Sciences
SLCP Saturn Launch Computer Program
      SF *Computer Sciences
          Data Processing
SLD   Ships Logistics Division
      SF Logistics
          *Military Sciences
SLD   Slim Line Diffuser
      SF *Metallurgy and Metallography
          Metalworks
SLE   Superheat Limit Explosion
      SF *Aeronautics
          Propellants and Fuels
SLF   System Library File
      SF *Computer Sciences
          Data Processing
SLIC Simulation Linear Integrated Circuits
      SF *Electronics and Electrical
          Engineering
          Solid-state Circuits
SLIS Shared Laboratory Information System
      SF *Computer Sciences
          Data Processing
SLOCOP Specific Linear Optimal Control
       Program
      SF *Computer Sciences
          *Engineering
          Marine Engineering
SLRV Surveyor Lunar Roving Vehicle
      SF *Engineering
          Mechanical Engineering
          Terramechanics
SLS   Segment Long Spacing
      SF *Biological and Medical Sciences
          Cytochemistry
SLS   Sidelobe Suppression
      SF *Aeronautics

        Air Traffic Control
        *Communication Systems
SLT   Solid Logic Technology
      SF *Computer Sciences
          Data Processing
SLTF Shortest Latency Time First
      SF *Computer Sciences
          *Electronics and Electrical
          Engineering
SLUR Share Library User Report
      SF *Computer Sciences
          Data Processing
SLW   Specific Leaf Weight
      SF *Agricultural Sciences
SM   Set Mode
      SF *Computer Sciences
SM   Shell Model
      SF Nuclear Physics
          *Nuclear Sciences
SM   Storage Mark
      SF *Computer Sciences
          Data Processing
SMA   Standard Methods Agar
      SF *Agricultural Sciences
          *Dairy Sciences
SMA   Surface Modeling and Analysis
      SF *Electronics and Electrical
          Engineering
SMAB Segment Receipt Inspection Building
      SF Civil Engineering
          *Engineering
          *Military Sciences
SMAB Solid Motor Assembly Building
      SF Civil Engineering
          *Engineering
SMAF Specific Microphage Arming Factor
      SF *Biological and Medical Sciences
SMATS Source Module Alignment Test Site
      SF *Space Sciences
          Space Simulation
SMAWT Short Range Man Portable Anti-Tank
       Weapon Technology
      SF *Military Sciences
          Rockets
SMC   Sheet Molding Compound
      SF *Materials
SMC   Small Magellanic Cloud
      SF *Astronautics and Astrophysics
          *Lunar Sciences
SMC   Systems Man and Cybernetics
      SF *Management
SMEAT Skylab Medical Experiments Altitude
       Tests
      SF *Space Sciences
SMEDP Standard Methods for the Examination
       of Dairy Products
      SF *Agricultural Sciences
          *Dairy Sciences
SMF   System Management Facilities
      SF *Computer Sciences

Data Processing

SMIC Study of Man's Impact on Climate
    SF *Geosciences
SML Symbolic Machine Language
    SF *Computer Sciences
        Data Processing
SMM Start of Manual Message
    SF *Computer Sciences
        Data Processing
SMMC System Maintenance Monitor Console
    SF *Aeronautics
        Air Traffic Control
        Radar Equipment
SMP Scanning Microscope Photometer
    SF *Photography
SMP Sucrose Monopalmitate
    SF *Agricultural Sciences
        Cereals
SMPTE Society of Motion Picture and
      Television Engineers
    SF *Photography
SMR Super Metal Rich
    SF *Astronautics and Astrophysics
        *Lunar Sciences
SMRE Safety Mines Research Establishment
      (UK)
    SF *Information Retrieval Systems
SMS Synchronous Meteorological Satellites
    SF *Aeronautics
        *Meteorology
        *Space Sciences
        *Telecommunications
SMS Systems Maintenance Service
    SF *Aeronautics
SMSA Standard Metropolitan Statistical Area
    SF *Military Sciences
SMT Silphamethazine
    SF *Dairy Sciences
SMTAG Standard Micro-Teaching Appraisal
      Guide
    SF Programmed Learning
        *Training
SMU Secondary Multiplexing Unit
    SF *Engineering
        Radio Engineering
        *Telecommunications
SMUF Simulated Milk Ultrafiltrate
    SF *Dairy Sciences
S/N Signal-to-Noise
    SF Photogrametric Engineering
        *Photography
SNAP Structural Network Analysis Program
    SF *Aeronautics
        Aircraft
SNF Solids Not Fat
    SF *Agricultural Sciences
        *Dairy Sciences
SNG Synthetic Natural Gas
    SF *Fuels
        *Transportation

SNHS Supraoptic Neurohypophysial System
    SF *Biological and Medical Sciences
SNJ Switching Network Junction
    SF *Engineering
        Radio Engineering
        *Telecommunications
SNP Sodium Nitroprusside
    SF *Nuclear Sciences
        Spectroscopy
SNPO Space Nuclear Propulsion Office
    SF *Nuclear Sciences
SNPS Satellite Nuclear Power Station
    SF *Engineering
        Mechanical Engineering
        *Nuclear Sciences
SNR Signal-to-Noise Ratio
    SF *Photography
        Radar
SNR Supernova Remnants
    SF *Astronautics and Astrophysics
        *Lunar Sciences
SNS Space Navigation System
    SF *Astronautics and Astrophysics
        Navigation
        *Space Sciences
SO Shift Out
    SF *Computer Sciences
        Data Processing
SO Signal Oscillator
    SF *Engineering
        Instruments
SO Slow Operate
    SF *Electronics and Electrical
          Engineering
        Switches
SOAF Sultan of Oman's Air Force
    SF *Aeronautics
        *Military Sciences
SOCE Staff Officer Construction Engineering
    SF Civil Engineering
        *Engineering
        *Military Sciences
SODACT Society of Authors and Composers of
      Tunisia
    SF *Copyright
SOH Start Of Heading
    SF *Computer Sciences
        Data Processing
SOIS Shipping Operations Information Systems
    SF *Transportation
SOLRAD Solar Radiation
    SF *Aeronautics
        Radiation
SON Supraoptic Nuclei
    SF *Biological and Medical Sciences
SOP Sum-of-Products
    SF *Computer Sciences
        Data Processing
SOS Sentinel On Station
    SF *Aeronautics

SOS   Silicon-On-Sapphire
      SF *Electronics and Electrical
             Engineering
          Solid-state Circuits
SOS   Start of Significance
      SF *Computer Sciences
          Data Processing
SOSS Shipboard Oceanographic Survey System
      SF *Naval Sciences
          Navigation
SOSTEL Solid State Electric Logic
      SF *Aeronautics
          *Electronics and Electrical
             Engineering
SOTA State Of The Art
      SF *Computer Sciences
          Data Processing
SP   Service Package
      SF *Computer Sciences
          Data Processing
SP   Summary Punch
      SF *Computer Sciences
          Data Processing
SP   Supervisory Package
      SF *Aeronautics
          Wind Tunnel
SP   Supervisory Printer
      SF *Computer Sciences
          Data Processing
SPA   Small Parts Analysis
      SF *Information Retrieval Systems
SPA   Standard Plate Agar
      SF *Dairy Sciences
SPACE Symbolic Programming Anyone Can Enjoy
      SF *Computer Sciences
          Data Processing
SPAD Simplified Procedures for Analysis
         of Data Systems
      SF *Engineering
          Mechanical Engineering
SPADATS Space Detection and Tracking System
      SF *Astronautics and Astrophysics
SPAM Satellite Processor Access Method
      SF *Computer Sciences
          Data Processing
SPAR Staff Payroll Allocations and Records
      SF *Management
SPASM System Performance and Activity
         Software Monitor
      SF *Computer Sciences
          Data Processing
SPC   Salkowski Positive Compounds
      SF *Agricultural Sciences
SPC   Standard Plate Count
      SF *Agricultural Sciences
          Dairy Sciences
SPC   Stored Program Control Exchange
      SF *Communication Systems
          *Computer Sciences
          Data Processing

SPD   Ship Project Directive
      SF Logistics
          *Military Sciences
SPD   Synchronous Phased Detector
      SF Radio Engineering
          *Telecommunications
spdt Single Pole Double Throw
      SF *Communication Systems
          *Computer Sciences
          *Electronics and Electrical
             Engineering
SPE   School of Preliminary Education
      SF Programmed Learning
          *Training
SPEC Speech Predictive Encoding
         Communication
      SF *Aeronautics
          *Communication Systems
SPEDE System for Processing Educational Data
         Electronically
      SF *Computer Sciences
          Data Processing
SPEED Special Program for Emergency
         Employment Development
      SF *Training
SPI   Single Program Initiator
      SF *Computer Sciences
          Data Processing
SPI   Symbolic Pictorial Indicator
      SF *Aeronautics
SPIDAC Specimen Input to Digital Automatic
         Computer
      SF *Computer Sciences
          Data Processing
SPIDACSYS SPIDAC System
      SF *Computer Sciences
          Data Processing
SPIN Selected Physics Information Notice
      SF *Information Retrieval Systems
SPIT Selective Printing of Items from Tape
      SF *Computer Sciences
          Data Processing
SPL   Sound Pressure Level
      SF *Aeronautics
          Aircraft
          *Communication Systems
SPL   Space Programming Language
      SF *Astronautics and Astrophysics
          *Computer Sciences
          Data Processing
SPM   Small Perturbation Method
      SF *Communication Systems
SPM   Solar Proton Monitor
      SF Solar Sciences
          *Telecommunications
SPMS Special Purpose Manipulator System
      SF *Telecommunications
SPO   System Program Office
      SF Civil Engineering
          *Engineering

```
                *Military Sciences
SPOOL Simultaneous Peripheral Operation
         On-Line
         SF   *Computer Sciences
              Data Processing
SPP   Standard Psychophysiological
         Preparation
         SF   *Biological and Medical Sciences
              Stress
SPR   Supervisory Printer Read
         SF   *Computer Sciences
SPRT  Standard Platinum Resistance
         Thermometers
         SF   *Engineering
SPRU  Science Policy Research Units
         SF   *Engineering
              Structural Mechanics
SPS   Secondary Power System
         SF   *Aeronautics
              Propulsion
SPSA  Signal Phase Statistical Analyzer
         SF   *Engineering
              Radio Engineering
              *Telecommunications
SPST  Single Pole Single Throw
         SF   *Computer Sciences
              Data Processing
              *Nuclear Sciences
              Reactors
SPT   Shared Page Table
         SF   *Computer Sciences
              Data Processing
SPT   Star Point Transfer
         SF   *Photography
SPTF  Sodium Pump Test Facility
         SF   *Nuclear Sciences
              Reactors
SPTU  Staff Pilot Training Unit
         SF   *Aeronautics
              *Training
SPWM  Singlesided Pulse-Width Modulation
         SF   *Engineering
              Radio Engineering
              *Telecommunications
SQA   System Queue Area
         SF   *Computer Sciences
              Data Processing
SQAT  Shim Qualification Assistance Team
         SF   *Military Sciences
              *Naval Sciences
SQF   Subjective Quality Factor
         SF   *Photography
SQUID Superconducting Quantum Interference
         Device
         SF   *Engineering
              Instruments
              Mechanical Engineering
SR    Scanning Radiometer
         SF   *Aeronautics
              *Communication Systems

SR    Semiregular
         SF   *Astronautics and Astrophysics
SR    Slow Release
         SF   *Electronics and Electrical
                 Engineering
              Switches
SR    Sorter Reader
         SF   *Computer Sciences
              Data Processing
SRA   Spring Research Association (UK)
         SF   *Information Retrieval Systems
SRA   Surveillance Radar Approaches
         SF   *Aeronautics
              Air Traffic Control
SRB   Sorter Reader Buffered
         SF   *Computer Sciences
              Data Processing
SRBC  Sheep Red Blood Cells
         SF   *Biological and Medical Sciences
SRC   Science Research Council (UK)
         SF   *General
              *Information Retrieval Systems
SRDS  System Research and Development
         Service
         SF   *Aeronautics
              *Communication Systems
SRF   Sorter Reader Flow
         SF   *Computer Sciences
              Data Processing
SRI   Stanford Research Institute (US)
         SF   *General
SRL   System Reference Library
         SF   *Computer Sciences
              Data Processing
SRM   Shock Remnant Magnetization
         SF   *Lunar Sciences
SRO   Short Range Order
         SF   *Non-crystalline Solids
              *Nuclear Sciences
SRS   Sodium Removal Station
         SF   *Nuclear Sciences
              Reactors
SRT   Secondary Ranging Test
         SF   *Aeronautics
              *Communication Systems
SRT   Standard Radio and Telefon
         SF   *Computer Sciences
              Data Processing
SRT   Supply Response Time
         SF   Logistics
              *Military Sciences
SS    Salmonella-Shigella
         SF   *Agricultural Sciences
              *Dairy Sciences
SS    Shigella Agar
         SF   *Agricultural Sciences
              *Dairy Sciences
SS    Sodium Salicylate
         SF   *Nuclear Sciences
              Alpha Rays
```

SS   Solid Solution
        SF *Ceramics
SS   Spherical Symmetry
        SF *Astronautics and Astrophysics
            *Lunar Sciences
SS   Stainless Steel
        SF *Metallurgy and Metallography
            Metalworks
SSA   Soaring Society of America
        SF *Aeronautics
SSA   Sulphosalicylic Acid
        SF *Agricultural Sciences
            Cereals
SSALS   Simplified Short Approach Light
          System
        SF *Aeronautics
            Approach and Landing
SSB   Single Side Band
        SF *Communication Systems
            *Electronics and Electrical
             Engineering
SSBAM   Single Sideband Amplitude Modulation
        SF *Engineering
            Radio Engineering
            *Telecommunications
SSC   Stellar Simulator Complex
        SF *Space Sciences
SSCA   Strobed Single Channel Analyser
        SF *Electronics and Electrical
             Engineering
SSCC   Spin Scan Cloud Camera
        SF *Photography
            *Telecommunications
SS-CPA Single-Site Coherent Potential
          Approximation
        SF *Non-crystalline Solids
SSD   SHARE Secretarial Distribution
        SF *Computer Sciences
            Data Processing
SSD   Solid State Detector
        SF *Nuclear Sciences
SSD   Space Systems Division
        SF *Military Sciences
            *Space Sciences
SSDR   Steady State Determining Routine
        SF *Computer Sciences
            Data Processing
SSF   System Support Facility
        SF *Aeronautics
            Radar Equipment
SSL   Sodium Stearoyl Laclylate
        SF *Agricultural Sciences
            Cereals
SSL   Software Sciences Limited
        SF *Computer Sciences
SSM   Single-sideband Signal Multiplier
        SF Radio Engineering
            *Telecommunications
SSMA   Spread Spectrum Multiple Access
        SF *Aeronautics

        *Communication Systems
        *Electronics and Electrical
         Engineering
SSP   Signalling and Switching Processor
        SF *Telecommunications
SSP   Sorghum Soy Pellets
        SF *Dairy Sciences
SSP   Sums of Squares and Products
        SF *Statistics
SSPF   Signal Structure Parametric Filters
        SF *Telecommunications
SSR   Secondary Surveillance Radar
        SF *Aeronautics
            Radar Beacon Systems
SSRA   Spread Spectrum Random Access
        SF *Telecommunications
SSS   Shipboard Survey Sub-system
        SF *Naval Sciences
            Navigation
S/SS   Steering and Suspension System
        SF *Engineering
            Mechanical Engineering
            *Transportation
SST   Sea Surface Temperature
        SF *Agricultural Sciences
            *Fisheries
SST   Set Strobe Time
        SF *Computer Sciences
            Testing
SST   Supersonic Transport
        SF *Aeronautics
            Aircraft
SSTR   Solid State Track Detectors
        SF *Electronics and Electrical
             Engineering
SSTV   Sea Skimming Test Vehicles
        SF *Military Sciences
            Missiles
SSU   Saybolt Seconds Universal
        SF *Nuclear Sciences
            Reactors
SSV   Supersonic Test Vehicles
        SF *Aeronautics
ST   Segment Table
        SF *Computer Sciences
            Data Processing
ST   Skin Temperature
        SF *Biological and Medical Sciences
            *Space Sciences
            Space Simulation
ST   Sound Trap
        SF *Metallurgy and Metallography
            Metalworks
ST   Sucrose Tallowate
        SF *Agricultural Sciences
            Cereals
STA   Seed Trade Association
        SF *Agricultural Sciences
            *Milling
STADAC Station Data Acquisition and Control

```
         SF  *Communication Systems
             Satellite Telemetry
             *Space Sciences
STAG  Strategy and Tactics Analysis Group
         SF  *Military Sciences
STAGG Small Turbine Advanced Gas Generator
         SF  *Aeronautics
             Aircraft
STAGS Structural Analysis of General Shells
         SF  *Aeronautics
             Aircraft
STAI  State Trait Anxiety Inventory
         SF  *Aeronautics
             Air Traffic Control
STAR  Standard Terminal Approach Route
         SF  *Aeronautics
             Approach and Landing
STARFIRE System to Accumulate and Retrieve
             Financial Information with
             Random Extraction
         SF  *Computer Sciences
             Data Processing
STARS Satellite Telemetry Automatic Reduction
         Systems
         SF  *Communication Systems
             *Space Sciences
START Space Technology and Advanced Re-entry
         Tests
         SF  *Astronautics and Astrophysics
STB   Segment Tag Bits
         SF  *Computer Sciences
STBR  Stirred Tank Biological Reactor
         SF   Bioengineering
             *Biological and Medical Sciences
STC   Sensitive Time Control
         SF  *Communication Systems
             Radar
STC   Standard Telephone Cables
         SF  *Computer Sciences
             Data Processing
STCAG Stanford Teacher Competence Appraisal
         Guide
         SF   Programmed Learning
             *Training
STD   Subscriber Trunk Dialling
         SF  *Computer Sciences
             Data Processing
STDN  Spacecraft Tracking and Data Network
         SF  *Communication Systems
             *Space Sciences
STE   Sterolesters
         SF   Biochemistry
             *Biological and Medical Sciences
STEP  Supervisory Tape Executive Program
         SF  *Computer Sciences
             Data Processing
STEP  Supplementary Training and Employment
         Program
         SF  *Training
STI   Scientific and Technical Information
```

```
         SF  *Computer Sciences
             *Information Retrieval Systems
ST-INV Static Inverter
         SF  *Electronics and Electrical
             Engineering
STM   Short Term Memory
         SF  *Aeronautics
             Human Factors
STM   Standard Thermal Model
         SF  *Non-crystalline Solids
STOL  Short Takeoff and Landing
         SF  *Aeronautics
             Aircraft
STP   Standard Temperature and Pressure
         SF  *Lunar Sciences
STR   Short Term Revitalization
         SF  *Building
STR   Standard Taxiway Routing
         SF  *Aeronautics
             Air Traffic Control
STR   Synchronous Transmitter Receiver
         SF  *Computer Sciences
             Data Processing
STRUDL Structural Design Language
         SF  *Engineering
             Mechanical Engineering
STS   Space Transportation Systems
         SF  *Space Sciences
             Spacecraft
STS   Standard Test Signal
         SF  *Engineering
             Radio Engineering
             *Telecommunications
STT   Standard Tube Test
         SF  *Dairy Sciences
STV   Separation Test Vehicles
         SF  *Aeronautics
STVW  Symmetrical Triangle Voltage Waveform
         SF  *Electronics and Electrical
             Engineering
             Solid-state Circuits
STX   Start of Text
         SF  *Computer Sciences
             Data Processing
SU    Station Units
         SF  *Engineering
             Radio Engineering
             *Telecommunications
SU    Syne Unit
         SF  *Engineering
             Radio Engineering
             *Telecommunications
SUB   Substitute
         SF  *Computer Sciences
             Data Processing
SUD   Sudden Unexpected Death
         SF  *Biological and Medical Sciences
SUMT  Sequential Unconstrained Minimization
         Techniques
         SF   Cybernetics
```

	*Electronics and Electrical Engineering
SUNI	Southern Universities Nuclear Institute (Can.)
	SF *Nuclear Sciences
SV	Synchronous Voltage
	SF *Engineering
	*Telecommunications
SVC	Supervisory Call
	SF *Computer Sciences
	Data Processing
SVCS	Star Vector Calibration Sensor
	SF *Aeronautics
	Flight Control
SVER	Spatial Visual Evoked Response
	SF Cybernetics
	*Electronics and Electrical Engineering
SVH	Solar Vacuum Head
	SF *Space Sciences
	Space Simulation
SVI	Stroke Volume Index
	SF Biochemistry
	*Biological and Medical Sciences
SVIB	Strong Vocational Interest Blank
	SF *Training
SVM	Silicon Video Memory
	SF *Astronautics and Astrophysics
	*Computer Sciences
	*Space Sciences
SVR	Slant Visual Range
	SF *Aeronautics
	Approach and Landing
SW	Sandwich Wound
	SF *Electronics and Electrical Engineering
	Switches
SWADS	Scheduler Work Area Data Set
	SF *Computer Sciences
	Data Processing
SWAT	Stress Wave Analysis Techniques
	SF *Metallurgy and Metallography
	Welding
SWB	Single Weight Baryta
	SF *Photography
SWBS	Ship Work Breakdown Structure
	SF *Computer Sciences
	Data Processing
SWD	Surface Wave Device
	SF *Aeronautics
	*Electronics and Electrical Engineering
swg	Standard Wire Gauge
	SF *Communication Systems
SWIFT	Strength of Wings Including Flutter
	SF *Aeronautics
	Aircraft
SWIR	Short Wave Infrared
	SF *Geosciences
SWL	Short Wave Listeners

	SF *Communication Systems
	*Engineering
	Radio Engineering
SWL	Surface Wave Lines
	SF Radio Engineering
	*Telecommunications
SWRA	Selected Water Resources Abstracts
	SF *Geosciences
	*Meteorology
	*Oceanography
SwRI	Southwest Research Institute
	SF *Nuclear Sciences
SWS	Short Wave Sleep
	SF *Biological and Medical Sciences
SWSI	Single Width Single Inlet
	SF *Metallurgy and Metallography
	Metalworks
SWW	Soft White Winter
	SF *Agricultural Sciences
	Cereals
SXT	Spacecraft Sextant
	SF *Astronautics and Astrophysics
	Navigation
SY	Stripping Yield
	SF *Agricultural Sciences
SY	Synchroscope
	SF *Electronics and Electrical Engineering
	Meters
SYNTAXSYS	SYNTAX System
	SF *Computer Sciences
	Data Processing
SYSCAP	System of Circuit Analysis Programs
	SF *Communication Systems
SYSGEN	System Generation
	SF *Computer Sciences
	Data Processing
SYSIN	System Input
	SF *Computer Sciences
	Data Processing
SYSOUT	System Output
	SF *Computer Sciences
	Data Processing
SYSRC	System Reference Count
	SF *Computer Sciences
	*Information Retrieval Systems

T

T   Triode
    SF *Electronics and Electrical
        Engineering
        Semiconductor Devices

TA   Tape Address
    SF *Computer Sciences
        Data Processing

TA   Time Analyzer
    SF Fission Chambers
        *Nuclear Sciences

TA   Triacetin
    SF *Nuclear Sciences
        Thermal Processes

TABSIM Tabulating Simulator
    SF *Computer Sciences
        Data Processing

TAC   Tacan
    SF *Aeronautics
        Approach and Landing

TaC   Tantalum Carbide
    SF Fuels
        *Nuclear Sciences

TAC   Telemetry and Command
    SF *Telecommunications

TAC   Terminal Control Area
    SF *Aeronautics
        Airports

TAC   Time Amplitude Converter
    SF *Electronics and Electrical
        Engineering
        *Nuclear Sciences

TAC   Total Available Carbohydrate
    SF *Agricultural Sciences

TACAN TACtical Air Navigation
    SF *Aeronautics
        Instrument Flying
        *Military Sciences
        Navigation

TACCO Tactical Coordinator
    SF *Aeronautics
        Human Factors

TACP   Tactical Air Control Party
    SF *Aeronautics
        Air Traffic Control
        *Communication Systems

        *Military Sciences

TACRV Tracked Air Cushion Research Vehicle
    SF *Transportation

TACS Tactical Air Control System
    SF *Aeronautics
        Computer Sciences

TACT Transonic Aircraft Technology
    SF *Aeronautics

TACV Tracked Air Cushion Vehicle
    SF *Transportation

TAEC Thiolated Aminoethyl Cellulose
    SF *Agricultural Sciences
        *Dairy Sciences

TALS Transfer Air Lock Section
    SF *Space Sciences
        Space Simulation

TAM   Terminal Access Method
    SF *Computer Sciences
        Data Processing

TAN   Tangent
    SF *Mathematics

TANS Tactical Air Navigation System
    SF *Aeronautics
        Navigation

TAPPI Technical Association of the Pulp
    and Paper Industry
    SF *Printing

TAS   True Air Speed
    SF *Aeronautics
        Avionics

TASC Tactical Articulated Swimmable Carrier
    SF *Engineering
        Mechanical Engineering
        Terramechanics

TASES Tactical Airborne Signal Exploitation
    System
    SF *Aeronautics
        Navigation

TASRA Thermal Activation Strain Rate
    Analysis
    SF *Physics

TATC Terminal Area Traffic Control
    SF *Aeronautics
        Air Traffic Control

TBA   Testbed Aircraft

	*Aeronautics
	Testing
TBA	Torsional Braid Analysis
	SF *Non-metallic Materials
	Plastics
TBC	Thermophilic Count
	SF *Agricultural Sciences
	*Dairy Sciences
TBO	Time Between Overhaul
	SF *Aeronautics
	*Military Sciences
TBPO	Tertiary Butyl Peroctoate
	SF *Non-metallic Materials
	Polymers
TBS	Tolerance for Bureaucratic Structure
	SF *Training
TC	Tape Command
	SF *Computer Sciences
	Data Processing
TC	Telescoping Collar
	SF *Metallurgy and Metallography
	Metalworks
TC	Temperature Coefficient
	SF *Electronics and Electrical
	Engineering
	Solid-state Circuits
TC	Tetracycline
	SF Biochemistry
	*Biological and Medical Sciences
TC	Threshold Circuit
	SF *Engineering
	Radio Engineering
	*Telecommunications
TC	Total Cholesterol
	SF Biochemistry
	*Biological and Medical Sciences
TC	Transmitting Circuits
	SF *Engineering
	Radio Engineering
	*Telecommunications
TC	True Complement
	SF *Electronics and Electrical
	Engineering
	Solid-state Circuits
TCA	Terminal Control Area
	SF *Aeronautics
	Air Traffic Control
	*Communication Systems
TCA	Tricarboxylic Acid
	SF Biochemistry
	*Biological and Medical Sciences
TCA	Trichloroacetic Acid
	SF *Agricultural Sciences
	*Biological and Medical Sciences
TCA	Turbulent Contact Absorber
	SF Chemical Engineering
	*Chemistry
TCAM	Telecommunications Access Method
	SF *Computer Sciences
	Data Processing

TCB	Task Control Block
	SF *Computer Sciences
	Data Processing
TCB	Terminal Control Block
	SF *Computer Sciences
	Data Processing
TCC	Technical Coordination Committee
	SF Industrial Property
	*Patents
TCC	Thermal Control Coatings
	SF *Metallic Materials
TCC	Transportation Commodity Classification
	SF *Transportation
TCCSR	Telephone Channel Combination and
	Separation Racks
	SF *Engineering
	Radio Engineering
	*Telecommunications
TCD	Time Code Division
	SF *Engineering
	Radio Engineering
	*Telecommunications
TCE	Tetrachloroethane
	SF *Non-metallic Materials
	Polymers
TCLE	Thermal Coefficient of Linear
	Expansion
	SF *Aeronautics
	Propellants and Fuels
TCM	Temperature Control Model
	SF *Space Sciences
	Space Simulation
TCM	Terminal Capacity Matrix
	SF *Mathematics
TCNE	Tetracyanoethylene
	SF *Photography
TCNQ	Tetracyanoquinodimethane
	SF *Photography
TCR	Temperature Coefficient of Resistance
	SF *Ceramics
	*Electronics and Electrical
	Engineering
	Instruments
TCRA	Telegraphy Channel Reliability
	Analyzer
	SF *Engineering
	Radio Engineering
	*Telecommunications
TCS	Terminal Communications Subsystem
	SF *Computer Sciences
	Data Processing
TCT	Trunk Coin Telephones
	SF *Engineering
	Radio Engineering
	*Telecommunications
	*Telephone Networks
TCTS	Trans-Canada Telephone System
	SF *Telecommunications
TCU	Transmission Control Unit
	SF *Computer Sciences

Data Processing
TD   Thiamin Deficient
       SF   *Biological and Medical Sciences
TD   Thoracic Duct
       SF   *Dairy Sciences
TD   Top Down
       SF   *Metallurgy and Metallography
             Metalworks
TD   Tracing Dye
       SF   Biochemistry
             *Biological and Medical Sciences
TD   Transmitter Distributor
       SF   *Computer Sciences
             Data Processing
TD   Tunnel Diode
       SF   *Engineering
             Radio Engineering
             *Telecommunications
TDC   Through Deck Cruisers
       SF   *Aeronautics
             Aircraft
TDC   Track Detection Circuit
       SF   *Electronics and Electrical
             Engineering
             Data Recording
TDH   Toxic Dose High
       SF   *Biological and Medical Sciences
             Drugs
TDI   Toluene Diisocyanate
       SF   *Non-metallic Materials
             Polymers
TDL   Toxic Dose Low
       SF   *Biological and Medical Sciences
             Drugs
TDM   Tertiary Dodecyl Mercaplan
       SF   *Non-metallic Materials
             Polymers
TDM   Time Division Multiplex
       SF   *Computer Sciences
             Data Processing
TDMA   Time Division Multiple Access
       SF   *Aeronautics
             *Communication Systems
             *Computer Sciences
             Data Processing
TDMS   Time-sharing Data Management System
       SF   *Computer Sciences
             Data Processing
TDN   Total Digestible Nutrient
       SF   *Agricultural Sciences
             *Dairy Sciences
TDP   Technical Development Plan
       SF   *Aeronautics
             Air Traffic Control
TDPAC Time Differential Perturbed Angular
       Correlation
       SF   *Nuclear Sciences
TDR   Teacher Demonstration Rating
       SF   Programmed Learning
             *Training

TDR   Torque Differential Receiver
       SF   *Communication Systems
             *Electronics and Electrical
             Engineering
TDS   Tertiary Data Set
       SF   *Computer Sciences
             Data Processing
TDS   Total Dissolved Solids
       SF   Civil Engineering
             *Engineering
TDSCC Tidbinbilla Deep Space Communication
       Complex
       SF   *Communication Systems
TDSS   Time Dividing Spectrum Stabilization
       SF   *Electronics and Electrical
             Engineering
TDT   Task Dispatch Table
       SF   *Computer Sciences
             Data Processing
TDT   Terminal Death Time
       SF   *Agricultural Sciences
             *Dairy Sciences
TDTL   Tunnel Diode Transistor Logic
       SF   *Computer Sciences
             Data Processing
TDX   Time Division Exchange
       SF   *Computer Sciences
             Data Processing
TDX   Torque Differential Transmitter
       SF   *Communication Systems
             *Electronics and Electrical
             Engineering
TDY   Temporary Duty
       SF   Air Force
             *Military Sciences
TDZ   Touchdown Zone
       SF   *Aeronautics
             Approach and Landing
TDZL   Touchdown Zone Lights
       SF   *Aeronautics
             Approach and Landing
TE   Electron Temperature
       SF   *Electronics and Electrical
             Engineering
             Lasers and Masers
TE   Terminal Exchange
       SF   *Engineering
             Radio Engineering
             *Telecommunications
TE   Transverse Electric
       SF   *Astronautics and Astrophysics
             Lunar Sciences
TE   Trunk Equalizers
       SF   *Engineering
             Radio Engineering
             *Telecommunications
TEA   Transferred Electron Amplifier
       SF   *Electronics and Electrical
             Engineering
             Solid-state Circuits

TEA   Transversely Excited Atmospheric
       SF *Electronics and Electrical
               Engineering
           Lasers and Masers
TEA   Triethylamine
       SF *Non-metallic Materials
           Polymers
TEAH   Tetraethylammonium
       SF Biochemistry
           *Biological and Medical Sciences
TEAOH Tetraethylammonium Hydroxide
       SF Biochemistry
           *Biological and Medical Sciences
TEC   Total Electron Content
       SF *Nuclear Sciences
           Reactors
TEC   Transearth Coast
       SF *Astronautics and Astrophysics
           Lunar Sciences
TEC   Transient Electron Current
       SF *Electronics and Electrical
               Engineering
           *Nuclear Sciences
TED   Thin Film Detector
       SF Alpha Particles
           *Nuclear Sciences
TE/DC Traffic Enforcement/Driver Control
       SF *Transportation
TEL   Tetra Ethyl Lead
       SF *Aeronautics
           Fuels
TELOPS Telemetry On-Line Processing System
       SF *Communication Systems
           *Space Sciences
TEM   Tomato Extract Medium
       SF *Dairy Sciences
TEM   Transmission Electron Microscopy
       SF *Biological and Medical Sciences
           Clinical Medicine
           *Nuclear Sciences
TENE   Total Estimated Net Energy Consumed
       SF *Dairy Sciences
TEO   Transferred Electron Oscillators
       SF *Electronics and Electrical
               Engineering
           Solid-state Circuits
TEP   Transmitter Experimental Package
       SF *Aeronautics
           *Communication Systems
TEP   Transportation Energy Panel
       SF *Transportation
TEPA   Tetraethylenepentamine
       SF *Non-metallic Materials
           Plastics
TER   Tergitol
       SF *Dairy Sciences
TESS   Thermocouple Emergency Shipment
           Service
       SF *Engineering
           Instruments

TET   Turbine Entry Temperature
       SF *Aeronautics
           Aircraft
TETA   Triethyleletetramine
       SF *Non-metallic Materials
           Polymers
TEWS   Tactical Electronic Warfare Systems
       SF *Aeronautics
           *Electronics and Electrical
               Engineering
           *Military Sciences
TEX   Target Excitation
       SF Elementary Particles
           *Physics
TF   Threshold Factor
       SF *Photography
TFA   Timing Filter Amplifier
       SF *Communication Systems
TFA   Transfer Function Analyser
       SF *Aeronautics
           Testing
TFA   Trifluoroacetic
       SF *Non-metallic Materials
           Polymers
TFR   Total Follicular Response
       SF *Dairy Sciences
TFT   Thin Film Technology
       SF *Computer Sciences
           Data Processing
TFT   Time-to-Frequency Transformation
       SF *Electronics and Electrical
               Engineering
           Solid-state Circuits
TFZ   Transfer Zone
       SF *Computer Sciences
           Data Processing
TG   Top Grille
       SF *Metallurgy and Metallography
           Metalworks
TG   Total Graph
       SF *Mathematics
TG   Triglyceride
       SF Biochemistry
           *Biological and Medical Sciences
TGE   Transmissible Gastroentritis
       SF *Agricultural Sciences
TGFA   Triglyceride Fatty Acids
       SF Biochemistry
           *Biological and Medical Sciences
TGS   Triglyncinsulphate
       SF *Engineering
           Radio Engineering
           *Telecommunications
TGSO   Tertiary Groups Shunt Operation
       SF *Engineering
           Radio Engineering
           *Telecommunications
THAM   Tri-Hydroxymethyl Aminomethane
       SF Biochemistry
           *Biological and Medical Sciences

THC   Thermal Converter
      SF *Electronics and Electrical
              Engineering
          Meters
THC   Transtetrahydro-Cannabinol
      SF *Biological and Medical Sciences
          Drugs
THE   Thunderstorm Event
      SF *Statistics
THF   Tetrahydro Furan
      SF *Non-metallic Materials
          Polymers
THFTDA Tetrahydrofuran Tetracarboxylic
          Dianhydride
      SF *Non-metallic Materials
          Polymers
THI   Total Height Index
      SF *Photography
THIS Total Hospital Information System
      SF *Biological and Medical Sciences
          Computer Sciences
          Data Processing
          *Information Retrieval Systems
THOR Tape Handling Option Routines
      SF *Computer Sciences
          Data Processing
TI   Ion Temperature
      SF *Electronics and Electrical
              Engineering
          Lasers and Masers
TIC   Task Interrupt Control
      SF *Computer Sciences
          Data Processing
TICAS Taxonomic Intra-Cellular Analytic
          System
      SF *Astronautics and Astrophysics
TICCIT Time Shared Interactive Computer
          Controlled Information Television
      SF *Communication Systems
TID   Total Ion Detector
      SF *Astronautics and Astrophysics
          Lunar Sciences
TIFS Total In-Flight Simulator
      SF *Aeronautics
          Approach and Landing
TIG   Tugstern Inert Gas
      SF *Nuclear Sciences
          Pressure Boundaries
TIG   Tungen Inert Gas
      SF *Metallurgy and Metallography
          Welding
TILS Tactical Instrument Landing System
      SF *Aeronautics
          Approach and Landing
TIN   Temperature Independent
      SF *Computer Sciences
          Data Processing
TINT Track in Track
      SF *Lunar Sciences
TIOM Telegraph Input Output Multiplexers

      SF *Aeronautics
          Ground Communication Networks
TIP   Tactile Information Presentation
      SF *Information Retrieval Systems
TIP   Technical Information Program
      SF *Computer Sciences
          Data Processing
TIPA Tetraisopropylpyrophosphoramide
      SF *Biological and Medical Sciences
          Cytochemistry
TIPTOP Tape Input/Tape Output
      SF *Computer Sciences
          Data Processing
TIS   Transponder Interrogation Sonar
      SF *Aeronautics
          *Naval Sciences
          Navigation
Tj   Junction Temperature
      SF *Electronics and Electrical
              Engineering
          Semiconductor Devices
TJID Terminal Job Identification
      SF *Computer Sciences
          Data Processing
TK   Thymidine Kinase
      SF *Biological and Medical Sciences
TKE   Track Angle Error
      SF *Aeronautics
          Instruments
TKF   TRIGA King Furnace
      SF *Nuclear Sciences
          Reactors
TKFF TRIGA King Furnace Facilities
      SF *Nuclear Sciences
          Reactors
TKP   Tonne Km Performed
      SF *Aeronautics
TL   Target Loss
      SF *Fisheries
TL   Thermoluminescence
      SF *Lunar Sciences
TL   Total Lipid
      SF Biochemistry
          *Biological and Medical Sciences
TLAS Tactical Logical Air Simulation
      SF Logistics
          *Military Sciences
TLC   Thin Layer Chromatography
      SF *Agricultural Sciences
          *Dairy Sciences
          *Chemistry
TLD   Thermoluminescence Dosimeter
      SF *Nuclear Sciences
TLD   Thermoluminescent Detectors
      SF *Nuclear Sciences
          Radiation
          Reactors
TLD   Thermoluminescent Dosimeters
      SF *Aeronautics
          Instruments

TLM   Telemeter
        SF   *Electronics and Electrical
                Engineering
             Meters
TLM   Thin Lipid Membranes
        SF   *Chemistry
             Physical Chemistry
TLO   Tracking Local Oscillators
        SF   *Aeronautics
             *Electronics and Electrical
                Engineering
TLP   Transient Lunar Phenomena
        SF   *Lunar Sciences
TLRV   Tracked Levitated Research Vehicles
        SF   *Astronautics and Astrophysics
             *Space Sciences
TLU   Table Look Up
        SF   *Computer Sciences
             Data Processing
TLW   Threshold Limit Value
        SF   *Biological and Medical Sciences
             Drugs
TM   Tape Mark
        SF   *Computer Sciences
             Data Processing
TM   Transverse Magnetic
        SF   *Astronautics and Astrophysics
             *Lunar Sciences
TMA   Terminal Movement Area
        SF   *Aeronautics
             Runways
TMA   Trimellitic Anhydride
        SF   *Photography
TMA   Trimethylamine
        SF   *Agricultural Sciences
             Dairy Sciences
TMAC   Tetramethylammonium Bicarbonate
        SF   *Aeronautics
             Aviation Medicine
             *Biological and Medical Sciences
TMAO   Trimethylamine Oxide
        SF   *Agricultural Sciences
             *Dairy Sciences
TMCB   Tetramethoxycarbonyl Benzophenone
        SF   *Non-metallic Materials
             Polymers
TMD   Tensor Meson Dominance
        SF   Elementary Particles
             *Nuclear Sciences
TME   Telemetric Equipment
        SF   *Engineering
             Radio Engineering
             *Telecommunications
TMEDA   Tetramethyl Ethylene Diamine
        SF   *Non-metallic Materials
             Polymers
TMIS   Television Measurement Information
             System
        SF   *Engineering
             Radio Engineering

             *Telecommunications
TMIS   Television Metering Information
             System
        SF   *Engineering
             Radio Engineering
             *Telecommunications
TMN   Trimethylamine Nitrogen
        SF   *Agricultural Sciences
             *Dairy Sciences
TMP   Thermal Mechanical Processing
        SF   *Metallurgy and Metallography
TMP   Terminal Monitor Program
        SF   *Computer Sciences
             Data Processing
TMP   Thermomechanical Process
        SF   *Metallurgy and Metallography
TMPAH   Trimethylphenenyl Ammonium Hydroxide
        SF   Biochemistry
             *Biological and Medical Sciences
TMS   Trimethylsilyl
        SF   *Biological and Medical Sciences
             Forensic Sciences
TMSC   Texas Male Steridity Cytoplasm
        SF   *Agricultural Sciences
             Cereals
TMSDEA Trimethyl Silyldiethylamine
        SF   *Chemistry
             Organic Chemistry
TMTU   Tetramethylthiourea
        SF   *Nuclear Sciences
TMV   Tobacco Mosaic Virus
        SF   *Biological and Medical Sciences
TMXO   Tactical Miniature Crystal Oscillator
        SF   *Computer Sciences
             *Electronics and Electrical
                Engineering
TNA   Transient Network Analyzer
        SF   *Electronics and Electrical
                Engineering
             Transmission Lines
TNBS   Trinitrobenzenesulphonic [Acid]
        SF   *Agricultural Sciences
             Cereals
TNC   Total Nonstructural Carbohydrate
        SF   *Agricultural Sciences
TNG   Tactical and Negotiations Game
        SF   *Behavioural Sciences
             Psychology
TNI   Traffic Noise Index
        SF   *Aeronautics
             Noise
TOA   Time of Arrival
        SF   *Aeronautics
             *Nuclear Sciences
             Measurements
TOC   Total Optical Colour
        SF   *Photography
TOC   Total Organic Carbon
        SF   Bioengineering
             *Biological and Medical Sciences

TOD   Technical Objective Documents
       SF   *Information Retrieval Systems
TOD   Time Of Day
       SF   *Computer Sciences
            Data Processing
TOD   Top Of Duct
       SF   *Metallurgy and Metallography
TOF   Time Of Flight
       SF   *Aeronautics
            Instruments
TOFL   Takeoff Field Length
       SF   *Aeronautics
            Airports
TOGW   Takeoff Gross Weight
       SF   *Aeronautics
            Aircraft
T-OH   Tyrosine Hydroxylase
       SF   *Biological and Medical Sciences
TOM   Topological Optimization Module
       SF   *Computer Sciences
            Data Processing
TOPICS Transport Operations for Increasing
            Capacity and Safety
       SF   *Transportation
TOPS   Telephone Order Processing System
       SF   *Computer Sciences
            *Information Retrieval Systems
TOS   Tactical Operating System
       SF   *Computer Sciences
            Data Processing
TOS   Tape Operating System
       SF   *Computer Sciences
            Data Processing
TOS   Test Operating System
       SF   *Computer Sciences
            Data Processing
TOS   Top Of Steel
       SF   *Metallurgy and Metallography
            Metalworks
TOST   Turbine Oxidation Stability Test
       SF   *Engineering
            Mechanical Engineering
TP   Terphenyl
       SF   *Nuclear Sciences
TP   Timing Pulse
       SF   *Electronics and Electrical
            Engineering
            Solid-state Circuits
TP   Total Protein
       SF   *Dairy Sciences
TPA   Terephthalic Acid
       SF   *Non-metallic Materials
            Polymers
TPC   Time Pickoff Controls
       SF   *Nuclear Sciences
TPCU   Thermal Preconditioning Unit
       SF   *Aeronautics
            *Naval Sciences
            Navigation
TPE   Teleprocessing Executive

       SF   *Computer Sciences
            Data Processing
            *Management
TPE   Tetraphenylethylene
       SF   *Biological and Medical Sciences
            Forensic Sciences
TPE   Two Pion Exchange
       SF   *Nuclear Sciences
TPF   Two Photon Fluorescence
       SF   *Electronics and Electrical
            Engineering
            Quantum Electronics
TPHC   Time to Pulse Height Converter
       SF   *Nuclear Sciences
tpi   Turns Per Inch
       SF   *Communication Systems
            Radio Communications
TPL   Total Phospholipid
       SF   Biochemistry
            *Biological and Medical Sciences
TPNH   Triphosphopyridine Nucleotide
       SF   *Agricultural Sciences
TPP   Thiamine Pyrophosphatase
       SF   *Biological and Medical Sciences
            Cytochemistry
TPR   Thermoplastic Recording
       SF   *Photography
TPR   Total Peripheral
       SF   Biochemistry
            *Biological and Medical Sciences
TPS   Telecommunications Programming System
       SF   *Computer Sciences
TPS   Thermal Protection System
       SF   *Space Sciences
            Space Shuttle
TPU   Time Pickoff Units
       SF   *Nuclear Sciences
TPWB   Three Program Wire Broadcasting
       SF   *Engineering
            Radio Engineering
            *Telecommunications
TQ   Turf Quality
       SF   *Agricultural Sciences
TQA   Total Quality Assurance
       SF   *Engineering
TR   Top Register
       SF   *Metallurgy and Metallography
            Metalworks
TR   Torque Receiver
       SF   *Communication Systems
            *Electronics and Electrical
            Engineering
TRA   Technical Requirements Analysis
       SF   *Engineering
            Automatic Support Systems
TRACAB Terminal RAdar-Control from Tower
            CAB
       SF   *Aeronautics
            Air Traffic Control
            Radar Beacon Systems

TRACALS Traffic Control and Landing
     System
    SF *Aeronautics
       Air Traffic Control
       *Communication Systems
TRACON Terminal Radar Control
    SF *Aeronautics
       Air Traffic Control
       *Communication Systems
TRADA Timber Research and Development
     Association (UK)
    SF *Information Retrieval Systems
TRAM Target Recognition Attack Multisensor
    SF *Military Sciences
TRAN Transmit
    SF *Computer Sciences
       Data Processing
TRANSIF Transient State Isoelectric Focusing
    SF Biochemistry
       *Biological and Medical Sciences
TRAPATT TRApped Avalanche Triggered Transit
    SF *Nuclear Sciences
       Microwave Oscillators
TRC   Technology Reports Centre (UK)
    SF *Information Retrieval Systems
TRF   Track Pick Fragments
    SF *Lunar Sciences
TRF   Tuned Radio Frequency
    SF *Communication Systems
       Radio Communications
TRIC Trachoma Inclusion Conjunctivitis
    SF *Biological and Medical Sciences
       Clinical Medicine
TRN   Television Relay Networks
    SF *Engineering
       Radio Engineering
       *Telecommunications
TRRA Tilt Rotor Research Aircraft
    SF *Aeronautics
TRS   Total Reducing Sugar
    SF *Agricultural Sciences
TRS   Terry Research Station (UK)
    SF *Information Retrieval Systems
TRSA Terminal Radar Service Area
    SF *Aeronautics
       Air Traffic Control
       Radar Beacon Systems
TRSB Time Reference Scanning Beacon
    SF *Aeronautics
       Approach and Landing
TRSBMLS Time Reference Scanning Beam
     Microwave Landing System
    SF *Aeronautics
       Approach and Landing
TRU   Total Recycle Unit
    SF *Agricultural Sciences
       *Dairy Sciences
TRW   Thompson-Ramo-Wooldrige
    SF Electron Temperature
       *Nuclear Sciences

TS   Tape Status
    SF *Computer Sciences
       Data Processing
TS   Target Strength
    SF *Fisheries
TS   Transformer Substations
    SF *Engineering
       Radio Engineering
       *Telecommunications
TS   Transition Sets
    SF *Engineering
       Radio Engineering
       *Telecommunications
TSA   Total Scan Area
    SF *Astronautics and Astrophysics
TSA   Trypticase Soy Agar
    SF *Dairy Sciences
TSB   Technical Support Building
    SF *Civil Engineering
       *Engineering
TSB   Trypticase Soy Broth
    SF *Agricultural Sciences
       *Dairy Sciences
TSC   Thermally Stimulated Currents
    SF *Astronautics and Astrophysics
       Lunar Sciences
TSC   Time Sharing Control
    SF *Computer Sciences
       Data Processing
TSC   Transmitter Start Code
    SF *Computer Sciences
       Data Processing
TSC   Transportation Systems Center
    SF *Aeronautics
       *Communication Systems
       *Transportation
TSCA Timing Single Channel Analyser
    SF *Electronics and Electrical
         Engineering
TSD   Thermally Stimulated Depolarization
    SF *Astronautics and Astrophysics
       *Lunar Sciences
TSD   Thermostimulated Depolarization
    SF *Non-crystalline Solids
TSD   Touch Sensitive Digitizer
    SF *Electronics and Electrical
         Engineering
TSE   Tactical Support Equipment
    SF *Computer Sciences
       Data Processing
TSE   Time Slice End
    SF *Computer Sciences
       Data Processing
TSEE Thermally Stimulated Emission of
     Exoelectrons
    SF *Astronautics and Astrophysics
       Lunar Sciences
TSFO Transportation Support Field Office
    (US)
    SF *Transportation

TSH   Thyroid Stimulating Hormone
      SF   *Biological and Medical Sciences
TSH   Thyrotropic Hormone
      SF   Biochemistry
           *Biological and Medical Sciences
TSI   Task Status Index
      SF   *Computer Sciences
           Data Processing
TSI   Triple Sugar Iron
      SF   *Agricultural Sciences
           *Dairy Sciences
TSN   Tryptone Sulphite Neomycin
      SF   *Agricultural Sciences
           Dairy Sciences
TSO   Technical Standard Order
      SF   *Aeronautics
           Air Traffic Control
           Radar Beacon Systems
TSO   Time Sharing Option
      SF   *Computer Sciences
           Data Processing
TSP   Titanium Sublimation Pump
      SF   *Engineering
           Instruments
TSR   Thyroid (Hormone) Secretion Rate
      SF   *Agricultural Sciences
           *Dairy Sciences
TSS   Time Sharing System
      SF   *Computer Sciences
           Data Processing
TSTA Tumour Specific Transplantation
         Antigens
      SF   *Biological and Medical Sciences
           Physiology
TSU   Tariff Selection Unit
      SF   *Engineering
           Radio Engineering
           *Telecommunications
TSX   Time Sharing Executives
      SF   *Computer Sciences
           Data Processing
TT   Teletypewriter
      SF   *Computer Sciences
           Data Processing
TT   Total Time
      SF   *Electronics and Electrical
              Engineering
           Meters
TTAC Telemetry Tracking and Command
      SF   *Telecommunications
TTC   Technical Training Centers
      SF   *Aeronautics
           *Training
TTC   Tetrazolium Chloride
      SF   *Agricultural Sciences
TTC   Thiatricarbocyanine
      SF   *Photography
TTC   Triphenyltetrazolium Chloride
      SF   *Agricultural Sciences
           *Dairy Sciences

TTG   Test Target Generator
      SF   *Aeronautics
           Air Traffic Control
TTL   Transistor Transistor Logic
      SF   *Computer Sciences
           Data Processing
           *Electronics and Electrical
              Engineering
           Radio Engineering
           *Telecommunications
TTMA Truck Trailer Manufacturers'
         Association
      SF   *Engineering
TTRC Thrust Travel Reduction Curve
      SF   *Engineering
           Mechanical Engineering
           Terramechanics
TTRM Transition Thermoremnant Magnetization
      SF   *Astronautics and Astrophysics
           Lunar Sciences
TTS   Teletypesetter
      SF   *Computer Sciences
           Data Processing
TTS   Temporary Threshold Shift
      SF   *Aeronautics
           Noise
TTS   Transportable Transformer Substations
      SF   *Electronics and Electrical
              Engineering
TTT   Time Temperature Transformation
      SF   *Lunar Sciences
TTU   Timing Terminal Unit
      SF   *Photography
TTY   Teletype
      SF   *Computer Sciences
           Data Processing
TTY   Teletypewriter
      SF   *Electronics and Electrical
              Engineering
TU   Tape Unit
      SF   *Computer Sciences
           Data Processing
TU   Top Up
      SF   *Metallurgy and Metallography
TU   Transfer Units
      SF   *Electronics and Electrical
              Engineering
           Radio Engineering
           *Telecommunications
TU   Turbopump Units
      SF   *Engineering
           Mechanical Engineering
TUCC Triangle Universities Computation
         Center
      SF   *Computer Sciences
           Data Processing
TURPS Terrestial Unattended Reactor Power
         System
      SF   *Nuclear Sciences
TV   Television

	SF *General
TV	Test Vector
	SF *Computer Sciences
TVA	Tennessee Valley Authority (US)
	SF *Transportation
TVAT	Television Air Trainer
	SF *Aeronautics
	Military Aviation
TVC	Control Tag Vector
	SF *Computer Sciences
	Data Processing
TVC	Total Viable Counts
	SF *Agricultural Sciences
	*Dairy Sciences
TVDR	Tag Vector Display Register
	SF *Computer Sciences
	Data Processing
TVF	Tape Velocity Fluctuations
	SF *Electronics and Electrical
	Engineering
	Radio Engineering
	*Telecommunications
TVG	Time Varied Gain
	SF *Computer Sciences
	Data Processing
TVM	Track Via Missile
	SF *Aeronautics
	Military Aircraft
	*Military Sciences
TVN	Total Volatile Nitrogen
	SF *Agricultural Sciences
	*Dairy Sciences
TVR	Response Tag Vector
	SF *Computer Sciences
	Data Processing
TVW	Word Tag Vector
	SF *Computer Sciences
	Data Processing
TW	Tape Word
	SF *Computer Sciences
	Data Processing
Tw	Typewriter
	SF *Computer Sciences
	Data Processing
TWA	Trans World Airways
	SF *Aeronautics
	*Transportation
TWAIT	Terminal Wait
	SF *Computer Sciences
	Data Processing
TWB	Typewriter Buffer
	SF *Computer Sciences
TWERLE	Tropical Wind Energy Conversion and
	Reference Level Experiments
	SF *Space Sciences
TWL	Total Weight Loss
	SF *Space Sciences
	Space Simulation
TWT	Travelling Wave Tube
	SF *Aeronautics

	*Electronics and Electrical
	Engineering
	*Naval Sciences
	Navigation
TWTA	Travelling Wave Tube Amplifier
	SF *Aeronautics
	*Communication Systems
TWX	Teletypewriter Exchange
	SF *Computer Sciences
	Data Processing
TX	Toilet Exhaust
	SF *Metallurgy and Metallography
	Metalworks
TX	Torque Transmitter
	SF *Communication Systems
	*Electronics and Electrical
	Engineering

U

UADPS Uniform Automated Data Processing
    SF   Logistics
        *Military Sciences
UADS   User Attribute Data Set
    SF *Computer Sciences
        Data Processing
UAF   Union Air Force
    SF *Aeronautics
        *Military Sciences
UAIMS United Aircraft Information
    Management System
    SF *Aeronautics
        *Information Retrieval Systems
        *Management
UAN   Unified Automatic Network
    SF *Engineering
        Radio Engineering
        *Telecommunications
UAO   Urban Automatic Office
    SF Radio Engineering
        *Telecommunications
UAP   Upper Air Project
    SF *Meteorology
        *Space Sciences
UARS   Unmanned Arctic Research Submersible
    SF *Oceanography
UAS   Upper Airspace
    SF *Aeronautics
        Air Traffic Control
UBFF   Urey Bradley Force Field
    SF *Non-metallic Materials
        Polymers
UC   Upper Case
    SF *Computer Sciences
        Data Processing
UC   Uranium Carbide
    SF *Fuels
        *Nuclear Sciences
UCBS   Unit Control Blocks
    SF *Computer Sciences
        Data Processing
UCC   University Computer Company
    SF *Computer Sciences
UCK   Unit Check
    SF *Computer Sciences

        Data Processing
UCNI   Unified Communications Navigation
    and Identification
    SF *Aeronautics
        *Communication Systems
        Navigation
UCS   Uniform Chromaticity Scale
    SF *Photography
UCS   Universal Character Set
    SF *Computer Sciences
        Data Processing
UCSTR Universal Code Synchronous Transmitter
    Receiver
    SF *Computer Sciences
        Data Processing
UDAS   Unified Direct Access System
    SF *Computer Sciences
        Data Processing
UDF   Union Defence Force
    SF *Aeronautics
        *Military Sciences
UDP   Uridine Diphosphate
    SF *Biological and Medical Sciences
        Cytochemistry
UDPG   Uridine Diphosphoglucose
    SF Biochemistry
        *Biological and Medical Sciences
UDPGA Uridine Diphosphoglucuronic Acid
    SF Biochemistry
        *Biological and Medical Sciences
UDR   Universal Document Reader
    SF *Computer Sciences
        Data Processing
UDT   Universal Document Transport
    SF *Computer Sciences
        Data Processing
UEP   Underwater Electric Potential
    SF *Naval Sciences
        Navigation
UET-RT Universal Engineer Tractor-Rubber
    Tired
    SF *Engineering
        Mechanical Engineering
        Terramechanics
UF   Ultrafiltration

```
        SF  *Agricultural Sciences
            *Biological and Medical Sciences
UF      Urea Formaldehyde
        SF  *Agricultural Sciences
UFA     Unesterified Fatty Acids
        SF   Biochemistry
            *Biological and Medical Sciences
UFRCC   Uniform Federal Regional Council
            City (US)
        SF  *Transportation
UHF     Ultra High Frequency
        SF  *Aeronautics
            Navigation
UHF     Universal High Frequency
        SF  *Aeronautics
            *Communication Systems
UHM     Upper Half Mean-Length
        SF  *Agricultural Sciences
UHT     Ultra High Temperature
        SF  *Agricultural Sciences
            *Dairy Sciences
UHV     Ultra High Vacuum
        SF  *Astronautics and Astrophysics
            *Lunar Sciences
UIEC    International Union of Cinematograph
            Exhibitors
        SF  *Copyright
            Patents
UJM     Uncorrelated Jet Model
        SF   Nuclear Physics
            *Nuclear Sciences
UK      United Kingdom
        SF  *General
UKAEA   United Kingdom Atomic Energy Authority
        SF  *Nuclear Sciences
UL      Upper Limit
        SF  *Computer Sciences
            Data Processing
UMD     Unit Management Document
        SF  *Military Sciences
UMR     Unipolar Magnetic Regions
        SF  *Astronautics and Astrophysics
            *Lunar Sciences
UMTA    Urban Mass Transportation
            Administration (US)
        SF  *Transportation
UN      Urban Network
        SF  *Engineering
            Radio Engineering
            *Telecommunications
UNB     United Nations Beacon
        SF  *Aeronautics
            Air Traffic Control
            Radar Beacon Systems
UNCITRAL United Nations Commission on
            International Trade Law
        SF  *Copyright
            Industrial Property
UNCTAD  United Nations Conference on Trade
            and Development
```

```
        SF  *General
UNDP    United Nations Development Programme
        SF  *General
UNICE   Union of Industries of European
            Community
        SF  *General
UNIDO   United Nations Industrial Development
            Organization
        SF  *General
UNNSAD  Unit Neutral Normalized Spectral
            Analytical Density
        SF  *Photography
UOD     Units of Optical Density
        SF   Bioengineering
            *Biological and Medical Sciences
UON     Unless Otherwise Noted
        SF  *Metallurgy and Metallography
            Metalworks
UP      Urea Phosphate
        SF  *Agricultural Sciences
UPAU    Uttar Pradesh Agricultural University
        SF  *Agricultural Sciences
UPE     Unnatural Parity Exchange
        SF   Elementary Particles
            *Physics
UPOV    Union for the Protection of Plant
            Varieties
        SF  *Copyright
            Industrial Property
UPT     Undergraduate Pilot Training
        SF  *Aeronautics
            *Training
UR      Unattended Repeaters
        SF   Radio Engineering
            *Telecommunications
URS     Unmanned Repeater Station
        SF  *Engineering
            Radio Engineering
            *Telecommunications
URTNA   Union of National Radio and
            Television Organization of Africa
        SF  *Communication Systems
            *Copyright
US      Underside of Slab
        SF  *Metallurgy and Metallography
            Metalworks
US      Unit Separator
        SF  *Computer Sciences
            Data Processing
US      United States
        SF  *General
USA     United States Army
        SF  *Military Sciences
USAEC   United States Atomic Energy Commission
        SF  *Nuclear Sciences
            Reactors
USAF    United States Air Force
        SF  *Aeronautics
            *Military Sciences
USARP   United States Atlantic Research Program
```

            SF   *Engineering
                 Mechanical Engineering
USASI United States of America Standard
      Institute
            SF   *Computer Sciences
                 Data Processing
USATACOM United States Army Tank Automotive
         Command
            SF   *Engineering
                 Mechanical Engineering
                 *Military Sciences
                 Terramechanics
USAWC United States Army War College
            SF   *Military Sciences
                 *Training
USB   Upper Side Band
            SF   *Communication Systems
                 Radio Communications
USCG United States Coast Guard
            SF   *Transportation
USGW Under Sea Guided Weapon
            SF   *Military Sciences
                 Missiles
USI   User System Interface
            SF   *Computer Sciences
                 Data Processing
USMA United States Military Academy
            SF   *Military Sciences
                 *Training
USMC United States Marine Corps
            SF   *Military Sciences
                 *Transportation
USN   United States Navy
            SF   *Military Sciences
                 *Naval Sciences
USPHS United States Public Health Service
            SF   *Biological and Medical Sciences
USPS United States Postal Service
            SF   *Telecommunications
                 *Transportation
USRA United States Railway Association
            SF   *Transportation
USRA United States Railroad Association
            SF   *Transportation
USSM United Systems Simulation Model
            SF   *Computer Sciences
                 Data Processing
USSR Union of Soviet Socialist Republics
            SF   *General
UT   Universal Time
            SF   *Aeronautics
                 Navigation
UTAP Unified Transportation Assistance
      Program (US)
            SF   *Transportation
UTC   Coordinated Universal Time
            SF   *Aeronautics
                 Navigation
UTCS Urban Traffic Control System
            SF   *Transportation

UTIAS University of Toronto Institute for
      Aerospace Studies
            SF   *Space Sciences
UTN   Urban Telephone Network
            SF   *Engineering
                 Radio Engineering
                 *Telecommunications
UTP   Upper Turning Point
            SF   *Electronics and Electrical
                 Engineering
UTS   Ultimate Tensile Stress
            SF   *Metallurgy and Metallography
                 Welding
UTS   Ultimate Tensile Strength
            SF   *Non-metallic Materials
                 Polymers
UTS   Universal Time-sharing System
            SF   *Computer Sciences
                 Data Processing
UTTAS Utility Tactical Transport Aircraft
      System
            SF   *Aeronautics
                 *Military Sciences
UUT   Unit Under Test
            SF   *Computer Sciences
                 Testing
UV   Ultraviolet
            SF   *General
UVC   Unidirectional Voltage Converter
            SF   *Engineering
                 Radio Engineering
                 *Telecommunications
UVDC Urban Vehicle Development Competition
            SF   *Engineering
                 Mechanical Engineering
UVDS Ultra-Violet Flame Detection System
            SF   *Aeronautics
                 Avionics

V   Voltmeter
     SF *Electronics and Electrical
          Engineering
          Meters
Va   Anode Voltage
     SF *Electronics and Electrical
          Engineering
          Semiconductor Devices
VA   Volt Ammeter
     SF *Electronics and Electrical
          Engineering
          Meters
VA   Volt-ampere
     SF *Electronics and Electrical
          Engineering
          Solid-state Circuits
VAAC Vanadyl Acetylacetonate
     SF   Crystallography
          *Nuclear Sciences
VACR Variable Amplitude Correction Rack
     SF *Engineering
          Radio Engineering
          *Telecommunications
VAL   Vehicle Authorization List
     SF *Military Sciences
VAM   Virtual Access Method
     SF *Computer Sciences
          Data Processing
VAN   Value Added Networks
     SF *Computer Sciences
          Data Processing
VAP   Video Audio Participative
     SF   Programmed Learning
          *Training
va(pk)max Maximum Peak Anode Voltage
     SF *Electronics and Electrical
          Engineering
VAPS Vertical-short-takeoff-landing
     Approach System
     SF *Aeronautics
          Navigation
VAR   Visual and Aural Range
     SF *Aeronautics
          *Communication Systems
          Navigation

VARES Vega Aircraft Radar Enhancing System
     SF *Aeronautics
          Radar
VASI Visual Approach Slope Indicator
     SF *Aeronautics
          Approach and Landing
VAST Versatile Avionics Shop Test
     SF *Aeronautics
          Avionics
VCI   Vehicle Cone Index
     SF *Engineering
          Mechanical Engineering
          Terramechanics
VCCS Voltage Controlled Current Sources
     SF *Electronics and Electrical
          Engineering
          Solid-state Circuits
VCD   Variable Center Distance
     SF *Computer Sciences
          Data Processing
VCE   Collective-Emitter Voltage
     SF *Electronics and Electrical
          Engineering
          Semiconductor Devices
VCM   Vacuum Condensible Material
     SF *Space Sciences
          Space Simulation
VCO   Voltage Controlled Oscillator
     SF *Electronics and Electrical
          Engineering
VCR   Video Cassette Recorder
     SF *Copyright
          Patents
VCR   Visual Control Room
     SF *Aeronautics
          Air Traffic Control
VCVS Voltage Controlled Voltage Source
     SF *Electronics and Electrical
          Engineering
          Solid-state Circuits
VD   Volume Damper
     SF *Metallurgy and Metallography
          Metalworks
VDS   Variable Depth-Towed Sonar
     SF *Fisheries

VDU   Visual Display Unit
      SF *Aeronautics
          *Computer Sciences
          Data Processing
VE   Value Engineering
      SF *Engineering
VE   Vibration Eliminator
      SF *Metallurgy and Metallography
          Metalworks
VEM   Virtual Electrode Model
      SF *Non-crystalline Solids
VEP   Visual Evoked Potential
      SF *Biological and Medical Sciences
          Physiology
VER   Visual Evoked Response
      SF *Electronics and Electrical
              Engineering
Vf   Frequency Voltage
      SF *Electronics and Electrical
              Engineering
          Semiconductor Devices
VFA   Volatile Fatty Acids
      SF *Agricultural Sciences
          *Dairy Sciences
VFC   Video Film Converter
      SF *Photography
vfo   Variable Frequency Oscillator
      SF *Communication Systems
          Radio Communication
VFR   Visual Flight Rules
      SF *Aeronautics
          Air Traffic Control
          *Communication Systems
          Navigation
VFU   Vertical Format Unit
      SF *Computer Sciences
          Data Processing
VG   Vertical Gyroscope
      SF *Aeronautics
          Navigation
VG   Voice Grade
      SF *Computer Sciences
          Data Processing
Vh   Heater Voltage
      SF *Electronics and Electrical
              Engineering
          Semiconductor Devices
VHDL Very High Density Lipoprotein
      SF Biochemistry
          *Biological and Medical Sciences
VHF   Very High Frequency
      SF *Aeronautics
          *Communication Systems
          Navigation
VHRR Very High Resolution Radiometer
      SF *Aeronautics
          *Telecommunications
VI   Volume Indicator
      SF *Electronics and Electrical
              Engineering

          Meters
VIB   Vertical Integration Building
      SF   Civil Engineering
          *Engineering
VICOM Visual Communications Management
      SF   Microfilms
          *Photography
VIDIAC Vidicon Input to Automatic Computer
      SF *Computer Sciences
          Data Processing
VIN   Vehicle Identification Numbers
      SF *Computer Sciences
          *Transportation
VINS Very Intense Neutron Source
      SF *Nuclear Sciences
          Reactors
VISSR Visible and Infrared Spin Scan
          Radiometer
      SF *Aeronautics
          *Communication Systems
          *Space Sciences
VITA Volunteers for International Technical
          Assistance
      SF *Engineering
          Mechanical Engineering
VITAL VAST Interface Test Application
          Language
      SF *Computer Sciences
          Data Processing
VLA   Very Large Array
      SF *Engineering
          Mechanical Engineering
          *Space Sciences
VLB   Very Long Baseline
      SF *Astronautics and Astrophysics
          *Communication Systems
VLBI Very Long Baseline Interferometry
      SF *Astronautics and Astrophysics
          *Lunar Sciences
          *Space Sciences
VLCC Very Large Crude Carrier
      SF *Transportation
VLDL Very Low Density Lipoprotein
      SF   Biochemistry
          *Biological and Medical Sciences
VLF   Very Low Frequency
      SF *Aeronautics
          *Communication Systems
          Navigation
VLO   Viable Parahaemolyticus
      SF *Agricultural Sciences
          *Dairy Sciences
VLPE Very Long Period Experiment
      SF *Geosciences
          Seismic Detection
VLS   Vapour Liquid Solids
      SF   Crystallography
          *Geosciences
VLT   Ventrolateral Tract
      SF *Biological and Medical Sciences

VM   Virtual Machine
        SF *Computer Sciences
VMA   Virtual Memory Allocation
        SF *Computer Sciences
            Data Processing
VMC   Vertical Motion Carriage
        SF *Engineering
            Mechanical Engineering
            Terramechanics
VMC   Visual Meteorological Conditions
        SF *Aeronautics
            *Meteorology
VMCB   Virtual Machine Control Block
        SF *Computer Sciences
            Data Processing
VMD   Vector Meson Dominance
        SF   Elementary Particles
            *Nuclear Sciences
VMID   Virtual Machine Identifier
        SF *Computer Sciences
            Data Processing
VMJ   Vertical Multijunction
        SF *Electronics and Electrical
                Engineering
VMM   Vertical Machine Monitor
        SF *Computer Sciences
            Data Processing
VMT   Video Matrix Terminal
        SF *Computer Sciences
VMTAB   Virtual Machine Table
        SF *Computer Sciences
            Data Processing
VN   Ventral Nozzle
        SF *Aeronautics
            Aircraft
VN   Volatile Nitrogen
        SF *Agricultural Sciences
VOD   Volume Discount
        SF *Computer Sciences
            Data Processing
vol   Volume
        SF *Mathematics
VOLFD   Volume Adjustable Fire Damper
        SF *Metallurgy and Metallography
            Metalworks
VOR   Very High Frequency Omnirange
        SF *Aeronautics
            Air Traffic Control
            *Communication Systems
            Navigation
VORTAC Very High Frequency Omnirange and
            Tactical Air Navigation
        SF *Aeronautics
            Navigation
VOSC   VAST Operating System Code
        SF *Computer Sciences
            Data Processing
VOX   Voice Operated Switching Device
        SF *Communication Systems
            Radio Communication

VP   Virtual Processor
        SF *Computer Sciences
            Data Processing
VPAM   Virtual Partitioned Access Method
        SF *Computer Sciences
            Data Processing
VPD   Vertical Polar Diagram
        SF *Aeronautics
            Radar Beacon Systems
VPSW   Virtual Program Status Word
        SF *Computer Sciences
            Data Processing
VRB   Violet Red Bile
        SF *Agricultural Sciences
            *Dairy Sciences
VRC   Vertical Redundancy Check
        SF *Computer Sciences
            Data Processing
VRC   Vertical Ride Control
        SF *Aeronautics
VRC   Visual Record Computer
        SF *Computer Sciences
            Data Processing
VRM   Viscous Remnant Magnetization
        SF *Astronautics and Astrophysics
            *Lunar Sciences
            *Oceanography
VRS   Volatile Reducing Substances
        SF *Agricultural Sciences
            Dairy Sciences
VS   Variable Stores
        SF *Computer Sciences
            Data Processing
VS   Vertical Sounding
        SF *Engineering
            Radio Engineering
            *Telecommunications
VSAM   Virtual Sequential Access Method
        SF *Computer Sciences
            Data Processing
VSAM   Virtual Storage Access Method
        SF *Computer Sciences
            Data Processing
VSCF   Variable Speed Constant Frequency
        SF *Aeronautics
            *Communication Systems
VSD   Vertical Situation Display
        SF *Aeronautics
            Displays
VSG   Vertical Sweep Generator
        SF *Engineering
            Radio Engineering
            *Telecommunications
VSPX   Vehicle Scheduling Program Extended
        SF *Computer Sciences
            Data Processing
VSR   Validation Summary Report
        SF *Computer Sciences
            Data Processing
VSTA   Virus Specified Tumour Antigens

```
          SF  *Biological and Medical Sciences
              Physiology
V/STOL Vertical/Short Takeoff and Landing
          SF  *Aeronautics
VSTT  Variable Speed Training Target
          SF  *Aeronautics
              *Military Sciences
VSWR  Voltage Standard Wave Ratio
          SF  *Electronics and Electrical
                  Engineering
              Measurements
VT    Vertical Tabulation
          SF  *Computer Sciences
              Data Processing
VTO   Vertical Takeoff
          SF  *Aeronautics
              Aircraft
VTOC  Volume Table of Content
          SF  *Computer Sciences
              Data Processing
VTOGW Vertical Takeoff Gross Weight
          SF  *Aeronautics
              Aircraft
VTOL  Vertical Takeoff and Landing
          SF  *Aeronautics
              Aircraft
VTPR  Vertical Temperature Profile
             Radiometer
          SF  *Aeronautics
              *Communication Systems
VU    Voice Unit
          SF  *Computer Sciences
              Data Processing
VUV   Vacuum Ultraviolet
          SF  *Chemistry
VVE   Vertical Vertex Errors
          SF  *Nuclear Sciences
              Wire Chamber Spectrometer
VXO   Variable Crystal Oscillator
          SF  *Communication Systems
              Radio Communication
Vz    Zener Voltage
          SF  *Electronics and Electrical
                  Engineering
              Semiconductor Devices
```

W   Wattmeter
     SF *Electronics and Electrical
           Engineering
           Meters

WABCO Westinghouse Air Brake Company
     SF *Engineering
           Mechanical Engineering
           *Transportation

WAC   World Aeronautical Chart
     SF *Aeronautics
           Navigation

WADC Wright Air Development Centre (UK)
     SF *Aeronautics

WANEF Westinghouse Astronuclear Experimental
       Facility
     SF *Nuclear Sciences
           Reactors

WANL Westinghouse Astronuclear Laboratory
     SF *Nuclear Sciences
           Reactors

WARC-ST World Administrative Radio
           Conference for Space
           Telecommunications
     SF *Engineering
           Radio Engineering
           *Telecommunications

WASP War Air Service Program
     SF *Military Sciences
           *Transportation

WATS Wide Area Telecommunications Service
     SF *Information Retrieval Systems
           *Telecommunications

WATS Wide Area Telephone Service
     SF *Communication Systems
           *Computer Sciences
           Data Processing

WBC   White Blood Cell
     SF *Biological and Medical Sciences

WC   Water Closet
     SF *Building

WCEE World Conference on Earthquake
       Engineering
     SF *Engineering
           Structural Engineering

WCG   Weakly Compactly Generated

     SF *Mathematics
WD   Write Direct
     SF *Computer Sciences
           Data Processing

WECO Western Electric Company
     SF *Aeronautics
           Air Traffic Control
           *Communication Systems

WED   Weak Exchange Degeneracy
     SF Elementary Particles
           *Physics

WEFAX Weather Facsimile Experiment
     SF *Meteorology

WEIS World Event Interaction Survey
     SF *General

WEP   Wideband Exciter and Processor
     SF *Aeronautics
           Radar Detection

WES   Waterway Experiment Station (US)
     SF *Engineering
           Mechanical Engineering
           Terramechanics

WGSC Wide Gap Spark Chamber
     SF *Electronics and Electrical
           Engineering
           Data Recording

WGTA Wisconsin General Testing Apparatus
     SF *Biological and Medical Sciences

WH   Watthour
     SF *Electronics and Electrical
           Engineering
           Meters

WHOI Woods Hole Oceanographic Institutions
     SF *Naval Sciences
           Navigation

WHRA Welwyn Hall Research Association (UK)
     SF *Information Retrieval Systems

WI   Welding Institute (UK)
     SF *Information Retrieval Systems

WIN   Work Intensive
     SF *Training

WIP   Work In Progress
     SF *Computer Sciences
           Data Processing

WIPO World Intellectual Property

```
              Organization                        Cereals
          SF  *Copyright           WSB  Wheat Soy Blend
              Patents                       SF  *Agricultural Sciences
WIRA  Wool Industries Research Association          Cereals
          (UK)                     WSCS Wide Sense Cyclo-Stationary
          SF  *Information Retrieval Systems    SF  *Computer Sciences
WKQDR Work Queue Directory                    *Electronics and Electrical
          SF  *Computer Sciences                  Engineering
              *Information Retrieval Systems WSE  Water Saline Extract
WLI   Wavelength Interval                  SF  *Biological and Medical Sciences
          SF  *Agricultural Sciences            Drugs
WM    Work Mark                  WSE  Weapon System Efficiency
          SF  *Computer Sciences            SF  *Military Sciences
              Data Processing        WSI  Water Solidity Index
WMO   World Meteorological Organization    SF  *Agricultural Sciences
          SF  *Meteorology                    Cereals
              *Geosciences           WSMR White Sands Missile Range (US)
WMS   Wire Mesh Screen                 SF  *Military Sciences
          SF  *Metallurgy and Metallography        *Space Sciences
WMSC  Weather Message Switching Center WSMV Wheat Steak Mosaic Virus
          SF  *Aeronautics                 SF  *Agricultural Sciences
              *Communication Systems WST  Weapon System Trainer
              *Meteorology                 SF  *Aeronautics
WOL   Wedge Opening Load                   Human Factors
          SF  *Nuclear Sciences      WSZ  Wrong Signature Zero
WPAFB Wright Patterson Air Force Base      SF  *Nuclear Sciences
          SF  *Aeronautics           WT   Water Tight
              *Military Sciences           SF  *Metallurgy and Metallography
WPC   Wheat Protein Concentrate             Metalworks
          SF  *Agricultural Sciences wt   Weight
              Cereals                      SF  *Mathematics
WPC   Whey Protein Concentrate       w/t  Wireless Telegraphy
          SF  *Agricultural Sciences       SF  *Communication Systems
WPESS Within-Pulse Electronic Sector          *Engineering
          Scanning                           Radio Engineering
          SF  *Fisheries             WTM  Write Tape Mark
WPM   Words Per Minute                     SF  *Computer Sciences
          SF  *Computer Sciences               Data Processing
              Data Processing        WTR  Western Test Range (US)
WPS   Water Phase Salt                     SF  *Space Sciences
          SF  *Agricultural Sciences WUE  Water Use Efficiency
              *Dairy Sciences              SF  *Agricultural Sciences
WQ    Water Quenched                 WVAS Wake Vortex Avoidance System
          SF  *Non-crystalline Solids      SF  *Aeronautics
WRA   Water Research Association (UK)          Turbulence
          SF  *Information Retrieval Systems WVE Water Vapour Electrolysis
WRAT  Wide Range Achievement Test          SF  *Aeronautics
          SF  Programmed Learning              Aviation Medicine
              *Training                        *Biological and Medical Sciences
WRD   Whole Rumen Digesta            ww   Wire Wound
          SF  *Agricultural Sciences       SF  *Communication Systems
              *Dairy Sciences                  *Engineering
WRSIC Water Resources Scientific Information      Radio Engineering
          Center (US)                WWF  Whole Wheat Flour
          SF  Civil Engineering            SF  *Agricultural Sciences
              *Engineering                     *Dairy Sciences
WS    Water Solid                    WWMCCS World Wide Military Command and
          SF  *Ceramics                     Control System
WS    Wire Shear                          SF  *Military Sciences
          SF  *Agricultural Sciences WWW  World Weather Watch
```

```
       SF  *Aeronautics
           *Meteorology
WXTRN Weak External Reference
       SF  *Computer Sciences
           Data Processing
```

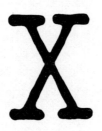

X

XBT Expendable Bathythermonograph
       SF *Agricultural Sciences
             *Fisheries
XDS Xerox Data Systems
       SF *Computer Sciences
             Data Processing
XIO Execute Input/Output
       SF *Computer Sciences
             Data Processing
XLDP Xylose-Lysine-Desoxycholatepeplon
         Agar
       SF *Agricultural Sciences
             *Dairy Sciences
XO   Xanthine Oxidase
       SF *Dairy Sciences
XPN External Priority Number
       SF *Computer Sciences
             Data Processing
XPT External Page Table
       SF *Computer Sciences
             Data Processing
XRF X-Ray Fluorescence
       SF *Lunar Sciences
XSPT External Shared Page Table
       SF *Computer Sciences
             Data Processing
XTSI Extended Task Status Index
       SF *Computer Sciences
             Data Processing

YAG   Yttrium Aluminium Garnet
      SF   *Electronics and Electrical
            Engineering
          Lasers and Masers
          Quantum Electronics
YES   Yeast Extract Sucrose
      SF   *Agricultural Sciences
          Cereals
YIG   Yttrium Iron Garnet
      SF   *Electronics and Electrical
            Engineering
          Instruments
YMC   Yeast Mold Count
      SF   *Agricultural Sciences
          *Dairy Sciences
YTL   Yarsley Technical Services (UK)
      SF   *Biological and Medical Sciences

Z

Z   Zero
        SF   *Computer Sciences
             Data Processing
ZAMS   Zero Age Main Sequence
        SF   *Astronautics and Astrophysics
             *Lunar Sciences
ZCS   Zone Communication Station
        SF   *Engineering
             Radar Engineering
             *Telecommunications
ZD   Zenith Distance
        SF   *Photography
ZF   Zone Finders
        SF   *Engineering
             Radio Engineering
             *Telecommunications
ZFS   Zero Field Splitting
        SF   *Biological and Medical Sciences
             Medical Ions
Zn   Zone
        SF   *Computer Sciences
             Data Processing
ZnO   Zinc Oxide
        SF   *Aeronautics
             Instruments
ZOTS   Zoom Optical Target Simulator
        SF   *Aeronautics
             Testing
ZP   Zero Point
        SF   *Nuclear Sciences
             Spectroscopy
ZRA   Zero Range Approximation
        SF   Nuclear Physics
             *Nuclear Sciences
ZTS   Zoom Transfer Scope
        SF   Instruments
             *Photography
             Photogrametric Engineering

Part Two

SUBJECT FIELDS

SUBJECT FIELDS

AERONAUTICS

AA	Armature Accelerator
AAA	Anti Aircraft Artillery
AABNCP	Advanced Airborne Command Post
AAC	Air Approach Control
AAC	Automatic Approach Control
AACB	Aeronautics and Astronautics Board
AACO	Arab Air Carrier Organization
AACS	Airways and Air Communications Service
AADA	Anti Aircraft Defended Area
AADC	Anti Aircraft Defence Commander
AAFCE	Allied Air Force Central Europe
AAFNE	Allied Air Force Northern Europe
AAFSE	Allied Air Force Southern Europe
AAG	Air Adjutant General
AAH	Advanced Attach Helicopter
AALMG	Anti Aircraft Light Machine Gun
AAOO	American Academy of Ophthalmology and Otolaryngology
AAPP	Auxiliary Airborne Power Plant
AAPU	Airborne Auxiliary Power Unit
AASR	Airport and Airways Surveillance Radar
AATC	Automatic Air Traffic Control
AATMS	Advanced Air Traffic Management System
AATO	Army Air Transport Organization
ABC	Advance Booking Charter
ABCCC	Airborne Battlefield Command and Control Center
AC	Advisory Circular
AC	Alternating Current
ACC	Air Control Centre
ACC	Air Coordinating Committee
ACC	Area Control Centers
ACDO	Air Carrier District Office (US)
ACE	Airspace Coordination Element
ACE	Altimeter Control Equipment
ACE	Automatic Clutter Eliminator
ACE	Automatic Computing Engine
ACF	Air Combat Fighter
ACF	Avion de Combat Futur
ACGB	Aircraft Corporation of Great Britain
ACIC	Aeronautical Chart and Information Center (US)
ACIR	Aviation Crash Injury Research
ACLS	Automated Control Landing System
ACM	Air Chief Marshal
ACM	Air Combat Maneuvering
ACP	Azimuth Change Pulse
ACR	Approach Control Radar
ACS	Adrenocortico Steroids
ACS	Aerodrome Control Service
ACS	Altitude Control System
ACTF	Altitude Control Test Facility
ACV	Air Cushion Vehicle
ACW	Aircraft Control Warning
ADAR	Advanced Design Array Radar
ADC	Aerodrome Control
ADC	Air Data Computer
ADC	Air Defense Command
ADCC	Air Defense Control Center
ADE	Air Defense Emergency (US)
ADEU	Automatic Data Entry Unit
ADF	Aerial Direction Finding
ADF	Automatic Direction Finder
ADI	Altitude Direction Indicator
ADI	Automatic Direction Indicator
ADIS	Automatic Data Interchange System
ADISP	Aeronautical Data Interchange System Panel
ADIZ	Air Defense Identification Zone
ADO	Air Defense Officer
ADOC	Air Defense Operations Centre
ADS	Accessory Drive System
ADS	Advanced Dressing Station
ADS	Air Defense Ship
ADS	Air Defence System
ADS	Aircraft Development Service
ADS	Automatic Door Seal
ADSM	Air Defence Suppression Missile
AE	Atmospheric Explorer
AEDC	Arnold Engineering Development Center (US)
AEEC	Airline Electronic Engineering Committee
AEEMS	Automatic Electric Energy Management System
AEG	Active Element Groups

AEROSAT Aeronautical Satellite
AEW   Airborne Early Warning
AEWC   Airborne Early Warning and Control
AFA   Air Force Association
AFA   Army Flight Activity
AFAR   Advanced Field Array Radar
AFB   Air Force Base
AFB   Anti Friction Bearing
AFBMD Air Force Ballistic Missile Division
AFC   Automatic Frequency Control
AFCAC African Civil Aviation Commission
AFCRL Air Force Cambridge Research
         Laboratory
AFCS   Air Force Communications Service
AFCS   Automatic Flight Control System
AFCS   Avionic Flight Control System
AFF   Army Field Force
AFFDL Air Force Flight Dynamics Laboratory
         (US)
AFFF   Aqueous Film Forming Foam
AFFTC Air Force Flight Test Center
AFHRL Air Force Human Resources Laboratory
AFLC   Air Force Logistics Command (US)
AFLCM Air Force Logistics Command Manual
AFM   Air Force Manual
AFMDC Air Force Missile Development Center
AFPAM Automatic Flight Planning and
         Monitoring
AFPAV Airfield Pavement
AFPRO Air Force Plant Representative Office
AFR   Air Force Regulation
AFRTC Air Force Reserve Training Center
AFS   Aeronautics Fixed Service
AFS   Air Force Specialty
AFS   Air Force Supply
AFSATCOM Air Force Satellite Communications
AFSCM Air Force Systems Command Manual
AFSWC Air Force Special Weapons Center (US)
AFTN   Aeronautical Fixed Telecommunications
         Network
AFWL   Air Force Weapon Laboratory
AFWTR Air Force Western Test Range
AGARD Advisory Group for Aeronautical
         Research and Development
AGC   Automatic Gain Control
AGCA   Automatic Ground Controlled Approach
AGD   Axil Gear Differential
AGDS   American Gage Design Standard
AGL   Above Ground Level
AGL   Altitude Above Ground Level
AGOS   Air Ground Operations Section
AGS   Air Gunnery School (UK)
AGS   Aircraft General Standards
AGS   Automatic Gain Stabilization
AGSAN Astronomical Guidance System for Air
         Navigation
AHRS   Altitude Heading Reference System
AHS   Airborne Hardware Simulator
AI   Airborne Interception
AI   Annoyance Index

AI   Anti Icing
AIA   Aeroplane Industries Association
AIAA   American Institute of Aeronautics
         and Astronautics
AIB   Accidents Investigation Branch
AIB   Agency Investigation Board
AIC   Aeronautical Information Circular
AIC   Automatic Intersection Control
AIDAS Advanced Instrumentation and Data
         Analysis System
AIDATS Army In-flight Data Transmission
         System
AIDS   Airborne Integrated Data System
AIEE   American Institute of Electrical
         Engineering
AIG   Accident Investigation
AIL   Airborne Instruments Laboratory
AILAS Automatic Instruments Landing System
AILS   Advanced Integrated Landing System
AIM   Airman's Information Manual
AIM   Alarm Indication Monitor
AIMIS Advanced Integrated Modular Instrument
         System
AIP   Aeronautical Information Publication
AIP   Allied Intelligence Publication
AIR   Airborne Intercept Radar
AIR   American Institute of Research
AIRLO Air Liaison Officer
AIRPASS Airborne Interception Radar and
         Pilot's Attack Sight System
AIS   Aeronautical Information Service
AIS   Altitude Indication System
AIT   Autoignition Temperature
AITE   Aircraft Integrated Test Equipment
ALARM Air Launched Advanced Ramjet Missile
ALARR Air Launched Air Recoverable Rocket
ALATD Assumed Latitude
ALBM   Air Launched Ballistic Missile
ALC   Automatic Level Control
ALCH   Approach Light Contact Height
ALMS   Aircraft Landing Measurement System
ALOTS Airborne Lightweight Optical Tracking
         System
ALPA   Airline Pilots' Association
ALQAS Aircraft Landing Quality Association
         Scheme
ALS   Approach Light System
ALS   Automatic Landing System
ALTA   Association of Local Transport
         Airlines
ALCC   Airborne Launch Control Center
AMA   Air Materiel Area
AMAD   Aircraft Mounted Accessory Drive
AMC   Acetylmethylcarbion
AMC   Aircraft Manufacturers' Council
AMC   Army Missile Command
AMCS   Airborne Missile Control System
AMIS   Aircraft Movement Information Service
AMK   Anti Misting Kerosine
AMO   Air Ministry Order (UK)

AMPR   Aeronautical Manufacturers Planning
         Report
AMPSS Advanced Manned Precision Strike
         System
AMS   Aeronautical Material Specification
AMS   Air Mail Service
AMST   Advanced Medium STOL Transport
ANBS   Air Navigation and Bombing School
ANC   Air Navigation Commission
ANC   Air Navigation Conference
ANCU   Airborne Navigation Computer Unit
AND   Air-Force Navy Design
ANDB   Air Navigation Development Board (US)
ANG   Air National Guard
ANG-CE Air National Guard Civil Engineering
ANIP   Army-Navy Instrumentation Program
ANIP   Army Navy Integrated Presentation
ANO   Air Navigation Order
ANP   Allied Navigation Publication
ANS   Air Navigation School
ANSI   American National Standards Institute
ANTAC Air Navigation Tactical Control
         System
ANU   Airplane Nose Up
AOC   Air Officer Commanding
AOCI   Airport Operators Council International
AOEW   Airplane Operating Empty Weight
AONS   Air Observer's Navigation School
AOP   Air Observation Post
AOPA   Aircraft Owners' and Pilots'
         Association
AOS   Air Observer's School
AP   Air Publication
AP   Assumed Position
AP   Autopilot
APACS Airborne Position and Altitude Camera
         System
APATS Automatic Programmers and Test System
APC   Approach Control
APC   Area Position Control
APC   Automatic Pressure Control
Apex   Advanced Purchase Excursion
APFD   Autopilot Flight Director
APG   Automatic Program Generation
APG   Azimuth Pulse Generator
APGC   Air Proving Ground Center
API   Air Position Indicator
API   Armour Piercing Incendiary
APIS   Army Photographic Interpretation
         Section
APP   Approach Control Office
APP   Auxiliary Power Plant
APPLE Associative Processor Programming
         Language Evaluation
APRIL Aqua Planning Risk Indicator for
         Landing
APT   Airman Proficiency Test
APT   Automatic Position Telemetering
APU   Auxiliary Power Unit
AQE   Airman Qualifying Examination

AR   Aerial Refuelling
AR   Army Regulation
ARA   Aircraft Research Association
ARADCOM Army Air Defence Command
ARAP   Aeronautical Research Associates of
         Princeton
ARB   Air Registration Board
ARB   Air Research Bureau
ARC   Aeronautical Research Council (UK)
ARC   Aircraft Radio Corporation
ARC   Airworthiness Requirements Committee
ARC   Atlantic Research Corporation
ARC   Automatic Remote Control
ARCAS Automatic Radar Chain Acquisition
         System
ARCH   Articulated Computer Hierarchy
ARDC   Air Research and Development Command
         (US)
ARI   Airborne Radio Instrument
ARIA   Advanced Range Instrumented Aircraft
ARINC Aeronautical Radio Incorporated (US)
ARL   Aerospace Research Laboratory (UK)
ARM   Anti Radar Missile
ARNOT Aera Notice
AROD   Airborne Range and Orbit Determination
ARODS Airborne Radar Orbital Determination
         System
ARP   Air Raid Protection
ARP   Azimuth Reset Pulse
ARQ   Automatic Response Query
ARS   Air Rescue Service
ARSR   Air Route Surveillance Radar
ARTC   Air Route Traffic Control
ARTC   Aircraft Research and Testing Committee
ARTCC Air Route Traffic Control Center (US)
ARTG   Azimuth Range and Timing Group
ARTOC Army Tactical Operations Centre
ARTS   Automatic Radar Terminal System
ASA   Air Security Agency
ASB   Air Safety Board
ASCC   Air Standardization Coordinating
         Committee
ASD   Aeronautical Systems Division
ASDE   Airport Surface Detection Equipment
ASDIC Anti Submarine Detection Investigation
         Committee
ASDIC Armed Services Documents Intelligence
         Center
ASEB   Aeronautics and Space Engineering
         Board
ASET   Aeronautical Services Earth Terminal
ASG   Aeronautical Standards Group
ASH   Assault Support Helicopter
ASI   Advanced Scientific Instrument
ASI   Air Speed Indicator
ASIP   Aircraft Structural Integrity Program
ASIR   Air Speed Indicator Reading
ASM   Air-to-Surface Missile
ASMC   Automatic Systems Management and
         Control

ASMI Airfield Surface Movement Indicator
ASMS Advanced Surface Missile System
ASO   Aviation Supply Office
ASOP Automatic Structural Optimization
        Program
ASR   Airport Surveillance Radar
ASR   Aviation Safety Regulation
ASROC Anti Submarine Rocket
ASST Advanced Supersonic Transport
ASSU Air Support Signal Unit
AST   Advanced Supersonic Technology
ASTC Airport Surface Traffic Control
ASTF Aero-propulsion System Test Facility
ASTRA Application of Space Techniques
        Relating to Aviation
ATS   Army Transport Service
AT   Air Temperature
ATA   Actual Time of Arrival
ATA   Air Transport Association
ATAA Air Transport Association of America
ATAC Air Transport Advisory Council
ATB   Air Transport Board
ATC   Air Traffic Control
ATC   Air Traffic Controller
ATC   Air Training Command
ATC   Aircraft Technical Committee
ATC   Army Training Center
ATC   Armament Training Camp
ATCAC Air Traffic Control Advisory Committee
ATCAP Air Traffic Control Automation Panel
ATCBI Air Transport Control Beacon
        Interrogator
ATCC Air Traffic Control Center
ATCO Air Traffic Control Officer
ATCRBS Air Traffic Control Radar Beacon
         System
ATCS Air Traffic Control Service
ATCS Air Traffic Controller Specialist
ATCSS Air Traffic Control Signalling System
ATCT Air Traffic Control Tower
ATDA Augmented Target Docking Adapter
ATDS Air Tactical Data System
ATE   Advanced Technology Engine
ATEC Automatic Test Equipment Complex
ATG   Air-To-Ground
ATI   Army Training Instruction
ATIS Automatic Terminal Information Service
ATK   Along Track Distance
ATK   Available Tonne-Km
ATLAS Abbreviated Test Language for
        Avionics Systems
ATLB Air Transport Licensing Board
ATO   Air Transfer Order
ATOM Apollo Telescope Orientation Mount
ATP   Accepted Test Procedure
ATP   Allied Technical Publication
ATR   Air Traffic Regulations
ATR   Aircraft Trouble Report
ATR   Anti-Transmit-Receive
ATRAN Automatic Terrain Recognition and
        Navigation
ATREPS Air Traffic Control Representatives
ATS   Air Traffic Service
ATS   Applications Technology Satellite
ATS   Armament Training Station
ATSD Airborne Traffic Situation Display
ATSU Air Traffic Service Units
ATT   Advanced Technology Transport
ATTITB Air Transport and Travel Industry
         Training Board
ATTP Advanced Transport Technology Program
AVA   Aerodynamische Versuchsanstalt
        (Ger.)
AVAS Automatic VFR Advisory Service
AVASI Abbreviated Visual Approach Slope
        Indicator
AVC   Automatic Volume Control
AVCS Advanced Vidicon Camera System
AVGAS Aviation Gasoline
AVM   Airborne Vibration Monitoring
AVSF Advanced Vertical Strike Fighter
AWACS Airborne Warning and Control System
AWCLS All Weather Carrier Landing System
AWG   American Wire Gage
AWOP All Weather Operation Panel
AWS   Air Warning System
AWS   Air Weapon System
AWS   Air Weather Service
BAA   British Airports Authority
BABS Blind Approach Beacon System
BAC   Barometric Altitude Control
BAC   British Aircraft Corporation
BADGE Base Air Defence Ground Experiment
BALPA British Airline Pilots' Association
BALS Blind Approach Landing System
BANS Basic Air Navigation School
BANS Bright Alphanumeric Subsystem
BARIG Board of Airline Representatives in
        Germany
BAS   Basic Airspeed
BAS   Blind Approach System
BAUA Business Aircraft Users' Association
BCA   Battery Control Area
BCAR British Civil Airworthiness
        Requirements
BCF   Bromochlorofluoromethane
BD   Blocker Deflector
BDI   Bearing Deviation Indicator
BDM   Bomber Defense Missile
BEA   British European Airways
BEF   Blunt End Forward
BGA   British Gliding Association
BGS   Bombing and Gunnery School
BIATA British Independent Air Transport
        Association
BIT   Built In Test
BITE Built In Test Equipment
BLAC British Light Aviation Centre
BLC   Boundary Layer Control
BLEU Blind Landing Experimental Unit

BLG   Breech Loading Gun
BM   Boundary Marker
BMEP   Brake Mean Effective Pressure
BMS   Boeing Materials Specification
BOAC   British Overseas Airways Corporation
BORAM Block Oriented Random Access Memory
BOSOR Buckling Of Shell Of Revolution
BPT   Blade Passage Tones
BREL   Boeing Radiation Effect Laboratory
BRG   Beacon Reply Group
BRGW   Brake Release Gross Weight
BRL   Ballistics Research Laboratory (US)
BSAA   British South American Airways
BUCLASP Buckling of Laminated Stiffened
          Plates
BUEC   Back-Up Emergency Communications
BUM   Back Up Mode
CAA   Civil Aeronautics Administration (US)
CAA   Civil Aviation Authority (UK)
CAAC   Civil Aviation Administration of
          China
CAARC Commonwealth Advisory Aeronautical
          Research Council
CAAS   Computer Aided Approach Sequencing
CAAS   Computer Assisted Approach Sequencing
CAB   Civil Aeronautics Board
CABATM Civil Aeronautics Board Air
          Transport Mobilization
CAC   Commonwealth Aircraft Corporation
          (Aust.)
CACAC Civil Aircraft Control Advisory
          Committee (UK)
CACAS Civil Aviation Council of Arab States
CADC   Control Air Data Computer
CAG   Civil Aviation Group
CAINS Carrier Aircraft Inertial Navigation
          System
CAL   Confined Area Landing
CAL   Cornell Aeronautical Laboratory
CAM   Civil Aeronautics Manual
CAM   Commercial Air Movement
CAMI   Civil Aeromedical Institute (US)
CAMI   Civil Aviation Medical Institute
CANS   Civilian Air Navigation School
CAP   Civil Air Patrol
CAP   Civil Aviation Planning Committee
CAP   Civil Aviation Publication
CAP   Combat Air Patrol
CAPC   Civil Aviation Planning Committee
CAPRI Coded Address Private Radio Intercom
CAR   Civil Air Regulation
CARA   Cargo and Rescue Aircraft
CARA   Combat Aircrew Rescue Aircraft
CARDE Canadian Armament Research and
          Development Establishment
CARF   Central Altitude Reservation Facility
CARP   Computed Air Released Point
CAS   Calibrated Air Speed
CAS   Close Air Support
CAS   Collosion Avoidance System
CAS   Control Augmentation System

CAS   Controlled Airspace
CASWS Close Air Support Weapon System
CAT   Civil Air Transport
CAT   Clear Air Turbulence
CATITB Civil Air Transport Industry
          Training Board
CAVU   Ceiling And Visibility Unlimited
CAWS   Common Aviation Weather System
CCA   Carrier Control Approach
CCECA Consultative Committee on Electronics
          for Civil Aviation
CCS   Communication Control System
CCTV   Closed Circuit Television
CCV   Control Configured Vehicles
CD   Common Digitizer
CDA   Command and Data Acquisition
CDC   Computer Display Channel
CDI   Control Deviation Indicator
CDI   Control Direction Indicator
CDI   Course Deviation Indicator
CDP   Communications Data Processor
CDR   Composit Damage Risk
CDU   Control Display Unit
CEAC   Committee for European Airspace
          Coordination
CEP   Probable Circular Error
CFAE   Contractor Furnished Aircraft
          Equipment
CFANS Canadian Forces Air Navigation School
CFF   Critical Flicker Frequency
CFL   Clear Flight Level
CFR   Code of Federal Regulations
CFR   Contact Flight Rules
CGA   Compagnie Générale d'Automatisme (Fr.)
CHAG   Chain Arrester Gear
CHD   Coronary Heart Disease
CHL   Chain Home Low
CIAP   Climatic Impact Assessment Program
CIC   Combat Information Center
CIDIN Common ICAO Data Interchange Network
CIFRR Common IFR Room
CIOM   Communications Input Output
          Multiplexer
CIRIS Complete Integrated Reference
          Instrumentation System
CIT   Cranfield Institute of Technology (UK)
CIU   Control Indicator Unit
CMACL Composite Mode Adjective Checklist
CMC   Command Module Computer
CMM   Computerised Modular Monitoring
CN   Cascade Nozzle
CNCS   Central Navigation Control School
CNI   Communication Navigation and
          Information
CNR   Composite Noise Rating
CNS   Central Navigation School
COAT   Corrected Outside Air Temperature
COD   Carrier Onboard Delivery
CODIS Controlled Digital Simulator
COMESA Committee on the Meteorological

Effects of Stratospheric Aircraft (UK)

COMLO	Compass Locater
COPAG	Collision Prevention Advisory Group
CORA	Coherent Radar Array
CORDS	Coherent-On-Receive Doppler System
CP	Control Panel
CPA	Closest Point of Approach
CPE	Circular Probable Error
CPI	Crash Position Indicator
CPILS	Correlation Protected Instrument Landing System
CPM	Central Processor Modules
CPU	Central Processor Unit
CRAF	Civil Reserve Air Fleet
CRC	Control and Reporting Center
CRP	Control and Reporting Post
CRT	Cathode Ray Tube
CSC	Chief Sector Control
CSD	Constant Simulus Differences
CSD	Constant Speed Drive
CSM	Command Service Module
CT	Current Transformer
CTD	Cross Track Distance
CTOL	Conventional Takeoff and Landing
CTS	Contralateral Threshold Shift
CTV	Control Test Vehicle
CUE	Computer Up-date Equipment
CW	Continuous Wave
CVF	Controlled Visual Flight
CVR	Cockpit Voice Recorder
DABS	Discrete Address Beacon System
DADS	Digital Air Data System
DAIS	Digital Avionics Information System
DARC	Direct Access Radar Channel
DARPA	Defence Advanced Research Project Agency
DAS	Data Acquisition Subsystem
DAVIE	Digital Alphanumeric Video Insertion Equipment
DAWNS	Design of Aircraft Wing Structures
DBP	Diastolic Blood Pressure
DCC	Display Channel Complex
DCCU	Data Communication Control Units
DCM	Defence Combat Maneuvering
DEDS	Data Entry and Display Subsystem
DEXAN	Digital Experimental Airborne Navigator
DF	Direction Finding
DFDR	Digital Flight Data Recorder
DG	Directional Gyroscope
DH	Decision Height
DIAN	Decca Integrated Airborne Navigation
DIANE	Digital Integrated Attack Navigation System
DILS	Doppler Inertial Loran System
DLC	Direct Lift Control
dLO	Longitudinal Difference
DME	Distance Measuring Equipment
DMET	Distance Measuring Equipment TACAN

DMLS	Doppler Microwave Landing Guidance System
DMS	Differential Maneuvering Simulator
DOA	Dominant Obstacle Allowance
DORA	Directorate of Operational Analysis
DOT	Department of Transportation
DP	Display Package
DPCT	Differential Protection Current Transformer
DPS	Data Processing Subsystem
DPSA	Deep Penetration Strike Aircraft
DRC	Damage Risk Contours
DRDTO	Detection Radar Data Take-Off
DRI	Descent Rate Indicator
DRIFT	Diversity Receiving Instrumentation for Telemetry
DRIR	Direct Readout Infrared
DRS	Detection Ranging Set
DSB	Double Side Band
DSCS	Defense Satellite Communications System
DST	Data System Test
DSU	Data Storage Unit
DTE	Development Test and Evaluation
DU	Display Unit
DVARS	Doppler Velocity Altimeter Radar Set
DWL	Downwind Localiser
EA	Enemy Aircraft
EAC	Approach Clearance Expect
EACS	Electronic Automatic Chart System
EADI	Electronic Attitude Director Indicator
EAGLE	Elevation Angle Guidance Landing Equipment
EAIR	Extended Area Instrumentation Radar
EANS	Empire Air Navigation School
EAR	Employee Appraisal Record
EARB	European Airlines Research Bureau
EAS	Equivalent Air Speed
EASAMS	E-A Space and Advanced Military System
EASCON	Electronics and Aerospace Systems Conference
EAT	Expected Approach Time
EATS	Empire Air Training Scheme
EBF	Externally Blown Flap
EBM	Electronic Bearing Marker
ECAC	Electromagnetic Compatibility Analysis Center
ECAC	European Civil Aviation Conference
ECCM	Electronic Counter-Counter Measure
ECF	Emission Contribution Fraction
ECG	Electrocardiograph
ECM	Electronic Countermeasures
ECS	Environmental Control System
ECT	Evans Clear Tunnel
ED	External Deflector
EDD	Electronic Data Display
EDRL	Effective Damage Risk Level
EEC	European Experimental Centre
EEG	Elecroencephalographic

EEPNL Estimated Effective Perceived Noise
      Level
EFATCA European Federation of Air Traffic
      Controllers Association
EFC   Expect Further Clearance
EFFE   European Federation of Flight
      Engineers
EGT   Exhaust Gas Temperature
EIDLT Emergency Identification Light
EIRP   Equivalent Isotropical Radiated Power
ELDO   European Launcher Development
      Organization
ELT   Emergency Location Transmitters
ELTAD Emergency Locator Transmitters
      Automatic Deployable
ELTAF Energy Locator Transmitters Automatic
      Fixed
ELTAP Emergency Locator Transmitters
      Automatic Portable
ELTR   Emergency Locator Transmitter Receiver
EMC   Electromagnetic Compatibility
EMD   Electronic Map Display
emf   Electromotive Force
EMG   Electromyographic
EMI   Ernst-Mach Institut (FR Germ.)
EMP   Electromagnetic Pulse
ENC   Equivalent Noise Charge
EOAB   Earth Observations Aircraft Program
EOD   Entry on Duty
EOPAP Earth and Ocean Physics Program
EOW   Engine Over the Wing
EPA   Environmental Protection Agency
EPC   Environmental Protection Control
EPNdB Equivalent Perceived Noise Level,
      Decibels
EPNL   Effective Perceived Noise Level
EPR   Engine Pressure Radio
EPR   Engine Pressure Ration
EPS   Electromagnetic Position Sensor
EPU   Emergency Power Unit
EREP   Earth Resources Experimental Package
EROS   Earth Resources Observation System
ERP   Effective Radiated Power
ERTS   Earth Resources Technology Satellite
ESME   Exited State Mass Energy
ESRO   European Space Research Organization
ETA   Estimated Time of Arrival
ETC   European Traffic Committee
ETD   Estimated Time of Departure
ETE   Estimated Time Enroute
ETF   Engine Test Facility
ETO25 Esso Tube Oil 25
ETS   Electronic Test Set
EUROCAE European Organization for Civil
      Aviation Electronics
EUROCONTROL European Organization for the
      Safety of Air Navigation
EWTR   Electronic Warfare Test Range
FAA   Federal Aviation Administration
FAA   Federal Aviation Agency

FAAP   Federal Aid Airport Program
FAAR   Forward Area Alerting Radar
FAC   Forward Air Control
FAC   Forward Air Controller
FADES Fuselage Analysis and Design
      Synthesis
FAF   Final Approach Fix
FAR   Federal Airworthiness Regulation (US)
FAR   Federal Aviation Regulation
FARR   Forward Area Refuelling and Rearming
FAWS   Flight Advisory Weather Service
FBRL   Final Bomb Release Line
FCA   Frequency Control and Analysis
FCC   Flat Conductor Cable
FCC   Flight Control Center
FCLP   Field Carrier Landing Practice
FCO   Flight Clearance Office
FCR   Fire Control Radar
FCS   Fire Control System
FCSS   Fire Control Sight System
FCU   Fares Calculating Unit
FD   Flight Director
FD   Frequency Diversity
FDAU   Flight Data Acquisition Unit
FDC   Flight Director Computer
FDDS   Flight Data Distribution System
FDEP   Flight Data Entry Panel
FDI   Field Director Indicator
FDI   Flight Director Indicator
FDMA   Frequency Division Multiple Access
FDP   Fast Digital Processor
FDP   Field Data Processing
FDR   Flight Data Recorder
FDSU   Flight Data Storage Unit
FEP   Front End Packages
FEP   Front End Processor
FF   Fuel Flow
FFT   Fast Fourier Transform
FGCS   Flight Guidance and Control Systems
FHS   Framingham Heart Study
FIC   Flight Information Center
FIDO   Fog Investigation and Dispersal
      Operation
FIILS Full Integrity Instrument Landing
      System
FIPS   Federal Information Processing
      Standards
FIR   Flight Information Region
FIS   Flight Information Service
FL   Flight Level
FLAR   Forward Looking Airborne Radar
FLIP   Floating Instrument Platform
FLIR   Forward Looking Infrared
FLTSATCOM Fleet Satellite Communication
FMC   Flutter Mode Control
FMA   Flight Manual Allowance
FOI   Follow-on Intercepter
FPL   Field Flight Plan
FPPS   Flight Plan Progressing System
FRC   Federal Radio Commission

FRC	Flight Research Center	HELMS	Helicopter Multifunction System
FRSB	Frequency Referenced Scanning Beam	HF	High Frequency
FRWI	Framingham Relative Weight Index	HIRL	High Intensity Runway Lights
FSAA	Flight Simulator for Advanced Aircraft	HITS	Holloman Infrared Target Simulator
FSF	Flight Safety Foundation	HL	Hearing Levels
FSS	Flight Service Station	HLH	Heavy Lift Helicopters
FSS	Flight Standards Service	HPD	Horizontal Polar Diagram
FTC	Fast Time Constant	HR	Heart Rates
FTHMA	Frequency Time Hoping Multiple Access	HSD	Horizontal Situation Display
FTS	Flying Training School	HSGTC	High Speed Ground Test Center
FVRDE	Fighting Vehicle Research and Development Establishment	HSI	Horizontal Situation Indicator
		HST	Hypervelocity Shock Tunnel
FWTT	Fixed Wing Tactical Transport	HT	Homing Transponders
GADO	General Aviation District Organization	HUD	Head-Up-Display
GAFAWG	General Aviation Fuel Allocation Working Group (UK)	HVIS	Hypervelocity Impact Symposium
		HVTS	Hypervelocity Techniques Symposium
GAM	Ground-to-Air-Missile	HYLO	Hybrid Loran
GAMA	General Aviation Manufacturers' Association	IA	Intermediate Amplifier
		IAF	Initial Approach Fix
GAPA	Ground-to-Air Pilotless Aircraft	IAF	Instrument Approach Fix
GAPAN	Guild of Air Pilots and Air Navigators	IAL	International Aeradio Limited
GAREX	Ground Aviation Radio Exchange System	IAOPA	International Aircraft Owners' and Pilots' Association
GARP	Global Atmospheric Research Program		
GAT	General Air Traffic	IANAP	Interagency Noise Abatement Program
GATE	Global Atlantic Tropical Experiment	IAS	Indicated Air Speed
GCA	General Control Approach	IAT	International Automatic Time
GCC	Ground Control Center	IATA	International Air Transport Association
GCI	Ground Controlled Interception	IAU	International Aeronautical Union
GCU	Generator Control Unit	IC	Instrument Correction
GDO	Gun Direction Officer	ICA	Initial Cruise Altitude
GDOP	Geometric Dilution of Precision	ICAF	International Committee on Aeronautical Fatigue
GENOT	General Notices		
GEON	Gyro Erected Optical Navigation	ICAMRS	International Civil Aviation Message Routing System
GETOL	Ground Effect Take-Off and Landing		
GFAE	Government Furnished Aeronautical Equipment	ICAN	International Commission for Air Navigation
		ICAO	International Civil Aviation Organization
GHA	Greenwich Hour Angle		
GLLD	Ground Laser Locator Designator	I-CAS	Independent Collision Avoidance System
GM	Guided Missile	ICHTF	Low Cycle High Temperature Fatigue
GMC	Ground Movement Controller	ICP	Indicator Control Panel
GMP	Ground Movement Planner	IDA	Integrated Digital Avionics
GNC	Global Navigation Chart	IDG	Integrated Drive Generator
GPAS	General Purpose Airborne Simulator	IDIIOM	Information Display Incorporation Input Output Machine
GPI	Ground Position Indicator		
GPM	Gallons Per Minute	IDSCS	Initial Defence Satellite Communications System
GPR	General Purpose Radar		
GPWS	Ground Proximity Warning System	IEIS	Integrated Engine Instrument System
GRU	Gyro Reference Unit	IFALPA	International Federation of Air Line Pilots' Associations
GS	General Schedule		
GSD	Generator Starter Drive	IFF	Identification Friend or Foe
GSE	Group Support Equipment	IFL	Initial Flight Level
GTC	Gain Time Control	IFR	Instrument Flight Rules
GTS	Global Telecommunications System	IGIA	Interagency Group for International Aviation
HAA	Height Above Aerodrome		
HAA	Height Above Airport	IISLS	Improved Interrogator Sidelobe Suppression
HAS	Hardened Aircraft Shelters		
HAS	Heading Altitude System	ILAAS	Integrated Light Attack Avionics System
HAT	Height Above Touchdown		
HDC	Hydrogen Depolarized CO_2 Concentrator	ILF	Integrated Lift Fan
HEF	High Expansion Foam		

ILS	Instrument Landing Systems		LEST	Low Energy Speed Transmission
ILS-LOC	Instrument Landing System Localizer		LF	Low Frequency
IM	Inner Marker		LGS	Landing Guidance System
IMC	Instrument Meteorological Conditions		LHA	Local Hour Angle
IME	International Magnetosphere Explorer		LHC	Left Hand Circular
IMI	Improved Manned Intercepter		LIOD	Laser Inflight Obstacle Detector
IMP	Interplanetary Monitoring Platform		LLLTV	Low Light Level Television
IMS	International Magnetospheric Study		LNG	Liquefied Natural Gas
IMU	Inertial Measurement Units		LOC	Localizer
INS	Inertial Navigation System		LOM	Locator at the Outer Marker
INTELSAT	International Telecommunications Satellite		LOP	Line of Position
			LPD	Landing Point Designator
INU	Inertial Navigation Unit		LR	Landing Radar
IOCE	Input Output Control Element		LRBA	Laboratoire de Recherches Balistiques et Aérodynamiques (Fr.)
IOP	Input Output Processor			
IPAD	Integrated Programs for Aerospace-Vehicles Design		LRC	Long Range Cruise Speed
			LRMTS	Laser Rangefinder and Marked Target Seeker
IPC	Intermittent Position Control			
IPNL	Integrated Perceived Noisiness Level		LRPA	Long Range Patrol Aircraft
IRATE	Interim Remote Area Terminal Equipment		LRRS	Long Range Radar Site
IRIG	Inter Range Instrument Group		LRU	Line Replacement Unit
ISEPS	International Sun-Earth Physics Programme		LSD	Large Screen Display
			LSI-MOS	Large Scale Integration of Metal Oxide Silicon
ISLS	Improved Sidelobe Suppression			
ISO	International Standards Organization		LTMR	Laser Target Marker Ranger
ISTS	International Shock Tube Symposium		LVRJ	Low Volume Ram Jet
ISU	Inertial Sensor Unit		LWF	Light Weight Fighter
ITA	Institut du Transport Aérien		MAC	Military Airlift Command
ITACS	Integrated Tactical Air Control System		MAC	Multi Access Computer
			MAD	Magnetic Azimuth Detector
ITNS	Integrated Tactical Navigation System		MADGE	Microwave Aircraft Digital Guided Equipment
ITPR	Infrared Temperature Profile Radiometer			
			MALS	Maximum Intensity Approach Light System
ITU	International Telecommunication Unit			
IUS	Initial Upper Stage		MAP	Minimum Audible Pressure
IUV	Iata Unit of Value		MAP	Missed Approach Point
JANAIR	Joint Army Navy Aircraft Instrumentation Research (US)		MAR	Minimal Angle of Resolution
			MASSTER	Mobile Army Sensor System Test Evaluation and Review
JARC	Joint Avionics Research Committee			
JATCRU	Joint Air Traffic Control Radar Units		MATS	Military Air Transport Service
JATO	Jet Assisted Take-Off		MATZ	Military Aerodrome Traffic Zone
JCASR	Joint Committee on Avionics Systems Research		MAU	Marine Amphibious Unit
			MAWS	Mobile Aircraft Weighing System
JCC	Joint Control Centers		MBP	Mechanical Balance Package
JPNL	Judged Perceived Noise Level		MCF	Mutual Coherence Function
KEAS	Knots Equivalent Air Speed		MCRT	Maximum Cruise Thrust
KIAS	Knots Indicated Air Speed		MCT	Maximum Continuous Thrust
KTSP	Knots True Air Speed		MDA	McDonnell Douglas Aeronautics
LAC	Lunar Aeronautical Charts		MDA	Minimum Descent Altitude
LAHS	Low Altitude High Speed		MDAL	McDonnell Douglas Aerophysics Laboratory
LAMS	Load Alleviation and Mode Stabilization			
LARS	London Airways Radar Station		MDC	McDonnell Douglas Corporation
LAT	Laser Acquisition and Tracking		MDT	Minimum Mean Downtime
LATCC	London Air Traffic Control Center		ME	Magnetic Estimation
LBCM	Locator at the Back Course Marker		MEA	Minimum Enroute Altitude
LCF	Low Cycle Fatigue		MECU	Master Engine Control Unit
LCL	Library Control Language		MEMAS	Microelectronic Modular Assemblies
LCLU	Land Control and Logic Unit		MF	Medium Frequency
LD	Liftover Drag		MFD	Multifunction Display
LDA	Localizer Directional Aid		MFV	Military Flight Vehicles

MHD	Magnetohydrodynamic	NCS	Numerical Category Scaling
MIUS	Modular Integrated Utility System	NCU	Navigation Computer Unit
MLC	Manoeuvre Load Control	NDB	Non-Directional-Radio Beacon
MLD	Masking Level Difference	NDRO	Non-Destructive Readout
MLGW	Maximum Landing Gross Weight	NDT	Non-Destructive Testing
MLS	Microwave Landing System	NE	Norepinephrine
MM	Middle Marker	NEACP	National Emergency Airborne Command Post (US)
MNR	Minimum Noise Routes		
MOC	Minimum Operational Characteristics	NEF	Noise Exposure Forecast
MOCA	Minimum Obstruction Clearance Altitude	NEMS	Nimbus E Microwave Spectrometer
		NESS	National Environmental Satellite Service
MODILS	Modular Instrument Landing System		
MOR	Mandatory Occurrence Reporting	NFDC	National Flight Data Center
MOTNE	Meteorological Operational Telecommunications Network Europe	NFO	Naval Flight Officers
		NGS	Nominal Guidance Scheme
MPD	Map Pictorial Display	NI	Noisiness Index
MPIP	Miniature Precision Inertial Platform	NIAG	NATO Industrial Advisory Group
MPP	Most Probable Position	NIPTS	Noise Induced Permanent Threshold Shift
MPT	Multiple Pure Tones		
MRA	Minimum Reception Altitude	NMC	National Meteorological Center
MRCA	Multi Role Combat Aircraft	nmi	Nautical Miles
MRR	Mechanical Reliability Reports	NNI	Noise Number Index
MRSA	Mandatory Radar Service Areas	NOAA	National Oceanographic Atmospheric Administration (US)
MRSL	Marconi Radar Systems Limited		
MRT	Modified Rhyme Test	NOESS	National Operational Environmental Satellite System
MSA	Minimum Sector Altitude		
MSFC	Marshall Space Flight Center	NOTAM	Notice To Air Men
MSL	Mean Sea Level	NPA	National Pilots' Association
MST	Mountain Standard Time	NPL	Noise Pollution Level
MTBCF	Mean Time Between Confirmed Failures	NPR	Nozzle Pressure Ration
MTBF	Mean Time Between Failure	NRC	Noise Rating Curves
MTBFC	Mean Time Between Flight Cancellation	NS	Navigation Subsystems
MTBMAS	Mean Time Between Maintenance Actions	NTDS	Naval Tactical Data Systems
		NTSB	National Transportation Safety Board
MTD	Moving Target Detector	NWEP	Nuclear Weapons Effects Panel
MTDS	Marine Tactical Data System	NYARTCC	New York Air Route Traffic Control Center
MTFA	Modulation Transfer Function Analyser		
MTI	Moving Target Indicator	OAFU	Observers' Advanced Flying Unit
MToGW	Maximum Takeoff Gross Weight	OASPL	Overall Sound Pressure Level
MTP	Minimum Time Path	OAT	Operational Air Traffic
MTR	Migration Traffic Rate	OBAWS	On Board Aircraft Weighing System
MUT	Minimum Mean Uptime	OBSPL	Octave Band Sound Pressure Level
MUX	Multiplexer Channel	OCI	Operator Control Interface
MWHGL	Multiple Wheel Heavy Gear Load	OCP	Obstacle Clearance Panel
NACA	National Advisory Committee for Aeronautics	OCS	Optical Contact Sensor
		ODIN	Optical Design Integration
NADC	National Air Development Center	OEW	Operating Empty Weight
NAFEC	National Aviation Facilities Experimental Center	OFT	Operational Flight Trainer
		OFZ	Obstacle Free Zone
NAM	Nautical Air Miles	OM	Operation and Maintenance
NAS	National Airspace System	OM	Outer Marker
NASA	National Aeronautics and Space Administration	ONERA	Office National d'Etudes et de Recherches Aéronautiques (Fr.)
NASM	National Air and Space Museum	OPLE	OMEGA Position Locating Equipment
NASP	National Airport System Plan	OSR	Over the Shoulder Rating
NASTRAN	NASA Structural Analysis Program	OTC	One-stop Tour Charter
NATSPG	North Atlantic Systems Planning Group	OTH	Over the Horizon
		OWE	Operating Weight Empty
NAUS	National Airspace Utilization Study	PALM	Precision Altitude and Landing Monitor
NBT	Narrow Beam Transducer	PAM	Peripheral Adapter Module
NCLT	Night Carrier Landing Trainer		

PAM	Pulse Amplitude Modulation
PANS	Procedures for Air Navigation Services
PAR	Precision Approach Radar
PBF	Potential Benefit Factor
PCD	Production Common Digitizer
PCI	Peripheral Command Indicator
PCI	Plant Control Interface
PCM	Pulse Code Modulation
PCR	Positively Control Routes
PCS	Power Conditioning System
PDD	Projected Data Display
PDD	Pulse Delay Device
PDR	Pilot's Display Recorder
PDU	Pilot's Display Unit
PED	Pulse Edge Discrimination
PEE	Proof and Experimental Establishment (UK)
PEP	Propulsion and Energetics Panel
PFA	Popular Flying Association
PFCS	Primary Flight Control System
PFP	Post Flight Processor
PHM	Patrol Hydrofoil Missile
PIBAL	Polytechnic Institute of Brooklyn Aerodynamics Laboratory (US)
PICAO	Provisional International Civil Aviation Organization
PLL	Peripheral Light Loss
PLL	Phase Locked Loop
PLRACTA	Position Location Reporting and Control Tactical Aircraft
PMGS	Predictable Model Guidance Scheme
PMIP	Postmaintenance Inspection Pilots
PMP	Pressure Measurement Package
PMS	Project Map System
PND	Pictorial Navigation Display
PNdB	Perceived Noise Decibels
PNL	Perceived Noise Level
PNP	Precision Navigation Processor
POT	Propeller Order Transmitter
PP	Plane Parallel
PPC	Patrol Plane Commander
PPFRT	Prototype Preliminary Flight Rating Test
PPI	Plan Position Indicator
PPL	Private Pilot Licence
PPO	Polyphenol Oxidase
PRF	Pulse Repetition Frequency
PRFD	Pulse Recurrence Frequency Discrimination
PRFS	Pulse Recurrence Frequency Stagger
PRI	Project Readout Indicator
PRP	Pulse Repetition Period
PRR	Pulse Repetition Rate
PRT	Primary Ranging Test
PSALI	Permanent Supplementary Artificial Lighting Installation
PSD	Power Spectral Density
PSK	Phase Shift Keyed
PSU	Power Supply Unit

PTACV	Prototype Tracked Air Cushion Vehicle
PTFS	Pilot to Forecast Service
PTI	Programmed Time of Arrival
PTR	Part Throttle Reheat
PUI	Pilot Under Instruction
PVD	Plan Video Display
PVD	Plan View Display
PVOR	Precision VOR
PWI	Pilot Warning Indicator
PWL	Power Level
PWT	Propulsion Wind Tunnel
QCSEE	Quiet Clean STOL Experimental Engine
QEAF	Qatar Emiri Air Force
QMR	Qualitative Materiel Requirement
QSATS	Quiet Shorthaul Air Transportation System
QSEE	Quiet STOL Experimental Engine
QUESTOL	Quiet Experimental STOL
RADC	Rome Air Development Center
RAE	Royal Aircraft Establishment (UK)
RAIL	Runway Alignment Indicator Lights
RAM	Radar Absorbing Material
RAPCON	Radar Approach Control
RARDE	Royal Armament Research and Development Establishment (UK)
RAREP	Radar Report
RB	Radio Beacon
RCAG	Remote Controlled Air /Ground
RCC	Rescue Coordination Center (US)
RCLS	Runway Centerline Light System
RCS	Radar Cross Section
RDAF	Royal Danish Air Force
RDF	Radio Direction Finding
RDP	Radar Data Processing
RDS	Robust Detection Scheme
RDTE	Research Development Test and Evaluation
REA	Radar Echoing Area
REIL	Runway End Identifier Lights
REM	Rapid Eye Movement
RENOT	Regional Notice
RF	Radio Frequency
RFDU	Reconfiguration and Fault Detection Unit
RFI	Radio Frequency Interference
RFL	Requested Flight Level
RFO	Radio Frequency Oscillator
RGCS	Revision of General Conception of Separation
RHC	Right Hand Circular
RMI	Radio Magnetic Indicator
ROD	Rate Of Descent
ROT	Reusable Orbital Transport
RPM	Revolutions Per Minute
RPS	Radar Plotting Sheet
RPV	Remote Pilotless Vehicle
RR	Rendezvour Radar
RSRA	Rotor Systems Research Aircraft
RSS	Relaxed Static Stability
RTOL	Reduced Takeoff and Landing

RTT	Reservoir and Tube Tunnel
RVP	Reid Vapour Pressure
RVR	Runway Visual Range
RVV	Runway Visibility Value
RWI	Radio Wire Integration
RWS	Receiver Waveform Simulation
SAC	Strategic Air Command
SAGE	Semi-Automatic Ground Environment
SALORS	Structural Analysis of Layered Orthotropic Ring-stiffened Shells
SALS	Short Approach Light System
SAM	Surface-to-Air Missiles
SAN	School of Air Navigation
SAR	Synthetic Aperture Radar
SARDA	State and Regional Disaster Airlift
SARPS	Standard and Recommended Practices
SAVES	Sizing of Aerospace Vehicle Structures
SBA	Standard Beam Approach
SBP	Strain Gauge Package
SBP	Systolic Blood Pressure
SCATANA	Security Control of Air Traffic and Air Navigation Aids
SCF	Satellite Control Facility
SCICON	Scientific Control
SCIM	Speech Communication Index Meter
SCP	Surveillance Communication Processor
SCR	Selective Chopper Radiometer
SCRAMJET	Supersonic Combustion Ramjet
SCU	Sulphur Coated Urea
SCV	Sub-Clutter Visibility
SCW	Super Critical Wing
SD	Standard Deviation
SDD	Synthetic Dynamic Display
SDF	Simplified Directional Facility
SDMA	Space Division Multiple Access
SDR	Space Drawing Rights
SDRT	Slot Dipole Ranging Tests
SE	Spherical Eyeball
SEAL	Signal Evaluation Airborne Laboratory
SECAL	Selective Calling
SECAR	Structural Efficiency Cones with Arbitrary Rings
SEF	Small End Forward
SEP	Separation Parameter
SFSS	Satellite Field Service Station
S/I	Signal-to-Interference
SIA	Standard Instrument Approach
SID	Standard Instrument Departure
SIF	Selective Identification Feature
SIL	Speech Interference Level
SIMNS	Simulated Navigation Systems
SITA	Société Internationale de Télécommunications Aéronautiques
SITE	Satellite Instructional Television Experiment
SLAR	Side Looking Airborne Radar
SLCM	Sea Launched Cruise Missile
SLE	Superheat Limit Explosion
SLS	Sidelobe Suppression
SLW	Specific Leaf Weight

SMMC	System Maintenance Monitor Console
SMS	Synchronous Meteorological Satellites
SMS	Systems Maintenance Service
SNAP	Structural Network Analysis Program
SOAF	Sultan of Oman's Air Force
SOLRAD	Solar Radiation
SOS	Sentinel On Station
SOSTEL	Solid State Electric Logic
SP	Supervisory Package
SPADATS	Space Detection and Tracking System
SPEC	Speech Predictive Encoding Communication
SPI	Symbolic Pictorial Indicator
SPL	Sound Pressure Level
SPS	Secondary Power System
SPTU	Staff Pilot Training Unit
SR	Scanning Radiometer
SRA	Surveillance Radar Approaches
SRDS	Systems Research and Development Service
SRT	Secondary Ranging Test
SSA	Soaring Society of America
SSALS	Simplified Short Approach Light System
SSF	System Support Facility
SSMA	Spread Spectrum Multiple Access
SSR	Secondary Surveillance Radar
SST	Supersonic Transport
SSV	Supersonic Test Vehicles
STAGG	Small Turbine Advanced Gas Generator
STAGS	Structural Analysis of General Shells
STAI	State Trait Anxiety Inventory
STAR	Standard Terminal Approach Route
STM	Short Term Memory
STOL	Short Takeoff and Landing
STR	Standard Taxiway Routing
STV	Separation Test Vehicles
SVCS	Star Vector Calibration Sensor
SVR	Slant Visual Range
SWD	Surface Wave Device
SWIFT	Strength of Wings Including Flutter
TAC	Tacan
TAC	Terminal Control Area
TACAN	TACtical Air Navigation
TACCO	Tactical Coordinator
TACP	Tactical Air Control Party
TACS	Tactical Air Control System
TACT	Transonic Aircraft Technology
TANS	Tactical Air Navigation System
TAS	True Air Speed
TASES	Tactical Airborne Signal Exploration System
TATC	Terminal Area Traffic Control
TBA	Testbed Aircraft
TBO	Time Between Overhaul
TC	Terminal Control Areas
TCLE	Thermal Coefficient of Linear Expansion
TDC	Through Deck Cruisers
TDMA	Time Division Multiple Access
TDP	Technical Development Plan

TDZ   Touchdown Zone
TDZL   Touchdown Zone Lights
TEL   Tetra Ethyl Lead
TEP   Transmitter Experimental Package
TET   Turbine Entry Temperature
TEWS   Tactical Electronic Warfare Systems
TFA   Transfer Function Analyser
TIFS   Total In-Flight Simulator
TILS   Tactical Instrument Landing System
TIOM   Telegraph Input Output Multiplexers
TIS   Transponder Interrogation Sonar
TKE   Track Angle Error
TKP   Tonne-Km Performed
TLD   Thermoluminescent Dosimeters
TLO   Tracking Local Oscillators
TMA   Terminal Movement Area
TMAC   Tetramethylammonium Bicarbonate
TNI   Traffic Noise Index
TOF   Time-Of-Flight
TOFL   Takeoff Field Length
TOGW   Takeoff Gross Weight
TPCU   Thermal Preconditioning Unit
TRACAB Terminal Radar Control from Tower CAB
TRACALS Traffic Control and Landing System
TRACON Terminal Radar Control
TRRA   Tilt Rotor Research Aircraft
TRSA   Terminal Radar Service Area
TRSB   Time Reference Scanning Beam
TRSBMLS Time Reference Scanning Beam
          Microwave Landing System
TSC   Transportation Systems Center
TSD   Thermally Stimulated Depolarization
TSO   Technical Standard Order
TTC   Technical Training Centers
TTG   Test Target Generator
TTS   Temporary Threshold Shift
TVAT   Television Air Trainer
TVM   Track Via Missile
TWA   Trans World Airways
TWT   Travelling Wave Tube
TWTA   Travelling Wave Tube Amplifier
UAF   Union Air Force
UAIMS   United Aircraft Information Management
          System
UAS   Upper Airspace
UCNI   Unified Communications Navigation
          and Identification
UDF   Union Defence Force
UHF   Ultra High Frequency
UHF   Universal High Frequency
UNB   United Nations Beacon
UPT   Undergraduate Pilot Training
USAF   United States Air Force
UT   Universal Time
UTC   Coordinated Universal Time
UTTAS   Utility Tactical Transport Aircraft
          System
UVDS   Ultra Violet Flame Detection System
VAPS   Vertical-short-takeoff-landing
          Approach System

VAR   Visual and Aural Range
VARES   Vega Aircraft Radar Enhancing System
VASI   Visual Approach Slope Indicator
VAST   Versatile Avionics Shop Test
VCR   Visual Control Room
VDU   Visual Display Unit
VFR   Visual Flight Rules
VG   Vertical Gyroscope
VHF   Very High Frequency
VHRR   Very High Resolution Radiometer
VISSR   Visible and Infrared Spin Scan
          Radiometer
VLF   Very Low Frequency
VMC   Visual Meteorological Conditions
VN   Ventral Nozzle
VOR   Very High Frequency Omnirange
VORTAC Very High Frequency Omnirange and
          Tactical Air Navigation
VPD   Vertical Polar Diagram
VRC   Vertical Ride Control
VSCF   Variable Speed Constant Frequency
VSD   Vertical Situation Display
V/STOL Vertical/Short Takeoff and Landing
VSTT   Variable Speed Training Target
VTO   Vertical Takeoff
VTOGW   Vertical Takeoff Gross Weight
VTOL   Vertical Takeoff and Landing
VTPR   Vertical Temperature Profile Radiometer
WAC   World Aeronautical Chart
WADC   Wright Air Development Centre (UK)
WECO   Western Electric Company
WEP   Wideband Exciter and Processor
WMSC   Weather Message Switching Center
WPAFB   Wright-Patterson Air Force Base
WST   Weapon System Trainer
WVAS   Wake Vortex Avoidance System
WVE   Water Vapor Electrolysis
WWW   World Weather Watch
ZnO   Zinc Oxide
ZOTS   Zoom Optical Target Simulator

AGRICULTURAL SCIENCES

AACC   American Association of Cereal Chemists
AC   Acetic Acid
ADA   Azodicarbonamide
ADD   Activated Dough Development
ADF   Acid Detergent Fiber
ADG   Average Daily Gain
ADSA   American Dairy Science Association
ADV   Acid Degree Values
AES   American Electrochemical Society
AHP   Aniline Hydrogen Phthalate
AHU   Accumulated Heat Unit
AI   Artificial Insemination
AIB   Aminoisobutyric Acid
AMCP   Abnormal Milk Control Program
AMF   Acid Modified Flour
AMHIC   Automatic Merchandising Health

	Industry Council	CVT	Crystal Violet Tetrazolium
AMPI	Associated Milk Producers'	CW	Clipping Weight
	Information (US)	CWC	Cell Wall Constituents
AN	Ammonium Nitrate	CZR	Center for Zoonoses Research (US)
ANOVA	Analysis Of Variation	DAPA	Diaminopimelic Acid
AOV	Analysis Of Variance	DC	Digestibility Coefficients
APC	Aerobic Plate Counts	DCP	Dicalcium Phosphate
APDC	Ammonium Pyrrolidine Dithiocarbamate	DE	Digestible Energy
ATP	Adenosine Triphosphate	DEPC	Diethylpyrocarbonate
AWC	Available Water Capacity	DES	Desoxycholate
AWHC	Available Water Holding Capacity	DHIA	Dairy Herd Improvement Association
B	Boron		(US)
BA	Bentonite Agglutination	DMA	Dry Matter Accumulation
BAA	Breed Age Average	DMC	Dichloromethyl Carbonol
BAI	Bentonite Agglutination Inhibition	DMD	Dry Matter Disappearance
BCPC	British Crop Protector Council	DMSCC	Direct Microscopic Somatic Cell Count
BGA	Brilliant Green Agar	DMSO	Dimethyl Sulphoxide
BGY	Bright Green Yellow	DNA	Deoxyribonucleic Acid
BHC	Benzene Hexachloride	DNMRT	Duncan's New Multiple Range Test
BHIA	Brain Heart Infusion Agar	DNP	Dexyribonucleoproteins
BOD	Biochemical Oxygen Demand	DNPH	Dinitrophenylhydrazin
BS	Bismuth Sulfite	DOA	Department of Agriculture
BSS	Basiodiacarp-inducing Substance(s)	DOMD	Digestible Organic Matter in Dry
BT	Bathythermograph	DSF	Defatted Soy Flour
BV	Benzyl Viologen	DSI	Dairy Society International
BW	Body Weight	DY	Dairy Yield
BWP	Brown Wrapping Paper	EAAFRO	East African Agriculture and Forest
CAFMNA	Compound Animal Feeding Stuffs		Research Organization
	Manufacturers' National Association	EBW	Empty Body Weight
CAP	Common Agricultural Policy	EC	Electric Conductivites
CAST	Council for Agricultural Science and	EDB	Ethylene Dibromide
	Technology	EDC	Ethylene Dichrorine
CC	Coliform Count	EDTA	Ethylenediaminetetraacete
CC	Conventional Color	EDTA	Ethylenediaminetetraacetic Acid
CD	Circular Dichroism	EIA	Endotoxin Inactivating Agent
CDF	California Division of Forestry	EM	Ethoxylated Monoglycerides
CEC	Cation Exchange Capacity	EMB	Eosine Methylene Blue
CER	Controlled Environment Rooms	EPTC	Ethyl Dipropylthiocarbamate
CF	Corn Flour	ES	Early Spring
CFT	Complement Fixation Test	ES	Exchangeable Sodium
CGR	Crop Growth Rate	ET	Evapotranspiration
CIAT	International Center for Tropical	ETSL	Estimated Total Shell Life
	Agriculture	EVA	Ethylene Vinyl Acetate
CIP	Cleaned-In-Place	FAD	Flavine Adenine Dinucleotide
CIRF	Corn Industries Research Foundation	FASEB	Federation of American Societies for
CKRS	Corn Kennel Red Steak		Experimental Biology
CMT	California Mastistis Test	FAT	Fluorescent Antibody Test
CNI	Conservation Need Inventory	FCA	Fluidized Computer Ash
COD	Chemical Oxygen Demand	FCC	Food Contaminants Commission (US)
COPA	Committee of Agricultural Organizations	FCVS	Free Calf Vaccination Service
CP	Crude Protein	FDA	Food and Drug Administration (US)
CPB	Competitive Protein Binding	FDWB	Fluorodinitrobenzene
CPW	Cooked Potato Weight	FE	Iron
CSM	Corn-Soy-Milk	FFA	Free Fatty Acids
CSO	Cotton Seed Oil	FFSF	Full-Fat Soy Flour
CSP	Concentrated Super-Phosphate	FMT	Flour Milling Technology
CTAB	Trimethylammonium Bromide	FNWC	Fleet Numerical Weather Central (US)
CTC	Carbon Tetrachloride	FOD	Flies-Odors Ducts
CTF	Cottonseed Flour	FPC	Fish Protein Concentrate
CV	Coefficient of Variation	FTU	Formazin Turbidity Units

GA	Gibberellic Acid	MS	Machine Stripping
GAD	Glutamic Acid Decarboxylase	MSA	Mannitol Salt Agar
GLC	Gas Liquid Chromatography	MSR	Medium Stocking Rate
GPC	Gel Permeation Chromatography	MSRS	Multiple Stylus Recording System
GR	Gypsum Requirement	MWPC	Moorepark Whey Protein Concentrates
G6PDH	Glucose-6-Phosphate Dehydrogenase	MY	Machine Yield
HCG	Human Chorionic Gonadotrophin	MYP	Mannito-egg Yolk Polymyxin
HD	Hepatosis Diaetetica	N	Nitrogen
HEAMF	Hydroxyethylated Acid Modified Flour	Na	Sodium
HMF	Hydroxymethylfuraldehyde	NACAM	National Association of Corn and Agricultural Merchants
HP	Hydroxyproline	NAN	Naphthalene Acetic Acid
HR	Hypersensitive	NAR	Net Assimilation Rate
HRS	Hard Red Spring	NBT	Nitroblue Tetrazolin
HRW	Hard Red Winter	NCN	Non-Casein Nitrogen
HS	Hand Stripping	NFB	Node of First-fruiting Branch
HSR	High Stocking Rate	NFDM	Non-Fat Dry Milk
IAA	Indole Acetic Acid	NFMS	Non-Fat Milk Solids
IAMS	International Association of Microbiological Societies	NIAB	National Institute of Agricultural Botany
IBA	Indole Butyvic Acid	NMC	National Mastitis Council
ICC	International Association for Cereal Chemistry	NMD	Nutritional Muscular Dystrophy
ICMSF	International Commission on Microbiological Specifications for Foods	NPN	Non-Protein Nitrogen
		ODR	Oxygen Diffusion Rate
		OFP	O-Fluorophonylalanine
IMF	Intermediate Moisture Food	OM	Organic Matter
INS	Initial Water Solubles	ORD	Optical Rotatory Dispersion
IP	Inorganic Phosphorus	OVX	Ovariectomized
IPLA	Interstate Producers' Livestock Association (US)	P	Phosphorus
		PAGE	Polyacrylamide Gel Electrophoresis
ISP	Isolated Soy Flour	PAP	p-Aminophenylamine
IVD	In Vitro Digestibility	PARP	Partially Acidulated Rock Phosphate
IVDMO	In Vitro Dry Matter Digestibility	PAS	Periodic Acid Schiff
IVOMD	In Vitro Organic Matter Digestion	PBC	Psychrotrophic Count
KRP	Krebs Ringer Phosphate	PBI	Protein Bound Iodine
La	Lactic Acid	PCB	Polychlorinated Biphenyl
LAD	Leaf Area Duration	PCI	Patterson Candy International
LAI	Leaf Area Index	PDA	Potato Dextrose Agar
LDH	Lactate Dehydrogenase	PDF	Protection Difference Fat
LIFE	League for International Food Education	PDM	Protected Difference Milk
		PE	Plant Extrusion
LNPK	Limestone Nitrogen Phosphorus and Potassium	PEBV	Pea Early Browning Virus
		PEG	Polyethylene Glycol
LPC	Laboratory Pasteurized Count	PEN	Penicillin
LSAI	Leaf Stem Area Index	PEP	p-Fluorophenylalanine
LSR	Low Stocking Rate	PER	Protein Efficiency Ratio
LVDT	Linear Variable Differential Transformer	PF	Peanut Flour
		PFA	Pulverized Fuel Ash
MAFWPB	Minimum Acceptable Flour for White Pan-Bread Production	PFM	Practice of Flour Milling
		PGRO	Pea Growing Research Organisation
MAP	Monoammonium Phosphate	PGUE	Polyacrylamide Gel Urea Electrophoresis
MCC	Modern Cereal Chemistry	PI	Preliminary Incubation
MCS	Multiple Compression Shear	PL	Psittacosis Lymphogranuloma
ME	Metabolizable Energy	PMA	Phenylmercuric Acetate
MEP	m-fluorophenylanine	PMS	Pregnant Mare's Serum
MH	Mulberry Heart	PPB	Pyrethrins Piperonyl Butoxide
MIW	Milk Ingredient Water	PPLO	Pleuro Pneumonia-Like Organisms
MLD	Mixed Layer Depth	PRI	Production Rate Indices
MMD	Mass Median Diameter	PTU	Propylthiouracial
MMD	Mean Maturity Dates	PVC	Polyvinyl Chloride

RBPT	Rose Bengal Plate Test		TSB	Tryticase Soy Broth
RF	Rice Flour		TSI	Triple Sugar Iron
RGR	Relative Growth Rates		TSN	Tryptone Sulphite Neomycin
RI	Refractive Index		TSR	Thyroid Hormone Secretion Rate
RIA	Radioimmunoassay		TTC	Tetrazolium Chloride
RO/UF	Reverse Osmosis Ultra Filtration		TTC	Triphenyltetrazolium Chloride
RPC	Rice Polishing Concentrate		TVC	Total Viable Counts
RUFAS	Remote Underwater Fisheries Assessment System		TVW	Total Volatile Nitrogen
RWC	Relative Water Content		UF	Ultrafiltration
RY	Residual Yield		UF	Urea Formaldehyde
SAT	Serum Agglutination Test		UHM	Upper-Half-Mean-Length
SBM	Soybean Meal		UHT	Ultra High Temperature
SC	Specific Conductivity		UP	Urea Phosphate
SCB	Selenite Cystine Broth		UPAU	Uttar Pradesh Agricultural University
SCC	Somatic Cell Concentration		VFA	Volatile Fatty Acids
SCLB	Southern Corn Leaf Bright		VLO	Viable Parahaemolyticus
SCN	Soybean Cyst Nematode		VN	Volatile Nitrogen
SDH	Succinate Dehydrogenase		VRB	Violet Red Bile
SDS	Sodium Dodecyl Sulphate		VRS	Volatile Reducing Substances
SDS-PAGE	Sodium Dodecyl Sulphate-Polyacrylamide Gel Electrophoresis		WLI	Wavelength Interval
			WPC	Wheat Protein Concentrate
SE	Starch Equivalent		WPC	Whey Protein Concentrate
SGE	Starch Gel Electrophoresis		WPS	Water Phase Salt
SGR	Short Growth Rate		WRD	Whole Rumen Digesta
Si	Silicon		WS	Wire Shear
SMA	Standard Methods Agar		WSB	Wheat Soy Blend
SMEDP	Standard Methods for the Examination of Dairy Products		WSI	Water Solidity Index
			WSMV	Wheat Steak Mosaic Virus
SMP	Sucrose Monopalmitate		WUE	Water Use Efficiency
SNF	Solids-Not-Fat		WWF	Whole Wheat Flour
SPC	Salkowski Positive Compounds		XBT	Expendable Bathythermonograph
SPC	Standard Plate Count		XLDP	Xylose-Lysine-Desoxycholatepeplon Agar
SS	Salmonella Shigella			
SS	Shigella Agar		YES	Yeast Extract Sucrose
SSA	Sulphosalicylic Acid		YMC	Yeast Mold Count
SSL	Sodium Stearoyl Laclylate			
SST	Sea Surface Temperature			
ST	Sucrose Tallowate		**ASTRONAUTICS AND ASTROPHYSICS**	
STA	Seed Trade Association			
SWW	Soft White Winter		AACB	Aeronautics and Astronautics Coordinating Board
SY	Stripping Yield			
TAC	Total Available Carbohydrate		AAP	Apollo Application Program
TAEC	Thiolated Aminoethyl Cellulose		AHCT	Ascending Horizon Crossing Time
TBC	Thermophilic Count		ALSEP	Apollo Lunar Surface Experiment Packages
TCA	Trichloroacetic Acid			
TDN	Total Digestible Nutrient		AM	Airlock Module
TDT	Terminal Death Time		ANS	Astronomical Netherlands Satellite
TGE	Transmissible Gastroenteritis		ARC	Advanced Reentry Concepts
TLC	Thin Layer Chromatography		ARC	Atlantic Research Corporation
TMA	Trimethylamine		ARIA	Apollo Range Instrumented Aircraft
TMAO	Trimethylamine Oxide		ARIS	Advanced Range Instrumentation SHIP
TMN	Trimethylamine Nitrogen		ARP	Advanced Reentry Program
TMSC	Texas Male Steridity Cytoplasm		ARS	Automatic Recovery System
TNBS	Trinitrobenzenesulfonic Acid		ARV	Armoured Recovery Vehicle
TNC	Total Nonstructural Carbohydrate		ASC	Automatic Sensitivity Control
TPNH	Triphosphopyridine Nucleotide		ASM	Apollo Service Module
TQ	Turf Quality		ASM	Apollo Systems Manual
TRS	Total Reducing Sugar		ASTP	Apollo Soyuz Test Project
TRU	Total Recycle Unit		ATDA	Augmented Target Docking Adapter
			ATM	Apollo Telescope Mount

ATO	Assisted Take-Off
ATOM	Apollo Telescope Orientation Mount
ATS	Astronomical Time Switch
AURA	Association of Universities for Research in Astronomy
AZS	Automatic Zero Set
COGS	Continuous Orbital Guidance System
COSPAR	Committee On Space Research
CTIO	Cerro Tololo Inter-American Observatory (Chile)
EFR	Emerging Flux Regions
EMF	Evolving Magnetic Features
FOV	Field Of View
FWHM	Full Width Half Maximum
GCVS	General Catalog of Variable Stars
GET	Ground Elapsed Time
GPS	Global Positioning System
GTS	Geostationary Technology Satellite
HAES	High Altitude Effects Simulation
HELOS	Highly Eccentric Lunar Occultation Satellite
HIRIS	High Resolution Interferometer Spectrometer
HPBW	Half Power Beamwidths
HVC	High Velocity Clouds
ICIASF	Instrumentation in Aerospace Simulation Facilities
ICP	Inter-Connected Processing
IGM	Intergalactic Medium
IITV	Image Intensified Television
ITRM	Inverse Thermoremnant Magnetization
IVC	Intermediate Velocity Clouds
LC	Lyman Continuum
LEM	Lunar Excursion Module
LMC	Large Megallanic Cloud
LMP	Lunar Module Pilot
LPM	Lunar Portable Magnetometer
LRL	Lunar Receiving Laboratory
LRV	Lunar Roving Vehicle
LSM	Lunar Surface Magnetometer
LSS	Lunar Soil Simulator
LST	Large Space Telescopes
LTE	Local Thermodynamic Equilibrium
LUT	Launcher Umbilical Tower
MA	Mass Analyzer
MAD	Mass Analyzer Detector
MARSAT	Maritime Satellite
MBF	Molecular Beam Facility
MCC-H	Mission Control Center Houston
MDA	Multiple Docking Adapter
MHD	Magnetohydrodynamics
MMF	Moving Magnetic Features
MOL	Manned Orbital Laboratory
MSFC	Marshall Space Flight Center
MSFN	Manned Space Flight Network
NAE	National Academy of Engineering (US)
NCAR	National Center for Atmospheric Research
NRAO	National Radio Astronomy Observatory
NRM	National Remnant Magnetization

OSO	Orbiting Solar Observatory
OWS	Orbital Workshop Station
PET	Pentaerythrital
PHA	Pulse Height Analysis
QSRS	Quasi Stellar Radio Sources
RA	Right Ascension
RDC	Recording Doppler Comparator
SAMSO	Space and Missile System Organization
SAO	Smithsonian Astrophysical Observatory
SEM	Scanning Electron Microscope
SFD	Sudden Frequency Deviation
SG	Supergranule
SID	Sudden Ionospheric Disturbance
SIM	Scientific Instrument Module
SMC	Small Magellanic Cloud
SMR	Super Metal Rich
SNR	Supernova Remnants
SNS	Space Navigation System
SPL	Space Programming Language
SR	Semiregular
SS	Spherical Symmetry
START	Space Technology and Advanced Re-entry Tests
SVM	Silicon Video Memory
SXT	Spacecraft Sextant
TE	Transverse Electric
TEC	Transearth Coast
TICAS	Taxonomic Intra Cellular Analytic System
TID	Total Ion Detector
TLRV	Tracked Levitated Research Vehicles
TM	Transverse Magnetic
TSA	Total Scan Area
TSC	Thermally Stimulated Currents
TSEE	Thermally Stimulated Emission of Exoelectrons
TTRM	Transition Thermoremnant Magnetization
UHV	Ultra High Vacuum
UMR	Unipolar Magnetic Regions
VLB	Very Long Baseline
VLBI	Very Long Baseline Interferometry
VRM	Viscous Remnant Magnetization
ZAMS	Zero Age Main Sequence

BEHAVIOURAL SCIENCES

CCBS	Center for Computer Based Behavioral Studies
LPC	Least Preferred Coworker
TNG	Tactical and Negotiations Game

BIOLOGICAL AND MEDICAL SCIENCES

AABP	Acetylaminobiphenyl
AAF	Acetylaminofluorene
AAMC	Association of American Medical Colleges
AB	Alcian Blue

AB	Aminoazobenzene	BL	Burkitt Lymphona
ABAF	Alcian Blue Aldehyde Fuchsin	BLC	Beef Liver Catalase
ABCC	Atomic Bomb Casualty Commission (Jap.)	BNL	Brookhaven National Laboratory (US)
ABP	Aminobiphenyl	BOD	Biological Oxygen Demand
ACA	Aminocephalosporanic Acid	BPB	Bromophenol Blue
ACD	Acid Citrate Dextrose	BSA	Bovine Serum Albumin
ACGIH	American Conference of Governmental Industrial Hygienists	BSTFA	Bistrimethylsilyl Trifluoroacetamide
		BTDU	Benzylthiodihydrouracil
ACh	Acetylcholine	BUN	Blood Urea Nitrogen
AChE	Acetylcholinesterase	BW	Biological Warfare
ACS	Adrenocortico Steroids	CA	Cellulose Acetate
ACTH	Adrenocorticotrophin	CA	Chromic Acid
ACTH	Adrenocorticotrophic Hormone	CaBP	Calcium Binding Protein
ADA	Adenosine Deaminase	CAM	Crassulacean Acid Metabolism
ADH	Antidiuretic Hormone	CAMI	Civil Aviation Medical Institute
ADP	Adenosine Diphosphate	CAMP	Computer Assisted Menu Planning
AEC	Aminoethyl Cellulose	CAMP	Cyclic Adenosine Monophosphate
AEC	Aminoethyl-Cysteine	CAP	Chloramphenicol
AEOC	Aminoethylhomocysteine	CBF	Cerebral Blood Flow
AF	Aldehyde Fuchsin	CD	Circular Dichroic
AFC	Atomic Fluid Cells	CDP	Cytioline Diphosphate Diacylglycerols
AFGP	Antifreeze Glycoproteins	CEA	Carcinoembryonic Antigens
AGL	Acute Granulocytic Leukaemia	CFC	Colony Forming Cells
ALA	Aminolaevulinate	CFPA	Chlorophenyl-trifluovomethyl Phenoxyacetate
ALB	Albumen		
ALL	Acute Lymphoblastic Leukaemia	CFU	Colony Forming Units
ALM	Applied Laboratory Methods	CGL	Chronic Granulocytic Leukaemia
ALS	Antilymphocyte Serums	CHD	Congenital Heart Disease
AMEDD	Army Medical Department	CHD	Coronary Heart Disease
AMEDS	Army Medical Sciences	ChE	Chrolinesterase
AMMoL	Acute Myelomonocytic Leukaemia	CHO	Carbohydrates
AMoL	Acute Monocytic Leukaemia	CHS	Chediak Higashi Syndrome
AMP	Adenosine Monophosphate	CI	Cardial Index
AMRL	Aerospace Medical Research Laboratory (US)	CI	Colloidal Iron
		CIA	Chemiluminescence Immunoassay
AMS	Army Medical Service	CK	Cleatine Kinase
ANC	Army Nurse Corps	CLL	Central Light Loss
ANL	Argonne National Laboratory	CLL	Chronic Lymphocytic Leukaemia
AP	Alkaline Phosphatase	CMHC	Community Mental Health Centres
AP	Anterior Pituitary	CMI	Cell Medicated Immunity
APA	Amino Penicillanic Acid	CML	Chronic Myelogenous Leukaemia
APRL	Automated Primate Research Laboratory	CMR	Carbon Magnetic Resonance
APRT	Adenine Phosphoribosyltransferase	CMV	Cytomegalovirus
AQ	Aminoquinoline	CN	Caudate Nucleus
AQO	Aminoquinoline Oxide	CNBr	Cyanogen Bromide
ARTC	Addiction Research and Treatment Corporation	CNS	Central Nervous System
		CNV	Contingent Negative Variation
ASCVD	Arteriosclerotic Cardiovascular Disease	COA	Conversion Of Acetyl
AT	Aminotriazole	COMT	Catechol-O-Methyltransferase
ATP	Adenosine Triphosphate	COPD	Chronic Obstructive Pulmonary Disease
ATS	Anti-Thymocyte Serum	CP	Continuous Phase
AWRE	Atomic Weapons Research Establishment	CPD	Carboxypeptidase
BA	Benzanthracene	CPD	Citrate Phosphate Dextrose
BAEE	Benzoyl Arginine Ethyl-Ester	CPED	Continuous Particle Electrophoresis Device
BBD	Bubble Bath Detector		
BCAA	Branched Chain Amino Acids	CPIB	Chlorophenoxisobutyrate
BCKA	Branched Chain a-Keto Acids	CPIB	Chlorophenoxyisophate
BGAV	Blue Green Algae Viruses	CR	Constant Rate
BHA	Butylated Hydroxy Anisole	CRF	Corticotropin Releasing Factor
BHT	Butylated Hydroxytoluene	CRO	Cathode Ray Oscilloscope

CS	Citrate Synthase	ECF	Extracellular Fluid
CSF	Cerebrospinal Fluid	ECG	Electrocardiograph
CSTF	Continuous Stirred Tank Fermentator	ECT	Electro Convulsive Shock Therapy
CSTR	Continuous Stirred Tank Reactor	EDC	Energy Distribution Curves
CT	Colloidal Thorium	EDTA	Ethylenediamine Tetra Acetate
CTA	Cystine Trypticase Agar	EEG	Electroencephalographic
CTO	Chlotetracycline	EKG	Electrocardiography
CTP	Cholinephosphate Cytidyltransferase	EL	External Lamina
CTP	Cytidine Triphosphate	ELD	Lethal Dose Embryos
CV	Condensing Vacuole	ELF	Extremely Low Frequency
CVP	Central Venous Pressure	ELS	External Lamina Substance
CWT	Critical Water Temperature	EMBO	European Molecular Biological Organization
DA	Dopamine	EMCRO	Experimental Medical Care Review Organization
DAB	Diaminobenzidine		
DBA	Dibenzathracene	EMS	Ethyl Methane Sulphorate
DBH	Dopamine Beta Hydroxylase	ENDOR	Electron Nuclear Double Resonance
DBHI	Dopamine B Hydroxylase Inhibitors	EOLM	Electron Optic Light Modulator
DBP	Diastolic Blood Pressure	EORTC	European Organization for Research on the Treatment of Cancer
DBP	Dibutyl Phthalate		
DCA	Direct Colorimetric Analysis	EPP	End Plate Potential
DCPIP	Dichlorophenolindophenol	EPR	Electron Paramagnetic Resonance
DCSS	Damage Control Suit System	ER	Endoplastic Recticulum
DDS	Distillers Dried Solubles	ESCA	Electron Spectroscopy for Chemical Analysis
DDT	Dichlorodiphenyl Trichloroethane		
DEN	Di-Ethyl Nitrosamine	ESPI	Electronic Speckle Pattern Interferometer
DES	Diethylsliboestrol		
DES	Dynamic Environment Simulator	ESR	Erythrocyte Sedimentation Rate
DG	Diacylglycerols	ESS	Earle's Salt Solution
DLT	Dorsolateral Tract	EtNC	Ethyl Isocyanide
DLVL	Diverted into Low Velocity Layer	FASEB	Federation of American Societies for Experimental Biology
DMBA	Dimethylbenzanthracene		
DMD	Dimethyl Oxozolidinedione	FC	Free Cholesterol
DMF	Dimethylformanide	FDA	Food Drug Administration (US)
DMI	Desmethylimipramine	FDAA	Fluorenyldiacetamide
DMN	Di-Methyl Nitrosamine	FDS	Fallout Decay Simulation
DMSO	Dimethyl Sulphoxide	FE	Flash Evaporation
DNA	Deoxyribonucleic Acid	FF	Filtration Faction
DNP	Deoxyribonucleoproteins	FFA	Free Fatty Acids
DNP	Dinitrophenol	FHS	Framingham Heart Study
DNT	Desmethylnortriplyline	FITC	Fluorescein Isothiocyanate
DO	Dissolved Oxygen	FMN	Flavin Mononucleotide
DOCA	Deoxycorticosterone Acetate	FPC	Fish Protein Concentrate
DOPA	Dihydroxyphenylalanine	FRWI	Framingham Relative Weight Index
DORF	Diamond Ordinance Radiation Facility	FS	Free Sterols
DP	Dispersed Phase	FS	Freeze Substitution
DPG	Diphosphoglycerate	FSH	Follicle Stimulating Hormone
DPH	Diphenylhydantoin	FSTC	Foreign Science and Technology Center (US)
DPNH	Diphosphopyridine Nucleotide		
DPTH	Diphenylthiohydantoin	FU	Fumarate Concentration
DS	Double Stranded	GA	Gibberellic Acid
DSC	Defense Scanning Calorimetry	GA	Glyoxylic Acid
DTA	Differential Thermal Analysis	GAISA	Gamma Aminobutyric Acid
dTMP	Thymidine Monophosphate	GARP	Global Atmospheric Research Program
DTT	Dithiotheitol	GBM	Glomerular Basement Membrane
dTTP	Thymidine Triphosphate	GC	Gas Chromatography
EAT	Ehrlich Ascites Tumour	GC-MS	Gas Chromatography - Mass Spectrometry
EATC	Ehrlich Ascites Tumour Cells	GDH	Glutamate Dehydrogenase
EBV	Epstein Barr Virus	GDP	Guanosine Disphosphate
EC	Enterochromaffin Cells	GFR	Glomerular Filtration Rate
EC	Esterified Cholesterol		

GH	Growth Hormone
GI	Gastrointestinal
GMA	Glycol Methacrylate
GOT	Glutamin Oxalacetic Transaminase
GPI	Glucose Phosphate Isomerase
GPT-C	Glutamic Pyruvic Transaminase-C
GTP	Guanoine Triphosphate
GVH	Graft Versus Host
HA	Hemagglutinin
HA	Hyalusonic
HAQO	Hydroxyaminoquinoline Oxide
HAT	Hypoxanthine Aminopterin and Thymidine
HBAg	Hepatitis B Antigen
HBFP	Hematoxylin Basic Fuchsin-Pecric
HBSS	Hanks Balanced Salt Solution
HCB	Hexachlorobenzene
HCG	Human Chorionic Gonadotrophin
HCHP	Harvard Community Health Plan (US)
HCL	Hydrogen Chloride
HDC	Hydrogen Depolarized CO_2 Concentrator
HDL	High Density Lipoprotein
HE	Heptachlor Epoxide
HEW	Health Education and Welfare (US)
HF	Hyperfine
HGPRT	Hypoxanthine Guanine Phosphoribosyl Transferase
HK	Hexakinase
HMP	Hexose Monophosphate
HNTD	Highest Non Toxic Dose
HPNS	High Pressure Nervous Syndrome
HQO	Hydroxyquinoline Oxide
HR	Heart Rates
HRR	Horseradish Peroxidase
HRSEM	High Resolution Scanning Electron Microscope
HT	Hydroxy Tryplamine
HTA	Hypophysiotropic Area
HTC	Hematocrit
IAA	Indole Acetic Acid
IAMS	International Association of Microbiological Societies
ICDH	Isocitrate Dehydrogenase
ICRP	International Commission on Radiological Protection
ICSU	International Council of Scientific Unions
IDH	Isocitrate Dehydrogenase
IDP	Ionsine Diphosphate
IEP	Isoelectric Point
IITV	Image Intensified Television
INDOR	Internuclear Double Resonance
IP	Imipramine
IPO-A	Indolephenoloxidase-A
ISR	Intersecting Storage Rings
IT	Intratracheal
IV	Intravascular Volume
JGA	Juxtaglomerular Apparatuses
KA	Kynurenic Acid
KLH	Keyhole Limpet Haemocyanin
LBNP	Lower Body Negative Pressure
LC	Lyman Continuum
LD	Lethal Dose
LDH	Lactate Dehydrogenase
LDH-A	Lactate Dehydrogenase-A
LDH-B	Lactate Dehydrogenase-B
LDL	Low Density Lipoprotein
LGV	Large Granular Vesicles
LGV	Lymphogranuloma Venereu
LH	Luteinizing Hormone
LIL	Large Ionic Lithophile
LM	Light Microscope
LME	Light Mitochondrial Extract
LNF	Liposoluble Neutral Fraction
LPL	Lipoprotein Lipid
LSD	Lysergic Acid Diethylamide
LSD	Lysergic Acid Diethylamine
LVL	Low Velocity Layer
LY	Lysosomes
MAA	Macroaggregates
MAB	Monomethylaminoazobenzene
MAM	Methylazoxymethanol
MAMAc	Methylazoxymethanol Acetate
MAO	Manoamine Oxidase
MC	Mast Cells
MCD	Magnetic Circular Dichroic
MCP	Microchannel Plate
MDMS	Methylene Dimethanesulphonate
MDP	Methylenedioxyphenyl
ME	Mateate Concentration
MECA	Molecular Emission Cavity Analysis
MeDAB	Methyl Dimethylaminoazobenzene
MEDAC	Medical Electronic Data Acquisition and Control
MEDLARS	Medical Literature Analysis and Retrieval System
MEM	Modified Eagle's Medium
MEP	Motor Evoked Potentials
MFO	Mixed Function Oxidase
MGL	Malachite Green Leucocyanite
MHA	Mueller Hinta Agar
MHD	Magnetohydrodynamic
MIF	Macrophage Inhibition Factor
MLF	Medium Longitudinal Fasciculus
MLSS	Mixed Liquid Suspended Solids
MLV	Moloney Leukaemia Virus
MM	Multiple Myeloma
MMH	Methylmercury Hydroxide
MMS	Methyl Methanesulphonate
MNNG	Methyl Nitro Nitrosoguanidine
MNU	Methyl Nitrosourea
MOI	Multiplicities of Infection
MOR	Magnetic Optical Rotation
MOR	Malate Oxidoreductase
MOTMX	Methoxy Trimethylxanthine
MPI	Mannose Phosphate Isomerase
MPO	Myeloperoxidase
MPS	Mucopolysaccharides
MRC	Mouse Erythrocytes
MRV	Maximum Relative Variation
MSH	Melanocyte Stimulating Hormone

MSS	Multispectral Scanner	PBI	Polybenzimidazole
MSUD	Maple Syrup Urine Disease	PBS	Phosphate Buffered Saline
MSV	Murine Sarcoma Virus	PC	Parvicellar
MTV	Mammary Tumour Virus	PC	Pyrurate Carboxylase
MU	Methylene Unit	PCG	Phonocardiogram
MV	Microvillus	PCM	Pulse Code Modulation
MVB	Multivesicular Bodies	PCPA	Para Chlorophenylalanine
MW	Molecular Weight	PDF	Pair Distribution Function
NAD	Nicotinamide Adenine Dinucleotide	PEP	Phosphoenolpyruvate
NADP	Nicotinamide Adenine Dinucleotide Phosphate	PEP	Primate Equilibrium Platform
		PEPCK	Phosphoenolpyruvate Carboxykinase
NCTRU	Naval Clothing and Textile Research Unit	PFC	Plaque Forming Cells
		PFCR	Plaque Forming Cell Response
NDC	National Drug Code	PFK	Phosphofructokinase
NDPase	Nucleoside Diphosphatase	PFT	Physical Fitness Test
NDT	Non-Destructive Testing	PFU	Plaque Forming Unit
NDV	Newcastle Disease Virus	PG	Photosphoglycollate
NE	Norepinephrine	PGI	Phosphoglucoisomerase
NEP	Nerve Ending Particles	PGK	Phosphoglycerate Kinase
NFE	Nearly Free Electron	PHS	Public Health Service
NGF	Nerve Growth Factor	PI	Pepsin Inhibitor
NHS	National Health Survey	PI	Propyl Isome
NIAMDD	National Institute of Arthritis Metabolism and Digestive Diseases	PK	Pyruvate Kinase
		PL	Phospholipids
NIH	National Institutes of Health (US)	PLA	Polylactic Acid
NIMH	National Institute of Mental Health	PLL	Peripheral Light Loss
NMJ	Neuromuscular Junctions	PM	Plasma Membrane
NMNH	National Museum of Natural History	PMA	Phorbol Myristate Acetale
NMR	Nuclear Magnetic Resonance	PMCM	Pulse Morse Code Modulation
NP	Nucleoside Phosphorylase	PMIS	Patient Medical Information System
NPC	Nasopharyngeal Carcinoma Tissue	PMN	Polymorphonuclear Leukocyte
NPPase	Nucleoside Diphosphatase	PMR	Proton Magnetic Resonance
NQ	Nitroquinoline	PMS	Pregnant Mare's Serum
NQO	Nitroquinoline Oxide	PNMT	Phenylethanolamine N-methyltransferase
NRS	Normal Rabbit Serum	POMR	Problem Oriented Medical Record
NT	Nortriptyline	PPP	Platelet Poor Plasma
OAC	Optimally Adaptive Control	PRE	Protein Relaxation Enhancement
OD	Optical Density	PRP	Plateler-Rich Plasma
OHA	Oxygen Haemoglobin Affinity	PRPP	Phosphorybosil Pyrophosphate
OHT	Oxygen at High Temperature	PS	Paradoxical Sleep
OM	Organic Matter	PTA	Phosphotungstic Acid
OPCM	Differential Pulse Code Modulation	PTAH	Phosphotungstic Acid Haematoxylin
OPT	Ophthaldialdehyde	PTT	Partial Thromboplastin Times
ORP	Oxidation Reduction Potential	PV	Polycythemia Vera
OSC	Optimally Sensitive Controller	PVN	Paraventricular Nuclei
OTC	Oxytetracycline	PVP	Polyvinylpyrrolidone
PA	Puromycin Aminonucleoside	QM	Quinacrine Mustard
PAA	Polyacrylamide	QO	Quinoline Oxide
PAF	p-Formaldehyde-Picric Acid	RAAP	Radford Army Ammunition Plant
BAG	Pre-Albumin Globulin	RAHTS	Rabbit Antihuman Thymocyte Serum
PAG	Protein Advisory Group (US)	RBC	Red Blood Cells
PAMD	Periodic Acid Mixed Diamine	RDTR	Radiographic Dielectric Track Registration
PAN	Polyacrylonitride		
PAP	Peroxidase Antiperoxidase	RER	Rough Endoplastic Reticulum
PAPD	Periodate Dimethylphenylenediamine	RES	Reticuloendothelial System
PAPS	Periodic Acid Phenylhydrazine Schiff	RFC	Rosette Forming Cells
PAS	Periodic Acid Schiff	RGR	Relative Growth Rates
PA-SM	Periodic Acid-Silver Methenamine	RIA	Radioimmunoassay
PB	Phenobarbital	RITC	Ramethylrhodamine Isothiocyanate
PB	Piperonyl Butoxide	RLC	Rotating Litter Chair

RM	Record Mark
RME	Reflex Milk Ejection
RNA	Ribonucleic Acid
RNase	Ribonuclease
RPC	Reversed Phase Chromatography
RPF	Renal Plasma Flow
RQ	Respiratory Quotient
RR	Ruthenium Red
RSV	Respiratory Syncytial Virus
RTA	Renal Tubular Acidosis
RVP	Renal Venous Pressure
SAODAP	Special Action Office for Drug Abuse Prevention
SARDA	State and Regional Disaster Airlift
SAREX	Search and Rescue Exercise
SBP	Systolic Blood Pressure
SBPT	Small-modular-weight Basic Protein Toxins
SC	Subcutaneously
SCFMO	Self Consistent Field Molecular Orbital
SDH	Succinic Dehydrogenase
SDS	Sodium Dodecyl Sulphate
SEM	Scanning Electron Micrographs
SEM	Scanning Electron Microscope
SER	Sebum Excretion Rates
SER	Smooth Endoplasmic Reticulum
SERV	Surface Effect Rescue Vehicle
SG	Secretory Granule
SGOT	SBPT Glutamin Oxalacetic Transaminase
SGV	Small Granular Vesicles
SHF	Super Hyperfine
SICA	Schizont Infected Cell Agglutin
SLS	Segment Long Spacing
SMAF	Specific Microphage Arming Factor
SNHS	Supraoptic Neurohypophysical System
SON	Supraoptic Nuclei
SPP	Standard Psychophysiological Preparation
SRBC	Sheep Red Blood Cells
ST	Skin Temperature
STBR	Stirred Tank Biological Reactor
STE	Sterolesters
SUD	Sudden Unexpected Death
SVI	Stroke Volume Index
SWS	Short Wave Sleep
TC	Tetracycline
TC	Total Cholesterol
TCA	Tricarboxylic Acid
TCA	Trichloroacetic Acid
TD	Thiamin Deficient
TD	Tracing Dye
TDH	Toxic Dose High
TDL	Toxic Dose Low
TEAH	Tetraethylammonium
TEAOH	Tetraethylammonium Hydroxide
TEM	Transmission Electron Microscopy
TG	Triglyceride
TGFA	Triglyceride Fatty Acids
THAM	Tri-Hydroxymethyl-Aminomethane

THC	Transtetrahydro-Cannabinol
TIPA	Tetraisopropylpyrophosphoramide
TK	Thymide Kinase
TL	Total Lipid
TLW	Threshold Limit Value
TMAC	Tetramethylammonium Bicarbonate
TMPAH	Trimethylphenyl Ammonium Hydroxide
TMS	Trimethylsilyl
TMV	Tobacco Mosaic Virus
TOC	Total Organic Carbon
TOH	Tyrosine Hydroxylase
TPE	Tetraphenylethylene
TPL	Total Phospholipid
TPP	Thiamine Pyrophosphatase
TPR	Total Peripheral Resistance
TRANSIF	Transient State Isoelectric Focusing
TRIC	Trachoma Inclusion Conjunctivitis
TSH	Thyroid Stimulating Hormone
TSH	Thyrotropic Hormone
TSTA	Tumour Specific Transplantation Antigens
UDP	Uridine Diphosphate
UDPG	Uridine Diphosphoglucose
UDPGA	Uridine Diphosphoglucuronic Acid
UF	Ultrafiltration
UFA	Unesterified Fatty Acids
UOD	Units of Optical Density
USPHS	United States Public Health Service
VEP	Visual Evoked Potential
VHDL	Very High Density Lipoprotein
VLDL	Very Low Density Lipoprotein
VSTA	Virus Specified Tumour Antigens
WBC	White Blood Cells
WSE	Water Saline Extract
WVE	Water Vapour Electrolysis
YTL	Yarsley Technical Services (UK)
ZFS	Zero Field Splitting

BREWERY

AAS	Atomic Absorption Spectroscopy
ABTA	Allied Brewery Traders' Association
APDC	Ammonium Pyrrolidine Dithiocarbamate
BOD	Biological Oxygen Demand
CEAC	Central European Analysis Commission
CM	Carboxymethyl
CMC	Carboxymethylcellulose
DHA	Dehydrated Humulinic Acid
EBC	European Brewery Convention
EDTA	Ethylenediamine Tatra Acetic
GA	Gibberellic Acid
MEA	Malt Extract Agar
MIBK	Methyl Isobutyl Ketone
NCYC	National Collection of Yeast Cultures (UK)
SASPL	Saturated Ammonium Sulphate Precipitation Limit
SDM	Schwarz Differential Medium
SG	Solution of Glucose

BUILDING

BRE	Building Research Establishment (UK)
CDA	Comprehensive Development Area
CPO	Compulsory Purchase Order
CS	Coal Store
DWD	District Works Department
HAC	High Alumina Cement
IAEE	International Association of Earthquake Engineers
LR	Living Room
LTR	Long Term Revitalization
PCC	Portland Cement Concrete
PFA	Pulverized Fuel Ash
PFIR	Part Fill In and Ram
RC	Reinforced Concrete
SC	Scullery
STR	Short Term Revitalization
WC	Water Closet

CERAMICS

CH	Calcium Hydroxid
CMS	Ca-Mg-Silicate
CP	Chemical Preparation
KHN	Knoop Hardness Number
LAS	Li Aluminosilicate
MO	Mixed Oxide
NS	Na Silicate
PTCR	Positive Temperature Coefficient of Resistivity
SS	Solid Solution
TCR	Temperature Coefficient of Resistance
WS	Water Solid

CEREALS

DNPH	Dinitrophenylhydrazin
EM	Ethoxylated Monoglycerides
GAD	Glutamic Acid Decarboxylase
SSL	Sodium Stearoyl Laclylate
ST	Sucrose Tallowate

CHEMISTRY

BSA	Bis-trimethylsilyl-acetamide
CP	Chemical Preparation
CPK	Creative Phosphokinase
DMM	Dimethylmercury
DNE	Dinitroethane
FIN	Field Iron Microscope
GC	Gas Chromatography
GC-MS	Gas Chromatography Mass Spectrometry
HMDS	Hexamethydisilazane
HVD	High Velocity Detonation
LRS	Laser Roman Scattering
LVD	Low Velocity Detonation

NMR	Nuclear Magnetic Resonance
NTA	Nitrilotriacetic Acid
PAA-PS	Polyacrylic Acid Polysulfone
PAC	Polycyclic Aromatic Hydrocarbons
PETN	Pentaerythritol Tetranitrate
PMDR	Phosphorescence Microwave Double Resonance
PPTP	Poly-p-Phenyleneterephtalamide
RENT	Reentry Nose Tip
SES	Superexcited Electronic States
TCA	Turbulent Contact Absorber
TLC	Thin Layer Chromatography
TLM	Thin Lipid Membranes
TMSDEA	Trimethyl-Silyldiethylamine
VUV	Vacuum Ultraviolet

COMMUNICATION SYSTEMS

AABNCP	Advanced Airborne Command Post
ABU	Asian Broadcasting Union
AEROSAT	Aeronautical Satellite
AF	Audio Frequency
AFC	Automatic Frequency Control
AFCS	Air Force Communications Service
AFSATCOM	Air Force Satellite Communications
AIDJEX	Arctic Ice Dynamic Joint Experiment
AMIS	Aircraft Movement Information Service
ant	Antenna
ARC	Aircraft Radio Corporation
ARE	Asymplotic Relative Efficiency
ARI	Airborne Radio Instrument
ARINC	Aeronautical Radio Incorporated (US)
ARPA	Advanced Research Projects Agency
ARQ	Automatic Repeat Request
ARSR	Air Route Surveillance Radar
ARTCC	Air Route Traffic Control Center (US)
ARTS	Automatic Radar Terminal System
ASC	Automatic Switching Center
ASET	Aeronautics Services Earth Terminal
ASTRA	Application of Space Techniques Relating to Aviation
ATCRBC	Air Traffic Control Radar Beacon
ATCSS	Air Traffic Control Signaling System
ATM	Apollo Telescope Mount
ATR	Air Transport Radio
ATR	Anti-Transit-Receive
ATREM	Average Time Remaining
ATS	Applications Technology Satellite
ATSD	Airborne Traffic Situation Display
ATU	Aerial Tuning Unit
AVAS	Automatic VFR Advisory Service
AVC	Automatic Volume Control
AVCS	Advanced Vidicon Camera System
AWACS	Airborne Warning and Control System
BA	Buffer Amplifier
BBC	British Broadcasting Corporation
BCI	Interference to Broadcast
BCRRA	British Commonwealth Radio Reception Award

BEBC	Big European Bubble Chamber
BFO	Beat Frequency Oscillator
BIS	Business Information System
BSC	Binary Synchronous Communication
BTSS	Basic Time Sharing System
CAPRI	Coded Address Private Radio Intercom
CARF	Central Altitude Reservation Facility
CAS	Close Air Support
CAS	Collision Avoidance System
CATV	Community Antenna Television
CBC	Canadian Broadcasting Corporation
CCC	Convert Character Code
CCITT	Comité Consultatif International Télégraphique et Téléphonique
CCITT	International Telegraph and Telephone Consultative Committee
CCP	Communication Control Package
CCS	Communication Control System
CCS	Hundred Call Seconds
CCTV	Closed Circuit Television
CDC	Computer Display Channel
CDP	Communications Data Processor
CDX	Control Differential Transmitter
CEAC	Committee for European Airspace Coordination
CESI	Centro Elettrotecnico Sperimentale Italiano
CF	Cathode Follower
CFAR	Constant False Alarm Rate
CFO	Critical Flashover
CFTD	Constant Fraction Timing Discriminator
CIAP	Climatic Impact Assessment Program
CNI	Communications Navigation and Identification
CO	Crystal Oscillator
COMCM	Communication Countermeasures
COMSAT	Communications Satellite
COMZ	Communication Zone
CORF	Committee on Radio Frequency
CORTEX	Communications Oriented Real Time Executive
CPM	Central Processor Modules
CPS	Cycles Per Second
CRC	Communications Research Centre
CRC	Control and Reporting Center
CRP	Control and Reporting Post
CSC	Communications Satellite Corporation
CSEF	Current Switch Emitter Follower
ct	Centre Tap
CT	Control Transformer
CTC	Communications Transistor Corporation (US)
CTFM	Continuous Transmission Frequency Modulated
CTS	Communications Technology Satellite
CVR	Cockpit Voice Recorder
CW	Carrier Wave
CX	Control Transmitter
DACOM	Data Communications
DARC	Direct Access Radar Channel
DC	Direct Current
DCC	Direct Computer Control
DCC	Display Channel Complex
DCC	Double Cotton Covered
DCCU	Data Communication Control Units
DDD	Direct Distance Dialing
DEDS	Data Entry and Display Subsystem
DICON	Digital Communication Through Orbiting Needles
DISCOS	Disturbance Compensation System
DPS	Data Processing Subsystem
DRIFT	Diversity Receiving Instrumentation for Telemetry
DRIR	Direct Readout Infrared
DRW	Defensive Radio Warfare
DSAP	Defence Systems Application Program
DSB	Double Side Band
DSFT	Detection Scheme with Fixed Thresholds
DSLT	Detection Scheme with Learning of Thresholds
DTAS	Data Transmission and Switching System
EBU	European Broadcasting Union
ECO	Electron Coupled Oscillator
ECS	European Communication Satellite
EIRP	Equivalent Isotropical Radiated Power
ELTAF	Energy Locator Transmitters Automatic Fixed
ELTR	Emergency Locator Transmitter Receiver
emf	Electromotive Force
EOAP	Earth Observations Aircraft Program
EREP	Earth Resources Experimental Package
ERP	Effective Radiated Power
ERTS	Earth Resources Technology Satellite
ESC	European Space Conference
ESRO	European Space Research Organization
ETS	Electronic Test Set
EVCS	Extravehicular Communication System
EXR	Execute and Repeat
FCC	Federal Communications Commission
FD	Frequency Diversity
fd	Frequency Doubler
FDMA	Frequency Division Multiple Access
FET	Field Effect Transistor
FETT	Field Effect Tetrode Transistor
FFT	Fast Fourier Transform
FLBE	Filter Band Elimination
FLTSATCOM	Fleet Satellite Communication
FM	Frequency Modulation
FRC	Federal Radio Commission
fsd	Full Scale Deflection
FTC	Fast Time Constant
GARD	General Address Reading Device
GAREX	Ground Aviation Radio Exchange System
GARP	Global Atmospheric Research Program
GATE	GARP Atlantic Tropical Experiment
GATE	Global Atlantic Tropical Experiment
GATR	Ground Air Transmitter Receiver

gb	Grid Bias	MESA	Marine Ecosystems Analysis
GDOP	Geometric Dilution of Precision	MEW	Microwave Early Warning
GPO	General Post Office	MF	Medium Frequency
GPS	Global Positioning System	MOC	Minimum Operational Characteristics
GRAN	Global Rescue Alarm Net	MOSFET	Metal Oxide Semiconductor Field
GSE	Ground Support Equipment		Effect Transistor
GSFS	Goddard Space Flight Center (US)	MOS/LSI	Metal Oxide Semiconductor/Large
HEMAC	Hybrid Electro Magnetic Antenna		Scale Integration
	Couplers	MPP	Mission Planning Program
HET	Health Education Telecommunications	MSS	Multispectral Scanning
HF	High Frequency	MTI	Moving Target Indicator
hp	High Pass	MTIL	Maximum Tolerable Insecurity Level
HSGTC	High Speed Ground Test Center	muf	Maximum Usable Frequency
IA	Intermediate Amplifier	NAS	National Airspace System
IC	Integrated Circuits	NAUS	National Airspace Utilization Study
ICAMRS	International Civil Aviation Message	nbfm	Narrow Band Frequency Modulation
	Routing System	NCS	National Communication System
ICSC	Interim Communications Satellite	NDS	Nonparametric Detection Scheme
	Committee	NEACP	National Emergency Airborne Command
IEE	Institution of Electric Engineering		Post (US)
IEEE	Institute of Electrical and Electronics	NEMS	Nimbus E Microwave Spectrometer
	Engineers	NESS	National Environmental Satellite
IFT	Intermediate Frequency Transformer		Service
IGIA	Interagency Group for International	nfm	Narrow Frequency Modulation
	Aviation	NMC	National Meteorological Center
ILS-LOC	Instrument Landing System Localizer	NOAA	National Oceanographic Atmospheric
IMP	Interplanetary Monitoring Platform		Administration (US)
INS	Inertial Navigation System	NPR	Noise Power Ratio
INTELSAT	International Telecommunications	NTDS	Naval Tactical Data System
	Satellite	OCC	Oceanic Control Centers
IOP	Input Output Processor	OCS	Optical Contact Sensor
IPC	Intermittent Positive Control	OD	Outside Diameter
ITACS	Integrated Tactical Air Control System	pa	Power Amplifier
ITNS	Integrated Tactical Navigation System	PABX	Private Automatic Branch Exchange
ITPR	Infrared Temperature Profile	PAM	Pulse Amplitude Modulation
	Radiometer	PCA	Polar Cap Absorption
ITT	International Telephone and Telegraph	PCB	Printed Circuit Board
JCC	Joint Communications Centre	PCI	Packet Communications Incorporated
JCC	Joint Control Centers	PCM	Pulse Code Modulation
kc/s	Kilocycle per Second	PCP	Programmable Communication Processors
KM	Kirchhoff Method	PCS	Power Conditioning System
kv	Kilovolts	pd	Potential Difference/Power Doubler
kw	Kilowatt	PLRACTA	Position Location Reporting and
LAT	Laser Acquisition and Tracking		Control Tactical Aircraft
LCL	Low Capacity Link	PM	Permanent Magnet
LF	Low Frequency	POS	Point Of Sale
LHC	Left Hand Circular	p-p	Peak-to-Peak
LIC	Linear Integrated Circuit	pp	Push-Pull
LPA	Linear Pulse Amplifier	PPI	Plan Position Indicator
LPS	Linear Pulse Sector	PRF	Pulse Repetition Frequency
lsb	Lower Side Band	PRFD	Pulse Recurrence Frequency
LST	Large Space Telescopes		Discrimination
lt	Lower Tension	PRFS	Pulse Recurrence Frequency Stagger
luf	Lower Usable Frequency	PRP	Pulse Repetition Period
luhf	Lower Usable High Frequency	PRT	Primary Ranging Test
MA	Main Amplifier	PRT	Pulse Repetition Time
MCI	Microwave Communications Inc.(US)	PTACV	Prototype Tracked Air Cushion Vehicle
MCT	Mobile Communication Terminal	QP	Quasi Peak
MCW	Modulated Continuous Ware	RACES	Radio Amateur Civil Emergency Service
MEM	Maximum Entropy Method	RAD	Relative Air Density

RAE   Radio Astronomy Explorer
RAL   Radio Annoyance Level
RAM   Random Access Memory
RAPCON Radar Approach Control
RAREP   Radar Reports
RASS   Rotating Acoustic Stereo Scanners
RCA   Radio Corporation of America
RCAG   Remote Controlled Air /Ground
rcc   Resistance Capacitance Coupling
RDS   Robust Detection Scheme
RF   Radio Frequency
rfc   Radio Frequency Choke
RFDU   Reconfiguration and Fault Detection
            Unit
RFI   Radio Frequency Interference
RHC   Right Hand Circular
RI   Radio Influence
ROC   Receiver Operating Characteristic
ROW   Right of Way
RPV   Remote Pilotless Vehicle
RRS   Radio Range/Range-Rate System
RSGB   Radio Society of Great Britain
RT   Radio Telephony
RTNE   Radio Technical New Entrant
RTTY   Radio Teletypewriter
RWI   Radio Wire Integration
RWS   Receiver Waveform Simulation
SAC   Strategic Air Command
SAMSO   Space and Missile System Organization
SAR   Search and Rescue
SARCEN Search and Rescue Central
SARCOM Search and Rescue Communicator
SAREX   Search and Rescue Exercise
SARSAT Search and Rescue Satellite
SCA   Single Channel Analyzer
SCATANA Security Control of Air Traffic
            and Air Navigation Aids
SCC   Single Cotton Covered
SCF   Satellite Control Facility
SCR   Selective Chopper Radiometer
SDMA   Space Division Multiple Access
SDRT   Slot Dipole Ranging Tests
SDS   Satellite Data System
SECAL   Selective Calling
SFSS   Satellite Field Service Stations
sg   Screen Grid
S/I   Signal-to-Interference
sic   Semiconductor Integrated Circuit
SITE   Satellite Instructional Television
            Experiment
SLS   Sidelobe Suppression
SPC   Stored Program Control Exchange
spdt   Single Pole Double Throw
SPEC   Speech Predictive Encoding
            Communication
SPL   Sound Pressure Level
SPM   Small Perturbation Method
SR   Scanning Radiometer
SRDS   System Research and Development
            Service

SRT   Secondary Ranging Test
SSB   Single Side Band
SSMA   Spread Spectrum Multiple Access
STADAC Station Acquisition and Control
STARS   Satellite Telemetry Automatic
            Reduction Systems
STC   Sensitive Time Control
swg   Standard Wire Gauge
SWL   Short Wave Listeners
SYSCAP System of Circuit Analysis Programs
TACP   Tactical Air Control Party
TCA   Terminal Control Areas
TDMA   Time Division Multiple Access
TDR   Torque Differential Receiver
TDSCC   Tidbinbilla Deep Space Communication
            Complex
TDX   Torque Differential Transmitter
TEP   Transmitter Experimental Package
TFA   Timing Filter Amplifier
TICCIT Time Shared Interactive Computer
            Controlled Information Television
tpi   Turns Per Inch
TR   Torque Receiver
TRACALS Traffic Control and Landing System
TRACON Terminal Radar Control
TRF   Tuned Radar Frequency
TSC   Transportation Systems Center
TWTA   Travelling Wave Tube Amplifier
TX   Torque Transmitter
UCNI   Unified Communications Navigation
            and Identification
UHF   Universal High Frequency
URTNA   Union of National Radio and Television
            Organization of Africa
USB   Upper Side Band
VAR   Visual and Aural Range
vfo   Variable Frequency Oscillator
VFR   Visual Flight Rules
VHF   Very High Frequency
VISSR   Visible and Infrared Spin Scan
            Radiometer
VLB   Very Long Baseline
VLF   Very Low Frequency
VOR   Very High Frequency Omnirange
VOX   Voice Operated Switching Device
vr   Voltage Regulator
VSCF   Variable Speed Constant Frequency
VTPR   Vertical Temperature Profile
            Radiometer
VXO   Variable Crystal Oscillator
WATS   Wide Area Telephone Service
WECO   Western Electric Company
WMSC   Weather Message Switching Center
w/t   Wireless Telegraphy
ww   Wire Wound

COMPUTER SCIENCES

AADC   All Applications Digital Computer

ABL   Atlantic Basic Language
ACA   American Communications Association
ACAU   Automatic Calling and Answering Unit
ACC   Abort Guidance Computer
ACCA   Asynchronous Communications Control
          Attachment
ACE   Automatic Computing Engine
ACID   Automated Classification and
          Interpretation of Data
ACL   Application Control Language
ACL   Automatic Circuit Layout
ACM   Association for Computing Machinery
          (US)
ACM   Associative Communication Multiplexer
ACPA   Association for Computer Programmers
          and Analysts
ACRT   Analysis Control Routine
ACT   Automatic Code Translation
ACTP   Advanced Computer Techniques Project
ACU   Arithmetic Control Unit
ACU   Automatic Calling Unit
AD   Account Directory
AD   Analog-to-Digital
ADA   Action Data Automation
ADA   Automatic Data Acquisition
ADAC   Automated Direct Analog Computer
ADAR   Automatic Data Acquisition Routine
ADBMS   Available Data Base Management System
ADC   Analog-to-Digital Converter
ADEPT   Automated Direct Entry Packaging
          Technique
ADP   Automatic Data Processing
ADPESO Automatic Data Processing Selection
          Office
ADSTAR Automatic Document Storage and
          Retrieval
ADT   Admission Discharge and Transfer
ADU   Automatic Data Unit
ADX   Automatic Data Exchange
AED   Automatic Engineering Design
AFCAL   Association Franchise de Calcul
AFG   Analog Function Generator
AFI   Automatic Fault Isolation
AFIPS   American Federation for Information
          Processing Societies
AFM   Analysis and Forecasting Mode
AGC   Automatic Gain Control
AH   Analog Hybrid
AIET   Average Instruction Executive Time
ALC   Adaptive Logic Circuit
ALGOL   Algorithmic Language
ALPAC   Automatic Language Processing
          Committee
ALPS   Advanced Linear Programming System
ALRR   Ames Laboratory Research Reactor
ALU   Arithmetic and Logic Unit
AM   Amplitude Modulation
AM   Associative Memory
AMA   American Management Association
AMR   Automatic Message Routing

AMTCL   Association for Machine Translation
          and Computational Linguistics
ANSL   American National Standard Labels
AOU   Automated Offset Unit
AP   Application Programs
AP   Array Processor
AP   Associative Processor
APAM   Array Processor Access Method
APATS   Automatic Programmer and Test System
APCS   Associative Processor Computer Systems
APDT   Allowed Project Time
APICS   American Production and Inventory
          Control
APPLE   Associative Processor Programming
          Language Evaluation
APR   Alternate Path Retry
APSP   Array Processor Subroutine Package
APT   Automatic Picture Transmission
APT   Automatic Programmed Tool
AQL   Acceptable Quality Level
AR   Arithmetic Register
AR   Associative Register
ARC   Augmentation Research Center (US)
ARCH   Articulated Computer Hierarchy
ARGUS   Automatic Routine Generating and
          Updating System
AROM   Associative Read Only Memory
ARPA   Advanced Research Project Agency
ARQ   Automatic Request for Repetition
ART   Advanced Research and Technology
ARU   Audio Response Unit
ASAP   Applied Systems and Personnel
ASC   Advanced Scientific Computer
ASCENT Assembly System for Central
          Processor
ASCII   American National Standard Code for
          Information Interchange
ASLT   Advanced Solid Logic Technology
ASP   Attached Support Processor
ASR   Automatic Send/Receive
ASRS   Automatic Storage and Retrieval Systems
AST   Auxiliary Segment Table
ASV   Automatic Self Verification
AT   Audit Trail
ATB   Access Type Bits
ATCCC   Advanced Technical Command Control
          Capability
ATE   Automatic Test Equipment
ATEC   Automated Technical Control
ATLAS   Abbreviated Test Language for
          Avionics Systems
ATN   Augmented Transition Network
AU   Arithmetic Unit
AUTODIN Automatic Digital Network
AUTOMAP Automatic Machining Program
AUTOPIC Automatic Personal Identification
          Code
AUTOPROMPT Automatic Programming of
          Machine Tools
AVM   Automatic Vehicle Monitoring

BAL	Basic Assembler Language	CAI	Computer Assisted Instruction
BAP	Basic Assembler Program	CAK	Command Access Keys
BAR	Buffer Address Register	CAK	Command Acknowledge
BASIC	Beginner's All Purpose Symbolic Instruction Code	CAL	Computer Aided Learning
		CALC	Cargo Acceptance and Load Control
BATS	Basic Additional Teleprocessing Support	CAM	Computer Aided Manufacturing
		CAM	Content Addressable Memory
BB	Building Blocks	CAN	Cancel
BBN	Bolt Beranek and Newman	CAN TRAN	Cancel Transmission
BCD	Binary Coded Decimal	CAP	Computer Analysts and Programmers
BCDC	Binary Code Decimal Counters	CAPDAC	Computer Aided Piping Design and Construction
BCL	Burroughs Common Language		
BCS	British Computing Society	CAPE	Communications Automatic Processing Equipment
BCSI	Biometric Computer Service Incorporation		
		CAPR	Catalog of Programs
BDC	Binary Decimal Counter	CAR	Channel Address Register
BEEF	Business and Engineering Enriched FORTRAN	CARP	Computer Air Released Point
		CASDAC	Computer Aided Ship Design and Construction
BEU	Basic Encoding Unit		
BEX	Broadband Exchange	CAST	Computerized Automatic System Tester
BIEE	British Institute of Electrical Engineers (see IEE)	CAT	Computer Average Transients
		CAU	Compare Alpha Unequal
BIM	Branch If Multiplexer	CAW	Channel Address Word
BIM	British Institute of Management	CAX	Community Automatic Exchange
BIMAG	Bistable Magnetic Core	CBOSS	Count Back Order and Sample Select
BIP	Binary Image Processor	CBT	Core Block Table
BIT	Built In Test	CCB	Command Control Block
BIT/S	Bits Per Second	CCC	Central Computational Computer
BLM	Basic Language Machine	CCC	Central Computer Complex
BMTT	Buffered Magnetic Tape Transport	CCC	Computer Control Complex
BORAM	Block Oriented Random Access Memory	CCD	Charged Coupled Device
BOS	Basic Operating System	CCH	Channel Check Handler
BOT	Beginning Of Tape	CCK	Channel Control Check
BPAM	Basic Partitioned Access Method	CCP	Communication Control Package
BPI	Bits Per Inch	CCP	Console Control Package
BPS	Basic Programming Support	CCS	Central Computer Station
BPS	Basic Programming System	CCS	Hundred Call Seconds
BPS	Batch Processing System	CCVS	COBOL Compiler Validation System
BQL	Basic Query Language	CCW	Channel Command Word
BRC	Branch Conditional	CD	Check Digit
BRD	Binary Rate Divider	CDA	Command and Data Acquisition
BRU	Branch Unconditional	CDC	Call Direct Code
BS	Backspace	CDC	Code Directing Character
BSAM	Basic Sequential Access Method	CDC	Computer Display Channel
BSC	Binary Synchronous Communication	CDC	Control Data Corporation
BTAM	Basic Telecommunications Access Method	CDE	Certified Data Educator
		CDK	Channel Data Check
BTM	Batch Time-Sharing Monitor	CDL	Computer Design Language
BTMF	Block Type Manipulation Facility	CDMS	COMRADE Data Management System
BUDWSR	Brown University Display for Working Set References	CDP	Certificate in Data Processing
		CDSF	COMRADE Data Storage Facility
BUGS	Brown University Graphic System	CE	Channel End
BUIC	Back Up Interceptor Control	CEM	Computer Education for Management
BYP	Bypass	CEP	Command Executive Procedures
CAD	Computer Aided Design	CERN	Organisation Européene pour la Recherche Nucléaire
CADA	Computer Aided Design Analysis		
CADAM	Computer-graphic Augmented Design And Manufacturing	CEU	Communications Expansion Unit
		CFMS	Chained File Management System
CADC	Central Air Data Computer	CFU	Current File User
CAE	Compare Alpha Equal	CG	Computer Graphics
CAI	Computer Aided Instruction		

CGRAM Clock Generator Random Access Memory
CHAR Character
CHKPT Checkpoint
CI   Call Indicator
CIA   Certified Internal Auditor
CIC   Communication Intelligence Channel
CICS Customer Information Control System
CIOCS Communications Input/Output Control
      System
CIOM Communications Input Output
      Multiplexer
CIOU Custom Input/Output Unit
Cir   Circulate
CL   Control Leader
CLC   Central Logic Control
CLC   Course Line Computer
CLI   Command Language Interpreter
CLK   Clock
CLS   Control and Launch Subsystems
CM   Communication Multiplexer
CMI   Computer Managed Instruction
CMS   Cambridge Monitor System
CMU   Computer Memory Unit
CNC   Computer Numerical Control
CNE   Compare Numeric Equal
CNU   Compare Numeric Unequal
COAM Customer Owned And Maintained
COBOL Common Business Oriented Language
CODASYL Conference on Data System Language
CODES Computer Design and Education System
CODES Computer Design and Evaluation System
CODIS Controlled Digital Simulator
COL   Computer Oriented Language
COMPAC Computer Program for Automatic Control
COMPACT Compatible Algebraic Compiler and
        Translator
COMPAY Computer Payroll
COMRADE Computer Aided Design Environment
CONHAN Contextural Harmonic Analysis
CONTRAN Control Translator
CORTEX Communications Oriented Real Time
       Executive
COSBA Computer Service and Bureaux
      Association
COSEC Culham One-line Single Experimental
      Consol
COSY Compiler System
COSY Correction System
CP   Central Processor
CP   Clock Pulse
CP   Command Processor
CPA   Certified Public Account
CPB   Channel Program Block
CPC   Channel Program Commands
CPCS Cheque Processing Control System
CPFMS COMRADE Permanent File Management
      System
CPI   Character Per Inch
CPID Computer Program Integrated Document
CPL   CAST Programming Language

CPL   Computer Projects Limited
CPM   Central Processor Molecules
CPM   Control Path Method
CPO   Concurrent Peripheral Operations
CPS   Character Per Second
CPS   Conversational Programming System
CPS   Cycles Per Second
CPSM Critical Path Scheduling Method
CPU   Central Processor Unit
CPU   Computer Processor Unit
CR   Card Reader
CR   Carriage Return
CR   Communications Register
CR   Control Routine
CRAM Card Random Access Memory
CRC   Cyclic Redundancy Checksum
CRCC Cyclic Redundancy Check Character
CRD   Card Reader
CRE   Current Ring End
CRJE Conversational Remote Job Entry
CRT   Cathode Ray Tube
CS   Cyclo-Stationary
CSC   Computer Science Corporation
CSC   Course and Speed Computer
CSD   Computer Science Division
CSECT Control Section
CSI   Computer Systems International
CSL   Computer Simulation Language
CSL   Control and Simulation Language
CSMP Continuous System Modelling Program
CSP   Control Switching Point
CSS   Computer Subsystem
CSS   Computer System Simulator
CSW   Channel Status Word
CTB   Computer Time Bookers
CTS   Common Test Subroutines
CTS/RTS Clear-to-Send/Request-to-Send
CU   Control Unit
CUE   Computer Up-date Equipment
CUE   Control Unit End
CUEA Coastal Upwelling Ecosystems Analysis
CVIS Computerized Vocational Information
      System
CW   Call Waiting
CW   Continuous Wave
CWTG Computer World Trade Group (UK)
CZE   Compare Zone Equal
CZU   Compare Zone Unequal
DA   Define Area
D-A   Digital-to-Analog
DA   Direct Access
DA   Discrete Address
DAA   .Data Access Arrangement
DA/C Data Acquisition
DAC   Digital-to-Analog Converter
DACOM Data Communication
DACU Digitizing and Control Unit
DADB Data Analysis Data Base
DADS Data Acquisition Display Subsystem
DAFT Digital Analogue Function Table

DAIR   Dynamic Allocation Interface Routine
DAK   Decision Acknowledge
DAR   Damage Assessment Routine
DARMS Digital Alternate Representation of
           Music Symbols
DART   Daily Automatic Rescheduling Technique
DAS   Data Acquisition Subsystem
DAS   Data Acquisition System
DAS   Data Acquisitioning System
DAS   Data Analysis System
DASD   Direct Access Storage Device
DAT   Dynamic Address Translator
DATICO Digital Automatic Tape Intelligence
           Checkout
DBA   Data Base Administrator
DBMS   Data Base Management Software
DBMS   Data Based Management Systems
DBMSPSM Data Base Management System Problem
           Specification Model
DBRN   Decibels Based Reference Noise
DBTG   Data Base Task Group
DBU   Digital Buffer Unit
DC   Device Control
DC   Direct Current
DCA   Driver Control Area
DCB   Data Control Block
DCB   Define Control Block
DCBD   Define Control Block Dummy
DCC   Digital Cross Correct
DCC   Direct Computer Control
DCCU   Data Communication Control Units
DCI   Data Communication Interrogate
DCR   Data Communication Read
DCS   Direct Coupled System
DCS   Distributed Computer System
DCTL   Direct Coupled Transistor Logic
DCU   Device Control Unit
DCW   Data Communication Write
DD   Data Definition
DDA   Data Differential Analyzer
DDC   Direct Digital Control
DDD   Direct Distance Dialing
DDI   Direct Dial In
DDL   Data Description Language
DDPL   Demand Deposit Program Library
DDR   Dynamic Device Reconfiguration
DDS   Digital Data Service
DE   Device End
DEB   Data Extension Block
DEC   Digital Equipment Corporation
DECB   Data Event Control Block
DECLAB Digital Equipment Company Laboratory
DEL   Delete
DEM   Demodulator
DEU   Data Entry Unit
DEUCE Digital Electronic Universal
           Calculating Engine
DEX   Deferred Execution
DF   Disk File
DFC   Disk File Check

DFCU   Disk File Control Unit
DFI   Disk File Interrogate
DFR   Disk File Read
DFSU   Disk File Storage Unit
DFT   Diagnostic Function Test
DFW   Disk File Write
DGBC   Digital Geoballistic Computer System
DIAM   Data Independent Architecture Model
DID   Distant Dependent
DIDS   Digital Information Display System
DIG   Digital Input Gate
DIM   Device Interface Module
DIO   Direct Input Output
DIOS   Distribution Information and
           Optimising System
DIP   Dual Inline Package
DISS   Digital Interface Switching System
DISTRO Distribution Rotation
DKI   Data Key Idle
DL   Dynamic Loader
DLCS   Data Line Concentrator System
DLE   Data Link Escape
DLT   Data Loop Transceiver
DLU   Data Line Unit
DMA   Direct Memory Access
DMC   Direct Multiplexed Control
DME   Distance Measuring Equipment
DML   Data Manipulation Language
DMM   Data Manipulation Mode
DMS   Database Management System
DMS   Display Management System
DNC   Direct Numerical Control
DOCSYS Display of Chromosome Statistics
           System
DOR   Digital Output Relay
DOS   Disc Operating System
DOS   Dix Operating System
DP   Data Processing
DPC   Data Processing Control
DPC   Display Processor Code
DPDT   Double Pole Double Throw
DPMA   Data Processing Management Association
DPS   Data Processing Subsystem
DPSA   Data Processing Supplies Association
DPST   Double Pole Single Throw
DRE   Data Recording Equipment
DRIDAC Drum Input to Digital Automatic
           Computer
DS   Data Set
DS   Digit Select
DSCB   Data Set Control Block
DSE   Data Set Extension
DSL   Data Set Label
DSS   Digital Sub-system
DSSM   Dynamic Sequencing and Segregation
           Model
DSU   Data Selector Units
DTCU   Data Transmission Control Unit
DTD   Data Transfer Done
DTF   Definite Tape File

DTL	Diode Transistor Logic	EOT	End of Transmission
DTR	Disposable Tape Reel	EOV	End of Volume
DTR	Distribution Tape Reel	EPDT	Estimated Project Duration Time
DTSS	Dartmouth Time Sharing System	EPN	External Priority Number
DTTU	Data Transmission Terminal Unit	EPR	Engine Pressure Radio
DTU	Data Transfer Unit	Eq	Equal
DTU	Data Transmission Unit	ER	Error Recovery
DUP	Disk Utility Programme	EREP	Environmental Recording Editing and Printing
DUT	Device Under Test		
DWB	Development Workbook	ERIC	Educational Resources Information Center
DX	Distance		
DX	Duplex	ES	Electronic Switch
EA	Effective Address	ESC	Escape Character
EAC	Error Alert Control	ESD	Ending Sequence Done
EAL	Electric Associates Limited	ESS	Electronic Switching System
EAM	Electronic Accounting Machine	ETB	End of Transmission Block
EAROM	Electrically Alterable Read Only Memories	ETIM	Elapsed Time
		ETX	End of Text
EASY	Efficient Assembly System	EXCP	Execute Channel Program
EAX	Electronic Automatic Exchange	EXEC	Executive
EBAM	Electron Beam Addressed Memory	EXR	Execute and Repeat
EBCDIC	Extended Binary Coded Decimal Information Code	EXTRN	External Reference
		FACE	Field Artillery Computer Equipment
EBCDIC	Extended Binary Coded Decimal Interchange Code	FADAC	Field Artillery Digital Automatic Computer
ECAP	Electronic Circuit Analysis Program	FAKs	File Access Keys
ECB	Event Control Block	FAP	Financial Analysis Program
ECL	Emitter Coupled Logic	FAX	Facsimile
ECM	Extended Core Memory	FCCTS	Federal COBOL Compiler Testing Service
ECMA	European Computer Manufacturers' Association	FCP	File Control Procedure
		FD	File Directory
ECT	Environment Control Table	FD	Floppy Disc
EDA	Electronic Differential Analyser	FD	Full Duplex
EDAC	Error Detection and Correction	FDDS	Flight Data Distribution
EDGE	Electronic Data Gathering Equipment	FDM	Frequency Division Multiplexer
EDP	Electronic Data Processing	FDP	Fast Digital Processor
EDPS	Electronic Data Processing System	FDP	Field Developed Program
EGIF	Equipment Group Interface	FDP	Flight Data Processing
EHF	Extremely High Frequency	FDS	Field Separator
EHV	Extra High Voltage	FDS	Frequency Division Separator
EKG	Electrocardiograph	FDT	Formated Data Tapes
ELD	Edge Lit Display	FDV	Fault Detect Verification
ELSIE	Electronic Letter Sorting and Indicating Equipment	FDX	Full Duplex
		FE	Format Effector
EM	End of Medium	FED	Front End Processor
EMBERS	Emergency Bed Request System	FEP	Financial Evaluation Program
EMU	Expanded Memory Unit	FEP	Front End Processor
ENIAC	Electronic Numerical Integrator and Calculator	FET	Field Effect Transistor
		FF	Flip Flops
ENQ	Enquiry	FF	Form Feed
EOA	End of Address	FFT	Fast Fourier Transform
EOB	End of Block	FID	Fédération International de Documentation
EOE	Error and Omission Excepted		
EOF	End of File	FIDAC	Film Input to Digital Automatic Computer
EOJ	End of Job		
EOL	End of Line	FIDACSYS	FIDAC System
EOM	End of Message	FIGS	Figures Shift
EOR	End of Reel	FINAC	Fast Interline None Active Automatic Control
EOT	End of Tape		
EOT	End of Task	FIND	File Interrogation of Nineteen

	Hundred Data
FIND	Forecasting Institutional Needs for Dartmouth
FIPS	Federal Information Processing Standards
FIT	File Information Table
FJCC	Fall Joint Computer Conference
FLIR	Forward Looking Infrared
FLOP	Floating Point
FM	Frequency Modulation
FMIS	Fiscal Management Information System
FNS	File Nesting Store
FORTRAN	Formula Translation
FOSDIC	Film Optical Sensing Device for Input to Computers
FPH	Floating Point Hardware
FPL	Fox Programming Language
FPL	Functional Problem Log
FPP	Floating Point Processor
FPQA	Fixed Portion Queue Area
FRED	Fractionally Rapid Electronic Device
FRU	Field Replacement Unit
FS	Field Separator
FS	File Separation
FSK	Frequency Shift Keying
FSR	Forward Space Record
FSU	Field Select Unit
FVN	Failed Vector Numbers
GAELIC	Grumman Aerospace Engineering Language for Instructional Checkout
GAM	Graphics Access Method
GaP	Gallium Phosphide
GAP	General Assembly Program
GATD	Graphic Analysis of Three-dimensional Data
GDG	General Data Group
GDMS	Generalized Data Management System
GE	Greater Than/Equal To
GECOS	General Comprehensive Operating Supervisory
GEIS	General Electric Information Service
GEORGE	General Organisational Environment
GIGO	Garbage In Garbage Out
GIS	Generalised Information System
GJP	Graphic Job Processor
GM	Group Mark
GMWM	Group Mark/Word Mark
GNC	Graphic Numerical Control
GPDC	General Purpose Digital Computer
GPLAN	Generalized Data Base Planning System
GPOS	General Purpose Operating System
GQE	Generalized Queue Entry
GRID	Graphical Interactive Display
GRIP	Grandmet Information Processing
GS	Group Separator
GSA	General Services Administration
GSP	General Syntactic Processor
GT	Greater Than
GTE	General Telephone and Electronics

HA	Half Add
HASP	High Level Automatic Scheduling Program
HASP	Houston Automatic Spooling Priority System
HCG	Hardware Character Generator
HD	Half Duplex
HD	High Density
HDX	Half Duplex
HGT	Hypergeometric Group Testing
HIR	Halden Internal Reports
HIS	Honeywell Information System
HLL	Higher Level Language
HLU	House Logic Unit
HO	High Order
HPR	Harden Project Reports
HRS	Host Resident Software
HSP	High Speed Printer
HSR	High Speed Reader
HT	Horizontal Tab
HV	Hardware Virtualizer
IAR	Instruction Address Register
IBM	International Business Machines
IC	Integrated Circuit
ICA	Institute of Chartered Accountants
ICA	International Communication Association
ICC	International Computation Center (Rome)
ICCP	Institute for Certification of Computer Professionals
ICES	Integrated Civil Engineering System
ICFC	Industrial and Commercial Finance Corporation
ICG	Interactive Computer Graphics
ICIP	International Conference on Information Processing
ICL	International Computer Limited
ICS	Input Control Subsystem
ICSMP	Interactive Continuous Systems Modeling Program
ICT	Interaction Control Table
IDF	Intermediate Distribution Frame
IDIOT	Instrumentation Digital On-line Transcriber
IDP	Integrated Data Processing
IDS	Integrated Data Store
IFILE	Interface File
IFIP	International Federation of Information Processing
IFS	Interchange File Separator
IGS	Integrated Graphic System
IGS	Interchange Group Separator
IH	Interaction Handler
ILC	Instruction Length Counter
IM	Item Mark
IMP	Interface Message Processors
IMS	Information Management System
INTERALIS	International Advanced Life Information System
INTIPS	Integrated Information Processing

System
I/O   Input/Output
IOBS   Input/Output Buffering System
IOC   Input Output Controller
IOCS   Input Output Control System
IOLS   Input Output Label System
IOM   Institute of Office Management
IOOP   Input Output Operation
IOP   Input Output Processor
IORB   Input Output Record Block
IOREQ   Input Output Request
IPL   Information Processing Language
IPL   Initial Program Load
IPM   Input Position Map
IPN   Initial Priority Number
IPS   Inches Per Second
IPU   Instruction Processing Unit
IRS   Interchange Record Separator
IS   Information Separator
ISA   Interrupt Storage Area
ISAM   Indexed Sequential Access Method
ISAT   Interrupt Storage Area
ISD   Initial Selection Done
ISD   Internal Symbol Dictionary
ISDS   Integrated Ship Design System
ISR   Image Storage Retrieval
ISVD   Information System for Vocational
          Decisions
ITC   Interval Time Control
ITE   Institute of Communications Engineers
ITF   Interactive Terminal Facility
ITS   Invitation To Send
ITT   International Telephone and Telegraph
ITU   International Telecommunication Unit
IUS   Interchange Unit Separator
IVM   Initial Virtual Memory
IW   Index Word
JCC   Joint Communications Centre
JCL   Job Control Language
JDL   Job Descriptor Language
JEQ   Jump Equal
JES   Job Entry Subsystem
JFET   Junction Field Effect Transistors
JNE   Jump Not Equal
JOVIAL Jules Own Version of the International
          Algorithmic Language
JSL   Job Specification Language
K   Kilo
KB   Keyboard
KB   Kilobits
KB   Kilobytes
KDS   Keydata Station
KSR   Keyboard Sent Receive
KWAC   Keyword And Context
KWIC   Keyword In Context
KWIT   Keyword In Title
KWOC   Keyword Out Of Context
LACES   London Airport Cargo EDP System
LAD   Lookout Assist Device
LAMSAC Local Authorities Management Services

        and Computer Committee
LASER   Light Amplification by Stimulated
          Emission of Radiation
LB   Line Buffer
LBTS   Land Based Test Site
LC   Lower Case
LCB   Line Control Block
LCS   Laboratory Computer Silence
LCS   Large Capacity Store
LCS   Large Core Storage
LCW   Line Control Word
LD   Low Density
LE   Leading Edge
LED   Light Emitting Diodes
LF   Line Feed
LFS   Logical File Structure
LIFO   Last In First Out
LISP   List Processor
LO   Low Order
LOD   Location Dependent
LOS   Loss Of Signal
LOW   Low Core Threshold
LP   Line Printer
LP   Linear Programming
LP   Low Pass
LPA   Link Pack Area
LPL   List Processing Language
LPM   Lines Per Minute
LPS   Line Per Second
LRC   Longitudinal Redundancy Check
LRS   Log and Reporting System
LRU   Least Recently Used
LSB   Least Significantly Bit
LSD   Language for Systems Development
LSD   Last Significant Digit
LSI   Large Scale Integration
LSQA   Local System Queue Area
LT   Less Than
LTRS   Letter Shift
LTU   Line Termination Units
M   Mega
M   Milli
M   Millimeter
MAC   Multi Access Computer
MACDAC Machine Communication with Digital
          Automatic Computer
MACDACSYS MACDAC System
MAD   Machine ANSI Data
MAP   Macro Assembly Program
MAP   Message Acceptance Pulse
MAR   Memory Address Register
MAT   Micro Alloy Transistor
MBS   Multiple Batch Station
MBU   Memory Buffer Unit
MCAR   Machine Check Analysis and Recording
MCC   Minichannel Communications Control
MCH   Machine Check Handler
MCM   Moving Coil Motor
MCP   Master Control Program
MCP   Message Control Program

MCR	Master Control Routine	MT/ST	Magnetic Tape Selectric Typewriter
MCRR	Machine Check Recording and Recovery	MTTR	Mean Time To Repair
MCS	Master Control System	MTU	Magnetic Tape Unit
MCT	Mobile Communication Terminal	MUI	Module Interface Unit
MCU	Memory Control Unit	MV	Measured Vectors
MCU	Microprogrammed Control Unit	MVM	Minimum Virtual Memory
MCU	Multiplexer Control Unit	MVT	Multi-programming Variable Tasks
MDA	Multi Dimensional Access	MWR	Magnetic Tape Write Memory
MDA	Multi Dimensional Array	NA	Not Assigned
MDC	Materials Distribution Center	NA	Not Available
MDD	Machine Dependence Data	NAK	Negative Acknowledgment
MDF	Main Distribution Frame	NC	Numbering Counter
MDP	Missile Data Processor	NC	Numerical Control
MDS	Mohawk Data System	NCC	National Computing Centre
MDT	Mean Down Time	NCC	Network Computer Center
MEDAC	Medical Electronic Data Acquisition and Control	NCR	National Cash Register
		NDC	National Data Communication
MFT	Multiprogramming Fixed Task	NDPS	National Data Processing Service
MIACS	Manufacturing Information and Control System	NDRO	Non-Destructive Readout
		NEAT	NCR Electronic Autocoding Technique
MIC	Master Interrupt Control	NEL	National Engineering Laboratory
MICR	Magnetic Ink Character Recognition	NEMA	National Electrical Manufacturers' Association
MICS	Manufacturing Information and Control System		
		NIC	Network Information Center
MIR	Music Information Retrieval	NIC	Nineteen-Hundred Indexing and Cataloguing
MISP	Medical Information Systems Program		
MIT	Master Instruction Tape	NICOL	Nineteen-Hundred Commercial Language
MITI	Ministry of International Trade and Industry	NIMMS	Nineteen-Hundred Integrated Modular Management System
MIX	Master Index		
ML	Machine Language	NIP	Nucleus Initialisation Procedure
MMR	Multiple Match Resolver	NIPS	NMCS Information Processing System
MN	Motor Number	NJCC	National Joint Computer Committee
MOE	Measure of Effectiveness	NL	New Line
MOL	Machine Oriented Language	NLP	Non-Linear Programming
MOP	Multiple On-line Programming	NMC	Network Measurement Center
MOS	Metal Oxide Semiconductor	NMCS	National Military Command System
MOS	Metal Oxide Silicon	NMSD	Next Most Significant Digit
MP	Measure Pragmetric	NPL	New Programming Language
MPPL	Multi-Purpose Programming Language	NRN	Negative Run Number
MPS	Modular-Runtimelinkable Programming System	NRZ	Non Return to Zero
		NRZI	Non Return to Zero Inverted
MPS	Multiprogramming System	NSV	Net Sales Value
MPSX	Mathematical Programming System Extended	OBR	Outboard Recorder
		OCI	Optically Coupled Isolator
MR	Memory Information Register	OCR	Optical Character Reader
MSAM	Multiple Sequential Access Method	OCR	Optical Character Recognition
MSB	Most Significant Bit	OCS	Output Control Subsystem
MSD	Most Significant Digit	OCT	Operational Cycle Time
MSF	Master Source File	OCU	Operational Control Unit
MSPLT	Master Source Program Library Tape	OEM	Original Equipment Manufacturer
MSR	Machine Status Register	OEMI	Office Equipment Manufacturers' Institute
MSU	Modern Sharing Unit		
MT	Magnetic Tape	OES	Order Entry System
MT	Message Table	OJT	On Job Training
MTBF	Mean Time Between Failure	OCPARS	On Line Pattern Analysis and Recognition System
MTCA	Multiple Terminal Communications Adapter		
		OLTEP	On-Line Test Executive Program
MTPT	Minimal Total Processing Time	OLTS	On-Line Test System
MTS	Michigan Terminal System	OMR	Optical Mark Reading
		OMR	Optical Mark Recognition

OPGENS Optical Pollution Surveillance Schedule Generating System
OPM   Operation Per Minute
OPM   Output Position Map
OPTIM Order Point Technique for Inventory Management
ORS   Operational Research Society
OS   Operating System
OSIL   Operating System Implementation Language
OSM   Option Select Mode
OSTI   Office for Scientific and Technical Information
OTU   Operational Taxonomic Unit
p   Print
PABX   Private Automatic Branch Exchange
PAC   Package Assembly Circuit
PACT   Project for the Advancement of Coding Techniques
PAD   Positioning Arm Disc
PAGE   Package Cram Executive
PAM   Process Automatic Monitor
PAM   Pulse Amplitude Modulation
PAR   Processor Address Register
PAT   Programmable Automatic Tester
PAT   Programmer's Aptitude Test
PATSY Programmer's Automatic Testing System
PAX   Private Automatic Exchange
PB   Peripheral Buffer
PBX   Private Branch Exchange
PC   Parametric Cubic
PC   Printed Circuit
PC   Processor Controller
PC   Program Computer
PC   Punch Card
PCB   Printed Circuit Board
PCC   Peripheral Control Computer
PCC   Power Control Center
PCI   Programmed Control Interrupt
PCL   Process Control Language
PCM   Pulse Code Modulation
PCM   Punched Card Machine
PCMI   Photochromic Microimage
PCOS   Process Control Operating System
PCP   Primary Control Program
PCP   Programmable Communication Processor
PCR   Program Control Register
PCS   Print Contrast System
PCU   Program Control Unit
PD   Performance Data
PDAID Problem Determination Aid
PDAPS Pollution Detection and Prevention System
PDL   Procedure Definition Language
PDM   Pulse Duration Modulation
PE   Processing Elements
PEP   Programme Evaluation Procedure
PERT   Program Evaluation Review Technique
PERT   Programme Evaluation Research Task
PF   Punch Off

PFN   Permanent File Name
PGLIN Page and Line
PI   Programmed Instruction
PI   Programmer's Interface
PIC   Process Interface Control
PICS   Production Information and Control System
PID   Pseudo Interrupt Device
PIOU   Parallel Input/Output Unit
PIP   Peripheral Interchange Program
PL   Programming Language
PLACE Programming Language for Automatic Checkout Equipment
PLAN   Programming Language Nineteen Hundred
PL/I   Programming Language One
PLUTO Parts Listing and Used On Techniques
PM   Post Mortem
PMB   Post Mortem Dump
PMD   Program Module Dictionary
PMS   Project Management System
PMS   Public Message Service
PN   Punch On
POC   Process Operater's Console
POGO   Programmer Oriented Graphic Operation
POL   Problem Oriented Language
POS   Product-of-Sums
POWU   Post Office Work Unit
pp   Parallel Processor
pp   Peripheral Processor
PP-DC Programming Panels and Decoding Circuits
PPI   Planar-Plug-In
PPM   Pulse Position Modulation
PPO   Precedence Partition and Outdegree
PPQA   Pageable Partition Queue Area
PPR   Precedence Partition and Random Assignment
PRL   Print Lister
PROFIT Program for Financed Insurance Techniques
PROM   Programmable Read Only Memory
PROMPT Production Reviewing, Organising and Monitoring of Performance Techniques
PROP   Profit Rating Of Projects
PROSPER Profit Simulation Planning and Evaluation of Risk
PROSPRO Process Systems Program
PRT   Program Reference Table
PS   Problem Specification
PS   Program Stores
PS   Programming System
PSA   Prefix Storage Area
PSECT Phototype Section
PSG   Programme Sequence Control
PSK   Phase Shift Keyed
PSL   Problem Specification Language
PSN   Public Switched Network
PSNS   Programmable Sampling Network Switch
PSP   Paper Tape Space
PSP   Programmable Signal Processor

PSU	Port Sharing Unit	ROS	Read Only Storage
PSW	Program Status Word	ROTR	Receive Only Typing Reperforator
PT	Paper Tape	RP	Record Processor
PTL	Process and Test Language	RPG	Report Program Generator
PTP	Paper Tape Punch	RPQ	Request for Price Quotation
PTP	Point to Point	RPS	Revolutions Per Second
PTR	Paper Tape Reader	RS	Reader Stop
PTT	Push To Talk	RS	Recorder Separator
PU	Processor Unit	RSDP	Remote Site Data
PVD	Plan Video Display	RSPI	Resident Shared Page Index
QAM	Queued Access Method	RT	Reperforator Transmitter
QC	Quantam Count	RTAM	Remote Terminal Access Method
QCB	Queued Control Block	RTE	Real Time Executive
QED	Quick Text Editor	RTI	Referred To Input
QISAM	Queued Indexed Sequential Access Method	RTL	Resister Transistor Logic
		RTM	Real Time Monitor
QL	Query Language	RTM	Response Time Module
QSAM	Queued Sequential Access Method	RTO	Referred To Output
QTAM	Queued Telecommunications Access Method	RTOS	Real Time Operating System
		RTS	Real Time Subroutines
RA	Replacement Algorithm	RTS	Remote Testing System
RAA	Random Access Array	RTTY	Radio Teletypewriter
RAAP	Residue Arithmetic Associative Processor	RTU	Remote Terminal Unit
		RTX	Real Time Executive
RAAP	Resource Allocation and Planning	RUN	Rewind and Unload
RAAR	RAM Address Register	R/W	Real Write
RAD	Rapid Access Device	SAFT	Shortest Access Time First
RAD	Rapid Access Disc	SAM	Sequential Access Method
RAM	Random Access Memory	SAP	System Assurance Program
RAMAC	Random Access Method of Accounting and Control	SBCA	Sensor Based Control Adapter
		SBT	Surface Barrier Transistor
RATE	Remote Automatic Telemetry Equipment	SBU	Station Buffer Unit
RBM	Real Batch Monitor	SCAN	Stock Control and Analysis
RBP	Registered Business Programmer	SCAN	Supermarket Computer Answering Service
RCS	Remote Control Station	SCARS	Software Configuration Accounting and Reporting System
RCT	Region Control Task		
RD	Read Direct	SCATS	Sequential Controlled Automatic Transistor Start
RDOS	Real Time Disc Operating System		
RDP	Radar Data Processing	SCB	Segment Control Bits
RDS	Relational Data System	SCB	Site Control Block
REFSYST	Reference System	SCBS	System Control Blocks
REGS	Registers	SCICON	Scientific Control
RENM	Request for Next Message	SCL	System Consultants
REQWQ	Requisition Work Queue	SCM	Smith Corona Merchant
RES	Remote Entry Service	SCM	Software Configuration Management
RES	Restore	SCM	Staran Control Module
REW	Rewind	SCOOP	Scientific Computation Of Optimum Programs
RFDU	Reconfiguration and Fault Detection Unit		
		SCU	Station Control Unit
RFP	Request for Proposals	SDA	Share Distribution Agency
RI	Read In	SDA	Source Data Automation
RIC	Relocation Instruction Counter	SDA	Symbolic Device Address
RIP	Ring Index Pointer	SDAT	Symbolic Device Allocation Tables
RJE	Remote Job Entry	SDBP	Small Data Base Package
RMC	Rod Memory Computer	SDCR	Source Data Communication Retrieval
RMS	Recovery Management Support	SDDTTG	Stored Data Definition and Translation Task Group
RMS	Root Mean Square		
RO	Receive Only	SDF	Ship Design File
ROC	Remote Operator's Console	SDF	Standard Data Format
ROM	Read Only Memory	SDI	Select Dissemination of Information

SDM   Staran Debug Module
SDR   Statistical Data Recorder
SDS   Shared Data Set
SDSW   Sense Device Status Word
SEA   Spherical Electrostatic Analyzer
SEP   Separation Parameter
SETF   STARAN Evaluation and Training
         Facility
SETM   Société d'Etudes et de Travaux
         Mécanographiques
SF   Stopping Factor
SFP   Slack Frame Program
SGJP   Satellite Graphic Job Processor
SHAS   Shared Hospital Accounting System
SHREAD Share Register and Dividend
         Warrants
SI   Sample Interval
SI   Shift In
SIA   Service Informatic Analysis
SID   Syntax Improving Device
SIGI   System for Interactive Guidance and
         Information
SIR   Selective Information Retrieval
SITE   Satellite Instructional Television
         Experiment
SJCC   Spring Joint Computer Conference
SKL   Skip Lister
SKP   Ship Line Printer
SLANG Systems Language
SLC   Simulated Linguistic Computer
SLCP   Saturn Launch Computer Program
SLF   System Library File
SLIS   Shared Laboratory Information System
SLOCOP Specific Linear Optimal Control
         Program
SLT   Solid Logic Technology
SLTF   Shortest Latency Time First
SLUR   Shane Library User Report
SM   Set Mode
SM   Storage Mark
SMF   System Management Facilities
SML   Symbolic Machine Language
SMM   Start of Manual Message
SO   Shift Out
SOH   Start Of Heading
SOP   Sum-of-Products
SOS   Start Of Significance
SOTA   State Of The Art
SP   Service Package
SP   Summary Punch
SP   Supervisory Printer
SPACE Symbolic Programming Anyone Can Enjoy
SPAM   Satellite Processor Access Method
SPASM System Performance and Activity
         Software Monitor
SPC   Stored Program Control Exchange
spdt   Single Pole Double Throw
SPEDE System for Processing Educational
         Data Electronically
SPI   Single Program Indicator

SPIDAC Specimen Input to Digital Automatic
         Computer
SPIDACSYS SPIDAC System
SPIT   Selective Printing of Items from Tape
SPL   Space Programming Language
SPOOL Simultaneous Peripheral Operation
         On-Line
SPR   Supervisory Printer Read
SPST   Single Pole Single Throw
SPT   Shared Page Table
SQA   System Queue Area
SR   Sorter Reader
SRB   Sorter Reader Buffered
SRF   Sorter Reader Flow
SRL   System Reference Library
SRT   Standard Radio and Telefon
SSD   SHARE Secretarial Distribution
SSDR   Steady State Determining Routine
SSL   Software Sciences Limited
SST   Set Strobe Time
ST   Segment Table
STARFIRE System To Accumulate and Retrieve
         Financial Information with
         Random Extraction
STB   Segment Tag Bits
STC   Standard Telephone Cables
STD   Subscriber Trunk Dialling
STDN   Spacecraft Tracking and Data Network
STEP   Supervisory Tape Executive Program
STI   Scientific and Technical Information
STR   Synchronous Transmitter Receiver
STX   Start of Text
SUB   Substitute
SVC   Supervisory Cell
SVM   Silicon Video Memory
SWADS Scheduler Work Area Data Set
SWBS   Ship Work Breakdown Structure
SYNTAXSYS SYNTAX System
SYSGEN System Generation
SYSIN System Input
SYSOUT System Output
SYSRC System Reference Count
TA   Tape Address
TABSIN Tabulating Simulator
TAM   Terminal Access Method
TC   Tape Command
TCAM   Telecommunications Access Method
TCB   Task Control Block
TCB   Terminal Control Block
TCS   Terminal Communications Subsystem
TCU   Transmission Control Unit
TD   Transmitter Distributor
TDM   Time Division Multiplex
TDMA   Time Division Multiple Access
TDMS   Time-sharing Data Management System
TDS   Tertiary Data Set
TDT   Task Dispatch Table
TDTL   Tunnel Diode Transistor Logic
TDX   Time Division Exchange
TFT   Thin Film Technology

TFZ	Transfer Zone	USASI	United States of America Standard Institute
THOR	Tape Handling Option Routines	USI	User System Interface
TIC	Task Interrupt Control	USSM	United Systems Simulation Model
TIN	Temperature Independent	UTS	Universal Time-sharing System
TIP	Technical Information Program	UUT	Unit Under Test
TIPTOP	Tape Input/Tape Output	VAM	Virtual Access Method
TJID	Terminal Job Identification	VAN	Value Added Networks
TLU	Table Look Up	VCD	Variable Center Distance
TM	Tape Mark	VDU	Visual Display Unit
TMP	Terminal Monitor Program	VFU	Vertical Format Unit
TMXO	Tactical Miniature Crystal Oscillator	VG	Voice Grade
TOD	Time Of Day	VIDIAC	Vidicon Input to Automatic Computer
TOM	Topological Optimization Module	VIN	Vehicle Identification Numbers
TOPS	Telephone Order Processing System	VITAL	VAST Interface Test Application Language
TOS	Tactical Operating System	VM	Virtual Machine
TOS	Tape Operating System	VMA	Virtual Memory Allocation
TOS	Test Operating System	VMCB	Virtual Machine Control Block
TPE	Teleprocessing Executive	VMID	Virtual Machine Identifier
TPS	Telecommunications Programming System	VMM	Virtual Machine Monitor
TRAN	Transit	VMT	Video Matrix Terminal
TS	Tape Status	VMTAB	Virtual Machine Table
TSC	Time Sharing Control	VOD	Volume Discount
TSC	Transmitter Start Code	VOSC	VAST Operating System Code
TSE	Tactical Support Equipment	VP	Virtual Processor
TSE	Time Slide End	VPAM	Virtual Partitioned Access Method
TSI	Task Status Index	VPSW	Virtual Program Status Word
TSO	Time Sharing Option	VRC	Virtual Redundancy Check
TSS	Time Sharing System	VRC	Visual Record Computer
TSX	Time Sharing Executives	VS	Variable Stores
TT	Teletypewriter	VSAM	Virtual Sequential Access Method
TTL	Transistor Transistor Logic	VSPX	Vehicle Scheduling Program Extended
TTS	Teletypesetter	VSR	Validation Summary Report
TTY	Teletype	VT	Vertical Tabulation
TU	Tape Unit	VTOC	Volume Table of Content
TUCC	Triangle Universities Computation Center	VU	Voice Unit
TV	Test Vector	WATS	Wide Area Telephone Service
TVC	Control Tag Vector	WD	Write Direct
TVDR	Tag Vector Display Register	WIP	Work In Progress
TVG	Time Varied Gain	WKQDR	Work Queue Directory
TVR	Response Tag Vector	WM	Work Mark
TVW	Word Tag Vector	WPM	Words Per Minute
TW	Tape Word	WSCS	Wide Sense Cyclo-Stationary
Tw	Typewriter	WTM	Write Tape Mark
TWAIT	Terminal Wait	WXTRN	Weak External Reference
TWB	Typewriter Buffer	XDS	Xerox Data System
TWX	Teletypewriter Exchange	XIO	Executive Input/Output
UADS	User Attribute Data Set	XPN	External Priority Number
UC	Upper Case	XPT	External Page Table
UCBS	Unit Control Blocks	XSPT	External Shared Page Table
UCC	University Computer Company	XTSI	Extended Task Status Index
UCK	United Check	Z	Zero
UCS	Universal Character Set	Zn	Zone
UCSTR	Universal Code Synchronous Transmitter Receiver		
UDAS	Unified Direct Access System		
UDR	Universal Document Reader	COPYRIGHT	
UDT	Universal Document Transport		
UL	Upper Limit	ABU	Asian Broadcasting Union
US	United Separator	AIPPI	International Association for the

Protection of Industrial Property

ALPI	International Literary and Artistic Association
ATPI	American Textbook Publishers Institute
BIRPI	International Bureaux for the Property of Intellectual Property
CEIF	Council of Europe Industrial Federation
CEPT	European Conference of Post and Telecommunications
CHC	Clearinghouse for Copyright
CICP	Committee to Investigate Copyright Problems
FIA	International Federation of Actors
FICPI	International Federation of Patent Agents
FIM	International Federation of Musicians
IBY	International Book Year
IDCAS	Industrial Development Center for Arab States
IFPI	International Federation of the Photographic Industry
IFTC	International Film and Television Council
ILAI	International Literary and Artistic Association
IPA	International Publishers' Association
IPC	International Classification of Patents
ISETU	International Secretariat of Entertainment Trade Unions
IWG	International Writers' Guild
LAFTA	Latin American Free Trade Association
PCT	Patent Cooperation Treaty
PRS	Performing Right Society
SODACT	Society of Authors and Composers of Tunisia
UIEC	International Union of Cinematograph Exhibitors
UNCITRAL	United Nations Commission on International Trade Law
UPOV	Union for the Protection of Plant Varieties
URTNA	Union of National Radio and Television Organizations of Africa
VCR	Video Cassette Recorder
WIPO	World Intellectual Property Organization

DAIRY SCIENCES

ACI	Adjusted Calving Interval
ADA	American Dairy Association
ADF	Acid Detergent Fiber
ADI	Accepted Daily Intakes
ADSA	American Dairy Science Association
ADV	Acid Degree Values
AEC	Aminoethyl Cellulose
AI	Artificial Insemination

ALM	Applied Laboratory Methods
AMC	Acetylmethylcarbon
AMCP	Abnormal Milk Control Program
AMHIC	Automatic Merchandising Health Industry Council
AMP	Adenosine Monophosphate
AMPI	Associated Milk Producers' Information (US)
ANOVA	Analysis of Variation
ANS	Aniline Naphthalene Sulfonate
APC	Aerobic Plate Counts
ASP	Antisena Seminal Plasma
AV	Artificial Vagina
BAA	Breed Age Average
BCB	Brown Cardboard
BCM	Bromochloromethane
BEV	Bovine Enterovirus
BGA	Brilliant Green Agar
BHA	Butylated Hydroxy Anisole
BHIA	Brain Heart Infusion Agar
BHIB	Brain Heart Infusion Broth
BML	Bovine Milk Lysozyme
BMS	Buttermilk Solids
BRT	Brucella Ring Test
BS	Bismuth Sulphite
BSA	Bovine Serum Albumin
BVD	Bovine Viral Diarrhoea
BWP	Brown Wrapping Paper
CaF	Calcium Free
CC	Coliform Count
CCC	Chlorochline Chloride
CF	Corn Flour
CF	Crude Fiber
CHO	Carbohydrates
CHY	Chymotrypsinogen
CIP	Cleaned-In-Place
CMT	California Mastitis Test
COD	Chemical Oxygen Demand
CPF	Colloidal Phosphate Free
CRSMP	Calcium Reduced Skim Milk Powder
CTF	Cottonseed Flour
CVM	Cervico Vaginal
CVT	Crystal Violet Tetrazolium
DCE-FPC	Dichloroethane Extracted Fish Protein Concentrate
DE	Digestible Energy
DEAE	Diethylaminoethyl
DEPC	Diethylpyrocarbonate
DES	Desoxycholate
DHI	Dairy Herd Improvement
DHIA	Dairy Herd Improvement Association (US)
DM	Dry Matter
DMD	Dry Matter Disappearance
DMSCC	Direct Microscopic Somatic Cell Count
DNA	Deoxyribonucleic Acid
DNMRT	Duncan's New Multiple Range Test
DSF	Defatted Soy Flour
DSI	Dairy Society International
DSP	Dextran Sulphate Precipitable

DTA	Differential Thermal Analysis	NSab	Nasal Secretion Antibody
DTT	Dithiotheitol	OD	Optical Density
DWCM	Dried Weight of Cell Mass	OVA	Ovalbumin
EDS	Estimated Daughter Superiority	OVX	Ovariectomized
EDTA	Ethylenediaminetetraacete	PAGE	Polyacrylamide Gel Electrophoresis
EMB	Eosine Methylene Blue	PBC	Psychotrophic Count
ENE	Estimated Net Energy	PBI	Protein Bound Iodine
ETSL	Estimated Total Shelf Life	PCMB	p-Chloromercuribenzoate
EWL	Egg White Lysozyme	PDF	Protected Difference Fat
FAT	Fluorescent Antibody Test	PDM	Protected Difference Milk
FCC	Food Contaminants Commission (US)	PDW	Partially Delactosed Whey
FCM	Fat Convected Milk	PDWP	Partially Delactosed Whey Powder
FFA	Free Fatty Acids	PEG	Polyethylene Glycol
FFSF	Full Fat Soy Flour	PEN	Penicillin
FOD	Flies-Odors-Ducts	PF	Peanut Flour
FPC	Fish Protein Concentrate	PHS	Paternal Half Sister
FSC	Free Secretory Component	PI	Preliminary Incubation
FTU	Formazin Turbidity Units	PMSG	Pregnant Mare Serum Gonadotrophin
GH	Growth Hormone	PSD	Paternal Sister Dam
GLC	Gas Liquid Chromatography	PTH	Parathyroid Hormone
GPABP	Guinea Pig Anti-Bovine Prolactin	RDA	Recommended Dietary Allowances
GPC	Gel Permeation Chromatography	RF	Rice Flour
GPCS	Guinea Pig Control Serum	RH	Relative Humidity
HCS	Human Chorionic Somatomammotropin	SAb	Serum Antibody
HGLF	High Grain Low Fibre	SAC	Sulphacetamide
HLA	Human Lymphocyte Antigens	SAGPGG	Sheep Anti-Guinea Pig Gamma Globulin
HMC	High Moisture Shelled Corn	SBM	Soybean Meal
HML	Human Milk Lysozyme	SCB	Selenite Cystine Broth
HP	Hydroxyproline	SCC	Somatic Cell Concentration
HTSM	High Temperature Skim Milk	SCL	Serum Cholesterol Level
IBR	Infectious Bovine Rhinotracheitis	SCM	Solid Collected Milk
ICMSF	International Commission on Microbiological Specifications for Food	SCS	Soybean Corn Silage
		SDS	Sodium Dodecyl Sulphate
		SEZ	Sulphaerhoxypyridizine
IN	Intranasally	SG	Suerglyceride
IOFC	Income Over Feed Cost	SGOT	Serum Glutamic Oxalic Transaminase
IR	Intraruminal	SMA	Standard Methods Agar
LBG	Locust Beam Gun	SMEDP	Standard Methods for the Examination of Dairy Products
LH	Luteal Hormone		
LH	Luteinizing Hormone	SMT	Sulphamethazine
LIA	Lysine Iron Agar	SMUF	Simulated Milk Ultrafiltrate
LPC	Laboratory Pasteurized Count	SNF	Solids Not Fat
LPL	Lipoprotein Lipase	SPA	Standard Plate Agar
ME	Mature Equivalent	SS	Salmonella Shigella
ME	Mercaptoethanol	SS	Shigella Agar
ME	Metabolizable Energy	SSP	Sorghum Soy Pellets
MGA	Melengestrol Acetate	STT	Standard Tube Test
MHA	Methionine Hydroxy Analog	TAEC	Thiolated Aminoethyl Cellulose
MIW	Milk Ingredient Water	TBC	Thermophilic Count
MSA	Mannitol Salt Agar	TD	Thoracic Duct
MTA	Milko Tester Automatic	TDN	Total Digestible Nutrient
MUF	Milk Ultrafiltrate	TDT	Terminal Death Time
MYP	Mannito-egg Yolk Polymyxin	TEM	Tomato Extract Medium
NAMA	National Automatic Merchandising Association	TENE	Total Estimated Net Energy Consumed
		TER	Tergitol
NEM	N-ethylmaleimide	TFR	Total Follicular Response
NFDM	Non-Fat Dry Milk	TLC	Thin Layer Chromatography
NFMS	Non-Fat Milk Solids	TMAO	Trimethylamine Oxide
NFN	Non-Fat Milk	TMN	Trimethylamine Nitrogen
NMC	National Mastitis Council	TP	Total Protein

TRU	Total Recycle Unit
TSA	Trypticase Soy Agar
TSB	Trypticase Soy Broth
TSI	Triple Sugar Iron
TSN	Tryptone-Sulphite-Neomycin
TSR	Thyroid [Hormone] Secretion Rate
TTC	Triphenyltetrazolium Chroride
TVC	Total Viable Counts
TVW	Total Volatile Nitrogen
UHT	Ultra High Temperature
VPA	Voltage Fatty Acids
VLO	Viable Parahaemolyticus
VRB	Violet Red Bile
WPS	Water Phase Salt
WRD	Whole Rumen Digesta
WWF	Whole Wheat Flour
XLDP	Xylose Lysine Desoxycholatepeplon Agar
XO	Xanthine Oxidase
YMC	Yeast Mold Count

ELECTRONICS AND ELECTRICAL ENGINEERING

A	Ammeter
a	Anode
AADC	All Applications Digital Computer
AC	Alternating Current
ACE	Area Control Error
ACL	Automatic Circuit Layout
ACP	Azimuth Charge Pulse
ACU	Automatic Calling Unit
AEEC	Airline Electric Engineering Committee
AEI	Associated Electrical Industries
AEP	American Electric Power
AES	Auger Electron Spectrum
AFT	Adaptive Ferroelectric Transformer
AGC	Automatic Gain Control
AH	Ampere Hour
AH	Analog Hybrid
AIDE	Automated Image Device Evaluation
AIEE	American Institute of Electrical Engineering
AIMIS	Advanced Integrated Modular Instrument System
ALU	Arithmetic and Logic Unit
AM	Analog Monolithic
APPG	Adjacent Phase Pulse Generator
AR	Arithmetic Register
AR	Associative Register
ARP	Azimuth Reset Pulse
ARQ	Automatic Request for Repetition
ASP	Attached Support Processor
AST	Auxiliary Segment Table
AT	Audit Trail
AU	Amplifier Unit
AWACS	Airborne Warning and Control System
B	Base
BASIC	Beginner's All Purpose Symbolic Instruction Code
BCD	Binary Coded Decimal

BCDC	Binary Code Decimal Counters
BCL	Burroughs Common Language
BEF	Band Elimination Filter
BEST	Business Electronics Systems Technique
BFER	Base Field Effect Register
BFO	Beat Frequency Oscillator
BLF	Band Limiting Filter
BP	Bandpass
BPF	Band Pass Filter
BRC	Branch Conditional
BRU	Branch Unconditional
BTAM	Basic Telecommunications Access Method
BTB	Bus Tie Breakers
BUGS	Brown University Graphic System
BUIC	Back Up Interceptor Control
C	Coulombmeter
CADA	Computer Aided Design Analysis
CAI	Computer Aided Instruction
CAPE	Communications Automatic Processing Equipment
CAPR	Catalog of Programs
CARN	Conditional Analysis for Random Networks
CAU	Compare Alpha Unequal
CAX	Community Automatic Exchange
CB	Coupled Biquad
CBT	Core Block Table
CCD	Charged Coupled Device
CCK	Channel Control Check
CCW	Channel Command Word
CD	Cage Dipole
CD	Check Digit
CDC	Call Direct Code
CDK	Channel Data Check
CDMA	Code Division Multiple Access
CDX	Control Differential Transmitter
CE	Channel End
CEADI	Coloured Electronic Altitude Director Indicator
CEGB	Central Electricity Generating Board
CEU	Communications Expansion Unit
CFD	Constant Fraction Discriminator
CFER	Collector Field Effect Register
CICD	Computer Aided Circuit Design
CIDA	Current Input Differential Amplifier
CLD	Constant Level Discriminator
CM	Common Mode
CM	Cross Modulation
CMA	Contact-Making Ammeter
CML	Current Mode Logic
CMOS	Contemporary Metal Oxide Semiconductor
CMR	Common Mode Rejection
CMTC	Coupled Monostable Trigger Circuit
CMV	Common Mode Voltage
CMV	Contact Making Voltmeter
CNU	Compare Numeric Unequal
COT	Cycleoctatetraene
CPM	Critical Path Method
CPS	Cycles Per Second
CPW	Coplanar Waveguide

CRO	Cathode Ray Oscillograph
CRO	Cathode Ray Oscilloscope
CRT	Cathode Ray Tube
CS	Cyclo-Stationary
CSECT	Control Section
CSML	Continuous Self Mode Locking
CT	Control Transformer
CT	Current Transformer
CTC	Communications Transistor Corporation (US)
CTTL	Complementary Transistor Transistor Logic
CUE	Control Unit End
CX	Control Transmitter
CZE	Compare Zone Equal
CZU	Compare Zone Unequal
d	Diode
d	Drain
DA	Delay Amplifier
DART	Daily Automatic Rescheduling Technique
DAT	Dynamic Address Translator
DB	Double Biased
DBM	Decibels Meter
DBRN	Decibel Based Reference Noise
DC	Direct Current
DCB	Drawout Circuit Breakers
DCTL	Direct Coupled Transistor Logic
DDL	Data Description Language
DDS	Digital Spectrum Stabilizer
DECM	Defence Electronic Countermeasures System
DECOR	Digital Electronic Continuous Ranging
DECTRA	Decca Tracking and Ranging
DEFT	Dynamic Error Free Transmission
DELRAC	Decca Long Range Area Coverage
DELTIC	Delay-Line Time Compression
DESC	Defense Electronic Supply Center
DEUCE	Digital Electronic Universal Calculating Engine
DHS	Data Handling System
DIAN	Decca Integrated Airborne Navigation
DLA	Distributed Lumped Active
DM	Demand Meter
DM	Differential Mode
DM	Digital Monolithic
DPCM	Differential Pulse Code Modulation
DPDT	Double Pole Double Throw
DPM	Digital Panel Meters
DPST	Double Pole Single Throw
DST	Data Summary Tape
DT	Deuterium and Tritium
DTAS	Data Transmission and Switching System
DTCP	Diode Transistor Compound Pair
DTL	Diode Transistor Logic
DTR	Demand Totalizing Relay
DVM	Digital Voltmeters
EADI	Electronic Altitude Director Indicator
EAL	Electronic Associates Limited
EAM	Electronic Accounting Machine
EASCON	Electronics and Aerospace Systems Conference

EAX	Electronic Automatic Exchange
EC	Electrical Conductivities
ECAC	Electromagnetic Compatibility Analysis Center
ECAP	Electronic Circuit Analysis Program
ECAR	East Central Area Reliability
ECM	Electronics Countermeasures
EDA	Electronic Differential Analyser
EDAC	Error Detection and Correction
EDCL	Electrical Discharge Correction Lasers
EDGE	Electronic Data Gathering Equipment
EDITAR	Electronic Digital Tracking and Ranging
EDP	Electronic Data Processing
EEG	Electroencephalographic
EEMTIC	Electrical and Electronic Measurement and Test Instruments Conference
EFAS	Electronic Flash Approach System
EFL	Emitter Follower Logic
EG	Electron Gun
EHV	Extra High Voltage
EIA	Electronic Industries Association
ELINT	Electronic Intelligent
ELSIE	Electronic Letter Sorting and Indicating Equipment
ELTAD	Emergency Locator Transmitters Automatic Deployable
ELTAP	Emergency Locator Transmitters Automatic Portable
EMC	Electromagnetic Compatibility
EMC	Excess Minority Carriers
EMM	Ebers Moll Model
ENIAC	Electronic Numerical Integrator and Calculator
EP	Electrically Polarized
EPD	Electronic Proximity Detector
EPSPs	Excitatory Post Synaptic Potentials
EPU	Emergency Power Unit
EQ	Equalizer
EQUATE	Electronic Quality Assurance Test Equipment
ER	Electronic Ram
ERA	Electrical Research Association (UK)
ERC	Electronic Research Center (US)
ES	Electronic Switch
ESS	Electronic Switching System
ETC	Electrothermal Integrated Circuits
ETM	Electronic Test and Measurement
EU	Electronic Unit
eV	Electronvolt
f	Filament
f	Frequency
f-	Filament Negative
FAV	Fast Acting Valve
FCA	Faraday Cup Array
fct	Filament Center Tap
FDM	Frequency Division Multiplexing
FDMA	Frequency Division Multiple Access
FDNR	Frequency Dependent Negative Register
FDNR	Frequency Dependent Negative Resistance

FDS	Field Separator	IMP	Interface Message Processor
FDS	Frequency Division Separator	IMS	International Magnetospheric Study
FET	Field Effect Transistor	IPSPS	Inhibitory Post Synaptic Potentials
FETT	Field Effect Tetrode Transistor	IRM	Image Rejection Mixer
FFT	Fast Fourier Transform	JCL	Job Control Language
FL-BE	Filter Band Elimination	JFET	Junction Field Effect Transistors
FL-BP	Filter Bandpass	KeV	Kilovolts
FLF	Follow the Leader Feedback	LED	Light Emitting Diodes
FL-HP	Filter High Pass	LES	Light Emitting Switch
FLIR	Forward Looking Infrared	LESC	Light Emitting Switch Control
FL-LP	Filter Low Pass	LFCM	Low Frequency Cross Modulation
FM	Frequency Modulation	LFFET	Low Frequency Field Effect Transistors
FM	Frequency Multiplier	LG	Linear Gate
FMICW	Frequency Modulated Intermittent Continuous Wane	LH	Linear Hybrid
		LIC	Linear Integrated Circuit
FPN	Fixed Pattern Noise	LLD	Low Level Discriminator
ft	Filament Positive	LM	Linear Monolithic
fT	Transistor Frequency	LP	Low Pass
FTFET	Four Terminal Field Effect Transistor	LSE	Longitudinal Section Electric
FTM	Folded Triangulator Monopole	LSI	Large Scale Integration
FTO	Folded Triangular Dipole	LSIC	Large Scale Integrated Circuits
g	Grid/Gate	LSL	Ladder Static Logic
GB	Gun Branch	LSM	Longitudinal Section Magnetic
GCB	General Circuit Breaker	LTP	Long Tailed Pair
GCR	General Control Relay	LVDT	Linear Variable Differential Transformer
GD	Ground Detector		
GDR	General Design Requirements	M	Magnetron
GE	Gaussian Elimination	MA	Milliammeter
GEC	General Electric Company	MA	Multi-channel Analyser
GEG	General Euclidean Geometry	MAS	Metal Aluminium Oxide
GEGB	General Electricity Generating Board	MB	Magnetron Branch
GIC	Generalized Immittance Converter	MCA	Multichannel Analyzer
GJE	Gauss Jordon Elimination	MEFET	Metal Semiconductor Field Effect Transistor
GPB	Ground Power Breader		
GTD	Geometrical Theory of Diffraction	MeV	Million Electron Volts
h	Heater	MHD	Magnetohydrodynamic
h	Heplode	MIC	Microwave Integrated Circuit
h	Hexode	MIS	Metal Insulator Semiconductor
hct	Heater Centre Tap	MISFETs	Metal Insulator Semiconductor Field Effect Transistors
hp	High Pass		
HSTCO	High Stability Temperature Compensated Crystal Oscillator	ML	Magnetic Latching
		MM	Monostable Multivibrator
htap	Heat Tap	MM	MOS Monolithic
HTL	High Threshold Logic	MMS	Magnetic Median Surface
HVAC	High Voltage Alternative Current	MNOS	Metal-Nitride Oxide Semiconductor
IC	Internal Connection	MNOS	Metal-Nitride Oxide Silicon
ICM	Integral Charge-control Model	MNOSFETs	Metal Nitride Oxide Semiconductor Field Effect Transistors
IDG	Integrated Drive Generator		
IEC	International Electrotechnical Commission	Mod	Modulator
		MOS	Metal Oxide Semiconductor
IEE	Institution of Electrical Engineers	MOS	Metal Oxide Silicon
IEEE	Institute of Electrical and Electronics Engineering	MOSFET	Metal Oxide Semiconductor Field Effect Transistor
		MOS/LSI	Metal Oxide Semiconductor/Large-Scale Integration
IEIS	Integrated Engine Instrument System		
IGFET	Insulated Gate Field Effect Transistor	MOST	Metal Oxide Semiconductor Transistor
IGS	Integrated Graphic System	MRPPS	Maryland Refutation Proof Procedure System
IL	Indication Lamps		
ILO	Injection Locked Oscillators	MSI	Medium Scale Integrated
IM	Intermodulation	MSS	Multispectral Scaling
IMD	Intermodulation Distortion		

MT	Master Time	RS	Resolver
MTF	Mean Time to Failure	RTL	Resistor Transistor Logic
MTL	Merged Transistor Logic	SBD	Schottky Barrier Diode
MTPT	Minimal Total Processing Time	SC	Set Clock
NB	No Bias	SC	Shaping Circuit
NC	No Connection	SCA	Single Channel Analyzer
NESC	National Electrical Safety Code	SCAM	Spectrum Characteristics Analysis and Measurement
NIPS	NMCS Information Processing System		
NM	Noise Margin	SCI	Short Circuit
NM	Noise Meter	SCI	Switched Collector Impedance
NMCS	National Military Command System	SCR	Silicon Controlled Rectifier
NOSHEB	North of Scotland Hydro-Electric Board	SCT	Schottky Clamped Transistor
		SCT	Surface Charge Transistor
NP	No Pin	SCT^2L	Schottky Clamped Transistor Transistor Logic
NPG	Normalized electron-Peak to Gamma-peak		
		SD	Synchronous Detector
NR	Non-Reactive	SDBP	Small Data Base Package
OCV	Open Circuit Voltage	SDM	Site Defence of Minuteman
OHM	Ohmmeter	SEA	Spherical Electrostatic Analyzer
p	Pentode	SER	Single Electron Response
PA	Preamplifier	SETE	Secretariat Electronic Test Equipment
PAA	Phase Antenna Arrays	SFSCL	Shunt Feedback Schottky Clamped
PAM	Peripheral Adapter Module	SHG	Second Harmonic Generation
PAM	Pulse Amplitude Modulation	sic	Semiconductor Integrated Circuit
PC	Printed Circuit	SLIC	Simulation Linear Integrated Circuits
PCS	Power Conditioning System	SLTF	Shortest Latency Time First
PEC	Platform Electronic Cards	SMA	Surface Modeling and Analysis
PED	Pulse Edge Discrimination	SO	Slow Operate
PES	Programmer Electronic Switch	SOS	Silicon-On-Sapphire
PF	Power Factor	SOSTEL	Solid State Electric Logic
PFD	Power Flux Density	spdt	Single Pole Double Throw
PFN	Pulse Forming Network	SR	Slow Releave
PFTE	Polytetrafluorethylene	SSB	Single Side Band
PG	Power Gate	SSCA	Strobed Single Channel Analyser
PH	Phasemeter	SSMA	Spread Spectrum Multiple Access
PI	Position Indicator	SSTR	Solid State Track Detectors
PID	Proportional Integral Derivative	ST-INV	Static Inverter
PLACE	Programming Language for Automatic Checkout Equipment	STVW	Symmetrical Triangle Voltage Waveform
		SUMT	Sequential Unconstrained Minimization Techniques
PLL	Phase-Locked Loop		
PM	Photomultiplier	SVER	Spatial Visual Evoked Response
POGO	Programmer Oriented Graphic Operation	SW	Sandwich Wound
POUT	Power Output	SWD	Surface Wave Device
PPDC	Programming Panels and Decoding Circuits	SY	Syncloroscope
		t	Triode
PRF	Pulse Repetition Frequency	TAC	Time Amplitude Converter
PSD	Pulse Shape Discrimination	TC	Temperature Coefficient
PSG	Phosphosilicate Glass	TC	True Complement
PSK	Phase Shift Keyed	TCR	Temperature Coefficient of Resistance
PTMT	Polyterephalate	TDC	Track Detection Circuit
PZT	Piezoelectric Translator	TDR	Torque Differential Receiver
RBV	Return Beam Vidicon	TDSS	Time Dividing Spectrum Stabilization
RTCL	Register Capacity Transistor Logic	TDX	Torque Differential Transmitter
RD	Recording Demand	TE	Electron Temperature
REBA	Relativistic Electron Beam Accelerator	TEA	Transversely Excited Atmospheric
REC	Recording	TEAs	Transferred Electron Amplifier
RF	Radio Frequency	TEC	Transient Electron Current
RF	Reactive Factor	TEOs	Transferred Electron Oscillators
RKHS	Reducing Kernel Hilbert Space	TEWS	Tactical Electronic Warfare Systems
		TFT	Time-to-Frequency Transformation

THC	Thermal Converter
TI	Ion Temperature
Tj	Junction Temperature
TLM	Telemeter
TLO	Tracking Local Oscillators
TMXO	Tactical Miniature Crystal Oscillator
TNA	Transient Network Analyzer
TP	Timing Pulse
TPF	Two Photon Fluorescence
TR	Torque Receiver
TSCA	Timing Single Channel Analyser
TSD	Touch Sensitive Digitizer
TT	Total Time
TTL	Transistor Transistor Logic
TTS	Transportable Transformer Substations
TTY	Teletypewriter
TU	Transfer Units
TVF	Tape Velocity Fluctuation
TWT	Travelling Wave Tube
UTP	Upper Turning Point
V	Voltmeter
Va	Anode Voltage
VA	Volt Ammeter
VA	Volt-ampere
va(pk)max	Maximum Peak Anode Voltage
VCCS	Voltage Controlled Current Sources
VCE	Collective-Emitter Voltage
VCO	Voltage Controlled Oscillator
VCVS	Voltage Controlled Voltage Source
VER	Visual Evoked Response
Vf	Frequency Voltage
Vh	Heater Voltage
VI	Volume Indicator
VMJ	Vertical Multijunction
VSWR	Voltage Standard Wage Ratio
Vz	Zener Voltage
W	Wattmeter
WGSC	Wide Gap Spark Chamber
WH	Watthour
WSCS	Wide Sense Cyclo-Stationary
YAG	Yttrium Aluminium Garnet
YIG	Yttrium Iron Garnet

ENGINEERING

AACD	Antennas Adjustable Current Distribution
AACS	Asynchronous Address Communications Systems
ACA	Ammoniacal Copper Arsenite
ACC	Acid Copper Chromate
ACF	Autocorrelation Function
ACS	Automatic Control System
ACSM	American Congress of Surveying and Mapping
AD	Adaptive Control
ADI	Alternating Direction Implicit
AE	Architect Engineer
AEC	American Engineering Council

AEC	Autocorrelation Functions
AEDC	Arnold Engineering Development Center (US)
AFIT	Air Force Institute of Technology (US)
AFLC	Air Force Logistics Command (US)
AFP	Adiabatic Fast Passage
AFR	Amplitude Frequency Responses
AFRCE	Air Force Regional Civil Engineer
AFWL	Air Force Weapon Laboratory
AGE	Aerospace Ground Equipment
AGMA	American Gear Manufacturers' Association
AID	Agency for International Development
AID	Automatic Interrogation Distorted
AIS	Automatic Intercity Station
AIT	Architect In Training
AITE	Automatic Intercity Telephone Exchange
AITS	Automatic Integrated Telephone System
AJ	Area Junction
AL	Amplitude Limiter
AL	Artificial Lines
AMC	Automatic Monitoring Circuit
AMMRC	Army Materiel and Mechanics Research Center (US)
ANG-CE	Air National Guard Civil Engineering
ANMC	American National Metric Council
ANPP	Army Nuclear Power Program
APC	Amplitude Phase Conversion
APC	Armoured Personnel Carrier
APD	Avalanche Photodiode
APSA	Automatic Particle Size Analyzer
ARDS	Advanced Remote Display Station
AS	Automatically Switching
ASCET	American Society of Certified Engineering Technicians
ASEB	Aeronautics and Space Engineering Board
ASEE	American Society of Engineering Education
ASME	American Society of Mechanical Engineering
ASP	American Society of Photogrametry
AST	Automatic Shop Tester
ASTM	American Society for Testing Materials
ASU	Automatic Switching Units
ASWG	American Steel Wire Gage
ATC	Automatic Through Centers
ATCA	Automatic Tuned Circuit Adjustment
ATCAA	Automatic Tuned Circuit Adjustment Amplitude
ATGSP	Advanced Test for Graduate Study in Business
ATJ	Automatic Through Junction
ATO	Automatic Trunk Offices
AURA	Association of Universities for Research in Astronomy
AVM	Automatic Vehicle Monitoring
B/A	Baron/Aluminium
BAM	Bituminous Aggregate Mixtures

BCE	Base Civil Engineer	CO	Crystal Oscillator
BCRA	British Ceramic Research Association	COF	Correct Operation Factor
BCRA	British Coke Research Association	CONC	Concrete
BEST	Ballastable Earthmoving Sectionized Tractor	COPEP	Committee of Public Engineering Policy (US)
BGIRA	British Glass Industry Research Association	CPG	Clock Pulse Generator
		CRCP	Continuously Reinforced Concrete Pavements
BHRA	British Hydromechanics Research Association	CRP	Constant Rate of Penetration
BMCS	Bureau of Motor Carrier Safety	CSI	Construction Specification Institute (US)
BOF	Basic Oxygen Furnace		
BRD	Binary Rate Divider	CTR	Collective Television Reception
BSA	Bimetal Steel Aluminium	CTR	Controlled Thermonuclear Reactor
BUT	Broadbend Unbalanced Transformer	CU	Consolidated Undrained
CAL	Cornell Aeronautical Laboratory	CUED	Cambridge University Engineering Department
CAM	Cellulose Acetate Methacrylate		
CAM	Cement Aggregate Mixture	CVS	Constant Volume Sampling
CAS	Central Amplifier Station	CZC	Chromated Zinc Chloride
CCA	Cement and Concrete Association	DC	Direct Connection
CCA	Chromated Copper Arsenate	DC	Dispatcher Console
CCB	Configuration Control Board	DCC	Double Cotton Covered
CCD	Controlled Current Distribution	DCC-MSF	Direct Contract Condensation Multistage Flash
CCE	Chief Construction Engineer		
CCF	Cross Correlation Function	DF	Distribution Feeders
CCIR	International Radio Consultative Committee	DFB	Distribution Feeders Branch
		DIFKIN	Diffusion Kinetics
CD	Coherent Detector	DL	Difference Limen
CdS	Cadmium Sulphide	DMF	Digital Matched Filter
CEBMCO	Corps Engineers Ballistic Missile Construction Office	DMV	Department of Motor Vehicles (US)
		DOA	Differential Operational Amplifiers
CEC	Consulting Engineers Council	DPolT	Differential Polarization Telegraphy
CEFAC	Civil Engineering Field Activities Center	DPSK	Differential Phase Shift Keying
		DPWM	Double Sided Pulse Width Modulation
CEI	Council of Engineering Institutions	DR	Defined Readout
CEMIRT	Civil Engineering Maintenance Inspection, Repair and Training	DS	Digital Signal
		DSS	Discrete Sync System
CES	Coordinate Evaluation System	DT	Data Transmission
CF	Cathode Follower	E	Emitter
CF	Correlation Function	ECO	Electron Coupled Oscillator
CFAP	Copenhagen Frequency Allocation Plan	EGD	Electrogas Dynamics
CFPHT	Constant Traction of Pulse Height Trigger	EHD	Electrohydrodynamic
		EIT	Engineer In Training
CGS	Control Guidance Subsystems	EJC	Engineers Joint Council
CIG	Cryogenic-In-Ground	ELE	Equivalent Logic Element
CIP	Civilian Institution Program	ELMS	Elastic Loop Mobility System
CIR	Characteristic Instants of Restitution	EPOs	Examination Procedure Outlines
CIRIA	Construction Industry Research and Information (UK)	EPR	Engine Pressure Ration
		ERS	Electric Resistant Strain
CISCO	Construction Information System Cost and Operation	ESD	Electronics Systems Division
		FCAP	Fluor Chrome Arsenate Phenol
CL	Cable Link	FCIA	Foreign Credit Insurance Association
CL	Chemiluminescence	FDNR	Frequency Dependent Negative Register
CL	Connecting Lines	FECP	Facility Engineering Charge Proposals
CMB	Concrete Median Barrier	FES	Floride Engineering Society
CMC	Contact Making Clock	FHWA	Federal Highway Administration (US)
CMC	Coordinal Manual Control	FMA	Facilities Management Analysis
CMD	Contract Management District	FPSK	Frequency and Phase Shift Keying
CMD	Coupled Mobility Devices	FRP	Fibre Reinforced Polyester
CMM	Coordinate Measuring Machines	FTC	Federal Trade Commission
CN-CA	Cellulose Nitrate Cellulose Acetate	FTMT	Final Thermomechanical Treatment

FTP	Federal Test Procedure
FUB	Facilities Utilization Board
GDR	Ground Delay Response
GIDEP	Government Industry Data Exchange Program
GLA	Gross Leasable Area
GPSS	General Purpose Simulation Program
GSCG	Ground Systems Coordination Group
GSU	Guaranteed Supply Unit
HIP	Hot Isostatic Pressing
HMC	Horizontal Motion Carriage
HSRI	Highway Safety Research Institute
HTGR	High Temperature Gas Cooled Reactor
HTR	High Temperature Reactors
HVG	High Voltage Generator
HVOSM	Highway Vehicle Object Simulation Model
IABSE	International Association of Bridge and Structural Engineering
IAEA	International Atomic Energy Agency
IAEE	International Association of Earthquake Engineers
IC	Integrated Circuits
ICBM	Inter Continental Ballistic Missiles
ICE	Institute of Civil Engineers (UK)
ICES	Integrated Civil Engineering System
ICSID	Industrial Council of Society of Industrial Design
IEC	International Electrotechnical Commission
IGS	Information Generator System
ILS	Integrated Logistic Support
IOS	International Organization of Standards
IPF	Indicative Planning Figures
IPQC	In Process Quality Control
IRB	Infinitely Rigid Bear
IRS	Infinitely Rigid System
ISM	Insulation System Modules
ISTVS	International Society for Terrain Vehicle Systems
ITL	Integrated Transfer Launch
ITMT	Intermediate Thermomechanical Treatments
LEM	Laser Exhaust Measurement
LH	Locating Head
LHSV	Liquid Hourly Space Velocity
LiF	Lithium Fluoride
LMEC	Liquid Metal Engineering Center (US)
LNG	Liquefied Natural Gas
LOBAT	Lunar Orbiter Block Triangulation
LOD	Locally One Dimensional
LOSAT	Lunar Orbiter Satellite
LPRE	Liquid Propellant Rocket Engines
LRV	Lunar Roving Vehicle
LSL	Ladder Static Logic
LSS	Lunar Soil Simulator
LUNR	Land Use and Natural Resources
MACS	Multi-Purpose Acquisition Control System

MAP	Military Assistance Program
MARV	Multi-Element Articulated Research Vehicle
MC	Main Channel
MCP	Military Construction Program
MCRN	Moscow City Relay Network
MDAI	Multidisciplinary Accident Engineering
MDAP	Machine and Display Application Program
MDCE	Monitoring and Duplicate Control Equipment
MERDC	Mobile Equipment Research and Development Center
METS	Modular Engine Test System
MFM	Multistage Frequency Multiplier
MFT	Multiposition Frequency Telegraphy
MG	Master Generator
MIACF	Meander Inverted Autocorrected Function
MO	Master Oscillator
MOS	Metal Oxide Semiconductor
MOSFET	Metal Oxide Semiconductor Field Effect Transistor
MOS/LSI	Metal Oxide Semiconductor/Large Scale Integration
MRS	Manned Repeater Station
MS	Mobile System
MSMLCS	Mass Service Main Line Cable Systems
MTIRA	Machine Tool Industry Research Association (UK)
muf	Maximum Usable Frequency
NAE	National Academy of Engineering (US)
NAL	National Accelerator Laboratory (US)
NAVFEC	Naval Facilities Engineering Command
nbfm	Narrow Band Frequency Modulation
NBFU	National Board of Fire Underwriters
NDF	Nonlinear Distortion Factor
NDIR	Non-Dispersive Infrared (Analyzers)
NDUV	Non-Dispersive Ultraviolet (Analyzers)
NHK	National Broadcasting Corporation (Jap.)
NIC	Negative Immitance Converters
NIT	Nonlinear Inertialess Three-pole
NJ	Network Junction
NSF	National Science Foundation (US)
NSPE	National Society of Professional Engineers
OCR	Overconsolidated Ratio
OD	Outside Diameter
OICC	Officer In Charge of Construction
OJT	On Job Training
OL	Overhead Links
OPSKS	Optimum Phase Shift Keyed Signals
OS	Oblique Sounding
OSHA	Occupational Safety and Health Act
OSHA	Occupational Safety and Health Administration
OSW	Office of Saline Water (US)
OTL	Order Trunk Lines

OTMJ	Outgoing Trunk Message Junctions	PVRC	Pressure Vessel Research Committee
OWD	Own Number Dialing	QCE	Quality Control Evaluation
OWF	Optimal Worked Frequency	RAL	Radio Annoyance Level
PAA	Phase Antenna Arrays	RANN	Research Applied to National Needs (US)
PAB	Pulse Adsorption Bed		
PACAF	Pacific Air Force	RC	Reinforced Concrete
PACF	Periodic Autocorrelation Function	RCI	Rating Core Index
PAFC	Phase-locked Automatic Frequency Control	RDT	Reactor Development and Technology
		RE	Ram Effect
PAIT	Program for the Advancement of Industrial Technology	rfc	Radio Frequency Choke
		RFR	Reduced Frequency Responses
PAM	Pozzolan Aggregate Mixture	RFU	Reference Frequency Unit
PAM	Pozzolanic Mixtures	RIS	Receipt Inspection Segment
PASNY	Power Authority of the State of New York	RL	Radio Links
		RMA	Reactive Modulation-type Amplifiers
PATCA	Phase-lock Automatic Tuned Circuit Adjustment	ROR	Release-on-Recognizance
		RPIE	Real Property Installed Equipment
PBE	Pulsed Bridge Element	RUC	Riverine Unity Craft
PC	Personal Call	SAE	Society of Automotive Engineers
PC	Premphasis Circuits	SAGE	Semi-Automatic Ground Environment
PCC	Portland Cement Concrete	SAS	Segment Arrival Storage
PCM	Pulse Code Modulation	SATAF	Site Activation Task Force
PCV	Positive Crankcase Ventilation	SBLG	Small Blast Load Generator
pd	Potential Difference/Power Doubler	SCC	Single Cotton Covered
PDF	Probable Density Functions	SCC	Stress Corrosion Cracking
PEPP	Professional Engineers in Private Practice	SCEO	Station Construction Engineering Officer
PERA	Production Engineering Research Association	SCEO	System Civil Engineering Office
		SCN	Shortest Connected Network
PERT	Program Evaluation Review Technique	SFG	Signal Frequencies Generator
PFA	Pulverized Fuel Ash	SFM	Switching-mode Frequency Multipliers
PFC	Phase Frequency Characteristics	SFR	Signal Frequency Receiver
PFTE	Polytetrafluoroethylene	SG	Screen Grid
PG	Pulse Generator	SG	Steam Generator
PGE	Primary Group Equipment	SGE	Secondary Group Equipment
PI	Proportional-plus Integral	SIP	Stay-In-Place
PIC	Polymer Impregnated Concrete	SIRA	Scientific Instruments Research Association
PM	Permanent Magnet		
PMC	Program Management Control	SKT	Skill Knowledge Test
POL	Problem Oriented Language	SL	Subscriber's Lines
pp	Polypropylene	SLOCOP	Specific Linear Optimal Control Program
pp	Push-Pull		
PPD	Pulse-type Phase Detector	SLRV	Surveyor Lunar Roving Vehicle
PPM	Pulse Position Modulation	SMAB	Segment Receipt Inspection Building
PPV	Polarized Platen Viewer	SMAB	Solid Motor Assembly Building
PRT	Personal Rapid Transit	SMU	Secondary Multiplexing Unit
PRVT	Production Reliability Verification Testing	SNJ	Switching Network Junction
		SNPS	Satellite Nuclear Power Station
PS	Phasing System	SO	Signal Oscillator
PSC	Power Supply Circuits	SOCE	Staff Officer Construction Engineering
PSC	Pulse and Signaling Circuit	SPAD	Simplified Procedures for Analysis of Data Systems
PSGC	Puget Sound Governmental Conference (US)		
		SPO	System Program Office
PSI	Present Serviceability Index	SPRT	Standard Platinum Resistance Thermometers
PSP	Planned Schedule Performance		
PSS	Power Supply System	SPRU	Science Policy Research Unit
PTL	Power Transmission Line	SPSA	Signal Phase Statistical Analyzer
PTMT	Polyterephalate	SPWM	Single-sided Pulse Width Modulation
PVC	Polyvinyl Chloride	SQUID	Superconducting Quantum Interference Device
PVC	Pulse Voltage Converter		

SSBAM Single Sideband Amplitude Modulation
S/SS Steering and Suspension System
STRUDL Structural Design Language
STS   Standard Test Single
SU   Station Units
SU   Syne Unit
SV   Synchronous Voltage
TASC Tactical Articulated Swimmable Carrier
TC   Threshold Circuit
TC   Transmitting Circuits
TCCSR Telephone Channel Combination and
      Separation Racks
TCD   Time Code Division
TCRA Telegraphy Channel Reliability
      Analyzer
TCT   Trunk Coin Telephones
TD   Tunnel Diode
TDS   Total Dissolved Solids
TE   Terminal Exchanges
TE   Trunk Equalizers
TESS Thermocouple Emergency Shipment
      Service
TGS   Triglyncinsulphate
TGSO Tertiary Groups Shunt Operation
TME   Telemetric Equipment
TMIS Television Measurement Information
      System
TMIS Television Metering Information
      Systems
TOST Turbine Oxidation Stability Test
TPWB Three Program Wire Broadcasting
TQA   Total Quality Assurance
TRA   Technical Requirements Analysis
TRN   Television Relay Networks
TS   Transformer Substations
TS   Transition Sets
TSB   Technical Support Building
TSP   Titanium Sublimation Pump
TSU   Tariff Selection Unit
TTMA Truck Trailer Manufacturers'
      Association
TTRC Thrust Travel Reduction Curve
TU   Turbopump Units
UAN   Unified Automatic Network
UET-RT Universal Engineer Tractor Rubber
      Tired
UN   Urban Network
URS   Unmanned Repeater Station
USARP United States Atlantic Research
      Program
USATACOM United States Army Tank-Automotive
      Command
UTN   Urban Telephone Network
UVC   Unidirectional Voltage Converter
UVDC Urban Vehicle Development Competition
VACR Variable Amplitude Correction Rack
VCI   Vehicle Cone Index
VE   Value Engineering
VIB   Vertical Integration Building
VITA Volunteers for International
          Technical Assistance
VLA   Very Large Array
VMC   Vertical Motion Carriage
VS   Vertical Sounding
VSG   Vertical Sweep Generator
WABCO Westinghouse Air Brake Company
WARC-ST World Administrative Radio
          Conference for Space
          Telecommunications
WCEE World Conference on Earthquake
          Engineering
WES   Water Experiment Station (US)
WRSIC Water Resources Scientific Information
          Center (US)
w/t   Wireless Telegraphy
ww   Wire Wound
ZCS   Zone Communication Station
ZF   Zone Finders

FISHERIES

CTFM Continuous Transmission Frequency
          Modulated
MLD   Mixed Layer Depth
MSRS Multiple Stylus Recording System
RFS   Regional Fisheries Survey
RUFAS Remote Underwater Fishery Assessment
          System
SL   Source Level
SST   Sea Surface Temperature
TL   Target Loss
TS   Target Strength
VDS   Variable Depth-Towed Sonar
WPESS Width-Pulse Electronic Sector-Scanning
XBT   Expandable Bathythermonograph

FUELS

EC   Ethyl Centralite
EMR   Engine Mature Ratio
EPGA Emergency Petroleum and Gas
          Administration
ESFA Emergency Solid Fuel Administration
ETO25 Esso Turbo Oil 25
NCB   National Coal Board (UK)
NIOC Iranian National Oil Company
SNG   Synthetic Natural Gas

GENERAL

AAAS American Association for the
          Advancement of Science
AC   Alternating Current
ADI   Accepted Daily Intakes
ADT   Average Daily Traffic
AIR   American Institute of Research
approx approximately

ARC	Automatic Remote Control	HEW	Health Education and Welfare (US)
ASA	American Standard Association	IADB	Inter American Development Bank
ASC	American Standard Code	IBRD	International Bank for Reconstruction and Development
AT	Air Temperature		
Auto	Automatic	ICIS	Interdepartmental Committee on Internal Security
BC	Benefit Cost		
BEMA	Business Equipment Manufacturers' Association	ID	Inner Diameter
		IEPB	Interagency Emergency Planning Board
Ca	Calcium	IEPC	Interagency Emergency Planning Committee
CA	Controlled Atmosphere		
CEPC	Canada Civil Emergency Planning Committee	IOC	Indirect Operating Cost
		ISO	International Standards Organization
CERD	European Committee on Research and Development	IU	International Unit
		JPG	Job Proficiency Guide
CLK	Clock	Mg	Magnesium
CMD	Contract Management District	MISC	Miscellaneous
COOP	Continuity of Operation Plan	Mn	Manganese
CPM	Critical Path Method	MNC	Multinational Corporations
CRT	Cathode Ray Tube	MNS	Modernized Number Services
CSC	Civil Service Commission	MOT	Ministry of Transport
CSIRO	Commonwealth Scientific and Industrial Research Organization (Aust.)	MPN	Most Probable Number
		MW	Molecular Weight
CU	Control Unit	MWD	Molecular Weight Distribution
Cu	Copper	N	Nitrogen
CV	Coefficient of Variation	Na	Sodium
DAS	Data Acquisition System	NAWAS	National Warning System (US)
DECOM	Delay Cost Model	NLRB	National Labor Relations Board (US)
DEL	Delete	NMB	National Mediation Board (US)
DHUD	Department of Housing and Urban Development (US)	NPU	Net Present Value
		NRC	National Research Council
DOC	Direct Operating Cost	NSF	National Science Foundation
DOI	Department of Interior (US)	OAR	Office of Research Analysis
DOL	Department of Labor (US)	OAS	Organization of American States
DORIS	Direct Order Recording and Invoicing System	OECD	Organisation for Economic Cooperation and Development
DOS	Decision Outstanding	OEO	Office of Economic Opportunity (US)
DSIR	Department of Science and Industrial Research (UK)	OMB	Office of Management and Budget (US)
		OTS	Out-of-Service
DTE	Development Test and Evaluation	PEAD	Presidential Emergency Action Document (US)
EDP	Experimental Development		
EEC	European Economic Community	PP	Present Position
EMA	Emergency Minerals Administration (US)	PPB	Parts Per Billion
		RAD	Radio Analysis Diagram
EOC	Emergency Operating Center (US)	RD	Research and Development
EOP	Executive Office of the President (US)	RDTE	Research Development Test and Evaluation
ESA	Economic Stabilization Administration (US)		
		ROI	Return On Investment
EXEC	Executive	SBA	Small Business Administration (US)
FCG	Federal Coordination Group (US)	SEN	Single Edge Notch
FDAA	Federal Disaster Assistance Administration (US)	SF	Subject Field
		SIDA	Swedish International Development Agency
Fe	Iron		
FEA	Federal Energy Administration (US)	SIP	Standard Information Package
FPC	Federal Power Commission (US)	SRC	Science Research Council (UK)
GAO	General Accounting Office	SRI	Standard Research Institute (US)
GMT	Greenwich Mean Time	TV	Television
GPC	Gross Profit Contribution	UK	United Kingdom
GPH	Gallons Per Hour	UNCTAD	United Nations Conference on Trade and Development
GPO	General Post Office		
GPO	Government Printing Office	UNDP	United Nations Development Programme
GRA	Government Report Announcement		

UNICE Union of Industries of European
       Community
UNIDO United Nations Industrial Development
       Organization
US   United States
USSR   Union of Soviet Socialist Republics
UV   Ultraviolet
WEIS   World Event Interaction Survey

GEOSCIENCES

ACIGY Advisory Council of the International
       Geophysical Year
AES   Atmospheric Environment Service
AFGWC Air Force Global Weather Center (US)
AIDJEX Arctic Ice Dynamic Joint Experiment
AIW   Auroral Infrasonic Wave
ALPA   Alaskan Long Period Array
AMSL   Above Mean Sea Level
BBB   Bisbenzimidazobenzophenanthrolines
BOMEX Barbados Oceanographic Meteorological
       Experiment
BUV   Backscatter Ultraviolet
CIAP   Clinical Impact Assessment Program
CTAB   Commerce Technical Advisory Board (US)
DCP   Data Collection Platform
DSA   Dynamic Spring Analysis
EDS   Environmental Data Service
EPC   Environmental Protection Control
ESSA   Environmental Survey Satellite
FAGS   Federation of Astronomical and
       Geophysical Services
GATE   GARP Atlantic Tropical Experiment
GESO   Geodetic Earth Orbiting Satellite
HAES   High Altitude Effect Simulation
HIRIS High Resolution Interferometer
       Spectrometer
IFYGL International Field Year for the
       Great Lakes
IHD   International Hydrological Decade
JHD   Joint Hypocenter Determination
LAWDS Loran-inertial Aided Weapon Delivery
       System
LCE   Land Covered Earth
MESA   Marine Ecosystems Analysis
MHD   Magnetohydrodynamic
MLW   Mean Low Water
NCAR   National Center for Atmospheric
       Research
NGSDS National Geophysical and Solar
       Terrestrial Data Center (US)
NSSL   National Severe Storms Laboratory (US)
NWS   National Weather Service
OCE   Ocean Covered Earth
PCA   Polar Cap Absorption
RAOB   Radio Observations
SMIC   Study of Man's Impact of Climate
SWIR   Short Ware Infrared
SWRA   Selected Water Resources Abstracts

VLPE   Very Long Period Experiment
VLS   Vapour Liquid Solid
WMO   World Meteorological Organization

INFORMATION RETRIEVAL SYSTEMS

ADSTAR Automatic Document Storage and
       Retrieval
ADT   Admission Discharge and Transfer
AFIPS American Federation for Information
       Processing Societies
APICS American Production and Inventory
       Control
ART   Average Retrieval Time
ASCA   Automatic Subject Citation Alert
ASRS   Automatic Storage and Retrieval System
ATIS   Automatic Terminal Information Service
BAL   Basic Assembler Language
BASEEFA British Approvals Service for
       Electrical Equipment in Flammable
       Atmospheres
BCRA   British Ceramic Research Association
BCRA   British Coke Research Association
BFMIRA British Food Manufacturing Industries
       Research
BGIRA British Glass Industry Research
       Association
BIBRA British Industrial Biological
       Research Association
BLL   British Library Lending
BLMRA British Leather Manufacturers'
       Research Association
BLRA   British Launderers' Research
       Association
BNFMRA British Non-Ferrous Metals Research
       Association
BSRA   British Ship Research Association
CCF   Central Communications Facility
CFMS   Chained File Management System
CFPRA Campden Food Preservation Research
       Association (UK)
CGLO   Commonwealth Geological Liaison
       Office (UK)
CIDST Committee for Information and
       Documentation on Science and
       Technology (UK)
CIRIA Construction Industry Research and
       Information (UK)
COM   Computer Output Microfilm
COSMIC Computer Software and Management
       Information Center
CPS   Conversational Programming System
CSMFRA Cotton, Silk and Man-made Fibres
       Research Association (UK)
CTRA   Coal Tar Research Association (UK)
CVIS   Computerized Vocational Information
       System
DAIR   Driver Aid Information and Routing
DAPP   Data Acquisition and Processing Program

DCS   Data Communication System
DDC   Defense Documentation Center
DFRA Drop Forging Research Association (UK)
DIDS Digital Information Display System
DRIC Defence Research Information Centre
ERA   Electrical Research Association (UK)
ERIC Educational Resources Information
      Center
FID   Fédération Internationale de
      Documentation
FIR   Flight Information Region
FIRA Furniture Industry Research
      Association (UK)
FMBRA Flour Milling and Baking Research
      Association (UK)
FMIS Fiscal Management Information System
FPRL Forest Products Research Laboratory
      (UK)
GRA   Government Reports Announcement
HATRA Hosiery and Allied Trades Research
      Association (UK)
HIS   Honeywell Information System
HVRA Heating and Ventilating Research
      Association
IDW   Institut für Dokumentationswesen
INTIPS Integrated Information Processing
      System
ISVD Information System for Vocational
      Decisions
LCS   Large Core Storage
LPL   List Processing Language
MDC   Materials Distribution Center
MDR   Mark-sense Document Reader
MIC   Management Information Centers
MICS Manufacturing Information and
      Control System
MIR   Music Information Retrieval
MIRA Motor Industry Research Association
      (UK)
MIS   Management Information System
MTIRA Machine Tool Industry Research
      Association (UK)
MTS   Michigan Terminal System
NLECS National Law Enforcement Communications
      System
NLL   National Lending Library (UK)
NRCd National Reprographic Centre for
      Documentation
NTIS National Technical Information Service
OCR   Optical Character Reader
OSTI Office for Scientific and Technical
      Information
OTIU Overseas Technical Information Unit
      (UK)
PICS Production Information and Control
      System
PIMISS Pennsylvania Interagency Management
      Information Support System
PIRA Paper Industries Research Association/
      Research Association for Paper

      and Board
PMIS Patient Medical Information System
PRA   Research Association of British
      Paints
PSMLG Public Service Microfilm Liaison
      Group (UK)
RAPRA Rubber and Plastic Research
      Association (UK)
REQWQ Requisition Work Queue
RHEL Rutherford High Energy Laboratory
SATRA Shoe and Allied Trade Research
      Association (UK)
SCRATA Steel Casting Research and Trade
      Association (UK)
SDCR Source Data Communication Retrieval
SEARCH System for Electronic Analysis and
      Retrieval of Criminal Histories
SIE   Science Information Exchange
SIGI System for Interactive Guidance
      and Information
SIR   Selective Information Retrieval
SMRE Safety in Mines Research Establishment
SPA   Small Parts Analysis
SPIN Selected Physics Information Notice
SRA   Spring Research Association (UK)
SRC   Science Research Council (UK)
STI   Scientific and Technical Information
SYSRC System Reference Count
TIP   Tactile Information Presentation
TOD   Technical Objective Documents
TOPS Telephone Order Processing System
TRADA Timber Research and Development
      Association
TRC   Technology Reports Centre
TRS   Terry Research Station
UAIMS United Aircraft Information System
WATS Wide Area Telecommunications Service
WHRA Welwyn Hall Research Association (UK)
WI   Welding Institute (UK)
WIRA Wool Industries Research Association
      (UK)
WKQDR Work QUEUE Directory
WRA   Water Research Association (UK)

LUNAR SCIENCES

AF   Alternating Fields
ALHT Apollo Lunar Hand Tool
APB   Antiphase Boundary Dormain
ARM   Anhysteretic Remnant Magnetization
BMR   Bipolar Magnetic Regions
BSO   Blue Stellar Objects
CCGE Cold Cathode Gauge Experiment
CCL   Core Current Layer
CESEMI Computer Evaluation of Scanning
      Electron Microscope Images
CL   Current Layer
CM   Command Module
CPLEE Changed Particle Lunar Environment

	Experiment
CSM	Command Service Module
DPV	Doppler Broadening Velocity
DCL	Duel Current Layer
DZA	Doppler Zeeman Analyser
ESR	Electron Spin Resonance
EVA	Extra Vehicular Activity
FOV	Field Of View
FWHM	Full Width, Half Maximum
GCVS	General Catalogs of Variable Stars
GET	Ground Elapsed Time
HELOS	Highly Eccentric Lunar Occultation Satellite
HG	Horizon Grow
HPBW	Half Power Beamwidths
HVC	High Velocity Clouds
IGM	Intergalactic Medium
IGY	International Geophysical Year
INAA	Instrumental Neutron Activation Analysis
IRM	Isothermal Remnant Magnetization
ITRM	Inverse Thermoremnant Magnetization
IVC	Intermediate Velocity Clouds
LCRU	Lunar Communications Relay Unit
LIL	Large Ionic Lithophile
LM	Lunar Module
LMC	Large Megallanic Cloud
LOSAT	Lunar Orbiter Satellite
LRL	Lunar Receiving Laboratory
LSM	Lunar Surface Magnetometer
LSPET	Lunar Sample Preliminary Examination Term
LSS	Lunar Soil Simulator
LTE	Local Thermodynamic Equilibrium
LVDT	Linear Variable Differential Transformer
M	Mira
MA	Mass Analyzer
MAD	Mass Analyzer Detector
MHD	Magnetohydrodynamic
MSFN	Manned Space Flight Network
NMR	Nuclear Magnetic Resonance
NRAO	National Radio Astronomy Observatory
NRM	Natural Remnant Magnetization
OSO	Orbiting Solar Observatory
PET	Pentaerythrital
PHA	Pulse Height Analysis
pp	Plane Parallel
PRM	Pressure Remnant Magnetization
PTRM	Partial Thermoremnant Magnetization
QSRS	Quasi Stellar Radio Sources
QSS	Quasi Stellar Sources
RA	Right Ascension
REE	Rare Earth Element
SFD	Sudden Frequency Deviation
SH	Scratch Hardness
SIDE	Suprathermal Ion Detector Experiment
SIM	Scientific Instrument Module
SMC	Small Magellanic Cloud
SMR	Super Metal Rich

SNRs	Supernova Remnants
SRM	Shock Remnant Magnetization
SS	Spherical Symmetry
STP	Standard Temperative and Pressure
TEC	Transearth Coast
TINT	Track in Track
TL	Thermoluminescence
TLP	Transient Lunar Phenomena
TM	Transverse Magnetic
TRF	Track Pick Fragments
TSD	Thermally Stimulated Depolarization
TTT	Time Temperature Transformation
UHV	Ultra High Vacuum
UMR	Unipolar Magnetic Regions
VLBI	Very Long Baseline Interferometry
VRM	Viscous Remnant Magnetization
XRF	X-Ray Fluorescence

MANAGEMENT

ACB	Army Classification Battery
AFM	Analysis and Forecasting Mode
BEST	Business Electronics Systems Technology
CAPER	Cost of Attaining Personnel Requirement
CARD	Compact Automatic Retrieval Display
CDMS	COMRADE Data Management System
CMC	Computer Machinery Company
CMG	Computer Management Group
COSBA	Computer Service and Bureaux Association
CSS	Computer Sale and Services
DMS	Database Management System
DOC	Direct Operating Cost
DTSS	Dartmouth Time Sharing System
EMBERS	Emergency Bed Request System
EMLC	Experimental Manpower Laboratory for Correction
ESPOL	Executive System Problem Oriented Language
FEP	Financial Evaluation Program
FIND	Forecasting Institutional Needs for Dartmouth
FOAMS	Forecasting, Order Administration, and Master Scheming
GDMS	Generalized Data Management System
GMM	General Matrix Manipulator
GPOS	General Purpose Operating System
GREMEX	Goddard Research and Engineering Management Exercise
IPSPS	Inhibitory Post Synaptic Potentials
MARS	Market Analysis Research System
MARS	Multi Access Retrieval System
MBO	Management By Objectives
MMS	Mobile Multiple-shopping Services
MOS	Military Occupational Speciality
MSS	Multiple Selling Service
NSTF	National Scholarship Trust Fund

OMB	Office of Management and Budget (US)
PCE	Program Cost Estimate
PERT	Program Evaluation Review Technique
PFC	Pack Feed and Converter
PIMISS	Pennsylvania Interagency Management Information Support System
PMS	Project Management System
RADC	Rome Air Development Center
ROC	Return On Capital
SHA	Software House Association
SMC	System Man and Cybernetics
SPAR	Staff Payroll Allocation and Records
TPE	Teleprocessing Executive
UAIMS	United Aircraft Information Management System

MATERIALS

ICHTF	Low Cycle High Temperature Fatigue
LCF	Low Cycle Fatigue
NDT	Nil-Ductility Transmission
SMC	Sheet Molding Compound

MATHEMATICS

AC	Alternating Current
ADH	Antidirected Hamiltonian
AE	Auxiliary Equation
AR	Autoregressive
AU	Arithmetic Unit
BHP	Brake Horsepower
calc	Calculated
CASME	Commonwealth Association of Science and Mathematics Educators
Chu	Centigrade Heat Unit
cf	Centripetal Force
cf	Contemporary Force
cg	Centre of Gravity
cm	Centimetre
Coeff	Coefficient
Coord	Coordinate
COS	Cosine
COSEC	Cosecant
cP	Centipoise
cS	Centistokes
C/S	Cycle per Second
cwt	Hundredweight
CY	Cubic Yard
DE	Differential Equation
dia	Diameter
dm	Decimetre
EHP	Effective Horsepower
emf	Electromotive Force
emu	Electromagnetic Unit
eqn	Equation
equiv	Equivalent
esu	Electrostatic Unit
eV	Electrovolt

EVTCM	Expected Value Terminal Capacity Matrix
ftlbf	Foot Pound-Force
G	Graph
GEG	Generalized Euclidean Geometry
GS	General Solution
GTD	Geometrical Theory of Diffraction
HNED	Horizontal Null External Distance
ID	Inside Diameter
IHP	Indicated Horsepower
in	Inch
IP	Imaginary Part
kcal	Kilocalorie
kg	Kilogramme
kl	Kilolitre
km	Kilometre
kw	Kilowatt
lb	Pound
LG	Line Graph
MA	Moving Average
MANOVA	Multivariate Analysis of Variance
max	Maximum
min	Minimum
ml	Millilitre
MLE	Maximum Likelihood Estimates
mm	Millimetre
MMF	Magnetomotive
mol-wt	Molecular Weight
MPM	Maximum Pionization Method
MSGs	Models Simulations and Games
mv	Mean Value
MVE	Multivariate Exponential Distribution
NHP	Nominal Horsepower
NRN	Negative Run Number
OD	Outside Diameter
OP	Orthogonal Polynomials
pd	Potential Difference
PDIs	Perfect Digital Invariants
PI	Particular Integral
PPDI	Pluperfect Digital Invariants
ppm	Parts Per Million
PSM	Parallel Slit Map
REV/MIN	Revolutions per Minute
rev/s	Revolutions per Second
RMS	Root Mean Square
rp	Real Part
sec	Secant
shm	Simple Harmonic Motion
SHP	Shaft Horsepower
sin	Sine
SISTM	Simulation Incremental Stochastic Transition Matrices
TAN	Tangent
TCM	Terminal Capacity Matrix
TG	Total Graph
Vol	Volume
WCG	Weakly Compactly Generated
wt	Weight

METALLIC MATERIALS

B/E	Baron-Epoxy
DHS	Dual Hardness Steel
TCC	Thermal Control Coatings

METALLURGY AND METALLOGRAPHY

AA	All Around
AC	Air Conditioning
ACA	Ammoniacal Copper Arsenite
ACC	Acid Copper Chromate
ACN	Asbestos Cloth Neck
AD	Access Door
AF	Air Filter
AF	Angle Frame
AFF	Above Finished Floor
AHU	Air Handling Unit
ALD	Automatic Louver Dumper
AMBD	Automatic Multiple Blade Damper
approx	Approximately
ASB	Asbestos
ASWG	American Steel Wire Gage
ATC	Acoustic Tile Ceiling
ATV	All Terrain Vehicle
AVC	Automatic Voltage Compression
AWS	American Welding Society
BCIRA	British Cast Iron Research Association
BD	Bottom Down
BEAMA	British Electrical and Allied Manufacturers' Association
BG	Bottom Grille
BI	Black Iron
BJ	Bar Joist
BLDG	Building
BOC	British Oxygen Company
BOD	Bottom Of Duct
BOS	Back Of Slip
BR	Bottom Register
BS	Below Slab
BU	Bottom Up
CCA	Chromated Copper Arsenate
CCT	Continuous Cooling Transformation
CCWBAD	Counterclockwise Bottom Angular Down
CCWBAU	Counterclockwise Bottom Angular Up
CCWBH	Counterclockwise Bottom Horizontal
CCWDB	Counterclockwise Down Blast
CCWTAD	Counterclockwise Top Angular Down
CCWTAU	Counterclockwise Top Angular Up
CCWTH	Counterclockwise Top Horizontal
CCWUB	Counterclockwise Up Blast
CD	Ceiling Diffuser
ceil	Ceiling
CEL	Carbon Equivalent Liquids
CFM	Cubic Feet per Minute
CH	Ceiling Height
ChPI	Chelyabinisk Polytechnic Institute
CIRC	Circumference
CLCOLL	Clinch Collar

CLR	Constant Load Rupture
COD	Clean Out Door
COGD	Circulator Outlet Gas Duct
COL	Column
CONC	Concrete
CONN	Connection
COP	Copper
CR	Ceiling Register
CS	Concrete Slab
CT	Cooling Tower
CTS	Controlled Thermal Severity
Cu	Copper
CWBAD	Clockwise Bottom Angular Down
CWBAU	Clockwise Bottom Angular Up
CWDB	Clockwise Down Blast
CWED	Cold Weld Evaluation Device
CWTAD	Clockwise Top Angular Down
CWTAU	Clockwise Top Angular Up
CWTH	Clockwise Top Horizontal
CWUB	Clockwise Up Blast
CZC	Chromated Zinc Chloride
DT	Drop Top
DT	Dust Turn
DT	Dynamic Tear
EA	Exhaust Air
EB	Electron Beam
EB	Equal Brake
EL	Elevation
EMMA	Electron Manual Metal Arch
ENG	Engineer
EPMA	Electron Probe Microanalysis
ESH	Electric Strip Heater
ET	Equal Taper
EXH	Exhaust
FA	Free Air
FA	Fresh Area
FAI	Fresh Air Intake
FB	Flat Bottom
FC	Flexible Connection
FC	Full Corners
FCAP	Fluor Chrome Arsenate Pheonol
FCP	Fatigue Crack Propagation
FD	Fire Damper
FFL	Finished Floor
FLBR	Fusible Link Bottom Register
FLTR	Fusible Link Top Register
FP	Fire Proofing
FPM	Feet Per Minute
FS	Flat Slip
FSAA	Flat Slips All Around
FSB	Flat Slip on Bottom
FST	Flat Slip on Top
FT	Flat Top
FTMT	Final Thermomechanical Treatment
FVD	Friction Volume Damper
GC	General Contractor
GI	Galvanized Iron
GPM	Gallons Per Minute
GTA	Gas Tungsten Arc
GYFM	General Yielding Fracture Mechanics

HAZ	Heat Affected Zone
HC	Hanging Ceiling
HC	Heating Coil
HP	High Pressure
HV	Heating and Ventilating
HVAC	Heating Ventilating and Air Conditioning
ID	Inside Dimension
IR	Infra-Red
ITMT	Intermediate Thermomechanical Treatment
KD	Knocked Down
KE	Kitchen Exhaust
LAMA	Locomotive and Allied Manufacturers' Association
LCC	Lead Coated Copper
LE	Large End
LEFM	Linear Elastic Fracture Mechanics
LH	Left Hand
LP	Low Pressure
LZT	Lead Zirconate Titanate
MA	Matched Angles
MB	Mixing Box
MD	Manual Damper
MIG	Metal Inert Gas
MMA	Manual Metal Arc
Mn	Manganese
MO	Masonry Opening
NC	Normally Closed
NDT	Non-Destructive Testing
NIC	Not in Contact
NO	Normally Open
NRC	Notch Root Contraction
NTS	Not to Scale
OA	Outside Air
OAI	Outside Air Intake
OAL	Overall Length
OBD	Open Blade Damper
OC	On Center
OD	Outside Dimension
OH	Opposite Hand
PBD	Parallel Blade Damper
RA	Return Air
RAD	Radio Analysis Diagram
RE	Raw End
RF	Roof Fan
RH	Right Hand
RHC	Reheat Coil
ROVD	Remotely Operated Volume Damper
RPM	Revolutions Per Minute
RT	Raise Top
SA	Submerged Arc
SD	Splitter Damper
SE	Slip End
SE	Small End
SEME	School of Electrical and Mechanical Engineering
SLD	Slim Line Diffuser
SS	Stainless Steel
ST	Sound Trap

SWAT	Stress Wave Analysis Techniques
SWSI	Single Width Single Inlet
TC	Telescoping Collar
TD	Top Down
TG	Top Grille
TIG	Tungen Inert Gas
TMP	Thermal Mechanical Processing
TMP	Thermomechanical Process
TOD	Top Of Duct
TOS	Top Of Steel
TR	Top Register
TU	Top Up
TX	Toilet Exhaust
UON	Unless Otherwise Noted
US	Underside of Slab
UTS	Ultimate Tensile Stress
VD	Volume Damper
VE	Vibration Eliminator
VOLFD	Volume Adjustable Fire Damper
WMS	Wire Mesh Screen
WT	Water Tight

METEOROLOGY

AFGWC	Air Force Global Weather Center (US)
ATS	Advanced Technology Satellites
AWADS	Adverse Weather Aerial Delivery System
AWN	Automatic Weather Network
AWOP	All-Weather Operations Panel
AWP	Allied Weather Publications
AWS	Air Weather Service
BOMEX	Barbados Oceanographic Meteorological Experiment
CAWS	Common Aviation Weather System
CIAP	Climatic Impact Assessment Program
CMC	Canadian Meteorological Centre
COMESA	Committee on the Meteorological Effects of Stratospheric Aircraft (UK)
CSTR	Committee on Solar Terrestial Research
ESSA	Environmental Survey Satellite
FAWS	Flight Advisory Weather Service
FIDO	Fog Investigation and Dispersal Operation
FNWC	Fleet Numerical Weather Central (US)
GARP	Global Atmospheric Research Program
GATE	GARP Atlantic Tropical Experiment
IGN	National Geographic Institute
IUCSTP	Inter-Union Commission on Solar Terrestial Physics
LCE	Land Covered Earth
LFM	Limited-area Fine-mesh Model
MOTNE	Meteorological Operational Telecommunications Network Europe
NEDN	Naval Environmental Data Network (US)
NOESS	National Operational Environmental Satellite System

NWP	Numerical Weather Prediction
NWS	National Weather Service
OCE	Ocean Covered Earth
OTSR	Optimum Track Ship Routing
RAOBs	Radio Observations
SMS	Synchronous Meteorological Satellites
SWRA	Selected Water Resources Abstract
UAP	Upper Air Project
VMC	Visual Meteorological Conditions
WMO	World Meteorological Organization
WEFAX	Weather Facsimile Experiment
WMSC	Weather Message Switching Center
WWW	World Weather Watch

MILITARY SCIENCES

AA	Anti Aircraft
AAA	Anti Aircraft Artillery
AAD	Advanced Ammunition Depot
AADA	Anti Aircraft Defended Area
AADC	Anti Aircraft Defence Commander
AAFCE	Allied Air Force Central Europe
AAFNE	Allied Air Force Northern Europe
AAFSE	Allied Air Force Southern Europe
AAG	Air Adjutant General
AAH	Advanced Attack Helicopter
AALC	Amphibious Assault and Landing Craft
AALMG	Anti Aircraft Light Machine Gun
AAM	Air-to-Missile
AAOR	Anti Aircraft Artillery Operations Room
AATO	Army Air Transport Organization
ABM	Anti Ballistic Missiles
ABMA	Army Ballistic Missile Agency
ABRES	Advanced Ballistic Reentry System
ACA	Armament Control Agency
ACB	Army Classification Battery
ACE	Allied Command Europe
ACF	Air Combat Fighter
ACI	Army Control Instruction
ACLANT	Allied Command Atlantic
ACM	Air Chief Marshal
ACOS	Assistant Chief of Staff
ACP	Allied Communications Publication
ACTICE	Authority for the Co-ordination of Inland Transport in Central Europe
ACTISUD	Authority for the Co-ordination of Inland Transport in Southern Europe
ACV	Armoured Command Vehicle
ACW	Aircraft Control Warning
ADC	Air Defense Command
ADCC	Air Defense Control Center
ADE	Air Defense Emergency
ADIZ	Air Defense Identification Zone
ADO	Air Defense Officer
ADOC	Air Defense Operations Centre
ADS	Air Defence Ship
ADS	Air Defence System

ADSM	Air Defence Suppression Missile
AFA	Air Force Association
AFA	Army Flight Activity
AFB	Air Force Base
AFBMD	Air Force Ballistic Missile Division
AFCE	Allied Forces Control Europe
AFCENT	Allied Forces Central
AFCRL	Air Force Cambridge Research Laboratory
AFCS	Air Force Communications Service
AFF	Army Field Force
AFFDL	Air Force Flight Dynamics Laboratory (US)
AFFTC	Air Force Flight Test Center
AFGWC	Air Force Global Weather Center (US)
AFHRL	Air Force Human Resources Laboratory
AFIT	Air Force Institute of Technology
AFLC	Air Force Logistics Command (US)
AFLCM	Air Force Logistics Command Manual
AFM	Air Force Manual
AFMDC	Air Force Missile Development Center
AFMED	Allied Forces Mediterranean
AFML	Air Force Materials Laboratory
AFMTC	Air Force Missile Test Center
AFN	American Forces Network
AFNORTH	Allied Forces North
AFPRO	Air Force Plant Representative Office
AFQT	Armed Forces Qualification Test
AFR	Air Force Regulation
AFRCE	Air Force Regional Civil Engineer
AFRTC	Air Force Research Training Center
AFS	Air Force Specialty
AFS	Air Force Supply
AFS	Army Fire Service
AFSATCOM	Air Force Satellite Communications
AFSC	Air Force Systems Command
AFSC	Armed Force Staff College
AFSCM	Air Force Systems Command Manual
AFSE	Allied Forces South Europe
AFSWC	Air Force Special Weapons Center (US)
AFV	Armoured Fighter Vehicle
AFWTR	Air Force Western Test Range
AGRA	Army Ground Royal Artillery
AGRE	Army Group Royal Engineers
AHQ	Allied Headquarters
AHWG	Ad Hoc Working Group
AI	Airborne Interception
AIC	Ammunition Identification Code
AICBM	Anti Intercontinental Ballistic Missile
AIDATS	Army Inflight Data Transmission System
AIIC	Army Imagery Intelligence Corps
AIP	Allied Intelligence Publication
AIRPASS	Airborne Interception Radar and Pilot's Attack Sight System
ALARM	Air Launched Advanced Ramjet Missile
ALARR	Air Launched Recoverable Rocket
ALBM	Air Launched Ballistic Missiles
ALCC	Airborne Launch Control Center

ALFCE Allied Land Forces Central Europe
ALSS Airborne Location and Strike System
ALT   Airborne Lasser Tracker
AMA   Air Materiel Area
AMC   Army Materiel Command
AMCA Advanced Materiel Concept Agency
AMCP Allied Military Communications Panel
AMCS Airborne Missile Control System
AMEDD Army Medical Department (US)
AMEDS Army Medical Science
AMMRC Army Materiels and Mechanics Research
        Center (US)
AMPSS Advanced Manned Precision Strike
        System
AMR   Atlantic Missile Range
AMS   Army Map Service
AMS   Army Medical Service
AMSP Allied Military Security Publications
AMST Advanced Medium STOL Transport
AMTRAC Amphibian Tractor
ANC   Army Nurse Corps
AND   Air-Force Navy Design
ANFCE Allied Naval Force Central Europe
ANG   Air National Guard
ANG-CE Air National Guard Civil Engineering
ANIP Army Navy Instrumentation Program
ANIP Army Navy Integrated Presentation
ANPP Army Nuclear Power Program
AOA   American Ordnance Association
AOC   Air Officer Commanding
AOD   Advanced Ordnance Depot
AOP   Allied Ordnance Publication
APC   Armoured Personnel Carrier
API   Armour Piercing Incendiary
APIS Army Photographic Interpretation
        Section
APT   Armour Piercing Tracer
AR   Army Regulation
ARADCOM Army Air Defense Command
ARM   Anti Radar Missile
ARNG Army National Guard
ARP   Air Raid Protection
ARTOC Army Tactical Operations Centre
ASA   Army Security Agency
ASDIC Anti Submarine Detection Investigation
        Committee
ASDIC Armed Service Documents Intelligence
        Center
ASM   Air-to-Surface Missile
ASMP Air Sol Moyenne Portée
ASMS Advanced Surface Missile System
ASP   Ammunition Supply Point
ASPR Army Services Procurement Regulations
ASROC Anti Submarine Rocket
ASSU Air Support Signal Unit
ASW   Anti Submarine Warfare
AT   Anti-Torpedo
ATAF Allied Tactical Air Force
ATC   Air Training Command
ATC   Army Training Center

ATG   Air-To-Ground
ATI   Army Training Instruction
ATP   Allied Technical Publication
ATP   Army Training Plan
ATS   Army Transport Service
AUM   Air-to-Underwater Missile
AUTEC Atlantic Undersea Test and Evaluation
        Center
AUV   Armoured Utility Vehicle
AVCS Assistant Vice Chief of Staff
AVLB Armoured Vehicle Launch Bridge
AVM   Air Vice Marshal
AVSF Advanced Vertical Strike Fighter
AW   Automatic Weapon
AWCS Air Weapons Control System
AWP   Allied Weather Publication
AWRE Atomic Weapon Research Establishments
AWS   Air Weapon System
AWS   American War Standards
BADGE Base Air Defense Ground Environment
BALMI Ballistic Missile
BAR   Browning Automatic Rifle
BATRE CON Battle Reconnaissance
BCE   Base Civil Engineer
BDM   Bomber Defense Missile
BDS   Bomb Disposal Squad
BDU   Bomb Disposal Unit
BFN   British Forces Network
BGS   Bombing and Gunnery School
BLG   Breech Loading Gun
BLR   Breech Loading Rifle
BOD   Base Ordnance Depot
BSD   Ballistic System Division
BSD   Base Supply Depot
BTO   Bombing Through Overcast
BW   Biological Warfare
CARA Combat Aircrew Rescue Aircraft
CARDE Canadian Armament Research and
        Development Establishment
CAS   Close Air Support
CAS   Control Augmentation System
CASWS Close Air Support Weapon System
CC   Camp Commandant
CC   Combat Commandant
CCB   Configuration Control Board
CCIP Continuous Computation of Impact
        Point
CCV   Control Configured Vehicles
CD   Civil Defence
CDA   Command and Data Acquisition
CEAC Committee for European Airspace
        Coordination
CEBMCO Corps Engineering Ballistic Missile
        Construction Office
CEFAC Civil Engineering Field Activities
        Center
CEMIRT Civil Engineering Maintenance
        Inspection, Repair and Training
CIC   Combat Information Center
CIC   Computer Intelligence Corps

CINC   Commander-in-Chief
CINCEUR Commander-in-Chief Europe
CINCPAC Commander-in-Chief Pacific
CIP   Civil Institution Program
CLAM   Chemical Low Altitude Missile
CNO   Chief of Naval Operation
CNP   Chief of Naval Personnel
COAMP   Cost Analysis of Maintenance Policies
COMATS Commander Military Air Transport
          Service
CONAD   Continental Air Defence
COS   Chief of Staff
CRAF   Civil Reserve Air Fleet
CRC   Control and Reporting Center
CRP   Control and Reporting Post
CSG   Combat Support Group
CTC   Compact Transpiration Cooling
CTV   Control Test Vehicle
CW   Chemistry Warfare
CWO   Chief Warrant Officer
DACOS   Deputy Assistant Chief of Staff
DAG   Deputy Adjutant General
DAMP   Downrange Anti-Missile Measurement
          Program
DAMS   Defense Against Missile Systems
DASA   Defense Atomic Support Agency (US)
DASH   Drone Anti-Submarine Helicopter
DCM   Defence Combat Maneuvering
DCPA   Defense Civil Preparedness Agency (US)
DCS   Defence Communications System
DCS/O   Deputy Chief of Staff, Operations
DDC   Defense Documentation Center
DECM   Defense Electronic Countermeasures
          System
DECOR   Digital Electronic Continuous Ranging
DECTRA Decca Tracking and Ranging
DEFCON Defense Readiness Condition
DELRAC Decca Long Range Area Coverage
DESC   Defense Electronics Supply Center
DEW   Distant Early Warning
DEWIZ   Distant Early Warning Identification
          Zone
DEFT   Dynamic Error Free Transmission
DIAC   Defense Industry Advisory Council
DIANE   Digital Integrated Attack Navigation
          System
DICBM   Defense Intercontinental Ballistic
          Missile
DLSC   Defense Logistics Service Center
DMET   Distance Measuring Equipment TACAN
DMO   Defense Mobilization Order (US)
DMS   Defense Management Simulation
DPC   Defense Planning Committee
DPS   Defense Printing Service (US)
DRL   Defense Research Laboratories (US)
DRS   Detection Ranging Set
DRW   Defensive Radio Warfare
DSA   Defence Shipping Agency
DSA   Defense Supply Agency (US)
DSARC   Defense Systems Acquisition Review

            Council
DSC   Defense Shipping Council
DSCS   Defense Satellite Communications
          System
DSEB   Defense Shipping Executive Board
DSSP   Deep Submergence Systems Project
DSV   Deep Submergence Vehicle
EA   Enemy Aircraft
ECM   Electronic Countermeasures
EMCCC   European Military Communication
          Coordinating Committee
ESD   Electronics Systems Division
ESSA   Environmental Science Services
          Administration
EUCOM   European Command
EWI   Education With Industry
EWTR   Electronic Warfare Test Range
FABMDS Field Army Ballistic Missile Defence
          System
FACE   Field Artillery Computer Equipment
FADAC   Field Artillery Digital Automatic
          Computer
FARR   Forward Area Refueling and Rearing
FBRL   Final Bomb Release Line
FCR   Facility Change Request
FDL   Fast Development Logistics
FEBA   Forward Edge of Battle Area
FECPs   Facility Engineering Change Proposals
FMA   Facilities Management Analysis
FMSO   Fleet Material Supply Office
FOBS   Fractional Orbital Bombardment System
FOI   Follow-on Intercepter
FUB   Facility Utilization Board
FVRDE   Fighting Vehicle Research and
          Development Establishment
FWTT   Fixed Wing Tactical Transport
GAM   Ground-to-Air-Missile
GDO   Gun Direction Officer
GEMM   Generalized Electronics Maintenance
          Model
GFM   Government Furnished Materials
GLLD   Ground Laser Locator Designator
GM   Guided Missile
GSCG   Ground Systems Coordination Group
HLH   Heavy Lift Helicopters
HOBOS   Homing Bomb System
HVD   High Velocity Detonation
ICBM   Inter Continental Ballistic Missiles
IDSCS   Initial Defense Satellite
          Communications System
ILP   International Logistics Program
IMI   Improved Manned Intercepter
IROS   Increase Reliability Operational
          System
ITL   Integrate Transfer Launch
JANAIR Joint Army-Navy Aircraft
          Instrumentation Research (US)
JCS   Joint Chief Staff
LAW   Light Antitank Weapon
LCRU   Landing Craft Retriever Unit

LRMTS Laser Rangefinder and Marked Target
        Seeker
LSFO Logistics Support Field Office
LTA   Light Than Air
LVRJ Low Volume Ram Jet
LWF   Light Weight Fighter
MAC   Military Airlift Command
MAP   Military Assistance Program
MAS   Military Alert System
MAST Military Assistance for Safety and
        Traffic
MATS Military Air Transport Service
MATZ Military Aerodrome Traffic Zone
MBFR Mutual and Balanced Force Reduction
MCP   Military Construction Program
MECU Master Engine Control Unit
MED COM Mediterranean Communications
MEECN Minimum Essential Emergency Network
        (US)
MFV   Military Flight Vehicles
MGGB Modular Guided Glide Bomb
MLOP Mid-Leth Overpressure
MODCAT Modified Catamaran
MOS   Military Occupational Speciality
MRCA Multi Role Combat Aircraft
MSC   Military Sealift Command
MSDS Marconi Space and Defence Systems
MTMTS Military Traffic Management and
        Terminal Service (US)
MVA   Modern Volunteer Army
NAC   North Atlantic Council
NAMSA NATO Maintenance and Supply Agency
NAVELECSYSCOM Naval Electronic Systems
        Command
NAVFEC Naval Facilities Engineering Command
NAVORD Naval Ordnance
NAVSEC Naval Ship Engineering Center
NAVSUP Naval Supply
NCA   National Command Authorities
NCSORG Naval Control of Shipping
        Organization
NCWA NATO Civil Wartime Agency
NDRF National Defense Reserve Fleet (US)
NEL   Navy Electronic Laboratory (US)
NIAG NATO Industrial Advisory Group
NIPS NMCS Information Processing System
NMCC National Military Command Center (US)
NMCS National Military Command System
NMCSSC National Military Command System
        Support Center
NOEB-E NATO Oil Executive Board-East
NOEB-W NATO Oil Executive Board-West
NOL   National Ordnance Laboratory (US)
NORAD North American Air Defense (US)
NRL   Naval Research Laboratory
NSRDC Naval Ship Research and Development
        Center
NUDET Nuclear Detection
NUSC Naval Underwater Systems Center
NWEP Nuclear Weapons Effects Panel

OCA   Operational Control Authority
ODR   Office of Defense Resources (US)
OES   Office of Emergency Service (US)
ONR   Office of Naval Research (US)
OPMS Officer Personnel Management System
OWE   Operating Weight Empty
PACAF Pacific Air Force
PACOM Pacific Command
PAD   Public Assistance Director (US)
PARM Participating Manager
PBEIST Planning Board for European Inland
        Surface Transport
PBOS Planning Board for Ocean Shipping
PCM   Penalty Cost Model
PELSS Precision Emitter Location Strike
        System
PERA Planning and Engineering for Repair
        and Alterations (US)
PERT Program Evaluation Review Technique
PHM   Patrol Hydrofoil Missile
PIV   Product Inspection Verification
PMC   Program Management Control
PMIP Postmaintenance Inspection Pilots
PMSE Program Management Simulation Exercise
PPC   Patrol Plane Commander
QCE   Quality Control Evaluation
QEAF Qatar Emiri Air Force
RAAP Radford Army Ammunition Plant
RACES Radio Amateur Civil Emergency Service
RAE   Royal Aircraft Establishment (UK)
RCC   Resources Control Centre
RDAF Royal Danish Air Force
RIS   Receipt Inspection Segment
ROC   Required Operational Capacity
RPG   Rocket Propelled Grenade
RPIE Real Property Installed Equipment
RSB   Regional Shipping Board
RURLAM Replacement Unit Repair Level
        Analysis Model
SACEUR Supreme Allied Command, Europe
SACLANT Supreme Allied Command, Atlantic
SALT Strategic Arms Limitation Talks
SAM   Surface-to-Air-Missiles
SAME Society of American Military
        Engineering
SAS   Segment Arrival Storage
SATAF Site Activation Task Force
SCEO Station Construction Engineering
        Officer
SCEO System Civil Engineering Office
SES   Surface Effect Ship
SESG Southern European Shipping Group
SHADCOM Shipping Advisory Committee
SHAPE Supreme Headquarters Allied Power,
        Europe
SHAPM Ships Acquisition Project Manager
SINK Simulated Interactive Naval Kriegspiel
SKT   Skill Knowledge Tests
SLBM Submarine Launched Ballistic Missile
SLCM Sea Launched Cruise Missile

SLD   Ships Logistics Division
SMAB   Segment Receipt Inspection Building
SMAWT Short Range Man Portable Anti-Tank
       Weapon Technology
SMSA   Standard Metropolitan Statistical Area
SOAF   Sultan of Oman's Air Force
SOCE   Staff Officer Construction Engineering
SPD   Ship Project Directive
SPO   System Program Office
SQAT   Skim Qualification Assistance Team
SRT   Supply Response Time
SSD   Space Systems Division
SSTV   Sea Skimming Test Vehicles
STAG   Strategy and Tactics Analysis Group
TACP   Tactical Air Control Party
TBO   Time Between Overhaul
TDY   Temporary Duty
TEWS   Tactical Electronic Warfare Systems
TLAS   Tactical Logical and Air Simulation
TRAM   Target Recognition Attack Multisensor
TVM   Track Via Missile
UADPS Uniform Automated Data Processing
UAF   Union Air Force
UMO   Unit Management Document
USA   United States Army
USAF   United States Air Force
USATACOM United States Army Tank-Automotive
       Command
USAWC United States Army War College
USGW   Under Sea Guided Weapon
USMA   United States Military Academy
USMC   United States Marine Corps
USN   United States Navy
UTTAS Utility Tactical Transport Aircraft
       System
VAL   Vehicle Authorization List
VSTT   Variable Speed Training Target
WASP   War Air Service Program
WPAFB Wright-Patterson Air Force Base
WSE   Weapon System Efficiency
WSMR   White Sands Missile Range (US)
WWMCCS World Wide Military Command and
       Control System (US)

MILLING

BOCM   British Oil and Cake Mills
CTC   Carbon Tetrachloride
CWP   Chorleywood Process
EDB   Ethylene Dibromide
EDC   Ethylene Dichorine
FM   Flour Milling
FMT   Flour Milling Technology
NACAM National Association of Corn and
       Agricultural Merchants
NMD   Nutritional Muscular Dystrophy
PFM   Practice of Flour Milling
PPB   Pyrethrins Piperonyl Butoxide
STA   Seed Trade Association

MUSIC

CONHAN Contextual Harmonic Analysis
DARMS Digital Alternate Representation of
       Music Symbols
FIM   International Federation of Musicians
MIR   Music Information Retrieval

NAVAL SCIENCES

ALOND Assumed Longitude
AOT   Alignment Optical Telescope
AT   Atomic Time
DOT   Deep Ocean Transponder
DR   Dead Reckoning
DRAI   Dead Reckoning Analyzer Indicator
DRM   Direction of Relative Movement
DRT   Dead Reckoning Tracer
DSRV   Deep Submergence Rescue Vehicle
DSSV   Deep Submergence Search Vehicle
DSV   Deep Submergence Vehicle
EL   Electroluminescent
EOT   Engine Order Telegraph
ET   Ephemeris Time
GEON   Gyro Erected Optical Navigation
HLAD   Hearing-Lookout Assist Device
HOE   Height Of Eye
IC   Instrument Correction
IIP   Instantaneous Impact Point
IMCO   Intergovernmental Marine Consultative
       Organization
LVRJ   Low Volume Ram Jet
MABS   Maritime Application Bridge System
MARAD Maritime Administration
MARR   Marine Accidents Requiring Rescue
MAU   Marine Amphibious Unit
MCS   Marine Casualty Statistics
MMC   Micro Meteoroid Capsule
MODCAT Modified Catamaran
MOUSE Manager-Owner-User System-Engineer
MTDS   Marine Tactical Data System
NA   Nautical Almanac
NASCO National Academy of Sciences Committee
       on Oceanography (US)
NAVELESYSCOM Naval Electronic System
       Command
NAVSAT Navigation Satellite
NBT   Narrow Beam Transducer
NCLT   Night Carrier Landing Trainer
NCSORG Naval Control of Shipping
       Organization
NCTRU Naval Clothing and Textile Research
       Unit
NFO   Naval Flight Officers
NM   Nautical Miles
NNSS   Navy Navigation Satellite System
NRL   Naval Research Laboratory
NSIA   National Security Industrial
       Association

NTDS	Naval Tactical Data Systems	ASPR	Average Specific Polymerization Rate
ODPCS	Oceanographic Data Processing and Control System	AZBN	Azobisisiobutyronitrile
ONR	Office of Naval Research (US)	BHET	Bishydroxyethyl Terephthalate
OPLE	OMEGA Position Locating Equipment	BLG	Benzyl-L-Glutamate
PMIP	Postmaintenance Inspection Pilots	BTDA	Benzophenone Tetracarboxylic Dianhydride
POT	Propeller Order Transmitter	CA	Cinnamic Acid
PPI	Plan Position Indicator	CCMD	Continuous Current Monitoring Device
PRR	Pulse Repetition Rate	COD	Crack Open Displacement
PTC	Passive Thermal Control	DAAM	Diacetone Acrylamide
RR	Rendezvour Radar	DADPS	Diamonodiphenylphone
RTCM	Radio Technical Commission for Marine Services	DCA	Dichloroacetic
		DCP	Dicumyl Peroxide
SBX	Subsea Beacon/Transponder	DETA	Diethylenetriamine
SEF	Small End Forward	DMA	Dimethyl Acetamide
SES	Surface Effect Ship	DME	Dimethyl Ethanolamine
SINS	Ship's Inertial Navigation System	DMT	Dimethyl Terephthalate
SOSS	Shipboard Oceanographic Survey System	DRP	Dense Random Packed
SQAT	Shim Qualification Assistance Team	DSC	Differential Scanning Calorimetry
SSS	Shipboard Survey Subsystem	EG	Ethylene Glycol
TIS	Transponder Interrogation Sonar	EM	Electron Microscopy
TPCU	Thermal Preconditioning Unit	EVA	Ethylene Vinyl Acetate
TWT	Travelling Wave Tube	FeAA	Ferric Acetylacetonate
UEP	Underwater Electric Potential	FFS	Flory Fox Schaefgen
USN	United States Navy	FRD	Fibre Resin Developments (UK)
WHOI	Woods Hole Oceanographic Institutions	FRP	Fiber Reinforced Polyester
		FRP	Fiberglass Reinforced Plastics
		GRP	Glass Reinforced Polyester
		HIPS	High Impact Polystyrene
		HM	Higher Melting

NON-CRYSTALLINE SOLIDS

CBOM	Current Break Off and Memory	HTPB	Hydroxy Terminated Polybutadiene
CCM	Chain Crossing Model	IPS	Impact Polystyrene
CP	Coherent Potential	LDPE	Low Density Polyethylene
CPA	Coherent Potential Approximation	LM	Lower Melting
CRN	Continuous Random Network	MA	Methyl Acrylate
DCA	Direct Colorimetric Analysis	MDA	Methylendianiline
ECD	Energy Conversion Devices	MLG	Methyl-L-Glutamate
HE	Hall Effect	MMA	Methyl Methacrylate
JDES	Joint Density of Electronic States	MPDA	Metaphenylene Diamine
NC	Non-crystalline	NR	Natural Rubber
NDC	Negative Differential Conductivity	PACA	Polyamide Carboxylic Acid
OAO	Orthogonalized Atomic Orbital	PC	Polycarbonate
RDF	Radial Distribution Function	PEA	Polyethyl Acrylate
RPM	Random Phase Model	PEG	Polyethylene Glycol
SAS	Small Angle Scattering	PEO	Polyethylene Oxide
SC	Splat-Cooled	PET	Polyethylene Terephthalate
SRO	Short Range Order	PLA	Poly Lalamine
SS-CPA	Single-Site Coherent Potential Approximation	PMA	Polymethyl Acrylate
		PMDA	Pyromellitic Dianhydride
STM	Standard Thermal Model	PMMA	Polymethyl Methracrylate
TSD	Thermostimulated Depolarization	PO	Polymerizable Oligomers
VEM	Virtual Electrode Model	PPO	Polyphenol Oxidase
WQ	Water Quenched	PTFE	Polytetrafluorethylene
		PTMEG	Polytetramethylene Oxide Glycol
		PTMO	Polytetramethylene Oxide
		PVC	Polyvinyl Chloride
		PVDC	Polyvinylidine Chloride

NON-METALLIC MATERIALS (PLASTICS, POLYMERS)

		PVDF	Polyvinylide Fluoride
ABS	Acrylonitrile Butadiene Styrene	PVF	Polyvinyl Fluoride
AIBN	Azobisiobutyronitrite	RSS	Ribbed Smoked Sheets
AMS	Aerospace Material Specification		

SAXS	Small Angle X-ray Scattering		BNFL	British Nuclear Fuels Limited
SF	Stockmayer Fixman		BNRL	British Nuclear Reactors Limited
TBA	Torsional Braid Analysis		BNW	Battelle Northwest
TBPO	Tertiary Butyl Peroctoate		BPD	Beam Positioning Drive
TCE	Tetrachloroethane		BRR	Battelle Research Reactor
TDI	Toluene Diisocyanate		BS	Beth Salpeter
TDM	Tertiary Dodecyl Mercaplan		BSLT	Blankenbecler and Sugar and Logunov and Tarhkelidze
TEA	Triethylamine			
TEPA	Tetraethylenepentamine		BTE	Baldwin Tate Emery
TETA	Triethylenetetramine		BWR	Boiling Water Reactors
TFA	Trifluoroacetic		C-A	Conventional-Alloy
THF	Tetrahydro Furan		CANDU-BLW	Canada Deuterium Uranium Boiling Light Water
THFTDA	Tetrahydrofuran Tetracarboxylic Dianhydride			
			CD	Displaced Central Trajectory
TMCB	Tetramethoxycarbonyl Benzophenone		CDR	Chemtob Durso and Riska
TMEDA	Tetramethyl Ethylene Diamine		CE	Coulomb Excitation
TPA	Terephthalic Acid		CEA	Commissariat à l'Energie Atomique (Fr.)
UBFF	Urey Bradley Force Field			
UTS	Ultimate Tensile Strength		CEF	Critical Experiments Facility
			CEGB	Central Electricity Generating Board
			CERN	Organisation Européene pour la Recherche Nucléaire

NUCLEAR SCIENCES

			CF	Combined Function
AAT	Analytic Approximation Theory		CFR	Commercial Fast Reactor
AC	Ammonium Citrate		CFT	Constant Fraction Trigger
AC	Anti-Coincidence Counters		CGN	Canadian General Electric
ACRS	Advisory Committee on Reactor Safeguards (US)		CHF	Critical Heat Flux
			CHT	Cycloheptatriene
ADAC	Analytical Development Associates Corporation (US)		CIBS	CERN-IHEP Boston Spectrometer
			CIDNP	Chemically Induced Dynamic Nuclear Polarization
ADS	Automatic Depressurization System			
AEC	Atomic Energy Commission (US)		CLD	Constant Level Descriptor
AECL	Atomic Energy of Canada Limited		CLEM	Closed Loop Ex-vessel Machine
AEG	Allgemeine Elekrizitatls-Gesellschaft (Ger.)		CLIRA	Closed Loop In-Reactor Assemblies
			CMRR	Common Mode Rejection Ratio
AES	Auger Electron Spectroscopy		CMS	Coincidence Mössbauer Spectroscopy
AFSR	Argonne Fast Source Reactor		CNG	Compressed Natural Gas
AGR	Advanced Gas-cooled Reactor		CP	Collision Probability
AI	Area of Intersection		CPC	Controlled Potential Coulometry
AMINCO	American Instrument Company		CPS	CERN Proton Synchrotron
ANI	Annular Isotropic Source		CRNL	Chalk River Nuclear Laboratories (Can.)
ANIM	Association of Nuclear Instrument Manufacturers		CSE	Containment Systems Experiment
			CSL	Constant Scattering Length
ANL	Argonne National Laboratory (US)		CTF	Controlled Thermonuclear Fission
ANPP	Army Nuclear Power Program		CTR	Controlled Thermonuclear Reactor
ANS	American Nuclear Society		CVD	Chemical Vapour Deposition
AP	Alkaline Permagnate		CVTR	Carolians Virginia Tube Reactors
APAC	Alkaline Permagnate Ammonium Citrate		DAC	Distance Amplitude Correction
			DAM	Dual Absorption Model
API	Automatic Priority Interrupt		DBA	Design Basic Accident
APRFR	Army Pulse Radiation Facility Reactor		DBDA	Dibenzyldodecylamine
ARHCO	Atlantic Richfield Hanford Company		DCD	Digital Coherent Detector
ARM	Accumulator Read-in Module		DD	Density Dependent
ASNDT	American Society for Non Destructive Tests		DEPE	Double Escape Peak Efficiency
			DFR	Dounveay Fast Reactor
ATR	Advanced Terminal Reactor		DHE	Dump Heat Exchangers
BC	Breeding Gain		DHX	Dump Heat Exchangers
BD	Blocking Device		DISC	Differential Isochronous Self-collimating Counter
BDNA	Benzyldinonylame			
BHT	Blowdown Heat Transfer		DL	Delay Line
BLTC	Bottom Loading Transfer Cast		DNA	Dinolylaniline

DNL	Differential Non Linearity		HIR	Halden Internal Reports
DOT	Discrete Ordinate Transport		HLH	High Level Heating
DP	Differential Pressure		HPCS	High Pressure Core Spray System
DPH	Diamond Pyramid Hardness		HPR	Halden Project Report
DT	Doubling Time		HSST	Heavy Section Steel Technology
DT	Dummy Target		HTGR	High Temperature Gas Cooled Reactor
DTA	Differential Thermal Analysis		HTR	High Temperature Reactors
DTD	Dimethyl Tin Diffluoride		HVE	Horizontal Vertax Errors
DTS	Double Thermostat and Safety		IAEA	International Atomic Energy Agency
DU	Delay Uniy		IAF	International Astronautical Federation
DUP	Disk Utility Programme		IC	Internal Conversion
DWBA	Distorted Ware Born Approximation		ICC	Internal Conversion Coefficients
EAC	Error Alert Control		ID	Isotope Dilution-mass
EBOR	Experimental Beryllium Oxide Reactors		IDS	Interim Decay Storage
EBR	Experimental Breeder Reactor		IHX	Intermediate Heat Exchanger
ECCS	Emergency Core Cooling System		IMPATT	Impact Avalanche Transit Time
ECM	Electro Chemical Machining		IMRAP	Infrared Monochromatic Radiation Pyrometer
ECNG	East Central Nuclear Group (US)			
ECR	External Control Registers		IRHS	Intact Reentry Heat Source
EDM	Electrical Discharge Machining		IRR-2	Israel Research Reactor-2
EDTA	Ethylenediaminetetraacetic Acid		IRS	Infrared Spectroscope
EFPD	Equivalent Full Power Days		IS	Isomer Shifts
EKS	Energic Komprimierendes System		ISR	Intersecting Storage Rings
ENEA	European Nuclear Energy Agency		ITR	In-core Thermionic Reactor
EPG	Electrostatic Particle Guide		IUPAC	International Union of Pure and Applied Chemistry
EPM	Economic Performance Monitoring			
EPNG	El Paso Natural Gas		IVHM	In-Vessel Handling Machine
EPR	Electron Paramagnetic Resonance		JCAE	Joint Committee on Atomic Energy
ESCA	Electron Spectroscopy for Chemical Analysis		JEN	Junta de Energia Nuclear (Spain)
			JNACC	Joint Nuclear Accident Coordinating Center
ET	Emf-Temperature			
ETR	Experimental Test Reactor		KUR	Kyote University Reactor
EXD	Exchange Degeneracy		LAREC	Los Alamos Reactor Economics Code
FCTC	Fuel Centerline Thermocouples		LCT	Linear Combination Technique
FEPE	Full Energy Peak Efficiency		LDF	Linear Discriminate Function
FFTF	Fast Flux Test Facility		LEED	Low Energy Electron Diffraction
FFTR	Fast Flux Test Reactors		LET	Leading Edge Trigger
FIOT	Flags and Input Output Transfer		LLFM	Low Level Flux Monitors
FLECHT	Full Length Emergency Cooling Heat Transfer		LLH	Low Level Heating
			LMEC	Liquid Metal Engineering Center (US)
FMSR	Finite Mass Sum Rules		LMFBR	Liquid Metal-Cooled Fast Breeder Reactor
FPCE	Fission Products Conversion and Encapsulation			
			LNG	Liquefied Natural Gas
FTE	Fracture Transition Elastic		LO	Local Oscillator
FWHM	Full Width Half Maximum		LOCA	Loss of Coolant Accident
GAI	Generalization Area of Intersection		LPCI	Low Pressure Coolant Injection System
GCFR	Gas Cool Fast Reactor		LPE	Loop Preparation Equipment
GEC	Generalized Equivalent Cylinder		LRL	Lawrence Radiation Laboratory (US)
GGA	Gulf General Atomic		LVDT	Linear Variable Differential Transformer
GGRT	Goddard Goldstone Rebbi and Thorn			
GLC	Gas Liquid Chromatography		LVDT	Linear Voltage Differential Transformer
GMN	LeGuillou Morel Navelet			
GTA	Gas Tungsten Arc		LWR	Light Water Reactor
H	Hexapole		MC-A	Modified Conventional Alloy
HBWR	Halden Boiling Heavy Water Reactor		MCPHA	Multichannel Pulse-Height Analyzer
HCEX	Hypercharge Exchange		MDH	Maximum Diameter Heat
HDM	Hidrodensimeter		MDT	Maximum Diameter of the Thorax
HFIR	High Flux Isotope Reactor		Me	Mössbauer Effect
HFS	Hyperfine Structure		MES	Mössbauer Effect Spectroscopy
HF-SCF	Hartree-Fock Self-Consistent-Field		MFBS	Multifrequency Binary Sequence

MHW	Multihundred Watt
MIRD	Medical Internal Radiation Dose
MLF	Multilateral Force
MMN	Metallurgie et Mécanique Nucléaires (Belg.)
MSAR	Mine Safety Appliance Research
MSF	Multi-Stage Flash
MSRE	Molten Salt Reactor Experiment
MTR	Materials Testing Reactor
MUCHA	Multiple Channel Analysis
NAN	Neutron Activation Analysis
NCRP	National Council on Radiation Protection (US)
NDT	Nil-Ductability Transmission
NDT	Non-Destructive Testing
NEPA	National Environmental Policy Act (US)
NERVA	Nuclear Energy Rocket Vehicle Application
NG-EGDN	Nitroglycerin-Ethylene Glycol Dinitrate
NIM	Nuclear Instrument Module
NINI	Nidbus to Nine
NMR	Nuclear Magnetic Resonance
NOSHEB	North of Scotland Hydro-Electric Board
NP	Neutrino Parents
NPSD	Neutron Power Spectral Density
NPT	Non-Proliferation Treaty
NQR	Nuclear Quadrupole Resonance
NSPP	Nuclear Safety Pilot Point
NSSS	Nuclear Steam Supply System
NTS	Nevada Test Site
NTS	Notch Tensile Strength
NUKEM	Nuklear Chemie und Metallurgie (Ger.)
NUMEC	Nuclear Material Equipment Corporation
O	Octopole
OBE	One-Brown Exchange
OCR	Organic Cooled Reactor
OD	Outside Diameter
OED	Quantum Electrodynamics
ONWARD	Organization of North West Authorities for Rationalized Design (US)
ORGDP	Oak Ridge Gaseous Diffusion Plant
ORNL	Oak Ridge National Laboratory
ORR	Oak Ridge Reactor
PBRF	Plum Brook Reactor Facility
PFR	Prototype Fast Reactor
PG	Pyrolytic Graphite
PHA	Pulse Height Analyzer
PHTC	Pulse Height to Time Converter
PM	Photomultiplier
PPS	Plant Protection System
PRBS	Psudorandom Binary Sequences
PRT	Platinum Resistance Thermometer
PRTR	Plutonium Recycle Test Reactor
PRTS	Pseudorandom Ternary Sequence
PSAR	Preliminary Safety Analysis Report
PUP	Plutonium Utilization Program
PVRC	Pressure Vessel Research Committee
PWR	Pressurized Water Reactor

PWR-FLECHT	Pressurized Water Reactor-Full Length Emergency Core Heat Transfer
QS	Quadrupole Splitting
RAS	Rutgers Annihilation Spectrometer
RCG	Radioactivity Concentration Guide
RD	Radiation Damage
REB	Relativistic Electron Beam
RED	Reflection Electron Diffraction
REM	Replacement Micrographs
RESAR	Reference Safety Analysis Report
RF	Release Fraction
RGLET	Rise-time Gated Leading Edge Trigger
RPH	Relative Pulse Height
RRTC	Retractable Replaceable Thermocouple
RTD	Resistance Temperature Detector
RTG	Radioisotope Thermoelectric Generator
RUDI	Restricted Use Digital Instrument
SAM	Strong Absorption Model
SARARC	Stable Auroral Red Arc
SBP	Shore Based Prototype
SC	Special Conventional-Alloy
SCE	Single Charge Exchange
SCR-CD	Silicon Controlled Rectifier, Direct Current
SEFOR	Southwest Experimental Fast Oxide Reactor
SEM	Scanning Electron Micrographs
SEPE	Single Escape Peak Efficiency
SEV	Sekundarelektronen Vervielfachern
SF	Separate Function
SGHWR	Steam Generating Heavy Water Reactor
SGZ	Surface Ground Zero
SHD	Slant Hole Distance
SI	Specific Inventory
SIP	Standard Information Package
SLAC	Stanford Linear Accelerator Center
SM	Shell Model
SNP	Sodium Nitroprusside
SNPO	Space Nuclear Propulsion Office
SNPS	Satellite Nuclear Power Station
SPST	Single Pole Single Throw
SPTF	Sodium Pump Test Facility
SRO	Short Range Order
SRS	Sodium Removal Station
SS	Sodium Salicylate
SSD	Solid State Detector
SSU	Saybolt Seconds Universal
SUNI	Southern Universities Nuclear Institute (Can.)
SwRI	Southwest Research Institute (US)
TA	Time Analyzer
TA	Triacetin
TaC	Tantalum Carbide
TAC	Time Amplitude Converter
TDPAC	Time Differential Perturbed Angular Correlation
TEC	Total Electron Content
TEC	Transient Electron Current
TED	Thin Film Detector

TEM   Transmission Electron Microscopy
TIG   Tugstern Inert Gas
TKF   TRIGA King Furnace
TKFF   TRIGA King Furnace Facilities
TLD   Thermoluminescence Dosimeter
TMD   Tensor Meson Dominance
TMTU   Tetramethythiourea
TOA   Time-of-Arrival
TP   Terphenyl
TPC   Time Pickoff Controls
TPE   Two Pion Exchange
TPHC   Time to Pulse Height Converter
TPU   Time Pickoff Units
TRAPATT Trapped Avalanche Triggered Transit
TRW   Thompson-Ramo-Wooldrige
TURPS   Terrestial Unattended Reactor Power
        System
UC   Uranium Carbide
UJM   Uncorrelated Jet Model
UKAEA   United Kingdom Atomic Energy Authority
USAEC   United States Atomic Energy Commission
VAAC   Vanadyl Acetylacetonate
VINS   Very Intense Neutron Source
VMD   Vector Meson Dominance
VVE   Vertical Vertex Errors
WANEF   Westinghouse Astronuclear Experimental
        Facility
WANL   Westinghouse Astronuclear Laboratory
WOL   Wedge Opening Load
WSZ   Wrong Signature Zero
ZP   Zero Point
ZRA   Zero Range Approximation

OCEANOGRAPHY

AMT   Audio Magnetotelluric
DCP   Data Collection Platform
DSDP   Deep Sea Drilling Projects
EERL   Earthquake Engineering Research
        Laboratory (US)
ERG   Electroretinogram
IDOE   International Decade of Ocean
        Exploration
IID   Intermittently Integrated Doppler
IOC   Intergovermental Oceanographic
        Commission
JHD   Joint Hypocenter Determination
LASA   Large Aperture Seismic Array
MLW   Mean Low Water
NOAA   National Oceanographic Atmospheric
        Administration (US)
NRM   Natural Remnant Magnetization
POL   Pacific Oceanographic Laboratory
SAGA   Short Arc Geodetic Adjustment
SWRA   Selected Water Resources Abstracts
UARS   Unmanned Arctic Research Submersible
VRM   Viscous Remnant Magnetization

PATENTS

ABCS   Advisory Board for Cooperative Systems
CISAC   International Confederation of
        Societies of Authors and Composers
ECE   Economic Commission for Europe
EIRMA   European Industrial Research
        Management Association
ICC   International Chamber of Commerce
ICF   International Contract Furnishing
        [Incorporated]
ICIREPAT International Cooperation in
        Information Retrieval among
        Patent Officers
IFIA   International Federation of Inventors
        Association
IIB   Institut International des Brevets
        [International Patent Institute]
LICCD   International League Against Unfair
        Competition
TCC   Technical Coordination Committee

PHOTOGRAPHY

AAS   Atomic Absorption Spectrophotometer
AEI   Aerial Exposure Index
AHU   Antihalation Undercoat
AIM   Aerial Independent Models
ANOVA   Analysis of Variants
APR   Airborne Profile Recorder
APTS   Automatic Picture Transmission System
ARDC   Air Research and Development Command
        (US)
AVCS   Advanced Vidicon Camera System
BDS   Benzenediazothioethers
BOD   Biochemical Oxygen Demand
BTCC   Benzothiazolocarbon-Cyanine
CADA   Cellulose Acetate Diethyl-Aminoacetate
CAT   Canon Auto Tuning
CC   Colour Compensating
CIE   Commission Internationale de
        l'Eclairage
CLC   Constant Light Compensating
COM   Computer Output Microfilm
COSATI Committee on Scientific and Technical
        Information
CP   Colour Printing
CPA   Concurrent Photon Amplification
CT   Charge Transfer
CTS   Cooke Troughton and Sims
CuLPCN Copper Leucophalocyanine
CVD   Creative Visual Dynamics
DIR   Development Inhibitor Releasing
DMF   Dimethylformanide
DMSO   Dimethyl Sulphoxide
DP   Degree of Polymerization
DQE   Detective Quantum Efficiency
DTR   Diffusion Transfer
ECO   Ektachrome Commercial

ELF	Electroluminescent Ferroelectric
END	Equivalent Neutral Density
ETD	Equivalent Transmission Density
EVR	Electronic Video Recording
FOSDIC	Film Optical Sensing Device for Input to Computer
HD	Horizontal Distance
HIRF	High Intensity Reciprocity Failure
HIRS	High-Resolution Infrared Radiation Sounder
HMO	Hiickel-approximation Molecular Orbital
HQ	Hydro Quinone
HS	Holographic Stereogram
ICA	International Cartographic Association
IEP	Image Edge Profile
IEP	Instrumental for Evaluation of Pictures
IFPI	International Federation of the Photographic Industry
ISCC	Inter Society Colour Council
ISO	International Society for Photogrammetry
ISP	International Society of Photogrammetry
ISS	Image Sharpness Scale
JCII	Japan Camera Inspection Institute
KMER	Kodak Metal Etch Resist
KTFR	Kodak Thin Film Resist
LES	Light Exposure Speed
LIRF	Low Intensity Reciprocity Failure
LSIG	Line Scan Image Generator
LTH	Low Temperature Herschel
MMF	Micromation Microfilm
MNP	N-Methyl-2-Pyrollidone
MS	Multispectral
MSS	Multispectral Scanner
MTCs	Modulation Transfer Curves
MTF	Modulation Transfer Function
NA	Numerical Aperture
NESC	National Environmental Satellite Centre
NMR	Nuclear Magnetic Resonance
NOS	National Ocean Survey (US)
NSPV	Number of Scans Per Vehicle
OBF	One-Bar-Function
OTD	Original Transmission Densities
OTF	Optical Transfer Function
PCMI	Photocromic Microimage
PD	Principal Distance
PDF	Probability Density Functions
PEG	Polyethylene Glycol
PEO	Polyethylene Oxide
PM	Photomultiplier
PMC	Princeton Microfilm Corporation
PMT	Pheny Mercaptote Trazole
PPI	Plan Position Indicator
PPM	Peak Programme Meters
PPV	Polarized Platen Viewer
PTAB	Photographic Technical Advisory Board

	(US)
PTF	Phase Transfer Function
PVA	Polyvinyl Acetate
PVA	Polyvinyl Alcohol
PVK	Poly-N-Vinylearbarbazole
PVK	Poly-N-Vinylearbazole
PVP	Polyvinylpyrrolidone
RBV	Return Beam Vidicon
RMS	Root Mean Square
ROC	Receive Operating Characteristic
RQE	Relative Quantum Efficiencies
RRB	Rapid Response Bibliography
RT	Room Temperature
SCP	Serial Character Printer
SDI	Select Dissemination of Information
SIA	Stereoimage Alternator
SID	Solubilization by Incipient Development
SLAR	Side Looking Airborne Radar
SMP	Scanning Microscope Photometer
SMPTE	Society of Motion Pictures and Television Engineers
S/N	Signal-to-Noise
SNR	Signal-to-Noise Ratio
SPT	Star Point Transfer
SQF	Subjective Quality Factor
SSCC	Spin Scan Cloud Camera
SWB	Single Weight Baryta
TCNE	Tetracyanoethylene
TCNQ	Tetracyanoquinodimethane
TF	Threshold Factor
THI	Total Height Index
TMA	Trimellitic Anhydride
TOC	Total Optical Color
TPR	Thermoplastic Recording
TTC	Thiatricarboxyanine
TTU	Timing Terminal Unit
UCS	Uniform Chromaticity Scale
UNNSAD	Unit Neutral Normalized Spectral Analytical Density
VFC	Video Film Converter
VICOM	Visual Communications Management
ZD	Zenith Distance
ZTS	Zoom Transfer Scope

PHYSICS

APL	Applied Physics Laboratory
AR	Antireflection
CEX	Central Excitation
C-V	Capacitance Voltage
DIPD	Double Inverse Pinch Device
EMF	Evolving Magnetic Features
ESP	Electron Spin Polarization
FKG	Fortuin Kasteleyn and Ginibre
GDL	Gas Dynamic Laser
ICTP	International Centre for Theoretical Physics
LCAO	Linear Combination of Atomic Orbitals

LEED Low Energy Electron Diffraction
LF   Limiting Fragmentation
MCD   Magnetic Circular Dichroism
NPE   Natural Parity Exchange
ODP   Optical Data Processor
PEX   Projectable Excitation
PIC   Particle-In-Cell
POTF Polychromatic Optical Thickness
        Fringes
SCS   Stimulated Compton Scattering
SEA   Statistical Energy Analysis
SED   Strong Exchange Degeneracy
TASRA Thermal Activation Strain Rate
        Analysis
TEX   Target Excitation
UPE   Unnatural Parity Exchange
WED   Weak Exchange Degeneracy

PRINTING

CAT   Computer Aided Typesetting
CB   Coated Back
CF   Coated Front
CFB   Coated Front and Back
DPS   Defense Printing Services (US)
EDTA Ethylenediaminetetraacetic Acid
EMPCO Electronic Mechanical Products Company
GATF Graphic Arts Technical Foundation
GBC   General Binding Corporation
GPO   Government Printing Office
IBB   International Brotherhood of
        Bookbinders
ICL   International Computer Limited
IPMA In-plant Printing Management
        Association
LPIU Lithographers and Photoengravers
        International Union
MARK Management Ability and Reprographic
        Know-how
MT/SC Magnetic Tape Selectric Composer
MT/ST Magnetic Tape Selectric Typewriter
NAPL National Association of Photo-
        Lithographers
NEPS National Printing Equipment Show
NPPS Navy Publication and Printing Services
PFC   Pack Feed and Converter
PIA   Printing Industries of America
PMT   Photochemical Transfer
PPC   Printers' Pension Corporation
RCA   Royal College of Art
TAPPI Technical Association of the Pulp
        Paper Industry

SECURITY

CIA   Central Intelligence Agency
CIC   Counter Intelligence Corps

SPACE SCIENCES

ABRES Advanced Ballistic Reentry System
ACS   Altitude Control System
AE   Atmospheric Explorer
AES   Artificial Earth Satellite
AGARD Advisory Group for Aeronautical
        Research and Development
AGE   Aerospace Ground Equipment
AIAA Aerospace Industries Association of
        America
AIAA American Institute of Aeronautics
        and Astronautics
AICBM Anti-Intercontinental Ballistic
        Missile
AMU   Astronaut Maneuvering Unit
ARL   Aerospace Research Laboratory (UK)
A/S   Ascent Stage
ASEB Aeronautics and Space Engineering
        Board
ASTP Apollo Soyuz Test Project
ATS   Advanced Technology Satellite
ATS   Applications Technology Satellite
AVA   Aerodynamische Versuchsanstalt (Ger.)
BMEWS Ballistic Missile Early Warning
        System
BREL Boeing Radiation Effect Laboratory
BRL   Ballistics Research Laboratory (US)
BSD   Ballistic System Division
CAV   Composite Analog Video
CCU   Contaminant Collection Unit
CIAP Climatic Impact Assessment Program
COGS Continuous Orbital Guidance System
CORF Committee on Radio Frequency
COSPAR Committee on Space Research
CRETC Combined Radiation Effects Test
        Chamber
CSC   Communications Satellite Corporation
CSM   Command Service Module
CSTR Committee on Solar Terrestrial Research
CTIO Cerro Tololo Inter-American
        Observatory (Chile)
CTR   Certified Test Requirements
CTS   Communications Technology Satellite
CVC   Consolidated Vacuum Corporation (US)
CWED Cold Weld Evaluation Device
DAMP Downrange Anti-Missile Measurement
        Program
DAMS Defense Against Missile Systems
DAS   Data Acquisitioning System
DBS   Direct Broadcast Satellite
DGBC Digital Geoballistic Computer System
DICBM Defense Intercontinental Ballistic
        Missile
DICON Digital Communication-Through Orbiting
        Needles
DICORAP Directional Controlled Rocket
        Assisted Projectiles
DISCOS Disturbance Compensation System
DRI   Descent Rate Indicator

DRIFT Diversity Receiving Instrumentation for Telemetry
DS   Descent Stage
DSAP Defence Systems Application Program
DSCS Defense Satellite Communications System
DSN   Deep Space Network
DST   Data System Test
ECG   Electrocardiogram
ECS   Environmental Control Subsystem
EDITAR Electronic Digital Tracking and Ranging
EEM   Earth Entry Module
EFAS Electronic Flash Approach System
EHF   Extremely High Frequency
ELDO European Launcher Development Organization
ELSS Extravehicular Life Support System
EMC   Electromagnetic Compatibility
EMU   Extravehicular Mobility Unit
EOAP Earth Observations Aircraft Program
EOPAP Earth and Ocean Physics Program
EPD   Electronic Proximity Detector
EPIC Earth Pointing Instrument Carrier
EROS Earth Resources Observation Satellite
EROS Earth Resources Observation System
ERTS Earth Resources Technology Satellite
ESC   European Space Conference
ESR   Electron Spin Resonance
ESRO European Space Research Organization
ESSCO Electron Space Structure Corporation
ESTEC European Space Technology Center
ETR   Eastern Test Range (US)
EUV   External Ultra Violet
EVA   Extra Vehicular Activity
EVCS Extravehicular Communication System
FABMDS Field Army Ballistic Missile Defence System
FBO   Fixed Base Operator
FDI   Flight Director Indicator
FITH Fire In The Hole
FLTSATCOM Fleet Satellite Communication
FMS   Force Measurement System
GARP Global Atmospheric Research Program
GATE Global Atlantic Tropical Experiment
GATV Gemini Agena Target Vehicle
GC   Gas Chromatography
GC-MS Gas Chromatography - Mass Spectrometry
GESO Geodetic Earth Orbiting Satellite
GPS   Global Positioning System
GSE   Ground Support Equipment
GSE   Group Support Equipment
GSFC Goddard Space Flight Center (US)
HEAO High Energy Astronomy Observatories
HEPA High Efficiency Particulate Air
HHMU Handheld Maneuvering Unit
IAF   International Astronautical Federation
ICCAIA International Coordinating Council of Aerospace Industries Association
IDSCS Initial Defense Satellite Communications System
IES   Internal Environmental Simulator
IME   International Magnetosphere Explorer
IMP   Interplanetary Monitoring Platform
IMS   International Magnetospheric Study
INTELSAT International Telecommunications Satellite
IPAD Integrated Programs for Aerospace-Vehicle Design
IRIG Inter Range Instrument Group
IRS   Infrared Spectroscopy
ISEPS International Sun-Earth Physics Programme
IUCSTP Inter Union Commission on Solar Terrestial Physics
IUE   International Ultraviolet Explorer
IUS   Initial Upper Stage
JPL   Jet Propulsion Laboratory (US)
JSC   Johnson Space Center
LES   Launch Escape System
LET   Launch Escape Tower
LET   Linear Energy Transfer
LM   Lunar Module
LST   Large Space Telescopes
LUT   Launcher Umbilical Tower
MFT   Monolayer Formation Time
MIUS Modular Integrated Utility System
MJS   Mariner Jupiter Saturn
MPIO Mission and Payload Integration Office
MPP   Mission Planning Program
MSC   Manned Spacecraft Center
MSFC Marshall Space Flight Center
MTF   Modulation Transfer Function
MVM   Mariner Versus Mercury
NAE   National Academy of Engineering (US)
NAS   National Academy of Science (US)
NAS   National Airspace System
NASA National Aeronautics and Space Administration
NASTRAN NASA Structural Analysis Program
NCAR National Center for Atmospheric Research
NOAA National Oceanographic Atmospheric Administration (US)
NOESS National Operational Environmental Satellite System
OALS Observer Air Lock System
OAO   Orbital Astronomical Observatories
ODIN Optical Design Integration
ONERA Office National d'Etudes et de Recherches Aéronautiques (Fr.)
OSR   Optical Solar Reflector
PADS Performance Analysis and Design Synthesis
PCG   Phonocardiogram
PGA   Pressure Garment Assembly
PLSS Portable Life Support System
PTM   Performance Test Model
PU   Propellant Utilization

QCM   Quartz Crystal Microbalance
QCMB   Quartz Crystal Microbalance Gravimetry
QSG   Quasi-Stellar Galaxy
QSO   Quasi-Stellar Objects
RAE   Radio Astronomy Explorer
RCS   Reaction Control System
RGA   Residual Gas Analyzer
RIMS   Radiation Intensity Meaning System
RTC   Reference Transfer Calibrator
SAB   Solar Alignment Bay
SAFE   San Andreas Fault Experiment
SAMTEC Space and Missile Test Center (US)
SAS   Small Astronomical Satellite
SATS   Solar Alignment Test Site
SAVES Sizing of Aerospace Vehicle Structures
SDMA   Space Division Multiple Access
SDS   Satellite Data System
SEP9   Solar Electric Propulsion System
SESL   Space Environment Simulation
       Laboratory (US)
SMATS Source Module Alignment Test Site
SMEAT Skylab Medical Experiments Altitude
       Tests
SMS   Synchronous Meteorological Satellites
SNS   Space Navigation System
SSC   Stellar Simulation Complex
SSD   Space Systems Division
ST   Skin Temperature
STADA Station Data Acquisition and Control
STARS Satellite Telemetry Automatic
       Reduction Systems
STDN   Spacecraft Tracking and Data Network
STS   Space Transportation Systems
SVH   Solar Vacuum Head
SVM   Silicon Video Memory
TALS   Transfer Air Lock Section
TCM   Temperature Control Model
TELOPS Telemetry On-Line Processing System
TLRV   Tracked Levitated Research Vehicles
TPS   Thermal Protection System
TWERLE Tropical Wind Energy Conversion and
       Reference Level Experiment
TWL   Total Weight Loss
UAP   Upper Air Project
UTCS   Urban Traffic Control System
UTIAS University of Toronto Institute for
       Aerospace Studies
VCM   Vacuum Condensible Material
VISSR Visible and Infrared Spin Scan
       Radiometer
VLA   Very Large Array
VLBI   Very Long Baseline Interferometry
WSMR   White Sands Missile Range (US)
WTR   Western Test Range (US)

STANDARDS

ANSI   American National Standards Institute
ASA   American Standards Association

ASC   American Standard Code
ASG   Aeronautical Standards Group
ASTA   Association of Short Circuit Testing
       Authorities
AWS   American War Standards
BASEC British Approval Service for Electric
       Cables
BEAB   British Eurotechnical Approval Board
BEMA   Business Equipment Manufacturers'
       Association
BSI   British Standards Institution
CESA   Canadian Engineering Standards
       Association
ISO   International Standards Organization
NBS   National Bureau of Standards

STATISTICS

CES   Constant Elasticity of Substitution
FES   Family Expenditure Survey
HPD   Highest Posterior Density
MLE   Maximum Likelihood Estimator
MST   Minimum Spanning Tree
MVLUE Minimum Variance Linear Unbiased
       Estimator
MVU   Minimum Variance Unbiased
PCV   Packed Cell Volume
POL   Problem Oriented Language
PSW   Processor State Word
RE   Relative Efficiency
SD   Second Difference
SSP   Sums of Squares and Products
THE   Thunderstorm Event

TELECOMMUNICATIONS

AACD   Antenna Adjustable Current Distribution
AACS   Asynchronous Address Communications
       Systems
ACF   Autocorrelation Function
ACS   Automatic Control System
ADSS   A Diesel Supply Set
AEI   Automatic Error Interrogation
AES   Atmospheric Environment Service
AFC   Amplitude Frequency Characteristic
AFC   Autocorrelation Functions
AFR   Amplitude Frequency Responses
AFTN   Aeronautical Fixed Telecommunications
       Network
AID   Automatic Interrogation Distorted
AIS   Automatic Intercity Station
AITE   Automatic Intercity Telephone
       Exchange
AITS   Automatic Integrated Telephone System
AJ   Area Junction
AL   Amplitude Limiter
AL   Artificial Lines
AM   Amplitude Modulation

AMC	Automatic Monitoring Circuit	DSS	Discrete Sync System
ANS	Astronomical Netherlands Satellite	DT	Data Transmission
APC	Amplitude Phase Conversion	EBU	European Broadcasting Union
APT	Automatic Picture Transmission	EC	Error Counter
ARRL	American Radio Relay League	ELE	Equivalent Logic Element
AS	Automatically Switching	EMU	Extravehicular Mobility Unit
ASU	Automatic Switching Units	EPIRB	Energy Position Indicating Beacon
ATC	Automatic Through Centers	ERSOS	Earth Resources Survey Operational Satellites
ATCA	Automatic Tunnel Circuit Adjustment	ERTS	Earth Resources Technology Satellite
ATCAA	Automatic Tuned Circuit Adjustment Amplitude	ESCES	Experimental Satellite Communication Earth Station
ATJ	Automatic Through Junction	ESRO	European Space Research Organization
ATO	Automatic Trunk Offices	ESSA	Environmental Science Services Administration
BAA	Broadband Antenna Amplifier	ESSCO	Electronic Space Structure Corporation
BSA	Bimetal Steel Aluminium	EUV	Extreme Ultra Violet
BUT	Broadband Unbalanced Transformer	FD	Frequency Demodulator
CAS	Central Amplifier Stations	FPSK	Frequency and Phase Shift Keying
CC	Comparison Circuit	FS	Frequency Synthesizer
CCD	Controlled Current Distribution	FSK	Frequency Shift Keying
CCF	Cross-Correlation Function	FTS	Federal Telecommunication System
CCIR	International Radio Consultative Committee	GDR	Ground Delay Responses
CEPT	European Conference of Post and Telecommunications	GDTA	Group Development of Aerospace Teledetection
CF	Correlation Function	GMS	Geostationary Meteorological Satellite
CFAP	Copenhagen Frequency Allocation Plan	GOES	Geostationary Operational Environmental Satellite
CIOT	International Telegraph Operation Centre	GSU	Guaranteed Supply Unit
CIR	Characteristic Instants of Restitution	GTS	Global Telecommunications System
CL	Cable Links	HET	Health Education Telecommunications
CL	Connecting Lines	HFPS	High Frequency Phase Shifter
COF	Correct Operation Factor	HIC	Hybrid Integrated Circuits
COTC	Canadian Overseas Telecommunication Corporation	HPA	High Power Amplifiers
CPG	Clock Pulse Generator	HSG	Horizontal Sweep Generator
CRAAM	Centre of Radio Astronomy and Astrophysics, Mackenzie University (Sao Paulo)	HVG	High Voltage Generator
		IBTE	Imperial Board of Telecommunications of Ethiopia
CS	Communication Satellites	IC	Input Circuit
CSC	Common Signalling Channel	ICO	Intercity Coin Offices
CTR	Collective Television Reception	IDM	Integral and Differential Monitoring
CTU	Channel Testing Unit	IF	Information Feedback
CU	Control Unit	IF	Intermediate Frequency
CVC	Current Voltage Characteristics	IFRB	International Frequency Registration Board
DASS	Demand Assigned Signalling and Switching	IGN	National Geographic Institute
DC	Direct Connections	IIRC	Interrogation and Information Reception Circuits
DC	Dispatcher Console	IMCO	Intergovernmental Marine Consultative Organization
DF	Distribution Feeders	INTELSAT	International Telecommunications Satellite
DFB	Distribution Feeders Branch		
DMF	Digital Matched Filter	IPTM	Interval Pulse Time Modulations
DOA	Differential Operational Amplifiers	IR	Intermediate Register
DPolT	Differential Polarization Telegraphy	ISC	Initial Slope Circuit
DPSK	Differential Phase Shift Keying	ISIS	International Satellite for Ionospheric Studies
DPWM	Double-Sided Pulse-Width Modulation	ISRO	Indian Space Research Organization
DR	Defined Readout	ISS	Ionosphere Sounding Satellite
DRID	Direct Readout Image Dissector	ITE	Institute of Telecommunications
DRTE	Defence Research Telecommunications Establishment		
DS	Digital Signal		

Engineers

ITMJ	Incoming Trunk Message Junction
ITOS	Improved Tiros Operational Satellite
ITU	International Telecommunication Unit
IUCAF	Inter-Union Commission on Allocation of Frequency
JE	Junction Exchanges
JO	Junction Office
JW	Junction Wide
LAS	Line Apparatus Shops
LCRU	Lunar Communications Relay Unit
LE	Logic Element
LF	Logic Function
LFPS	Low Frequency Phase Shifter
LNFB	Linear Negative Feedback
LNR	Low Noise Receivers
LPA	Log Periodic Antennas
LPD	Linear Phasing Device
LPF	Low Pass Filter
LSF	Lumped Selection Filters
MAACS	Multi-Address Asynchronous Communication System
MC	Main Channel
MCC	Mixing Cross-bar Connectors
MCRN	Moscow City Relay Network
MDCE	Monitoring and Duplicate Control Equipment
MFM	Multistage Frequency Multiplier
MFT	Multiposition Frequency Telegraphy
MG	Master Generator
MIACF	Meander Inverted Autocorrelated Function
MIC	Monolithic Integrated Circuits
MIS	Metering Information System
MMP	Monitoring Metering Panel
MMW	Main Magnetization Winding
MO	Master Oscillator
MO	Mobile Object
MOS	Metal Oxide Semiconductor
MOTNE	Meteorological Operational Telecommunications Network Europe
MRS	Manned Repeater Station
MS	Mobile System
MSMLCS	Mass Service Main Line Cable Systems
MWB	Multiprogram Wire Broadcasting
NEC	Nippon Electric Company
NHK	National Broadcasting Corporation (Jap.)
NIC	Negative Immitance Converters
NIT	Nonlinear Inertialess Three-pole
NJ	Network Junction
NTSK	Nordiska Tele-Satelit Kommitton
NTV	Network Television
OL	Overhead Links
OMJ	Outgoing Message Junction
OPSKS	Optimum Phase Shift Keyed Signals
OS	Oblique Sounding
OTC	Overseas Telecommunications Commission
OTL	Order Trunk Lines
OTMJ	Outgoing Trunk Message Junctions
OWD	Own Number Dialing
OWF	Optimal Worked Frequency
PAA	Phase Antenna Arrays
PACF	Periodic Autocorrelation Function
PAFC	Phase-locked Automatic Frequency Control
PATCA	Phase-lock Automatic Tuned Circuit Adjustment
PBE	Pulsed Bridge Element
PC	Personal Call
PC	Pre-emphasis Circuits
PFC	Phase Frequency Characteristics
PFSS	Particles and Field Sub-Satellite
PG	Pulse Generator
PGE	Primary Group Equipment
PI	Proportional-plus Integral
POLANG	Polarization Angle
PPD	Pulse-type Phase Detector
PPM	Pulse Position Modulation
PS	Phasing System
PSA	Parametric Semiconductor Amplifiers
PSC	Power Supply Circuits
PSC	Pulse and Signalling Circuit
PSK	Phase Shift Keyed
PSP	Planned Schedule Performance
PSS	Power Supply System
PTL	Power Transmission Line
PVC	Pulse Voltage Converter
RADA	Random Access Discrete Address
RC	Remote Control
RDF	Radio Direction Finding
RFR	Reduced Frequency Responses
RFU	Reference Frequency Unit
RL	Radio Links
RMA	Reactive Modulation Amplifiers
RO	Reference Oscillator
RPG	Random Pulse Generator
RRL	Radio Relay Link
RRR	Range and Range Rate
RRS	Radio Relay Stations
RTL	Resister Transistor Logic
RTS	Rural Telephone System
RTV	Remote Television
SARPS	Standard and Recommended Practices
SAS	Support Amplifier Station
SCN	Shortest Connected Network
SCPC	Single Channel Per Carrier
SCS	Satellite Communication Systems
SD	Square-law Detector
SEC	Studio Equipment Complex
SFG	Signal Frequencies Generator
SFM	Switching-mode Frequency Multipliers
SFR	Signal Frequency Receiver
SGE	Secondary Group Equipment
SIGOP	Signal Operation
SIRS	Satellite Infrared Spectrometer
SITA	Société Internationale de Télécommunications Aéronautiques
SL	Subscriber's Lines
SMS	Synchronous Meteorological Satellites

SMU   Secondary Multiplexing Unit
SNJ   Switching Network Junction
SPD   Synchronous Phased Detector
SPM   Solar Proton Monitor
SPMS   Special Purpose Manipulator System
SPSA   Signal Phase Statistical Analyzer
SPWM   Single-sided Pulse Width Modulation
SSBAM   Single Sideband Amplitude Modulation
SSCC   Spin Scan Cloud Camera
SSM   Single-sideband Signal Multiplier
SSP   Signalling and Switching Processor
SSPF   Signal Structure Parametric Filters
SSRA   Spread Spectrum Random Access
STS   Standard Test Signal
SU   Station Units
SU   Syne Unit
SV   Synchronous Voltage
SWL   Surface Ware Lines
TAC   Telemetry and Command
TC   Transmitting Circuits
TCCSR   Telephone Channel Combination and
            Separation Racks
TCD   Time Code Division
TCRA   Telegraphy Channel Reliability
            Analyzer
TCTS   Trans Canadian Telephone System
TD   Tunnel Diode
TE   Terminal Exchange
TE   Trunk Equalizers
TGS   Triglyneinsulphate
TGSO   Tertiary Groups Shunt Operation
TME   Telemetric Equipment
TMIS   Television Measurement Information
            System
TMIS   Television Metering Information
            Systems
TPWB   Three Program Wire Broadcasting
TRN   Television Relay Networks
TS   Transformer Substations
TS   Transition Sets
TSU   Tariff Selection Unit
TTAC   Telemetry Tracking and Command
TTL   Transistor Transistor Logic
TU   Transfer Units
TVF   Tape Velocity Fluctuations
UAN   Unified Automatic Network
UAO   Urban Automatic Office
UN   Urban Network
UR   Unattended Repeaters
URS   Unmanned Repeater Station
USPS   United States Postal Service
UTN   Urban Telephone Network
UVC   Unidirectional Voltage Converter
VACR   Variable Amplitude Correction Rack
VHRR   Very High Resolution Radiometer
VS   Vertical Sounding
VSG   Vertical Sweep Generator
WARC-ST World Administrative Radio
            Conference for Space
            Telecommunications

WATS   Wide Area Telecommunications Service
ZCS   Zone Communication Station
ZF   Zone Finders

TRAINING

AFQT   Armed Forces Qualification Test
AGS   Air Gunnery School (UK)
AIS   Advanced Instructional Systems
AIT   Advanced Individual Training
AIT   Architect In Training
ANBS   Air Navigation and Bombing School
ANS   Air Navigation School
AONS   Air Observer's Navigation School
AOS   Air Observer's School
AQE   Airman Qualifying Examination
ASEE   American Society of Engineering
            Education
ATV   Air Training Command
ATC   Armament Training Camp
ATC   Army Training Center
ATI   Army Training Instruction
ATP   Army Training Plan
ATS   Armament Training Station
BANS   Basic Air Navigation School
BGS   Bombing and Gunnery School
BRL   Behavioural Research Laboratories
CAI   Computer Aided Instruction
CAI   Computer Assisted Instruction
CANS   Civilian Air Navigation School
CAPER   Cost of Attaining Personnel Requirement
CAPI   Computer Administered Programmed
            Instruction
CATITB Civil Air Transport Industry Training
            Board
CCC   Civilian Conservation Corps
CDC   Career Development Course
CEM   Computer Education for Management
CEMIRT Civil Engineering Maintenance,
            Inspection, Repair and Training
CFANS   Canadian Forces Air Navigation School
CNS   Central Navigation School
CTS   Computerized Training System
DOT   Dictionary of Occupational Titles
DTA   Dental Therapy Assistant
EANS   Empire Air Navigation School
EIT   Engineer In Training
ERE   Edison Responsive Environment
FTS   Flying Training School
GPA   Grade Point Average
JOBS   Job Opportunities in the Business
            Sector
MODIA   Methods of Designing Instructional
            Alternatives
MVA   Modern Voluntary Army
NOTAP   Naval Occupational Task Analysis
            Program
NPTRL   Naval Personnel and Training Research
            Laboratory

NSTF   National Scholarship Trust Fund
OAFU   Observers' Advanced Flying Unit
OJT   On Job Training
PICLS Purdue International and Computational
       Learning System
POP   Partially Ordered Program
POS   Partially Ordered Set
PPL   Private Pilot Licence
PSO   Performance Structure Oriented
QA   Quasi Algorithms
RPT   Recruit Performance Tests
SAN   School of Air Navigation
SCOOP Student Controlled On-line Programming
SEP   System Engineering Process
SES   Socio Economic Status
SMTAG Standard Micro-Teaching Appraisal
       Guide
SPE   School of Preliminary Education
SPEED Special Program for Emergency
       Employment Development
SPTU   Staff Pilot Training Unit
STCAG Stanford Teacher Competence Appraisal
       Guide
STEP   Supplemented Training and Employment
       Program
SVIB   Strong Vocational Interest Blank
TBS   Tolerance for Bureaucratic Structure
TDR   Teacher Demonstration Rating
TTC   Technical Training Centers
UPT   Undergraduate Pilot Training
USAWC United States Army War College
USMA   United States Military Academy
VAP   Video Audio Participative
WIN   Work Intensive
WRAT   Wide Range Achievement Test

TRANSPORTATION

AASHO American Association of State
       Highway Officials
AATO   Army Air Transport Organization
ACDO   Air Carrier District Office (US)
ACT   Activity Center Transportation
ACTICE Authority for the Co-ordination of
       Inland Transport in Central Europe
ACTISUD Authority for the Co-ordination of
       Inland Transport in Southern
       Europe
AFCENT Allied Forces Central
AMVER Automated Merchant Vessel Reporting
ANRC   American National Red Cross
APT   Advanced Passenger Train
APT   Advanced Passenger Transport
ARDA   American Railway Development
       Association
ATA   Air Transport Association
ATA   American Taxicab Association
ATA   American Transit Association
ATAA   Air Transport Association of America

ATAC   Air Transport Advisory Council
ATB   Air Transport Board
ATLB   Air Transport Licensing Board
ATT   Advanced Technology Transport
ATTITB Air Transport and Travel Industry
       Training Board
BART   Bay Area Rapid Transit
BCABP Bureau of Competitive Assessment and
       Business Policy (US)
BDC   Bureau of Domestic Commerce
BDSA   Business and Defense Services
       Administration (US)
BEA   British European Airways
BIC   Bureau of International Commerce
BOAC   British Overseas Airways Corporation
BPR-Thm Bureau of Public Roads - Transport
       Highway Mobilization (Can.)
BSAA   British South American Airways
CAA   Civil Aeronautics Administration (US)
CAA   Civil Aviation Authority (UK)
CAB   Civil Aeronautics Board (US)
CABATM Civil Aeronautics Board Air Transport
       Mobilization
CALC   Cargo Acceptance and Load Control
CAP   Civil Air Patrol
CCEEP Canadian Committee for Coordination
       of Emergency Economic Planning
CCI   Consolidated City of Indianapolis
CEP   Civil Emergency Planning
CEPC   Canada Civil Engineering Planning
       Committee
CHP   California Highway Patrol
COMATS Commander Military Air Transport
       Service
CPR   Canadian Pacific Railway
CRAF   Civil Reserve Air Fleet
CSA   Central Supply Agency
CTAB   Commerce Technical Advisory Board (US)
CTS   Cleveland Transit System
DAIR   Driver Aid Information and Routing
DCPA   Defense Civil Preparedness Agency (US)
DDTV   Dry Driver Transport Vehicle
DECOM Delay Cost Model
DEFCON Defense Readiness Condition
DEPA   Defense Electric Power Administration
       (US)
DIOS   Distribution Information and
       Optimising System
DMO   Defense Mobilization Order (US)
DM/PRT Dual-Mode Personal Rapid Transit
DOC   Department of Commerce (US)
DOT   Department of Transportation (US)
DOTCOOP Department of Transportation
       Continuity of Operations Plan
DPC   Defense Planning Committee
DSA   Defence Shipping Agency
DSB   Demand Scheduled Bus
DSC   Defense Shipping Council
DSEB   Defense Shipping Executive Board
DSR   Danish State Railways

DWT   Deadweight Tonnage
EARB   European Airlines Research Bureau
ECAC   European Civil Aviation Conference
EHTR   Emergency Highway Transport Regulation
EOC   Emergency Operating Center (US)
EOF   Emergency Operating Facility (US)
ERGS   Electronic Route Guidance System
ESO-FHWA Federal Highway Administration
        Emergency Standby Order (US)
ETA   Estimated Time of Arrival
ETD   Estimated Time of Departure
FHWA   Federal Highway Administration (US)
FLPC   Federal Local Port Controller (US)
FRA   Federal Railroad Administration (US)
GPMTD   Greater Peovia Mass Transit District
HGV   Heavy Goods Vehicle
HSRI   Highway Safety Research Institute
HVOSM   Highway Vehicle Object Simulation
        Model
ICAO   International Civil Aviation
        Organization
ICC   Interstate Commerce Commission
ICC-TM Interstate Commerce Commission
        Transport Mobilization (US)
ICHCA   International Cargo Handling
        Coordination Association
IECG   Interagency Emergency Coordinating
        Group
IETC   Interagency Emergency Transportation
        Committee
ITA   Institut du Transport Aérien
ITE   Intercity Transportation Efficiency
lcl   Lowest Car Load
LNG   Liquefied Natural Gas
LPG   Liquefied Petroleum Gas
LPTB   London Passenger Transport Board
LSFO   Logistics Support Field Office
MAC   Military Airlift Command
MARAD   Maritime Administration
MAS   Military Alert System
MAST   Military Assistance for Safety and
        Traffic
MAT   Mobile Assistance Team
MA-TPM Maritime Administration Transport
        Planning Mobilization (US)
MATS   Military Air Transport Service
MCL   Mathematics Computation Laboratory
        (US)
MDAI   Multidisciplinary Accident
        Investigation
MEECN   Minimum Essential Emergency Network
        (US)
MOT   Ministry of Transport
MRO   Maintenance Repair and Operations
MSC   Military Sea Command
MSE   Modern Ship Equipment
MTMTS   Military Traffic Management and
        Terminal Service (US)
NAMSA   NATO Maintenance and Supply Agency
NAVSEC Naval Ship Engineering Center

NCA   National Command Authority
NCS   National Communication System
NCSORG Naval Control of Shipping
        Organization
NCWA   NATO Civil Wartime Agency
NDF   Nonlinear Distortion Factors
NDRF   National Defense Reserve Fleet (US)
NETC   National Emergency Transportation
        Center (US)
NFT   Niagara Frontier Transit
NHTSA   National Highway Traffic Safety
        Administration (US)
NMB   National Mediation Board (US)
NOAA   National Oceanographic Atmospheric
        Administration (US)
NOEB-W NATO Oil Executive Board - West
NSA   National Shipping Authority (US)
NSRDC   Naval Ship Research and Development
        Center
OCA   Operational Control Authority
ODR   Office of Defense Resources (US)
OEP   Office Emergency Preparedness (US)
OST   Office of Secretary of Transport (US)
OSTCOOP Office of the Secretary of
        Transportation Continuity of
        Operations Plan (US)
OTSR   Optimum Track Ship Routing
PBEIST Planning Board for European Inland
        Surface Transport
PBOS   Planning Board for Ocean Shipping
PRR   Pennsylvania Railroad
PRT   Personal Rapid Transit
RCC   Rescue Coordination Center (US)
RETC   Regional Emergency Transportation
        Center (US)
RETCO   Regional Emergency Transportation
        Coordinator
RETREP Regional Emergency Transportation
        Representation
RHA   Road Haulage Association (UK)
RIETCOM Regional Interagency Emergency
        Transportation Committee (US)
RPC   Regional Preparedness Committee (US)
RR   Railroads
RRB   Railroad Retirement Board (US)
RSB   Regional Shipping Board
SAE   Society of Automotive Engineers
SAR   Search and Rescue
SCRTD   South California Rapid Transit
        District
SESG   Southern European Shipping Group
SHADCOM Shipping Advisory Committee
SHAPE   Supreme Headquarters Allied Power,
        Europe
SNG   Synthetic Natural Gas
SOIS   Shipping Operations Information
        Systems
S/SS   Steering and Suspension System
TACRV   Tracked Air Cushion Research Vehicle
TCC   Transportation Commodity Classification

TE/DC Traffic Enforcement/Driver Control
TEP   Transportation Energy Panel
TOPICS Transport Operations Programs for
       Increasing Capacity and Safety
TSC   Transportation Systems Center
TSFO   Transportation Support Field Office
       (US)
TVA   Tennessee Valley Authority (US)
TWA   Trans World Airways
UFRCC Uniform Federal Regional Council City
       (US)
UMTA   Urban Mass Transportation
       Administration (US)
USCG   United States Coast Guard
USMC   United States Marine Corps
USPS   United States Postal Service
USRA   United States Railway Association
UTAP   Unified Transportation Assistance
       Program (US)
VIN   Vehicle Identification Numbers
VLCC   Very Large Crude Carrier
WABCO Westinghouse Air Brake Company
WASP   War Air Service Program